Walter Brown Gibson (1897-1985)

*M*an of *M*agic and *M*ystery:

A Guide to the Work of Walter B. Gibson

by
J. RANDOLPH COX

The Scarecrow Press, Inc.
Metuchen, N.J., & London
1988

British Library Cataloguing-in-Publication data available

Library of Congress Cataloging-in-Publication Data

Cox, J. Randolph.

   Man of magic and mystery.

   Includes indexes.
   1. Gibson, Walter Brown, 1897- . --Bibliography. 2. Detective
and mystery stories, American--Bibliography. 3. Shadow (Fictitious
character)--Bibliography. 4. Magic--Bibliography. I. Title.
Z8341.5.C69 1988   016.813'52   88-31917
[PS3513.I2823]
ISBN 0-8108-2192-3

Dedication

To the memory of my father, John Clarence Cox, who was always there when I needed him most.

To my mother, Augusta Onsum Cox, who saved the treasures of childhood for me.

To my brother, James Onsum Cox, a fellow member of Chick Carter's Inner Circle, even though he didn't always take it so seriously he would leave his play to listen to every episode of the radio serial.

TABLE OF CONTENTS

ILLUSTRATIONS

Walter Brown Gibson (1897-1985)   frontispiece

Walter Gibson's greatest creation was The Shadow. His adventures appeared in Street & Smith magazines for nearly twenty years. Gibson wrote a total of 283 pulp novels, one paperback original, and two short stories about his hero.

At the peak of his popularity, The Shadow appeared in two versions, the original novels and comic book adaptations. Gibson wrote both.

Three generations of magicians were promoted in books by Walter Gibson to the delight of all ages.

A George Sully edition of a Gibson title. Bindings were uniform. (See **A.11.**)

This program book was produced to be sold at Blackstone's stage show.   (**A.44.**)

Magic for the masses; the science of illusion. (**A.91.**)

During a wave of interest in the occult, Walter Gibson produced a shelf of volumes on the subject.

Gibson wrote a handful of mysteries about magician detectives. A rare paper-covered edition. (**A.52.**)

*   *   *   *   *

When **The Shadow Magazine** ceased publication, Gibson turned to the True Crime field.   page 186

Credit goes where credit is due. Other names are on the cover, but this is still a Gibson title. (A.50.)   page 189

A fine tribute to the master. This was the official badge at Pulpcon XV in 1986. (Courtesy of Frank Hamilton)   page 278

Who would guess the master of magic and mystery would try historical fiction? (A.90.)
                                        page 280

Among the many magazines with which Gibson was associated, this was his short-lived science fiction series. (B.801.)   page 282

Foreword ☞

As is indicated by the table of contents, the material by Walter Gibson is divided into sections: books and pamphlets, stories and articles in magazines, introductions and essays in books by others, syndicated newspaper features, scripts for comic books and newspaper comic strips, radio scripts and miscellaneous material. Within each section the arrangement is chronological where dates are given, alphabetical where they are not. For the convenience of those who want to see how much he contributed to a single issue of a magazine, the material is arranged in the same order as it appeared in that issue. That is, according to the original table of contents, not re-arranged alphabetically by title. I hope this somewhat nontraditional approach is acceptable.

Where Walter Gibson's name is not included in an entry, it means his own name appears on the article in the magazine or on the title page of the book. Where a name other than his own, or in addition to his own, appears on the publication this has been indicated. His name appears in brackets [] following the pseudonym used. Where a publication is unsigned, his name, and his name only, appears in brackets. In these instances, it has not seemed necessary to include the word "by" in front of his name.

I have not included every edition beyond the first edition. I have noted some reprints of his works which seemed of interest to collectors or to clarify a point or to indicate the need for future studies. Entries for comic books may seem excessively detailed, but no standard bibliographic form has been established for this type of material. I have tried to include information that describes the publication and can be used by anyone who needs to locate a copy of a particular issue.

Each entry has been provided with a distinctive sequence number corresponding to the section in which it appears. An appropriate index follows the appendices.

In the course of planning the work, some thought was given to providing an index to the magic tricks, but since this would involve indexing individual books as well as magazine articles, cooler heads prevailed. To move in that direction, it was felt, would take this work into the realm of becoming a concordance.

It has not seemed useful to maintain consistencies in all matters, but to represent the material as it was published originally. Therefore, both spellings of Miss Lane's first name ("Margo" and "Margot") appear according to usage in the work under discussion.

Unless otherwise noted, I have seen and examined each item or have been provided with a satisfactory photo copy or detailed notes from the owner of the item.

Acknowledgements

All covers and illustrations from Walter
Gibson's works appear by courtesy of the publishers
or Mrs. Walter Gibson. **Dunninger's Secrets**, Lyle
Stuart, Inc.; **Junior Magic**, Sterling Publishing
Co.; **Walter Gibson's Big Book of Magic for All Ages**
and **Blackstone's Secrets of Magic**, Doubleday & Co.;
Houdini on Magic, Dover Publications, Inc.;
Houdini's Fabulous Magic, Mrs. Walter B. Gibson
(for Chilton Books). All text, advertisements, and
illustrations from and about **The Shadow** magazine
are reprinted courtesy of The Conde Nast
Publications, Inc.

There are so many people to whom I owe so much
that I'm afraid to list any for fear of missing
someone, but here goes. Walter Gibson himself for
answering questions and telling me stories; Litzka
Gibson for putting me up (and putting up with me)
when she didn't know where it would end (and was
afraid sometimes that it wouldn't); Frank Hamilton
(for his illustrations and the permission to use
them here); Don Bratland (for his photography and
the imagination with which he enhanced this book);
Wendell Gibson; Dick Sardo; Sidney H. Radner; Jay
Marshall; Fred Cook (who had all the right
magazines); Albert Tonik (for locating the story
from **The Wissahickon**); Bob Sampson (whose book, **The
Night Master**, was a gold mine of information); Tom
Fagan (stalwart companion) who convinced me I
should annotate the comic book stories in this list
and who made other valuable suggestions; Micky
Murphy; Bill Rauscher; Will Murray; Anthony Tollin;
Carolyn Davis (and the Street & Smith Archives at
Syracuse University); Paul Bonner, Jr. of Conde
Nast Publications; Leonard Beck of the Library of
Congress; many other unsung librarians at various
institutions including Walter Gibson's alma mater,
Colgate; the editors and contributors to **Echoes,
Golden Perils**, and **Xenophile**, as well as **Bronze
Shadows**, and **Pulp**; Helen and Jack Deveny (who had
magazines I could not resist); Steve T. Miller;
Geoffrey Wynkoop; Brian Kenknight of Fine Groove
Records (for saving articles for me and adding to
my collection of Popular Culture); Steve Stilwell
(with whose help this might have been completed
sooner); Jim Goodrich (who helped more with the
index than shows here); Edward S. Lauterbach (who
taught me much, if not all, of what I know about

Bibliography; Rex Miller of Supermantiques; the people at Sinister Cinema; Dan McCoy of McCoy's Recordings; Gretchen Hardgrove, Connie Gunderson and the Minitex Inter-Library Loan system at St. Olaf College; John Marshall and Al Finholt of the St. Olaf Chemistry Department for introducing me to the more arcane functions of WordPerfect (Al made house calls); Louis Janus, Scott Narveson, and Don Tarr (who also made house calls), for their various types of assistance in getting this formatted for the laser printer; anyone else whom I have overlooked; and to my wife, Janice, who advised me on just about everything except how to type the final manuscript. Without her tutorials in the use of a PC this might have been done differently, but not nearly so well.

Introduction ☜

One

Walter Brown Gibson was one of the most prolific writers of this century. He also possessed one of the most gifted imaginations of this or any century. He saw possibilities for stories, for word games, for explanations of the unusual, everywhere in the world around him. The past, the present, the future, they were all one to him.

As a confidant and ghost writer for some of the greatest stage magicians of his time he interpreted so much of their lore to the public that no accurate history of the art of illusion should omit his name.

As a story-teller he created one of the great mythic figures of popular culture, The Shadow. The author of nearly 300 full length novels about the character, Gibson's creation and many of the ideas behind the stories transcend the literary merit of the individual episodes in the fictional career of the master of darkness.

The full story of Walter Gibson's life and work has not been told, nor is this book to be even an attempt to tell that story. This is merely the rough outline of a remarkable literary career. In most sections the material has been arranged chronologically so that his works may be studied in the order in which they reached the public. In this way, we may see just what he was doing in any one year in each of several media, book, magazine, comic book, or radio script.

It was in the Summer of 1977 that I met Walter Gibson in Akron, Ohio, at the annual Pulpcon. This convention for collectors and students of the pulp magazines of the early 20th century has been held every year since 1972. Gibson had been a guest of honor at a previous Pulpcon and had returned in that capacity this year. I was there as part of a research trip to gather information for a study of the Nick Carter stories. I knew that Gibson had had a hand in that series, as the bibliography below demonstrates, and I asked him about his work on the radio version of the character. He was extremely friendly and we spent much time talking during the convention. At the end of the convention he invited me to visit his home in Eddyville, New York.

On that visit, a few weeks later, I realized how many books and stories that had been childhood favorites of mine were the work of this genial white-haired gentleman from Philadelphia. The breadth of his knowledge and the depth of his imagination appealed to me. I certainly hoped someone would capture the spirit of this amazing man in some way, perhaps a biography, but certainly a bibliography of his works. I did not expect to be the person to attempt the latter.

In 1980 I elected to devote a sabbatical leave from St. Olaf College to preparing an annotated bibliography of Walter Gibson's works. As often happens, the work took much longer than it should have and appears here in a format considerably different from the original concept. Unfortunately, the subject is no longer with us to pass judgement on this tribute to his place in popular letters. He had a lively interest in the occult and it is tempting to speculate on the guidance which his spirit rendered me, looking over my shoulder as I typed.

Two

[Below is part of the journal I kept during my sabbatical. It has been edited to make it more comprehensible to a wider readership.]

October 3, 1980. I arrived at Eddyville by car ready and eager to begin serious work on this book. It was not long before I discovered just

what kept Walter Gibson busy...Dick Sardo, an old
friend [of Gibson's] who served as driver and
companion for many conventions and trips was
helping Walter pack for a trip to Wallingford and
Bridgeport, Connecticut. I brought a few things
into the house, said hello to Litzka Gibson,
Walter's wife, unstrapped and parked the bicycle I
had brought along in the garden shed, rearranged my
luggage and drove off in my car following Dick and
Walter. I parked my car at a Holiday Inn at
Fishkill, New York, transferred two knapsacks, my
camera and tape recorder, and the big suitcase to
Dick's car and off we went. I took advantage of
having someone else do the driving to sleep for
part of the trip.

     We arrived at Wallingford and looked for the
magic shop near the old railroad station which was
to be the site of Walter's lecture. [Walter was
often invited to address groups of magic
enthusiasts, to demonstrate methods and to
autograph books.] We weren't able to go down one
street because there were fire trucks fighting a
fire in the attic of a house there. When we went
around the block and found a parking place we
discovered the fire was across the street from the
magic shop for which we were looking.

     Introductions and drinks all around and then
we went into the living quarters next to the magic
shop (which was really a part of the house) and had
dinner--quiche as I recall.

     There was lots of shop talk about magic and I
was introduced once more to Sid Radner, the expert
on crooked gambling, whom I had met earlier and to
Chet Karkut, another magic buff. After dinner we
went to the railroad station and set up shop in the
auditorium...where Walter displayed a stock of some
of his books ready to be sold and autographed.
This was not my first opportunity to watch Walter
among members of the magic fraternity. I had
attended a meeting of the Magic Collectors in
Chicago a year or so earlier.

     Sid Radner showed the documentary film "The
Truth About Houdini" (I taped the sound track as
well as parts of Walter's talk with a portable,
battery-powered tape recorder). Dick and Walter
performed a routine with a newspaper cone and a

pitcher of milk. Then Walter performed the passe
pass bottle trick, reciting from memory the patter
he himself had written for it at least 50 years
earlier. In the midst of the presentation, Sid
Radner warned Walter he ought to take a rest before
going on. Walter took the break and resumed the
lecture a few minutes later.

During the question and answer session someone
asked him about the Shadow radio show, and I
realized how often people confused that Shadow with
the pulp one which Gibson had created. The
question was repeated several times during the next
few weeks.

We drove to Chet Karkut's house afterwards and
looked at his collection of magic memorabilia. He
had an old scrapbook with some entries from
Walter's "Miracles--Ancient and Modern" newspaper
series pasted into it. The book had once belonged
to Dr. Pierce, editor of The Magic World, and had
the words "Gibson Gas Works" on the cover. It was a
ledger from the company originally owned by Walter
Gibson's father. All of us were asked to sign it.

I spent part of the night on the living room
couch while the others discussed magic until the
early hours of the morning. Sid Radner and I drove
to Bridgeport to claim the motel room reserved for
Walter for the Friends of Old Time Radio
convention. In the morning we breakfasted and
registered for the convention. I browsed among the
exhibits in the dealers' room and bought some
cassettes of magic-related radio shows, including
Gibson's own Blackstone, the Magic Detective.

One of the more interesting aspects of the
convention was the opportunity to watch re-
enactments of radio plays with professional radio
actors taking the parts. Walter gave a strong
reading as the announcer for his own ABC radio
series Strange and later accepted an award for his
contributions to radio at the banquet. (I was
introduced as the foremost authority on Nick
Carter.)

We drove back to Fishkill after the convention
where I collected my car and scraped the frost off
its windshield. Walter and Dick decided to have
one last drink before they parted company [and Dick

drove to his own home] while I went in search of a
cup of black coffee to help me stay awake for the
drive back to Eddyville.   I found this to be
strangely elusive, especially in a bar.

     We all slept late on Sunday, having arrived in
Eddyville about 2 a.m.   The day was spent in
talking with Walter and Litzka, and in looking over
Walter's study and planning my approach to the
project.

     It was on Monday, October 6, that we were in
the attic room he called the "Up Study" and I was
shown the issue of **Saint Nicholas** which contained
his first published piece--a puzzle in the October
1905 issue, on page 1151.

                         Enigma
                           4
     Change this figure to another system of
     notation and it will give the name of a
     rare old plant.
          W.B. GIBSON (Age 7) (League Member)

     The first thing that needed to be done was to
clear a table to serve as my desk.   We carried
piles of xeroxes of articles about Walter's career
to the Up Study from the second floor study and
arranged them on the large table there. (Walter, I
soon discovered, was fond of making multiple copies
of articles.   They might come in handy some day, he
reasoned.   I was given a set of these for my
files.)

     Once the second floor table had been cleared I
began pulling copies of his books from the shelves
to arrange them in stacks, title by title.   I soon
filled the table and began piling the books on the
floor in rows across the room.   Between meals and
conversations this occupied my time for the next
two or three days.   Most of the conversations
involved listening to Walter's stories, of which he
had an endless supply.

     While the conversation concerned his work in
the main, he did not live entirely in the past.   He
had opinions on just about everything in the world
around him.

We fell into the habit of having dinner at a Chinese restaurant in nearby Kingston and the same day that I was shown the puzzle in **Saint Nicholas**, Litzka questioned my motives in doing the bibliography. I assured her that I only wanted to see that Walter received proper credit for all his work, even his fugitive pieces. The realities of academic publishing made it a safe bet that expenses incurred would outweigh any future royalties. Walter came to my defense and assured her that I was a genuine scholar and not a mercenary.

The following day, Tuesday, October 7, was my 44th birthday, which I spent happily sorting and shelving books, setting aside duplicate copies to go into storage. We drove to nearby Ulster County Community College where I made xerox copies of some of Walter's Thurston columns and of the pamphlet, **After Dinner Tricks**, his first book.

Walter and I did some shopping for apples at a roadside stand; he bought half a bushel which was more than was needed and I became the beneficiary of much of the excess when we returned to Litzka's kitchen. As we drove through the countryside, he pointed out some of the more significant scenery, including some that had served as background for The Shadow's adventures.

That evening there was a birthday card at my place at the table and we had dinner at a French restaurant.

Soon afterwards I left the Gibson house for about a week in pursuit of some other aspects of my research. On my return (October 12) I found the door locked and no car in the drive. I let myself in with the key I had been given when I'd left the week before (after knocking first) and startled Litzka who had been upstairs and had not heard my knock.

The ubiquitous and very welcome cup of tea and light lunch were put in front of me and I told her something of the events and travels of the past few days. Soon, the car pulled into the drive and Walter, Charlie Struck (a neighbor), and Art Emerson (a magic buff and travel agent) got out,

fresh from a convention at Tannen's, the well known
magic dealer.

Over the next two days I continued to sort
Walter's books, filling seven shelves with first
editions (hardcover and paperback) as well as the
significant reprints from among his own titles.
Duplicates were sent to storage in the "Up Study".
I then began to re-arrange and re-shelve his magic
collection along the shelves in the alcove behind
the work table.

And so the days passed with sorting books,
stopping to take notes, reading a passage here and
there, and listening to backstage gossip about the
magic profession.

I next left the Gibson home for a brief visit
to the Library of Congress where I paid a courtesy
call on Leonard Beck of the Rare Book Room and
looked at the Houdini and McManus-Young
collections. The Houdini Collection was made up
primarily of books on spiritualism and seemed
disappointing somehow. There were discussions on
other topics with other people over the next few
days and then I was on my way back to Eddyville for
the last major part of this research trip.

October 24. I arrived at Eddyville at 2:52
p.m. and it took a while to tell Walter and Litzka
a little of my adventures. Walter had been at the
typewriter when I came in (whether a letter or the
introduction to a new edition of one of his books,
I cannot recall). Plans were laid for the weekend
when we were to be visited by an old friend of
Walter's, Bill Rauscher, who combined a fascination
for magic with a calling as an Episcopal priest.
He was accompanied by a friend of his from seminary
days, Bob Lewis.

Even in a house the size of the Gibsons' there
were limited sleeping accommodations and I elected
to stay for a few days with Jim Goodrich, a friend
and fellow librarian, who lived at New Paltz, not
far away.

Work continued on the Bibliography. It was a
bit difficult to get much accomplished with the
additional people in the house. The new guests
came upstairs frequently to see how I was getting

along...and I was only too glad of the opportunity
to stop scribbling notes and talk.

     At my new lodgings that night I realized I was
telling the same stories over and over and boring
myself. I left my suitcase at Jim Goodrich's house
and drove back to Gibson's house in the morning.
When it came time to return in the evening I
discovered I had a flat tire. I spent the night in
a borrowed pair of Walter's capacious pajamas
sleeping on the couch in the room off the dining
area (on the way to the central stairway) where his
collection of biographical sources was kept.

     When the tire had been repaired the next day
(the nail was removed and a new valve stem
attached), I drove over to Larchmont for a visit
with Fred Dannay (Ellery Queen) and his wife, Rose.
I returned quite late. In the morning, Litzka said
I'd make a good Raffles as she hadn't even heard me
come in.

     Since my pacing from the second floor had been
a source of disturbance to my hosts earlier, this
was welcome news. However, I soon adopted the
practice of taking materials I needed into the
guest bedroom when I had to work late at night.

     I spent Hallowe'en at the Gibsons. There was,
of course, much talk of Houdini who had died on
Hallowe'en and I had Walter sign my copies of some
of the books he'd written about the master escape
artist. I also modelled my cloak and slouch hat
which I'd brought along so I could appear as The
Shadow in the annual Rutland, Vermont, Hallowe'en
Parade. [I had changed my plans about attending
the Parade in order to spend more time with the
Gibsons.] Some "Trick or Treaters" made their way
up the hill to knock on the back door. The Gibsons
pretended to be very put out by the bother of it
all, but played the game and gave out apples and
quarters to the children.

     My final excursion of note with the Gibsons
was to attend the annual dinner of the Delaware and
Hudson Canal Society, held at Mohonk, the nearby
mountain resort. Walter had been a member of the
society for several years. During the program
after dinner, Litzka arranged for Walter to be
invited to recite from memory a comic poem he had

read as a boy in **Saint Nicholas**. It was one in which a little boy is asked to say a piece and the result is a combination of lines from several famous verses, such as "The Wreck of the Hesperus" and "Barbara Fritchie."

There were still some notes to be taken on material found in the second floor study, but eventually I took my leave on November 4. I made my final xeroxes (the people at Copyland had begun to expect to see me every day) and discovered some more of Walter's titles which had eluded me before. The parting was in the early afternoon of that Tuesday.

Although I was to make two later visits they did not have the same aura as this extended sabbatical visit. The next visit was the following year when I arrived with Tom Fagan, a psychic researcher and fellow comic art fan. This also involved an appearance at Pulpcon in Cherry Hill, New Jersey, on the occasion of the 50th anniversary of the publication of the first Shadow novel. Much occurred that was interesting and new discoveries were made about aspects of Walter's work, but there is a magic about first impressions that can never be repeated.

I saw Walter Gibson for the last time in the Summer of 1985. He was much changed, having experienced a stroke and a period of hospitalization. But the fire was still in his imagination and he talked of the projects he hoped to complete. Although he still worked on his Autobiography (his "Memoirs" as he called it) and had begun a new Shadow novel, I realized that none of this was likely to be completed. For him to complete an autobiography was to accept that life was nearly over.

We parted after I had had a chance to show him the Bibliography in its still rough form. The final gap in the chain of publications had been closed earlier that day when I found a folder containing tear sheets and some complete magazine issues from his true crime writing. I shall be ever grateful to the sprite who placed it on the coffee table in the "biography room." I spent much of the night sitting up in bed, reading over the magazine stories and taking notes.

When news came of his death, December 6, 1985, I wept. I had lost a mentor and a friend. It was as though my father had died a second time.

Three

Walter Gibson saved everything, literally. In the early days he meticulously prepared scrapbooks of his clippings and kept lists of his articles and where they had appeared. It is this instinct for preservation that accounts for the thoroughness of this Bibliography.

The format of the Bibliography was partly dictated by my desire to be as informative as possible while being true to my subject by being entertaining as well. The new technologies provided by the computer and the laser printer required me to reshape my own approach to writing. For one who composes best with a sharpened pencil and a pad of yellow paper, this was not an insignificant step.

I will not use this introduction to belabor the obvious, but allow each user to come to his or her own conclusions based on its contents. It will become apparent that such a prolific writer as Walter Gibson recycled plots, story ideas, concepts, and gimmicks. An idea for The Shadow often turns up in a plot for a Blackstone adventure. His love for word games and intellectual puzzles is demonstrated again and again. A good magic trick will be used in more than one book or situation. Each time it seems to be reworked to fit its new format (especially when it turns up as a plot device in a work of fiction). I have indicated some of this recycling, but have not felt it necessary to constantly indicate the fact. I leave that to the future student of Gibsoniana.

This may be the place to dispel one myth about Walter Gibson and his alter ego, Maxwell Grant. While Street & Smith may not have advertised the fact that the two were one and the same, they did little to suppress the truth. There is ample evidence to support the thesis that any reader who paid attention would have known who "Maxwell Grant" really was.

Item: **The Seven Circles,** vol 2 no. 1, for October 1931, page 4. "You have heard of The Shadow, the master of mystery. His adventures are recounted by Maxwell Grant, who in real life is Walter B. Gibson." On page 11 is an illustration of the cover for **The Shadow** for November 1931 which contains the novel, "The Red Menace." **The Seven Circles,** the official publication of the International Magic Circle of Kalamazoo, Michigan, was edited by Walter B. Gibson. A little advertising doesn't hurt.

Item: **Street & Smith's Bulletin,** undated, but ca 1933, a trade journal, with an advertisement for Corona typewriters..."A New World's Record...1,440,000 words were written by Maxwell Grant in less than 10 months on a Corona typewriter in the creation of the sensational character, The Shadow, featured in **The Shadow Magazine,** a Street & Smith Publication...Corona is a good typewriter, but Maxwell Grant is a great type writer--and The Shadow is one of the most amazing types in all fiction." The photograph of Maxwell Grant is the young Walter Gibson.

Item: The **Portland Sunday Telegram and Sunday Press Herald** (Portland, Maine) for October 25, 1936, contains a long article about the man behind The Shadow, clearly identified in photo and text as Walter B. Gibson, alias, "Maxwell Grant." The article may not have circulated far beyond the state line, but the facts are made clear, including Gibson's choice of that state as a retreat for his writing. His mother had been a Maine resident. It was the Summer of 1936 when Gibson came to Maine and had a cabin built at Little Sebago Lake. (There is no mention of his having a typewriter stand built for him from scrap lumber.)

Item: **New York World-Telegram,** May 15, 1937. An article-interview with Maxwell Grant, author of The Shadow novels. While Gibson's name is not used in the article, there is a photograph of the author at his typewriter.

Item: **The Writer's Digest,** March 1941. An article called "A Million Words a Year for Ten

Straight Years," signed by "Walter (The Shadow) Gibson," in which our hero tells how he went about the task of supplying Street & Smith with enough material so they could publish **The Shadow Magazine** twice a month. This article appeared on the 10th anniversary of The Shadow. A little advertising doesn't hurt.

There they are. Anyone paying attention over the years should not have been surprised to learn the identity behind Maxwell Grant.

In October 1957 I wrote a letter to Street & Smith in which I asked if "Maxwell Grant" was a "house name." I was told that all of the novels about The Shadow were the work of one man. When I told this story to Walter Gibson in the 1970s he replied, "They should have been."

Someone is bound to ask me what I consider to be the "best" of Walter Gibson's many books and articles. It is difficult to make a choice, but were I to be asked I would have to list such diverse titles as the original Shadow trilogy (**The Living Shadow, The Eyes of The Shadow,** and **The Shadow Laughs**). Of the many books about Houdini in particular those in which he demonstrated the ability to capture Houdini's peculiar talent for showmanship (**Houdini's Escapes** and **Houdini's Magic**); **The Master Magicians;** the Blackstone duo (**Blackstone's Secrets of Magic** and **Blackstone's Modern Card Tricks**); certainly the two volumes on card magic and close-up magic. For any of these a lesser writer would be proud to be remembered. But there is a small volume which I prize, one which introduced me to the world of magic and to the name of Walter Gibson, for which I should have to leave room---**Magic Explained**, which came my way when I was a boy of thirteen. To me it was equivalent to the time when Walter Gibson himself followed that string to a box of tricks when he was a boy.

J. Randolph Cox
Northfield, Minnesota

A. Books and Pamphlets by Walter B. Gibson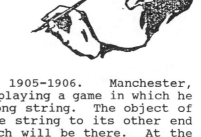

Chapter One

A New Rising Card

1897-1921

Christmas season. 1905-1906. Manchester, Vermont. A small boy is playing a game in which he is handed one end of a long string. The object of the game is to follow the string to its other end to collect the prize which will be there. At the other end of Walter Gibson's string is a box of simple magic tricks. Of such are the ways of Fate.

*   *   *   *   *

September 12, 1897. 2:00 pm. Germantown, Pennsylvania. Walter Brown Gibson is born to Alfred Cornelius and May (Whidden) Gibson. His father is the owner of the Gibson Gas Fixture Works.

1905. Young Walter discovers L. Frank Baum's latest book, **Queen Zixi of Ix**. While fond of the more famous Oz books, **Queen Zixi** remains his

1

favorite and he never tires of announcing that he is an Ixian before he is an Ozian.

October 1905. A puzzle he wrote when he was seven and submitted to the St. Nicholas League section of the famous **St. Nicholas Magazine** is published. In its entirety, it reads:

"(4) Change this figure to another system of notation and it will give the name of a rare old plant."

The answer is the Roman Numeral IV which can be pronounced ivy, the name of a plant.

In later years he will attribute his inspiration to his reading of the Baum book. If the Roman Numeral IX inspired Baum to create the land of Ix, the child, Walter, then saw the Roman Numeral IV as a word as well.

1912. As a student at Chestnut Hill Academy he writes a short story, "The Hidden Will," for the school magazine, **The Wissahickon.** Published in the January 1913 issue it is, prophetically enough, a mystery story. He also discovers a magic shop and begins his greater involvement in magic.

1913. Age 16. While visiting his aunt in New York City he meets Joseph Dunninger at the Eden Musee, the famous waxworks museum on 23d Street, where he is working as a magician. Dunninger is 17 years old.

1915. Young Walter publishes his first article on magic, the description of a trick, in **The Sphinx**, one of the leading magical magazines. He continues to write for the magical magazines throughout high school and college and places some 217 articles in all.

1916. Writes "The Remuda," another mystery story, which wins a literary prize, personally presented to him by former President William Howard Taft at his graduation ceremonies at the Peddie School, Hightstown, New Jersey. Taft tells young Walter that he hopes the story will be the beginning of a long literary career. (Records at Chestnut Hill Academy indicate he was graduated officially from Northeast High, Philadelphia.

Opinions differ on whether "The Remuda" was ever
published. Even the correct title is in doubt. It
has been cited also as "The Romuda," which may be a
misspelling or some play on words understood only
by the author of the story.)

1920. On being graduated from Colgate
University, Hamilton, New York, Gibson applies for
a job as reporter on the Philadelphia **North
American**. Told there will not be an opening until
the Fall, he works at a traveling carnival during
the Summer where he meets sketch artist, John
Duffy. Duffy will illustrate some of Gibson's
syndicated newspaper features. As a reporter he
learns to write quickly and succinctly, and to keep
several projects going simultaneously. He also
follows the example of his brother, Arthur, in
working for the Connecticut General insurance
company where he teaches himself how to type.
Among his jobs is typing out insurance policies.

1921. Gibson joins the staff of the
Philadelphia **Evening Public Ledger**, where he
creates his first feature for the Ledger Syndicate,
After Dinner Tricks. He appears on the radio,
broadcasting a series of puzzles and tricks from
Station WIP, Philadelphia, solving the puzzles and
explaining the tricks twice weekly. Eventually he
will be promoted in the advertising pages of the
paper as a creator of crossword puzzles and
something of a writing phenomenon. He publishes
his first book, a collection of material selected
from his syndicate feature.

Chapter Two

Early Magic

1921-1930

By now Gibson had published enough in
magazines and newspapers so that book publication
became a natural consequence, either with original
material or collections of his magazine pieces.
His first book

A.1.   After Dinner Tricks
Columbus, Ohio: Magic Publishing Co., 1921.
30p. illus. paper covers,

was a collection of 54 tricks gathered from the
syndicated feature of the same name and grouped by
subject. While the cover indicates this was to be
the first of a series of collections, there were no
more issued.   Gibson is cited in the book as the
author of **Easy Magic, Miracles--Ancient and Modern,**
and **Practical Card Tricks,** but this was a reference
to the syndicated features bearing those titles and
not the collections in book form.   Those were yet
to come.

His next book was patterned after a series he
had done for **The Magic World** (1920-1921), but was
not a collection of tricks taken directly from that
magazine.

A.2.   Practical Card Tricks
Hika, Wisconsin: E. R. Mill, 1921.
12p. paper covers,

became book one of the **Practical Card Trick** series.
The set of four was completed by 1928.

5

Gibson's interest in simple tricks which did not require elaborate apparatus is apparent in many of his magic books.

A.3. Money Magic
Philadelphia: Cooper Printing Co., 1926.
14p. illus. paper covers,

was no exception. The 18 tricks in this pamphlet use only coins and paper money as apparatus.

1926 was the first in a series of "peak years" in Gibson's writing. That is, it was the first year in which he published more than one book. Most novelists seem prolific if they can produce a book each year, but Gibson may have decided he couldn't succeed without doing better than that.

A.4. Popular Card Tricks
New York: E. I. Company, nd [1926].
48p. illus. paper covers,

was a more elaborate version of **Practical Card Tricks** and included 91 tricks arranged in five categories: Self-working card tricks; Methods for locating and appearing cards; Mysterious card tricks performed without the aid of special systems; Tricks requiring pre-arrangement; and Miscellaneous card mysteries. It was all accompanied by a Preface with suggestions for presenting the tricks and some concluding remarks.

Popular Card Tricks had been planned as the first in a series of books on simple magic to be issued under Houdini's name and sold with the Houdini Show. As such, it was the first of several works which were to be "ghosted" by Gibson under more famous names. When Houdini died in 1926, the magician's estate allowed Gibson to publish the book under his own name.

The second volume of the **Practical Card Tricks** series was published that same year.

A.5. Twenty New Practical Card Tricks
Hika, Wisconsin: E. R. Mill, 1926.
13-28p. paper covers,

was indeed a continuation of the series as indicated by the pagination continued from that of

Book One. It was intended that the purchaser have
the volumes bound together for easy reference.

Gibson's most comprehensive book to that time
is undoubtedly the one he ghosted for Howard
Thurston. While Gibson's own name does not appear
on the cover or title page of

A.6. Howard Thurston's [Walter B. Gibson]
200 Tricks You Can Do
New York: George Sully and Co., 1926.
xiii, 126p. illus. cloth,

the brief biography of the magician which serves as
an introduction is signed "Walter B. Gibson,
President, Philadelphia Assembly, Society of
American Magicians."

Once again, the tricks are arranged by
categories, with a minimum of suggested patter. To
Gibson, patter was such an individual thing that he
felt each practitioner should develop his own to
suit his personality. While many are very simple,
each requires a certain amount of practice before
performing.

The book has retained a durable place in the
libraries of amateur magicians. It also has a
complex bibliographic history. By itself, in
combination with its sequel (**200 More Tricks You
Can Do, A.15**), or in several editions of selected
tricks, it has rarely, if ever, been out of print.

A British edition was published by C. Arthur
Pearson, London, in two volumes: **100 Tricks You Can
Do** (1931) and **100 More Tricks You Can Do** (1932).
The combined edition appeared under the title, **400
Tricks You Can Do** (Blue Ribbon Books, 1939) and was
re-issued with new pagination by Garden City
Publishing in 1948. There have been various later
printings with variations on the title (**400
Fascinating Magic Tricks You Can Do**, Los Angeles:
Wilshire Books, nd, is obviously the complete
collection in one volume.) Selections from the
combined edition were published as **300 Tricks You
Can Do** (New York: Comet Books, 1948).

The ghosting and promotional work Gibson
intended doing for Houdini was transferred to
Howard Thurston (1869-1936) who toured the world

with his stage show in the first quarter of this century. His name does not have the charisma today that Houdini's name has, but has been kept alive to the general public through the work of Walter Gibson who knew both of them.

No less than ten books were produced by Gibson in the following year, 1927, the author drawing on material from his syndicated features for many of them.

A.7. The Book of Secrets, Miracles Ancient and Modern With Added Chapters on Easy Magic You Can Do
Scranton, Pa.: Personal Arts Co., [1927].
159p. illus. cloth,

was composed of material collected from two syndicated features, "Miracles- Ancient and Modern" and "Easy Magic You Can Do." The illustrations by a Ledger Syndicate artist named Gruger were retained from the feature, but the text was rewritten. Animal hypnotism, the Babylonian idol, Bel, which ate the meals placed before it at night, the Greek temple whose doors opened of their own accord followed by a thundering noise, the production of "ghosts" by medieval sorcery, the Indian rope trick, and Spirit Photographs are among the 56 "miracles" described briefly in a format which had each page of text faced with an illustration. In addition, 39 magic tricks of all categories, including coin and card tricks are included. The format of the published book (7 3/4" high by 9 3/4" wide, opening the long way) was chosen to fit the size of the illustrations and set a pattern for other books of its day. (A later edition was published by Mason Publishing Co., of New York.)

A.8. The Bunco Book
Philadelphia: Walter B. Gibson, 1927.
96p. illus. paper covers,

was published by the author himself and as such is a re-working of the 50 articles syndicated (1923- 24) as "Bunco Games to Beware of." With some re- arrangements and title changes, the 50 original articles became 66 entries in the book. It was re- issued with a new introduction (Holyoke, Mass.: Sidney H. Radner, 1946) and thirty years later

republished as two paper covered volumes, **The Bunco
Book** and **Carnival Gaffs,** with 3 of the 66 entries
omitted (Las Vegas: Gamblers Book Club, 1976).

The Gold Brick Swindle, methods of "short
change" artists, the old shell game, bets that seem
to be too good to be true, the methods of card
sharps, constitute one category of the short essays
in the book while the working of carnival games
make up   another.   The original articles were
illustrated by that artist from Columbus, Ohio,
John Duffy.   Most of these were retained in the
book and lend a certain "period" charm to the work,
especially in its later editions.

The first book which Gibson wrote under a pen
name which was not that of a real person was

A.9.   Wilber Gaston's [Walter B. Gibson]
First Principles of Astrology
New York: George Sully and Co., 1927.
186p cloth.

His first entry into the world of the occult, it
was not made up of previously published material.
It is a practical guide for applying astrological
principles   to   everyday   life   and   includes
instructions   for   casting   ones   own   horoscope
according to an "Astroscientific basis."   It was
re-issued as **Astrology Explained**   (New York: Vista
House, 1959) under Gibson's own name, printed from
a photo-enlargement of the original pages.   Thus,
the running head on the left-hand page in that
edition retains the original book title.   All of
the Sully editions of Gibson are uniform in size
and binding (7 1/2" x 5 1/4").   The Vista House
edition measures 9 1/4" x 6 1/4".

Sully had published three other Gibson titles
that year, so they may have suggested he use a pen
name on this one.   It was the only time that name
was used.

A good, workmanlike job with no flamboyant
style of writing, **First Principles of Astrology** is
a model for the handbooks and other self-help
manuals which Gibson wrote in the 1950s and 1960s.

That same year, Gibson assembled a collection
of about 60 tricks and puzzles taken from his own

articles as well as from material in Houdini's files.

A.10. Houdini's Book of Magic and Party Pastimes
New York: Stoll & Edwards Co., Inc., 1927.
32p. illus. paper covers,

has a very complicated bibliographic and publishing history. The same year that the Stoll & Edwards edition was published it was expanded and re-issued as **Houdini's Big Little Book of Magic Easy for Everyone**, by Whitman Publishing, Racine, Wisconsin as one of their Big Little Books. The 295 pages (alternating text on the left-hand page with the illustration on the right-hand page) required 90 tricks, of which 70 were Gibson originals and not Houdini reprints. The title page on the Stoll and Edwards edition reads: **Book of Magic and Party Pastimes, Fascinating Puzzles, Tricks, and Mysterious Stunts** while the Whitman edition reads: **Book of Magic, Fascinating Puzzles, Tricks, and Mysterious Stunts**, selected by Houdini, the World's Greatest Magician. It had a further edition in 1976 as **Houdini's Book of Magic** (New York: Pinnacle Books), with an introduction signed by Gibson. This edition contains 94 tricks, most of them written by Gibson, especially in the section, "Tricks of Magic by Other Magicians" on pages 41 to 110. A similar section appears in the Big Little Book on pages 115 to 295.

A.11. The Magic Square: Tells Your Past-Present-Future
New York: George Sully and Co., 1927.
vi, 167p. cloth,

is a straight parlor game built around the science of "Arithmancy" or divination by numbers. The reader is told to select a question from a table of 60 questions, turn to one of seven "magic squares" (a grid of 49 smaller squares, each bearing a different number) which corresponds to the day of the week, and choose a number at random. The answer to the question is found under that number in the Table of Answers which makes up the bulk of the book.

A companion volume to **The Magic Square,**

**A.12. The Science of Numerology: What Numbers
Mean to You**
New York: George Sully and Co., 1927.
x, 186p. illus. cloth,

explains the significance of numbers as well as the
science and history of Numerology. It includes a
detailed explanation of the importance of these
numbers for people.

Gibson turned once again to the mainstream of
magic with his other four books for 1927.

A.13. Howard Thurston's [Walter B. Gibson]
Book of Magic (New Edition-Number Nine)
Philadelphia: Edward J. Murray, 1927.
16p. illus. paper covers,

is really the program book for Thurston's magic
show "comprising Thurston's Life Story, Thurston's
New 'Easy Pocket Tricks,' Thurston's Astrological
Charts, Thurston's Secrets of Indian Magic, and
Thurston's Dream Book." Of the several "numbers"
of this publication (corresponding to new editions)
this is the only one to which Gibson made
substantial contributions. The cover title reads:
Thurston, the Great Magician, but the folio book is
generally referred to as **Thurston's Book of Magic.**

According to Gibson there were two versions of
this "number" with differing contents. The one
examined has a devil's face surrounded by
illustrations of various magic acts.

Book Three of the Practical Card Trick series
appeared under the title

A.14. Two Dozen Effective Practical Card Tricks
Hika, Wisconsin: E. R. Mill, 1927.
29-44p. paper covers.

Again the pagination was continued from the
previous volume. Correspondence with Gibson has
verified the suggestion that this was intended as a
book in parts, the three to be bound together as a
single entity.

The companion volume to **200 Tricks You Can Do** was published as

A.15. Howard Thurston's [Walter B. Gibson]
200 More Tricks You Can Do
New York: George Sully and Co., 1927.
187p. illus. cloth,

with 16 categories of tricks.   For additional publishing history, see book **A.6.**

While not as widely disseminated as the two Thurston books, the title of Major Collection from his Early Years must be awarded to

A.16.   The World's Best Book of Magic
Philadelphia: Penn Publishing Co., 1927.
319p. illus. cloth,

in which literally hundreds of tricks appear under six categories.   Drawn from the daily columns, weekly articles, and other material with which Gibson had supplied the magical magazines for the previous 12 years, the book was issued as a volume in Penn's "World's Best Book" series.   This has caused some confusion about its proper title. Gibson submitted it as **The Book of Magic**, but the series title quickly became part of it so that it is generally referred to as **The World's Best Book of Magic**.   Gibson might not have claimed it to be quite that superlative.   It was re-issued under its correct title by Baronet Publishing Co. New York, in 1978.

As with earlier collections of tricks, Gibson included some essays on the romance of magic, the art of misdirection, and classes of magic.   Having requested that Howard Thurston provide a Foreword, Gibson then wrote it himself, reversing the arrangement in the first of the **Tricks You Can Do** titles.   Here Gibson wrote the entire work, signing Thurston's name only to the Foreword; there he also wrote the entire work, but signed his own name to the Introduction and Thurston's name to the rest of the book.

The following year he published a more elaborate version of the program book for the Thurston show under the title

A.17. Howard Thurston's [Walter B. Gibson]
Fooling the World
New York: Howard Thurston, 1928
96p. illus. paper covers.

It is sub-titled "A Book of Mystery, Magic and
Adventure, containing important events and
experiences in the career of the famous magician."
In addition to Thurston's Life Story (found also in
A.13) there is Thurston's World Tour; Rulers of the
World (whom Thurston Entertained); Thurston's
Inventions; Thurston's Adventures; Easy Pocket
Tricks; Famous Magicians-Past and Present;
Thurston's Astrological Charts; "Signification" of
Dreams; Numerology; and Fortune Telling with Cards.
The contents varied from season to season so that
there are differences between printings of this
title. A 64 page version appeared in 1930 as **The
Book of Mystery**. The running heads and the title
page read: **Fooling Millions**, an early title altered
prior to release when only a new cover was
prepared.

The fourth and final section of the **Practical
Card Trick** series appeared as

A.18. **Sixteen Master Card Mysteries**
Hika, Wisconsin: Edward R. Mill, 1928.
16p. paper covers,

with pagination not continued from the earlier
books so that it stands alone.

A.19. Howard Thurston's [Walter B. Gibson]
The Thurston Magic Lessons
New York: Howard Thurston, 1928.
37p. illus. paper covers,

includes everything to help plan an evening of
magic among its eight lessons, including a partial
listing of magic dealers such as Walter B. Gibson,
Inc, 709 Chestnut Street, Philadelphia. It was
advertised as a "$10 Method for $1" and sold
through the program book for the Thurston show. It
has exhibited a considerable durability and has
been reprinted and serialized in the pages of
Gibson's own **Conjurors' Magazine** as well as other
magical magazines.

The following year Gibson began writing for another of the major stage magicians of the twentieth century, Harry Blackstone, born Henri Bouton (1885-1965), who was fast coming into prominence with his elaborate show.

A.20. Harry Blackstone's [Walter B. Gibson]
Blackstone's Annual of Magic
Philadelphia: Cooper Printing Co., 1929.
48p. illus. paper covers

was designed as a sedate version of the traditional program book (Blackstone's more flamboyant, illustrated programs would come later). It was sub-titled "A Compendium of Up-to-Date Conjuring including Master Methods of Magic, Practical Card Tricks, and The Magical Miscellany." Material signed by Gibson (although much of the rest must have been by him as well): "Practical Card Tricks" (those left out of the four booklet series) and the short story, "The Man of Mysteries."

Gibson produced several minor collections of tricks using Blackstone's name, but the most durable have been two longer volumes from this period. The first one

A.21. Harry Blackstone's [Walter B. Gibson]
Blackstone's Secrets of Magic
New York: George Sully and Co., 1929.
xv, 265p. illus. cloth

contains seven chapters covering more than 100 tricks from close-up magic to elaborate stage illusions. Such traditional tricks as the linking rings and the cups and balls are not forgotten. Combined with its "sequel", **Blackstone's Modern Card Tricks**, it was re-issued in 1941 by Garden City Publishing Co. Revised, abridged, and "brought up-to-date" it was re-published by Doubleday in 1958. It has remained in print to this day.

Similar, but more "light weight" in appearance, was another Blackstone title

A.22. Harry Blackstone's [Walter B. Gibson]
Blackstone's Tricks and Entertainments
New York: Jacobsen Publishing Co., 1929.
98p. illus. paper covers.

In the "Note to the Reader" the intent of the book
is stated as explaining "tricks and diversions
which you can learn to perform without skill or
special apparatus-and without the need of lengthy
practice."   The second category-the diversions-
includes shadow picture stories (how prophetic!),
match stick tricks, eye teasers, puzzling problems,
unusual games, and catch questions.

     Gibson's final service for Howard Thurston was
to collaborate with him on his autobiography.

     A.23.   Howard Thurston's
     My Life of Magic [as told to Walter B. Gibson]
     Philadelphia: Dorrance and Co., 1929.
     273p. illus. cloth

was Gibson's first substantial contribution to the
history of magic.   Thurston had been inspired to
become a magician when he saw Herrmann the Great in
Columbus, Ohio; later he was billed as "The Man
That Mystified Herrmann."   According to his
account, Thurston ran away from home to become a
jockey, returned to study to become a medical
missionary, but decided on a career in magic
following a re-encounter with Herrmann.   Tent shows
and dime museums lead to an engagement at Tony
Pastor's in 1899, a tour of the country, and four
weeks at the Palace Theatre in London.   Taking nine
months off, he developed a more elaborate show
which opened at Keith's Theatre in Boston, May
1902.   One third of the book is devoted to his tour
of Australia, India, and the Far East (1902-1908).
He ends with an account of his year with Harry
Kellar (1849-1922) and anecdotes of his
performances during World War I and the incident
when he nearly smashed President Coolidge's watch
for real.

     Dictated to Gibson at Thurston's Long Island
home, this is essentially his own story in his own
words.   Short on specific dates and the names of
people he encountered, Thurston nevertheless
presents his Life as a Story worth the Telling.   In
addition, it is a vivid account of life at the turn
of the century.

     There is no index, but a list of "Persons
Mentioned in Thurston's Life of Magic" (otherwise
unidentified) is included.   The first 23 chapters

also appeared in **Collier's Weekly** (May 11-June 8, 1929) as "Nothing Up My Sleeve" while the remaining chapters contain anecdotes found in other articles published under Thurston's name. Contrary to the usual practice, the book was written first and followed by the magazine version.

Another work for Blackstone, slight when compared to the Thurston autobiography, was

> **A.24.** Harry Blackstone's [Walter B. Gibson]
> **Blackstone's Magic: A Book of Mystery**
> Philadelphia: Shade Publishing Co., 1930.
> 64p. illus. paper covers.

This promotional booklet carries no author on the title page, but includes the life story of Harry Blackstone, "the greatest magician the world has ever known" as well as Blackstone's tricks for everyone; Magic of the East (methods of wonder workers); an illustrated display of Blackstone escaping from a locked box dropped in the ocean; Tricks of hypnotism; Card tricks for everyone; Fake mediums and their methods; and Mental Mysteries. It contains a little bit of everything in which Gibson had been interested for the past 15 years. There are 5 pages of advertisements, including one for **Blackstone's Annual of Magic (A.20)** and another for the Magic Circle of Three Rivers, Michigan, of which Blackstone was president. The cover illustration is a full face portrait of Blackstone. Gibson said there were two variants of this title with differing contents. Cover title: **Blackstone's Magic: Every Trick Illustrated.**

One of Gibson's syndicated features from the early years was called "Your Brains If Any" (it was also known as "Brain Tests") which appeared in the New York **Evening Post**. 150 tests were collected as

> **A.25. Brain Tests; or, Your Brains, If Any**
> Boston: L. C. Page & Co., 1930.
> xiii, 224p. illus. cloth

and "designed for one definite purpose: to provide interesting diversion and worth while entertainment for persons of intelligence." Adapted from the intelligence tests used in institutions of higher education to measure mental aptitude they were shortened, revised, and popularized to test ingenuity, accuracy, speed, judgment, observation, as well as knowledge of subjects like history, literature, and mathematics. Gibson's brother, Anthony, a philosophy instructor at the University of Pennsylvania designed a number of the tests.

At some time in 1929 or 1930, Gibson met and arranged to write material for Professor Alfred Francis Seward (1877-193?) whose name had appeared as author and publisher on books of astrology as early as 1915.   (**The Star Gazers of Egypt**, **The Zodiac and its Mysteries**, **Prof. Seward's Planetary Handbook**, as well as **Planting, Harvesting and Surgical Operations...According to the Signs of the Zodiac**)   Having dealt with some of the more enduring names in the field of conjuring, Gibson now turned to someone whose name is little known today. We will probably never know just what drew him to ghost books for this astrologer. Seward is remembered primarily for the fact that it was he who introduced Walter Gibson to Harry Blackstone.

A.26. Prof. A[lfred] F[rancis] Seward's
[Walter B. Gibson]
Facts about Brunettes and Blondes
Chicago: A. F. Seward & Co., 1930.
ii, 108p. illus. paper covers

is based on the theory that success, happiness, and a thorough understanding of others can be achieved only through a study of racial differences and national ideals. Then the psychology of groups can be applied to the individual. The distinctive differences of blondes and brunettes as observed in groups enables us to analyze each person according to a certain formula. The book includes tables of characteristics and a formula for determining an individual's "vibrations." Cover title: **Facts About Brunettes and Blondes and How to Read Them.**

Among Gibson's greatest contributions to the history and lore of magic was his work on behalf of the legacy of Houdini. The first of these was

A.27. Houdini's Escapes
New York: Harcourt, Brace & Co., 1930.
xiv, 317p. illus. cloth.

Prepared from Houdini's private notebooks and memoranda with the assistance of Beatrice (Bess)

Houdini (1876-1943) and Bernard M. L. Ernst (1879-1939), this may be the definitive account of the escape artist's methods.   Rope ties and chain releases, box escapes, underwater escapes, and walking through a brick wall are all included along with an account of the notes from which they were compiled.   According to the introduction to the later edition, the original notes no longer exist so this book is the only first-hand account of the master's methods.   As such it has served as source material for all later writers who have approached Houdini as a subject.   Bernard Ernst was Houdini's lawyer and the president of the parent assembly of the Society of American Magicians.

The book was re-issued in a combined edition with **Houdini's Magic (A.29)** by Blue Ribbon Books in 1932, and with the addition of an introduction by magician Milbourne Christopher (1914-1984) it was reprinted by Funk & Wagnalls as well as by Bantam Books in 1976.

Chapter Three

CASTING SHADOWS

1931-1940

The decade of the 1930s was not a period of great productivity on Gibson's part, but only if you look at his published books and pamphlets. Twelve titles, scarcely one every year. Four were works ghosted for others and four others were made up of material previously published in periodicals or from a Ledger Syndicate series.

Of course, the majority of Gibson's output in the decade appeared in periodicals, for this was when he established his position as a writer of fiction by creating The Shadow magazine series for Street and Smith. The story of the creation of The Shadow has been dealt with extensively and exhaustively by others and will be touched on in these pages only briefly.

According to Will Murray in **The Duende History of The Shadow Magazine**, Gibson wrote 9 Shadow novels the first year, in 1931, which explains to some extent why he published no books that year. Much of his writing was concerned with developing his new character. Prior to writing the lead novel for **The Shadow Magazine** he had edited **True Strange Stories** for MacFadden Publications as well as editing and publishing **Tales of Magic and Mystery**. By the time he came to Street and Smith, he had acquired a certain practical knowledge of the magazine business.

As though to make up for lost time, he published four books in 1932, among them the companion volumes to **Blackstone's Secrets of Magic (A.21)** and **Houdini's Escapes (A.27)**.

A.28. Harry Blackstone's [Walter B. Gibson]
Blackstone's Modern Card Tricks
New York: George Sully and Co., 1932.
xiv, 204p. illus. cloth,

contains more than 75 tricks with cards arranged in
seven   chapters: preliminary   sleights,   card
locations, card discoveries, spelling tricks, easy
card tricks, advanced card tricks, and special card
tricks.   Combined   with   **Blackstone's Secrets of
Magic**, it was re-issued by Garden City Publishing
Company in 1941.   It has been re-printed several
times;   in   1958   it   was   revised,   abridged,   and
brought "up-to-date" by Doubleday.

Another   significant   contribution   to   the
history and lore of magic is found in

A.29. **Houdini's Magic**
New York: Harcourt, Brace & Co., 1932.
xi, 316p. illus. cloth,

where preference is given to those magic illusions
(as   distinct   from   escapes)   which,   judging   from
Houdini's notes, were his own.   Impromptu tricks,
card tricks, slate tricks, message reading, second
sight tricks, stage tricks, effects and illusions,
anti-spiritualistic   effects,   some   escapes   not
included in the previous collection, and notes on
Kellar's magic appear in the book.   Prepared from
Houdini's   private   notebooks   and   memoranda,   this
constitutes as definitive an account as we possess.
Like its companion volume, it has served as source
material for all subsequent studies of Houdini.

Combined   with   its   predecessor,   the   book   was
published   in   one   volume   by   Blue   Ribbon   Books
(1932), and re-issued with a new introduction by
Milbourne Christopher in 1976 by Funk & Wagnalls.
For   other   notes   on   its   publishing   history,   see
A.27.

Gibson   returned   to   his   earlier   theme,   the
simple   magic   trick   which   may   be   performed   with
common objects in

A.30. Magic Made Easy
Springfield, Mass.: McLoughlin Bros., Inc.,
1932. 121p. illus. paper covers.

No special apparatus is required, the author promises, nor is skill necessary. There are actually 119 pages of tricks, two per page, collected from Gibson's "Magic Made Easy" series syndicated by the Ledger and reproduced here in facsimile. The tricks include "The Balanced Egg," "The Rising Card," "The Magic Loop," and "The Vanishing Thimble." A pamphlet of 12 selections from the syndicate feature was issued as an advertising flier under the title, **A Book of Magic for Boys and Girls.**

A.31. A[lfred] F[rancis] Seward's
[Walter B. Gibson]
Periodicity, the Absolute Law of the Universe
Atlantic City & Chicago: A. F. Seward & Co.,
1932. 154p. paper covers,

was another book ghosted for the Chicago astrologer. It contains lessons in attuning ones life with nature through the study of the correct "active laws" and the "rhythm of the world" along with those conditions which govern the affairs of all living beings. The cover title reads: **Periodicity or Cycles of Destiny.**

According to correspondence from Gibson to this writer, there was another book for Prof. Seward, **How to Be Happy**, a revision of an earlier title, but this has not been located.

A.32. Magician's Manual
New York: The Magician's League of America,
1933. 140p. illus. cloth,

is something of a gimmick, almost a non-book, before the day when that term came into general use. It was designed as an introduction to magic for the uninitiated with the apparatus needed for each trick either in cellophane envelopes or on special colored cardboard sheets inserted next to the directions. This may have proved too expensive to produce (each copy needed to be assembled by hand) for in the second edition the cellophane envelopes were replaced with special pages of

apparatus to be cut out. The reprint published by
A. L. Burt followed the format of the second
Magician's League edition.

When the first issue of **The Shadow** Detective
Magazine proved to be a sell-out and readers still
requested copies of the story from it, Street and
Smith responded with

A.33. Maxwell Grant's [Walter B. Gibson]
The Living Shadow: A Detective Novel
New York: Street & Smith, nd [1934].
245p. paper on boards,

proclaimed on the spine of the pictorial cover as a
volume in "The Ideal Library."

Murder, stolen jewels, and a Chinatown setting
form the structure of the first novel about The
Shadow. In it we are introduced to Harry Vincent,
Joe Cardona, and Diamond Bert Farwell, all of whom
return in later stories. While not a typical
Shadow plot, nevertheless the novel has many of the
elements which Gibson developed further in later
stories. It resembles the classic body-in-the-
library mysteries so typical of the Golden Age of
detective fiction.

Originally published in **The Shadow** Detective
Magazine for April-June 1931, it was reprinted in
1942 in the first **Shadow Annual,** and had four
subsequent editions as a separate work: Bantam
Books (1969), Pyramid Books (1974), New English
Library of London (1976), and Jove Books (1977).

When **The Living Shadow** was reprinted by the
Ideal Library, a Foreword signed Maxwell Grant was
added, the final paragraph was dropped and three
new paragraphs substituted. This new ending was
retained in **The Shadow Annual** edition for 1942, but
the entire text was revised and abridged by Morris
Ogden Jones, a Street and Smith staff editor. This
version has 33 chapters compared to the original
magazine version with 37 chapters. Some of the
original chapters were compressed and combined.

The original pulp magazine text has been
preserved in the Bantam, Pyramid, New English
Library, and Jove paperback editions.

When the demand for the early Shadow novels could not be met by reprinting the magazines, the second novel was also added to the Ideal Library as

A.34.   Maxwell Grant's [Walter B. Gibson]
The Eyes of The Shadow: A Detective Novel
New York: Street & Smith, nd [1935].
252p. paper on boards.

A fortune in gems is sought by criminal lawyer Isaac Coffran in this novel which also introduces Lamont Cranston as the alter ego of The Shadow. Other recurring characters include Bruce Duncan and Red Mike.   The story is set in part in the Cobalt Club and the Black Ship (a waterfront bar), which became recurring settings in some of the later stories.

Originally published in **The Shadow** Detective **Magazine** for July-September 1931, the novel was reprinted only once as a separate work in later years, by Bantam Books in 1969.   Again, the Ideal Library edition contains a Foreword signed Maxwell Grant which was not in the original pulp magazine. Otherwise, the text appears unchanged.

Reprinting magazine stories in book form in a "Library" edition was not a new concept for Street and Smith.   Dime Novel series such as the Frank Merriwell stories from the **Tip Top Weekly** and the Nick Carter stories in the **Nick Carter Weekly** and **Nick Carter Stories** gained extended life in the early twentieth century in paper covered series like the **Medal Library** and the **Magnet Library**. Street and Smith was not a firm to forget a good idea once discovered.   The first three novels from **Doc Savage Magazine** followed The Shadow into Ideal Library editions as well.

The final volume in the original Shadow trilogy was added to the Ideal Library as

A.35.   Maxwell Grant's [Walter B. Gibson]
The Shadow Laughs: A Detective Novel
New York: Street & Smith, nd [1935].
252p. paper on boards.

An innocent man is murdered, a police detective is lured to his death, and the man behind the plot turns out to be an old enemy of The Shadow.   The novel introduces Vic Marquette of the Secret Service and establishes Lamont Cranston and The Shadow as separate entities.

Originally published in **The Shadow Detective Monthly** (the new title for the magazine) in October 1931, the novel was later reprinted as a separate work by Bantam Books in 1969. Once more, the Ideal Library edition contains a Foreword signed Maxwell Grant which was not in the original pulp magazine.

During that busy decade, Gibson found time to serve as some time ghost writer for an upcoming new psychic entertainer, mentalist Joseph Dunninger (1896-1975). He also found a new publisher, David Kemp and Co.

> **A.36.** Joseph Dunninger's [Walter B. Gibson]
> **Inside the Medium's Cabinet**
> New York: David Kemp and Co., 1935.
> vi, 228p. illus. cloth,

is, according to its dust jacket "a daring expose of fraudulent mediums and the trickery of so-called supernatural phenomena... every statement of fact is based on first-hand investigation in the spook parlors and shrouded haunts of the modern wonder workers themselves." Included are accounts of the activities of a medium during the Lindbergh kidnapping case, the attempts to contact Houdini's spirit, as well as the work of mediums Nino Pecoraro and Frank Decker.

The following year, Gibson published a companion volume in

> **A.37.** Joseph Dunninger's [Walter B. Gibson]
> **How to Make a Ghost Walk**
> New York: David Kemp and Co., 1936.
> viii, 82p. illus. cloth,

which seems to have been written with tongue in cheek as well as a distinctively light touch. It is the practical aspect of spiritualism with chapters on staging a seance for fun and profit. The seance is presented as just another type of stage illusion.

Not one to allow a good idea to lie fallow, Gibson revised his **Magician's Manual** of 1933 and published

A.38. The New Magician's Manual
New York: David Kemp and Co., 1936.
143p. illus. cloth,

as a collection of 71 tricks and routines with instructions for performances by the amateur. Most of the tricks require only common objects like kitchen matches or playing cards. The emphasis is on deception rather than sleight of hand. Eight sheets of colored cardboard ready to cut out contain the apparatus for many of the tricks. The book gained a wider audience when it was reprinted in facsimile by Dover Publications in 1975. Drawings to illustrate the methods are by William H. Hanna.

By 1936, **The Shadow Magazine** with a slightly altered title was appearing twice a month. Gibson's original agreement with Street and Smith for four novels a year had been replaced by a contract calling for 24 novels each year. Faced with the task of supplying that amount there was no time to write fresh material to be published in book form. For the next decade Walter Gibson concentrated on feeding the insatiable appetite of publisher and public with stories for pulp magazines and comic books as well as an occasional script for the new medium of radio. Not all of these were involved with The Shadow and not all of it has been properly identified. Much of his radio work was in developing concepts or creating plot ideas which would be fleshed out by others.

The Shadow had been transferred back to radio (where he had originated) with notable success. He was not such a success on the screen, as the two Grand National films starring Rod LaRocque (**The Shadow Strikes**, 1937; **International Crime**, 1938) attest. However, at the beginning of the new decade, a more faithful film adaptation was released in the 15 chapter Columbia serial, **The Shadow**, starring Victor Jory and Veda Ann Borg. That same year, 1940, one of the more recent pulp novels was published as a separate work.

A.39.   Maxwell Grant's [Walter B. Gibson]
The Shadow and the Voice of Murder
Los Angeles: Bantam Books, 1940.
100p. paper covers,

has a plot which concerns the murder of Frank
Barstead for which Ted Lycombe is unjustly accused.
The novel is something of a milestone in the
evolving saga of The Shadow for in the story
Commissioner Weston appears to have finally
accepted the dark avenger as a real person and not
a legend.

The novel was published originally as "Voice
of Death" in **The Shadow Magazine** for February 15,
1940.   Two editions of this scarce book were
printed, one with a pictorial cover and a second
with a plain cover without an illustration.

Chapter Four

Greater Magic

1941-1949

   Primarily concerned with continuing The Shadow
saga for Street and Smith, Gibson published only 15
books in the decade of the 1940s.   Several were
barely pamphlets, some bore other names than his on
the title pages, and three were made up of novels
collected from **The Shadow Magazine.** He wrote two
original novels about magician-detectives following
the concept of the Norgil stories which he had
written for Street and Smith pulps as Maxwell Grant
during the previous decade.   These new works were
signed with his own name, but not so the
novelization of the movie, **The Sin of Harold
Diddlebock.**

   Gibson had expanded his role at Street and
Smith to include writing scripts for **Shadow Comics,**
an idea he claimed as largely his own.   He also
wrote scripts for the Blackstone and Elliman
stories in **Super-Magician Comics** and in connection
with this prepared

   A.40.   The Great Blackstone's [Walter B. Gibson]
   Complete Magic Show
   [New York:] [Street & Smith,] 1941.
   16p. illus. paper covers.

The pamphlet contains patter and instructions for
six tricks intended to make up an entire magic show
for young people: Paper Prestidigitation, The
Magician at the Circus, Conclave of the Aces, A
Tale of India, The Magic Chef, and Black and White.
This small publication (which measures 6 3/4" high
by 3 5/8" wide) includes the rules of the
Blackstone Junior Magicians.   Accompanied by a

27

membership card in the BJM, it was distributed by
Street and Smith to the readers of **Super-Magician
Comics.**

In 1942 Street and Smith published the first
of their Shadow "annuals" which collected three of
the more popular and hard to find novels from past
issues of the magazine.

A.41. Maxwell Grant's [Walter Gibson]
The Shadow Annual [1942]
New York: Street & Smith, 1942.
160p. illus. paper covers,

boasts a cover illustration showing Lamont Cranston
in formal dress casting an ominous shadow.
Previously used on **The Shadow Magazine** for January
1, 1939 for the novel, **Silver Skull**, it was a
fitting cover for this work which collects **The
Living Shadow** (1931), **The Ghost Makers** (October 15,
1932), and **The Black Hush** (August 1, 1933).

The success of the venture prompted the
publisher to repeat the performance the next year
with

A.42. Maxwell Grant's [Walter B. Gibson]
The Shadow Annual [1943]
New York: Street & Smith, 1943.
160p. illus. paper covers.

This time the cover has a framed portrait of Lamont
Cranston in a pin stripe suit casting the shadow of
his alter ego.

The selection of novels reprinted was again
from early issues of the magazine, **The Voodoo
Master** (March 1, 1936), **Hidden Death** (September
1932), and **The Grey Ghost** (May 1, 1936). The first
novel introduced Dr. Rodil Mocquino, a figure who
appeared in three Shadow novels and several comic
book stories.   The other two novels about Dr.
Mocquino are   **City of Doom** (May 15, 1936) and
Voodoo Trail (June 1, 1938).

The shortage of paper for magazines and books
during the second world war prevented Street and
Smith from following the two annuals with a third
one the next year.   The third and final **Shadow
Annual** did not appear until 1947.

In the meantime, Gibson collected a series of
newspaper articles on mind reading which he had
written, revised them slightly, and published them
as

A.43. [Joseph] Dunninger's [Walter B. Gibson]
What's On Your Mind?
Cleveland and New York: World Publishing
Co., 1944.
192p. illus. cloth.

The series, and the book, explain the mysteries and
methods of mental telepathy according to master
mentalist, Joseph Dunninger. An introduction on
Dunninger's life and work, signed by Gibson, was
added to the book.

One of Gibson's projects during the decade was
his promotion work for the Blackstone show. He
drafted scripts with Nancy Webb (her husband was
writer, Jean Francis Webb) for a radio series
called **Blackstone the Magic Detective**, provided
simple tricks for Blackstone to explain to the
audience, and wrote the program books for the stage
show. Blackstone was portrayed on the air by actor
Edwin Jerome. Several of his publications during
this period were tied in with these pursuits.

A.44. [Anonymous]
**Blackstone, World's Super Magician: Souvenir
Program and Illustrated Trick Book**
New York: Wm. C. Popper, nd [1945],
20p. illus. paper covers,

was the show book for the Blackstone (Stage) Magic
Show. As such it resembled an up-dated version of
the show book for Thurston, with the life story of
the magician, anecdotes about the show, the
illusions to be performed, and a dozen or more
simple tricks explained. The title, cover design,
and content varied from year to year. There are
five known "editions": 1945, as described above,
with the cover drawn by C. C. Beck around a three-
quarter view, cameo photo of Blackstone; 1946:
Blackstone, World's Master Magician, cover by E. C.
Stoner, profile cameo photo of Blackstone; 1947:
same title, but a different cover drawing by
Stoner; 1948: same title, but a photographic cover
only; 1949: **Blackstone** (as title) with a
photographic cover. The later editions were used

when Blackstone was no longer a comic book hero as
well as a stage magician but was merely a magician.

   **A.45.   Secrets of Magic. A New Book of Tricks
   You Can Do.**
   New York: Wm. C. Popper and Co., 1945.
   50p. illus. paper covers,

contains seven categories of simple tricks: Mind
Over Mind, Mathementalix, Two Minds as One, Its in
the Cards, Magicoddities, Hypnomagic, and
Gagmentalia.   More than 80 tricks which require no
apparatus, but do demand practice, are arranged two
or three to a page, with line drawings to
illustrate them.   This material is similar to that
used in the Blackstone Show program books, but
includes the addresses of selected magic dealers.
An abridged edition (61 tricks only) was published
as **My Secrets of Magic**, by Blackstone, World's
Foremost Magician (Blackstone Magic Enterprises,
1947).   A later printing of this bears the title,
Mysteries of Magic.

   A.46. [Anonymous]
   **Blackstone the Magic Detective Reveals Magic
   Tricks Everyone Can Do**
   New York: Blackstone Magic Enterprises,
   Inc., 1946,
   8p. illus. paper covers,

is a slim collection of 36 tricks illustrated with
line drawings in a format similar to that of **After
Dinner Tricks.**   The tricks require little if any
apparatus.   Distributed by Richfield Gasoline
dealers this was designed to advertise the radio
series.

       Gibson had worked with Julian J. Proskauer
when he was editor of **Conjurors' Magazine.** Now he
collaborated with him on a book about the negative
aspects of the spirit medium business

   A.47.   Julian J. Proskauer's [Walter B. Gibson]
   The Dead Do Not Talk
   New York: Harper and Brothers, 1946
   xvii, 198p. cloth.

Here is the fascinating story of how the illusions
of stage magicians, designed to entertain, are used
by charlatans to prey on those who have suffered

personal loss through death and hope to communicate
with the spirits of the departed.

More traditional and with great similarities
to work he had done before for Thurston and
Blackstone is

A.48.   Professional Magic for Amateurs
New York: Prentice-Hall, 1947
xvi, 225p. illus. cloth.

Fifty easy, but effective, tricks are presented for
the beginner to practice while developing a well-
rounded repertoire. The author explains how the
trick is done as well as how it is supposed to
appear from the audience. It has been extended
beyond the content of the Thurston collections (200
Tricks You Can Do) and Blackstone volumes (Secrets
of Magic) to include some traditional, well-known
stage illusions.

The post-war years saw the beginning of the
decline in popularity of the pulp magazine. Street
and Smith revived their annual collection of the
best of the Shadow stories from recent years one
more time with

A.49.   Maxwell Grant's [Walter B. Gibson]
The Shadow Annual [1947]
New York: Street & Smith, 1947.
144p illus. paper covers.

While collecting No Time for Murder (December
1944), Toll of Death (March 1944), and Murder By
Magic (August 1945), this annual also includes
short stories by other writers: "No Game for a Poor
Man," by Richard Dermody (Shadow, December 1944, as
by Richard Deming) and "The Seeing Eye," by
Franklin Gregory (Shadow, January 1946). An
effective cover design shows a brooding Shadow
towering over the city he is protecting.

Probably the greatest departure for Gibson at
the time was to be asked to write a novelization
for Harold Lloyd's final feature motion picture,
Mad Wednesday, which had originally been given the
title, The Sin of Harold Diddlebock.

A.50. Harry Hershfield's [Walter B. Gibson]
The Sin of Harold Diddlebock
New York: Bartholomew House, 1947.
155p. illus. endpapers. paper covers,

is the story of the rise to fame and fortune of a
young college football star turned clerk in an
advertising agency.   Based on the screenplay by
Preston Sturges, Gibson wrote the novel from the
script handed him by Hershfield which did not
indicate who the actor playing the lead would be.
With his resemblance to a comic Frank Merriwell or
one of Horatio Alger's young heroes, Harold
Diddlebock may have appealed to Gibson who had been
familiar with both of them in his youth.

    Gibson gathered some material from earlier
books (especially A.28.) to promote Blackstone in

A.51. Harry Blackstone's [Walter B. Gibson]
Blackstone's Tricks Anyone Can Do
New York: Permabooks, 1948.
xvii, 232p. illus. pictorial board covers,

which resembles one of the Thurston books with its
200 simple feats of magic to mystify and entertain.
It includes bafflers; table tricks; card sleights,
locations, and discoveries; cigarette magic;
divination and spelling tricks; strings and ropes;
mental mysteries, and a miscellany labelled
"different tricks."   The preface is signed by Harry
Blackstone, and a biographical note about
Blackstone is signed by Julian J. Proskauer, Past
National President, Society of American Magicians.

    If there was a previous magazine appearance
for

A.52. **A Blonde for Murder**
New York: Vital Publications, 1948.
128p. paper covers,

it has not been discovered. The cover calls it "An
Ardini Story" suggesting that Gibson had intended
writing more than this one. It is also labelled as
"Atlas Publication No. 2" and copyrighted by
Current Detective Stories, Inc. which seems to
refer to the title of a magazine. A pulp-action
thriller involving jewel thieves and spiritualism,
this case for Magician-detective, Ardini, also

known as John Arden, was written during Gibson's
hiatus from The Shadow series.

    A similar work which suggests a prior
publication (also not traced) is

    A.53. Looks That Kill!
    New York: Current Detective Stories,
    Inc., 1948. 128p. paper covers,

which is labelled "Atlas Publication No. 5." Both
titles were written directly for book publication,
in spite of the suggestions by the publisher to the
contrary.   Based in part on the Dunninger radio
show which made its debut on ABC, September 12,
1943, the second novel has a murder occurring
during a broadcast of a show starring Valdor, the
Mighty Mind.   The hero needs the ability of a
detective as well as a mentalist to solve the case.

    In 1949, **The Shadow Magazine** ceased
publication and Gibson lost his most steady source
of income. He had returned to the series (after a
hiatus of 15 issues) for the final numbers, but the
publisher decided that the day of the pulp fiction
magazine was over. One by one the magazines ceased
publication: **Doc Savage, Detective Story, Western
Story.** All that remained of the fiction factory
that had been   Street and Smith was **Astounding
Science Fiction.** Gibson's final book for the decade
before he plunged into   writing articles for the
true crime magazines was

    A.54. Magic Explained
    New York: Permabooks, 1949.
    188p. illus. paper covers.

The book contains 100 magic tricks to be performed
with common household objects like handkerchiefs,
coins, matches, playing cards, thimbles, and
string. Gibson traces the origins of many of the
tricks to the routines of magicians of the past.
His anecdotes about Blackstone, Ching Ling Foo,
Chung Ling Soo, Devant, Herrmann, Houdini, Kellar,
Neff, Raymond, Thurston, and others enliven the
work and raise it above the level of being just
another collection of tricks, however creatively
they are presented.

The book was re-issued, as an enlarged photo reprint with running heads added, in both board and paper covered editions by Vista House in 1958. It was later re-issued by Frederick Fell in 1977 under the title, **Mastering Magic: Secrets of the Great Magicians Revealed.**

Chapter Five

After the Shadow

1950-1959

Freed of the responsibility for providing 12 to 24 novels about The Shadow each year, but needing another source of income equally as dependable, Gibson explored some related fields of writing. Instead of writing crime fiction he concentrated on factual crime articles for magazines on the one hand while turning out self-help manuals on a variety of subjects for the Key Publishing Company on the other. The first project took him on trips throughout the United States (primarily in New England) because he preferred to actually talk with the law enforcement officials and others native to the areas where the crimes had been committed. He could just as easily have written his articles from the comfort of his study, using newspaper accounts for reference, but being on the scene helped him to find the right angle from which to approach the story. This gave his stories a greater degree of believability. He had not forgotten his days as a newspaperman.

The self-help manuals were another matter. Most of them were written at home with frequent consultation of his growing reference library of books on gambling, the occult, horse-racing, and other topics as well as regular recourse to his own prodigious memory. Ever on the alert for the odd fact or anecdote to enliven his account, he turned often to the volumes in the **American Notes and Queries** series which stood on the shelves in the room next to the dining room.

A.55. Walter B. Gibson's and Morris N. Young's
Houdini on Magic
New York: Dover Publications, 1953.
xv, 280p. illus. cloth and paper covered
editions,

was another gathering of material from the escape
artist's published writings and unpublished notes.
As such it approaches autobiography in being
Houdini's own account of his escapes, dealings with
spiritualists, stage tricks, and the history of
magic. The introduction and commentary which link
the selections from Houdini are readily
identifiable as they are signed by Gibson.

Prior to the Presidential election of 1956,
Gibson prepared an elementary reference work,

A.56. **The Book of the Presidents of the
United States**
New York: Vital Publications, 1956.
36p. (including cover) illus. paper covers.

There are brief biographical sketches of the
Presidents from Washington through Eisenhower,
nicknames of the Presidents, how the 48 states
voted since 1912, how the President is elected and
a quiz.

A pair of booklets which might have been
issued together because the subject matter is so
similar are

A.57. Sy Seidman's [Walter B. Gibson]
Fun with Optical Illusions
New York: Padell Book Co., 1956.
32p. illus. paper covers,

A.58. Bill Barnum's [Walter B. Gibson]
Fun with Stunts, Tricks and Skits
New York: Padell Book Co., 1956.
32p. illus. paper covers.

The first is a collection of fifty optical
illusions which prove that seeing is not always
believing. Examples of the illusions are
determining which of two printed lines is longer,
cubes that appear to appear different, but are the
same in size and structure, and gazing at a figure
which then appears before you on the wall. The

second collection, similar to some of Gibson's
syndicate features and magical magazine fillers is
a selection of stunts and skits guaranteed to make
you the life of the party. Gibson's fondness for
puns is evident in his choice of pen names for
these.

An arrangement with Key Publishing lead to
Gibson's agreeing to write nearly two dozen self-
help manuals on a variety of subjects from the
occult and paranormal to astronomy and camplife.
Most of them were published under his own name, but
he enjoyed making up pen names for a number of
them. They were written to a formula (the term he
often used was "knocking off a book"), but this
does not mean they are dull or that Gibson didn't
try to put his best work into them. Those on
subjects toward which he had a greater affinity
transcend the formula. Such a title is

A.59.   The Key to Hypnotism
New York: Key Publishing Co., 1956.
96p. illus. paper covers,

which is more of an historical study than a
practical handbook. As such it is a survey of
hypnotism as a science with fundamentals not too
difficult for the lay person to understand. The
description of practical methods are enlivened by
case histories of past practitioners: Dr. James
Braid, Maury, Rahman Bey, Tahra Bey, Professor
Edward B. Tichener, and others.

Another name in magic for whom Gibson served
as ghost writer was the Holyoke, Massachusetts
collector of magic and escape apparatus, Houdini
scholar, and exposer of frauds and crooked
gamblers, Sidney H. Radner. Their first
collaboration,

A.60.   Sidney H. Radner's [Walter B. Gibson]
Magic for Fun
New York: Padell Book Co., 1956.
93p. illus. paper covers,

contains clear descriptions of more than 100 magic
tricks with hints for patter, the importance of
misdirection and with keeping up in the field. The
usual gathering of tricks with handkerchiefs,
coins, cards, cigarettes, string, are presented
alongside mental mysteries, memory tricks, spirit

tricks, and a look at larger illusions. A note on Radner's career is included.

A related work signed by Gibson himself is

A.61. What's New in Magic
Garden City, New York: Hanover House, 1956.
222p. illus. boards,

with nearly 100 new and improved feats of magic using common and not so common objects. The use of special devices or "gimmicks" is discussed in the section called "Magic with Skill."   The British edition (London: Nicholas Kaye, 1957) adds a glossary of terms on pages 223-224.

Gibson combined the art of numbers and their ancient meanings with modern horse racing in

A.62.   Rufus Perry's [Walter B. Gibson]
How to Win with Racing Numerology
New York: Key Publishing Co., 1957.
92p. illus. paper covers.

Vibratory influences are described along with names and numbers linked in actual races with full details of the results. The very latest in racing numerology is the result of reducing a famous oriental system to simple terms and adapting it to the American track. The cover title is **How to Beat the Races by Numerology.**

Since gambling was the special field of Sidney H. Radner it is not surprising that Gibson's titles on poker, roulette, and dice were written under that name while "Rufus Perry" was reserved for the most part for books on horse racing.   It is tempting to wonder if Gibson ever thought of "Rufus Perry" as a relative to the "Bernard Perry" pseudonym he had used in **Tales of Magic and Mystery** in 1927.

A.63.   Sidney H. Radner's [Walter B. Gibson]
How to Play Poker and Win
New York: Key Publishing Co., 1957.
94p. illus. paper covers,

is a guide to poker as a game of skill and not chance and luck. The chapters include Basic Poker, the Draw in Poker, Betting and Bluffing, Five Card

Stud, Poker Gone Wild, and the methods of poker
sharps. The text is liberally filled with
anecdotes to explain the different games. It was
re-issued as **The Key to Playing Poker and Winning**
by Ottenheimer in 1964.

> **A.64.** Rufus Perry's [Walter B. Gibson]
> **How to Play the Horses and Win**
> New York: Key Publishing Co., 1957.
> 94p. illus. paper covers,

has a more scientific basis than the earlier work
using numerology to predict the outcome of a horse
race. This is an introduction for the novice with
descriptions of the different types of horse-racing
and how to gather information before placing a bet.
A simple, sure, winning system is presented along
with a more advanced selective odds system, special
progressive systems, playing overlays, and picking
and winning on longshots. Filled with good
anecdotes it has a glossary of racing terms as
well. It was re-issued and enlarged as **Play the
Horses and Win** by Padell in 1973.

A variant on this is

> **A.65.** Rufus Perry's [Walter B. Gibson]
> **How to Play the Trotters and Win**
> New York: Key Publishing Co., 1957.
> 91p. illus. paper covers,

which describes harness racing and how to bet on
that category of horsemanship. It is not on record
whether Gibson himself ever used any of these
betting methods to advantage.

> **A.66.** Sidney H. Radner's [Walter B. Gibson]
> **How to Spot Card Sharps and Their Methods**
> New York: Key Publishing Co., 1957.
> 95p. illus. paper covers,

is an expose of the crooked cards, devices, and
methods used by gamblers to cheat at card games.
Anecdotes enhance the text which explains how cards
are marked, how crooked deals are made, and how to
use fake shuffles and cold decks.

"Rufus Perry" enlarged his repertoire to
include a volume on card games in

A.67.   Rufus Perry's [Walter B. Gibson]
How to Win at Pinochle and Other Games
New York: Key Publishing Co., 1957.
92p. illus. paper covers,

which is a simplified guide to the game with
suggestions on how to value the hand and the widow,
how much to bid and when. Advice on gin rummy, red
dog and black jack is given along with how to
detect and avoid card sharps in these games. A
revised edition was published as **How to Win at
Pinochle**, edited by Eli S. Garber (New York: Max
Padell, 1972).

Contests and quizzes would seem to be right up
Gibson's alley and so the appearance of a
publication related to the famous CBS television
quiz show, "The $64,000 Challenge," shouldn't
appear out of place in his bibliography. The
anecdotal life story of Theodore Nadler, a 1956
contestant on the show appeared as

A.68.   Teddy Nadler's [Walter B. Gibson]
Secrets of My Million Dollar Memory
New York: Jersam Publishing Corp., 1957.
64p. illus. paper covers.

Memory tricks were something that Gibson was also
fond of and the similarity between the A-I-R
(Application, Interest, Retention) memory system
here and one in **Kreskin's Mind Power Book (A.166.)**
is not likely to be merely coincidental.

The next book written under Radner's name was

A.69.   Sidney H. Radner's [Walter B. Gibson]
Sidney H. Radner on Dice
New York: Key Publishing Co., 1957.
96p. illus. paper covers.

Again, it is intended to supply a great amount of
information in a few pages. From private games to
ones in the club or casino for high stakes, right
bets and wrong bets, the odds and probabilities of
each roll and point are included. The Radner name
assures the reader that crooked dice games and
sucker bets will be included as areas to avoid.
Odds and probabilities were another item with which
Gibson's memory was stored. The book has the
simple cover title, **Radner on Dice**, and was re-

issued in 1962 by Ottenheimer as **The Key to Winning at Dice.**

The last Radner title for the decade was the more optimistically titled work

> **A.70.**   Sidney H. Radner's [Walter B. Gibson]
> **How to Win at Roulette and Other Casino Games**
> New York: Key Publishing Co., 1958.
> 96p. illus. paper covers,

which attempts to cover such topics as the House Percentage and systems designed to even the odds for the players, slot machines, Blackjack, and Craps. The cover title reads: **Radner on--Roulette and Other Casino Games** and the book was re-issued as **The Key to Roulette, Blackjack, One-Armed Bandits** by Ottenheimer in 1963.

The titles alone are indicative of the contents of most of the "Key to..." manuals and the rest of these for the decade may be listed here with only a few comments.

> **A.71.   The Key to Astronomy**
> New York: Key Publishing Co., 1958.
> 96p. illus. paper covers.

> **A.72.   The Key to Camplife**
> New York: Key Publishing Co., 1958.
> 95p. illus.paper covers.

This addition to the list takes on an interesting aspect when one realizes that the adult Walter Gibson was one of the least likely candidates for living the strenuous life exemplified by Theodore Roosevelt. His mind and his typing fingers received maximum exercise. He purposely did not use hand or power tools for fear his hands might be injured because his hands were **his** tools as they pounded out saleable material on a manual typewriter. Among the chapters is one on how **not** to get lost. Cooking and recipes for the trail were supplied by Pearl L. Raymond, **i.e.,** Litzka R. Gibson, Walter Gibson's wife.

> **A.73.**   Ishi Black's [Walter B. Gibson]
> **The Key to Judo and Jiujitsu** [sic]
> New York: Key Publishing Co., 1958.
> 95p. illus. paper covers,

is the sort of manual The Shadow or his agents
might have found useful. The cover title is merely
The Key to Judo and it was re-issued by Ottenheimer
in 1962 under that title.

> **A.74.   The Key to Space Travel**
> New York: Key Publishing Co., 1958.
> 96p. illus. paper covers,

has certainly dated in many respects since it was
published, but it may be all the more valuable for
that with its statement of the popular view on the
subject at the dawn of the Space Age.   On the other
hand, some of the illustrations have proven to be
surprisingly prophetic.   Gibson is cited on the
title page as "Member: Interplanetary Exploration
Society."

> **A.75.   The Key to Yoga**
> New York: Key Publishing Co., 1958.
> 160p. illus. paper covers,

was re-issued by Ottenheimer, but the precise date
of that edition is uncertain.   Gibson was not a
practitioner of the art no matter how authoritative
he may have written on the subject.

Since he had written of astronomy under his
own name, Gibson chose a pen name under which to
write of astrology for the "Key" series,

> **A.76.   Felix Fairfax's [Walter B. Gibson]**
> **The Key to Astrology**
> New York: Key Publishing Co., 1959.
> 95p. illus. paper covers.

The redoubtable "Rufus Perry" was revived for
one final publication,

> **A.77.   Rufus Perry's [Walter B. Gibson]**
> **The Key to Better Bowling**
> New York: Key Publishing Co., 1959.
> 95p. illus. paper covers,

thereby proving himself adept at more subjects than
horse racing and gambling.

"Andrew Abbott" was used as a pen name for
only two books,

A.78. Andrew Abbott's [Walter B. Gibson]
The Key to Better Memory
New York: Key Publishing Co., 1959
95p. illus. paper covers,

A.79. Andrew Abbott's [Walter B. Gibson]
The Key to Character Reading
New York: Key Publishing Co., 1959.
95p. illus. paper covers.

The first reflects Gibson's fascination with memory
and mnemonic devices, some of which will be found
in the book he wrote for Kreskin (A.166.) as well.
The second is an updated version of the type of
material he wrote for Prof. Seward in the 1930s.
Facial formations, profiles, and head shapes are
discussed as ways to judge the traits of
individuals.

Gibson had a lot of fun devising pen names,
but sometimes he didn't give them enough thought or
he failed to learn if there was another writer
using the name he had chosen. When he chose the
name "Roy Masters" for

A.80. Roy Masters' [Walter B. Gibson]
The Key to Chess Simplified
New York: Key Publishing Co., 1959.
96p. illus. paper covers,

he wanted a name to suggest a "chess master."
Later he discovered there was someone of that name
who wrote in the field of human relations. If **The
Key to Chess** has been overlooked as a title in
Gibson's bibliography it has appeared as a work in
the bibliography of the real Roy Masters. It was
re-issued in 1964 by Ottenheimer.

Gibson tells the related story on himself in
which another "Walter Gibson," author of a book
about World War II, **The Boat** (Houghton Mifflin,
1953), was mistakenly identified with The Shadow's
creator. Finding he was being praised for writing
another man's book, our Gibson became even more
scrupulous about using his middle initial when he
signed his name to something.

He may have had a pun in mind when choosing
the pen name used on

A.81.   Walter Glass's [Walter B. Gibson]
The Key to Knots and Splices
New York: Key Publishing Co., 1959,
94p. illus. paper covers

for the instructions for making and using hundreds
of knots, ties, lashes, and splices for every
conceivable need are indeed presented quite
clearly.

In the next decade Gibson was more productive
than ever with even greater variety in his work.
He returned to a form which he had come to find
congenial, the writing of fiction.   He also
returned to his greatest literary creation, The
Shadow.

Chapter Six

The Shadow Returns

1961-1970

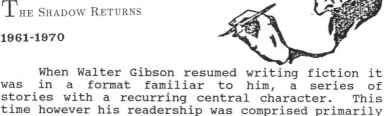

When Walter Gibson resumed writing fiction it was in a format familiar to him, a series of stories with a recurring central character. This time however his readership was comprised primarily of boys and not adults.

Grosset and Dunlap, long known for the publication of such series as Franklin W. Dixon's The Hardy Boys and Carolyn Keene's Nancy Drew, as well as Victor Appleton's Tom Swift, planned a new series of adventure stories for boys. Walter Gibson was one of several writers hired to contribute to the series and it was his first novel which established the concept and lead off the Biff Brewster adventures.

> **A.82.** Andy Adams' [Walter B. Gibson]
> **Brazilian Gold Mine Mystery**
> New York: Grosset and Dunlap, 1960.
> 182p. illus. paper on boards.

The major producer of juvenile series books in the twentieth century was the Stratemeyer Syndicate. Founded early in the century by Edward Stratemeyer, author and creator of the Rover Boys stories, it was a fiction factory designed to supply publishers with juvenile adventure stories. In 1960, the Syndicate was in the custody of Stratemeyer's daughter, Harriet Adams, and Andrew Svenson. The Biff Brewster stories, however, were not products of the Stratemeyer Syndicate. The pseudonym chosen as the house name for the series may reflect authorial or publisher attitudes toward the Syndicate monopoly of the field. With tongue in cheek, someone chose "Andy Adams" to be the "author", the first name from Andrew Svenson, the second from Harriet Adams.

45

Biff Brewster is sixteen, blond, and lives in Indianapolis with his parents and the eleven-year-old twins, Ted and Monica. Since his parents believe in the importance of travel to one's education, Biff is encouraged to spend his vacation months on trips to other countries. The series as planned was part adventure and part travelogue requiring Gibson to research each country to which he sent his young hero.

In the first novel, Biff flies to Brazil to join his father who is on a jungle safari. The trip is offered as a birthday present and it turns out to be a memorable one. Ostensibly on a rubber-hunting expedition, the elder Brewster is in reality on the trail of a fabulous Inca mine discovered by two prospectors during the second world war.

The series was one of the last new juvenile series produced by Grosset and Dunlap and contains thirteen titles published between 1960 and 1965. Of those thirteen titles, Gibson wrote only five. Two of the remaining eight were written by Peter Harkins who had collaborated with Hal Goodwin in creating the Rick Brant series of science-adventure stories, published between 1947 and 1968 under the pseudonym John Blaine.

The first ten volumes in the set were issued in two bindings, blue-gray paper on boards with a pictorial dust jacket and pictorial covers without dust jackets. The earlier printings of those titles are those with the dust jackets, of course.

Sometimes when we realize just how many titles Gibson could squeeze out of one or two basic subjects we may be justified in wondering if he isn't repeating himself. A comparison of the texts often demonstrates that either he had so much material left over after completing the first book that he felt it a shame to have it go to waste or that he just enjoyed trying new approaches to old topics. So it is that

A.83. Fell's Official Guide to Knots and
How to Tie Them
New York: Frederick Fell, 1961.
127p. illus. cloth,

is not the same book he wrote for Key Publishing as
"Walter Glass," no matter how much the subject
matter may overlap. Nor is

A.84. Walter B. Gibson's and Morris N. Young's
Houdini's Fabulous Magic
Philadelphia & New York: Chilton Books, 1961.
viii, 214p. illus. cloth,

identical to any of his previous books on Houdini.
It serves as a companion volume to Houdini on Magic
(A.55.) and draws on both Houdini's Escapes (A.27.)
and Houdini's Magic (A.29.), but it is not a carbon
copy of either.   It is supplemented by rare
photographs, additional historical information, a
16 page biographical sketch and a three page
selective bibliography.

     Gibson's second book on hypnotism,

A.85. Hypnotism Through the Ages
New York: Vista House, 1961.
173p. illus. boards,

is an another anecdotal history of the subject.
The chapters include "Mesmer and His Methods,"
"Ways of Inducing Hypnosis," "Crime and Hypnosis,"
"Hypnosis and Sex," and "Stage Hypnosis." Like the
others, The Key to Hypnosis (A.59.) and Hypnotism
(A.134), Hypnotism Through the Ages is strictly for
the layman and the three titles may be read as
variations on a theme.

     Gibson's second book on judo was like the
first (A.73.) written under a pen name,

A.86. Maborushi Kineji's [Walter B. Gibson]
Judo: Attack and Defense
New York: Vista House, 1961.
136p. illus. boards.

In direct step-by-step style, this treatment of the
time-honored science emphasizes individual methods
and stratagems rather than the lore and origins of
judo.

Gibson took young Biff Brewster to Mexico in his next contribution to the juvenile series.

A.87. Andy Adams' [Walter B. Gibson]
Mystery of the Mexican Treasure
New York: Grosset and Dunlap, 1961.
182p. illus. paper on boards,

was actually published as volume four in the series and did not immediately follow volume one.

Biff's father is acting as a consultant to a group of archaeologists searching for a treasure-house of Aztec antiquities. A talking statue, a legendary war god, a fire opal, a dagger, and a mask are the "forces of destruction" which threaten the lives of everyone at the excavation site.

The last two books Gibson wrote for Sidney Radner cover Bridge and Canasta and not crooked gambling, although there is advice on guarding against cheating in Bridge.

A.88. Sidney H. Radner's [Walter B. Gibson]
Radner on Bridge
New York: Padell Book Co., 1961.
96p. paper covers.

A.89. Sidney H. Radner's [Walter B. Gibson]
Radner on Canasta, including Samba, Bolivia, Calypso and Other Games
New York: Key Publishing Co., 1961.
95p. illus. paper covers.

Gibson chose a new pen name for his novel about the life and times of the female pirate, Anne Bonny.

A.90. Douglas Brown's [Walter B. Gibson]
Anne Bonny, Pirate Queen: The True Saga of a Fabulous Female Buccaneer
Derby, Conn.: Monarch Books, 1962.
138p. paper covers,

is fictional in spite of the sub-title and not nearly as spicy in content as the cover blurb promises ("she fought like a man-and loved like a woman-with the tools provided her by nature"). It was issued as part of Monarch's American Series. "Douglas Brown," a strangely subdued name for one

who often designed pen names which were anagrams of
his own, was used only one other time, five years
later, for a book on solitaire (A.121.).

As should be obvious by now, some of Gibson's
books are not in traditional book format.   Many
collectors overlook

A.91.   [Walter B. Gibson and Others]
Science and Mechanics Magic Handbook:
1962 Edition
Chicago: Science and Mechanics Publishing
Co.,1961. 160p. illus. paper covers,

because it resembles a magazine.   Likewise, they
may overlook the second printing as it was re-
issued in 1967 with some textual changes as the
"1968 edition."   The original is **"Science and**
Mechanics Handbook No. 18, 1961-No. 589" and
contains 100 "Life of the Party" tricks, with
articles on how to build magical apparatus, how to
present a magic show, and comments on the appeal of
magic to the public.   A note on page four reads:
"The editors sincerely thank William (sic) B.
Gibson, Sidney H. Radner, Litzka Raymond, and
Victor D. Dressner for their invaluable assistance
in the preparation of this book."

An approach to achieving a superior memory by
taking full advantage of your natural memory and
then bolstering it by acquiring artificial memory
aids is found in

A.92.   Walter B. Gibson's and Morris N. Young's
How to Develop an Exceptional Memory
New York: Chilton, 1962.
x, 266p. cloth.

Included in the book are anecdotes about ten men
with exceptional memories.

India and Egypt are the settings for Biff
Brewster's next adventures in

A.93. Andy Adams' [Walter B. Gibson]
Mystery of the Ambush in India
New York: Grosset and Dunlap, 1962.
170p. illus. paper on boards.

A.94. Andy Adams' [Walter B. Gibson]
Egyptian Scarab Mystery
New York: Grosset and Dunlap, 1963.
170p. illus. paper on boards.

In the first (no. 7 of the series), Biff is on his
way to meet his father when a mysterious message
makes him take a detour through the New India
Bazaar in Calcutta.   Entrusted with a blood-red
ruby, the Light of the Lama, Biff sets out to
return it to its rightful owner, the Chonsi Lama,
ruler of a lost city.

Ancient magic, a "living" mummy, and an
archaeological expedition are among the ingredients
in the second title, published as no. 9 of the
series. It is obvious how much of the old settings
and concepts from The Shadow novels were being used
to intrigue Gibson's young readers here.

A new area for Gibson is found in

A.95. **Fell's Guide to Papercraft Tricks, Games
and Puzzles**
New York: Frederick Fell, 1963.
125p. illus. paper on boards,

for, while games and puzzles had long fascinated
him he had not done anything with paper-folding or
handicrafts.

Much of the material gathered for the books on
card tricks or for the two Radner card game books
must have been revised and reorganized for

A.96. **Hoyle's Simplified Guide to the Popular
Card Games**
Garden City, New York: Doubleday, 1963.
267p. illus. cloth.

The book marked the beginning of his long
association with Doubleday as his publisher.

A.97. Magic Made Simple
Garden City, New York: Doubleday, 1963.
160p. illus. paper covers,

was part of a series of "Made Simple Books" and was
still another example of how magic could be brought
to the general public and did not have to be
reserved for the elite.   It was re-issued over a
decade later in a revised edition as **Junior Magic**
(Sterling, 1977).

Gibson's reliability and past work for Grosset
and Dunlap may have been responsible for his being
assigned to write the thirteen short stories for

A.98.   Rod Serling's [Walter B. Gibson]
The Twilight Zone
New York: Grosset and Dunlap, 1963.
vi, 207p. illus. boards.

While the title page gives him credit for the
stories ("adapted by Walter B. Gibson"), none of
them resembles any of the original scripts for the
television series in either title or plot. In this
writer's hearing he said once that he was
particularly proud of these stories, because they
were all his own.   His use of the theme of the
strange and uncanny is well within the territory of
the famous television series.   Gibson's photo was
used on the endpaper design in the original
hardcover edition.

The collection has achieved a certain
durability in later years. Selections of the
stories from the original edition have appeared
under various titles: **Chilling Stories from Rod
Serling's Twilight Zone** (Tempo Books, 1965) omits
three stories while Rod Serling's **The Twilight
Zone**, Abridged Edition (Grosset and Dunlap, 1974)
omits three different stories.   Complete contents:
The Ghost of Ticonderoga; Back There; The Ghost-
Town Ghost; Judgment Night; The Curse of Seven
Towers; The Tiger God; The Avenging Ghost; Return
from Oblivion; The House on the Square; Death's
Masquerade; The Riddle of the Crypt; Dead Man's
Chest; and The Thirteenth Story.

The collection has also appeared in a combined
edition with Rod Serling's **Twilight Zone Revisited**
(**A.108.**), published by Bonanza Books in 1984.

During the Fall of 1963, many browsers at news-stands must have experienced a pleasant surprise at the sight of a familiar figure on the cover of a new paperback novel. Both cover blurb and actual title proclaimed the

A.99. Return of The Shadow
New York: Belmont Books, 1963.
140p. paper covers,

to a waiting world. This final Shadow novel by his creator was the first to be intentionally signed "Walter B. Gibson" and not "Maxwell Grant," and also the first one to appear as a "paperback original" with no previous magazine publication. (The novel in **The Shadow**, June 1944, had appeared with Gibson's own name inadvertently left on the first page.) The plot concerns an international abduction ring which houses its victims in a castle on the Hudson River. Against this familiar setting many of the figures from Shadows past make their re-appearance.

The novel was intended to be the first of a series written by Gibson alternating new stories with reprints of some of the classic novels from the past. The agreement between the author and the publisher, Conde Nast Publications (the successor to Street and Smith), and a literary entrepreneur named Lyle Kenyon Engel did not last. Subsequent novels were written by Dennis Lynds under the old signature of Maxwell Grant. (See Appendix C for a listing of these.)

Another unexpected title among Gibson's works appeared the following year

A.100. Helen Wells' [Walter B. Gibson]
The Brass Idol Mystery
New York: Grosset and Dunlap, 1964.
173p. frontis. boards,

as volume 16 in the **Vicki Barr, Air Stewardess** series. Our heroine, stewardess for Worldwide Airways, makes an unexpected flight to New Delhi instead of her usual turnaround at Teheran, stumbles into a mystery involving a local big shot, a strange girl who drops a purse containing an initialed pin, and a brass idol of Lakshmi, goddess of wealth and plenty.

Since there was a real Helen Wells behind the Vicki Barr series we don't know why Gibson was asked to step in and contribute this novel. There were earlier writers who "ghosted" for Helen Wells and Gibson's volume is the final one in the series.

Sometimes Gibson could arrange a project for a publisher which resulted in half a dozen titles with a similarity among them making them seem like sections cut from a larger unit. Such a project was the one undertaken for Treasure Books. The six "Fun and Activity" books are identical in format, consisting of word, number, and picture puzzles, tricks, brain teasers, riddles, mazes, cutouts, indoor and outdoor games, and board games. Each was re-issued, but abridged and with a title change, by Grosset and Dunlap.

A.101.   Famous Lands and People Fun and Activity Book
New York: Treasure Books, 1964.
80p. illus. paper covers,

was re-issued as **People, Places, and Things Fun and Activity Book** (Grosset and Dunlap, nd) while

A.102.   Fifty States Fun and Activity Book
New York: Treasure Books, 1964.
80p. illus. paper covers,

re-appeared as **The United States Fun and Activity Book** (Grosset and Dunlap, nd).

Card games were not forgotten and formed the basis for the next two books,

A.103.   How to Win at Solitaire
Garden City, New York: Doubleday, 1964.
vi, 152p. illus. cloth,

A.104.   Hoyle Card Games: Reference Crammer
New York: Ken Publishing Co., 1964.
160p. paper covers with spiral binding.

In the first there are 31 of the most popular Solitaire games, selected for their finer points of play and presented with step-by-step instructions that allow the reader to learn and play while reading. It was re-issued as **How to Play Winning Solitaire** by Frederick Fell.

The second, the Hoyle **Reference Crammer** is a handbook to popular modern card games, arranged alphabetically by topic with a separate glossary of terms. According to Gibson, this formed the basis for his larger reference volume, **Hoyle's Modern Encyclopedia of Card Games** (A.145.).

It was followed by three more of the "Fun and Activity" books. This time there was

A.105. **Puzzles and Pastimes Fun and Activity Book**
New York: Treasure Books, 1964.
80p. illus. paper covers,

later re-issued as **Tricks, Games, and Puzzles Fun and Activity Book** by Grosset and Dunlap in an abridged edition.

A.106. **World Wide Fun and Activity Book**
New York: Treasure Books, 1964.
80p. illus. paper covers,

appeared later, abridged, as **Travel Time Fun and Activity Book** while

A.107. **Year-Round Fun and Activity Book**
New York: Treasure Books, 1964.
80p. illus. paper covers,

was re-issued in an abridged form as **Four Seasons Fun and Activity Book**. As usual, the publisher was Grosset and Dunlap.

The success of the first volume of stories from **The Twilight Zone** made a second collection possible.

A.108. Rod Serling's [Walter B. Gibson]
The Twilight Zone Revisited
New York: Grosset and Dunlap, 1964.
208p. illus. boards,

contained another thirteen stories of Gibson's own creation written on the Twilight Zone theme. Contents: Two Live Ghosts; The Ghost of the **Dixie Belle**; The Purple Testament; The Ghost Train; Beyond the Rim; The Ghost of Jolly Roger; The Man in the Bottle; The Mirror Image; The Man Who Dropped By; The Edge of Doom; The Fiery Spell; The

16-Millimeter Shrine; and The House on the Island.
Like its predecessor, **The Twilight Zone**, it was re-
issued with four stories omitted (The Edge of Doom,
The Fiery Spell, The 16-Millimeter Shrine, and The
House on the Island) by Tempo Books in 1967.   It
was   published   in   a   combined   edition   with   **The
Twilight Zone** by Bonanza Books in 1984.

As   was   true   of   the   stories   in   the   first
volume,   none   of   these   was   based   on   the   actual
television   scripts.   In   that,   the   two   volumes   do
not resemble the collections of Rod Serling's own
short stories from the series published by Bantam
Books.   (**Stories   from   The   Twilight   Zone**,   1960;
More Stories from The Twilight Zone, 1961; and **New
Stories from The Twilight Zone**, 1962.)   The Grosset
Twilight   Zone   volumes   were   written   for   young
readers   while   the   Bantam   Books   were   intended   for
adults.   All   of   the   volumes   would   appear   to   have
been read and enjoyed by both groups.

The last of the "Fun and Activity" books came
out the following year.

A.109.   Space and Science Fun and Activity Book
New York: Treasure Books, 1965.
80p. illus. paper covers,

was republished, abridged, by Grosset and Dunlap as
Out of This World Fun and Activity Book.   Knowing
how   much   the   author   enjoyed   creating   puzzles   and
games, it is intriguing to imagine the hours of fun
he   had   combing   books   and   magazines   for   material,
asking   friends   and   acquaintances   for   suggestions
for   these   collections.   He   never   treated   them
lightly; they were as important to his livelihood
as any other assignment.

Gibson's   experience   as   a   magazine   editor   was
valuable   when   he   edited   four   volumes   of   true   crime
articles for Grosset and Dunlap in 1965 and 1966.
Drawing   on   a   wealth   of   material   by   some   of   the
noted   authorities   such   as   Herbert   Asbury,   Stewart
Holbrook,   Alan   Hynd,   and   Edmund   Pearson,   Gibson
contributed   introductory   notes   for   each   to   set   the
historic context.   The first one was

A.110.   The Fine Art of Murder
New York: Grosset and Dunlap, 1965.
xi, 236p. illus. cloth.

Besides an introduction by the editor, the book contains eleven stories: Herbert Asbury's "The Monster of Sixty-Third Street," Stewart H. Holbrook's "Belle of Indiana," A. J. Liebling's "The Case of the Scattered Dutchman," Carl Carmer's "The Tale of the Murderous Philologist with but One Big Toe," Archie McFedries' "The Case of the Little Exterminator," Cleveland Moffatt's "The Rock Island Express," Edmund Pearson's "The End of the Borden Case," Gibson's own "The Ghost from the Grave," Avery Hale's "The She-Devil of Nagyrev," S. N. Phillips' "The Man Who Came Back," and Alan Hynd's "The Monster of Aurora."

The second collection was on the theme of spying, a very popular one of the day. It was the only one of the four to achieve a paperback edition (Tempo Books, 1967).

A.111. The Fine Art of Spying
New York: Grosset and Dunlap, 1965.
x, 243p. illus. cloth,

included nine stories besides Gibson's introduction. Well-known episodes from history as well as some less well-known ones appeared: Kurt Singer's "Prisoner in the Legation," W. Somerset Maugham's "The Traitor," Alan Hynd's "Encounter at Treasure Island," Winston Churchill's "I Escape from the Boers," Franz von Rintelen's "The Dark Invader," Joseph Gollomb's "The Spy Who Had to Die," Anthony Abbot's "A Very Special Agent," Thomas Johnson's "The Master," and Fletcher Pratt's "The Cryptographer's War."

In 1965 Gibson collaborated once again with his friend Morris N. Young in another kind of self-help manual.

A.112. Morris N. Young's and Chesley V. Young's
[Walter B. Gibson]
How to Read Faster and Remember More
West Nyack, N. Y.: Parker Publishing Co., 1965.
239p. cloth.

The ways and means for increasing ones reading rate and improving the retention of what is read are described in precise terms. The book includes the unique "Read-O-dometer" (a small card with slots of varying size) for use in practicing concentration

on words and increasing the speed of ones reading.
The book was re-issued in 1972 by Frederick Fell.
Gibson's work on the book was represented on the
title page by the name of Morris Young's wife and
collaborator Chesley.

A.113.   The Man from U.N.C.L.E.:
The Coin of El Diablo Affair
New York: Wonder Books, 1965.
48p. illus. paper covers,

was a tie-in with the well-known television series.
Ilya Kuryakin and Napoleon Solo of the United
Network Command for Law and Enforcement meet the
would-be emperor of the Caribbean, another tool in
the hands of THRUSH.

A.114.   Monsters: Three Famous
Spine-Tingling Tales
New York: Wonder Books, 1965.
48p. illus. paper covers.

The three stories adapted and abridged by Gibson
are "The Strange Case of Dr. Jekyll and Mr. Hyde,"
"Frankenstein," and "Dracula."

Gibson's last contribution to the Biff
Brewster series was published as volume 13 in the
set,

A.115.   Andy Adams' [Walter B. Gibson]
Mystery of the Alpine Pass
New York: Grosset and Dunlap, 1965.
170p. illus. pictorial boards.

Biff is in Switzerland where his Uncle Charlie is
surveying Swiss railways and tramways when a
mysterious stranger vanishes from an aerial tram
over a mountain pass.

A.116.   David Hoy's [Walter B. Gibson]
Psychic and Other ESP Party Games
Garden City, New York: Doubleday and Co., 1965.
141p. illus. cloth,

was ghosted for a professional mentalist. The book
explains how to play games which involve mind-
reading, clairvoyance, precognition, and other
forms of extrasensory perception.

A.117.   Walter B. Gibson's and Litzka R.
Gibson's **The Complete Illustrated Book
of the Psychic Sciences**
Garden City, New York: Doubleday and Co., 1966.
xx, 403p. illus. cloth,

was Gibson's most ambitious book to date and the
first one done in collaboration with his wife.
Mrs. Gibson had been the widow of the Great
Raymond, a noted magician.

This is a comprehensive history and survey of
the psychic and mystic sciences from star-gazing to
ESP and yoga. The introductory chapter defines 50
terms, most of which are then taken up for closer
scrutiny in the bulk of the work: Astrology,
Cartomancy, Colorogy. Dice Divination, Domino
Divination, Dreams, Graphology, Numerology,
Moleosophy, Palmistry, Phrenology, Physiognomy,
Radiesthesia, Superstitions and Omens, Teacup
Reading, and Telepathy. There is a good index in
the work. With British, Spanish, Japanese, and
Italian editions, it was also distributed as a
selection of Doubleday's Universe Book Club.

The tetralogy of true crime story collections
was completed by the publication of two additional
volumes. The first was

A.118.   **The Fine Art of Robbery**
New York: Grosset and Dunlap, 1966.
vi, 254p. illus. cloth,

with its introduction, historical notes, and
fifteen stories.   Edward D. Radin's "The Phantom
Safe-Crackers," Herbert Asbury's "Stewart's Bones,"
Ned Hickey's "A Present from Daddy," Joseph
Gollomb's "The Art Burglar," Edwin Valentine
Mitchell's "Cops and Robbers," Carl Carmer's "Rube
Burrow: Alabama Robin Hood," F. W. Waldo's "Captain
Lightfoot," Eugene B. Block's "The Gentleman
Bandit," S. N. Phillips' "Circumstantial Evidence,"
William T. Brannon's "Rendezvous at Rondout," Rene
Cassellari's "The Theft of the Mona Lisa," Alan
Hynd's "Money Car Mob," Cleveland Moffatt's "The
Destruction of the Renos," James L. Collier's "A
Very Bad Apple Named Adam," and Major Arthur
Griffith's "Orrock and Renard" make up the contents
of this third collection. Many of the authors are

familiar names to readers of American magazines
from the first third of the century.

The fourth and final volume was

A.119.   The Fine Art of Swindling
New York: Grosset and Dunlap, 1966.
255p. illus. cloth.

The introduction and notes accompany fourteen
stories this time.   The roster is comprised of
James L. Collier's "The Man Who Stole a Country,"
Carl Carmer's "The Cardiff Giant," A. J. Liebling's
"The American Golconda," Meyer Berger's "Broadway
Chiseler," Craig Thompson's "The Great Corporation
Swindle," Elmer L. Ivey's and William J. Slocum's
"Abandon All Beasts!", P. T. Barnum's "Riza Bey,"
St. Clair McKelway's "Old 880," Herbert Asbury's
"Any Number Can Lose," Alan Hynd's "The   Pied Piper
of Boston," William T. Brannon's "The Fabulous
Drake Swindle," Beverly Smith, Jr.'s "The Crook
Everyone Liked," U. E. Baughman's and Leonard
Wallace Robinson's "Coin Makers and Con Men," and
Major   Arthur   Griffith's   "Confidence   Tricks
Extraordinary."   In keeping with the unifying
theme, these stories are lighter in tone than most
of those in the other three volumes.

The theme of the next work,

A.120.   How to Bet the Harness Races
Garden City, New York: Doubleday and Co., 1966.
148p. paper covers,

might once have been reason enough for Gibson to
use a pen name, "Rufus Perry" perhaps.   But this
guide to betting on one of the oldest of American
sports appeared under its author's own name. In
1975 it was re-issued by the Gambler's Book Club of
Las Vegas.

Gibson's next book was published under a pen
name he had used once before.

A.121.   Douglas Brown's [Walter B. Gibson]
The Key to Solitaire
New York: Crown, Ottenheimer, 1966.
142p. illus. paper covers,

is compact and informative with 150 ways to play
the game.   An alphabetically arranged table of
contents   is   in   reality   a   topical   index.
Definitions of terms are included.

To some extent, Gibson's prolific writing can
be explained by referring to the type of books he
produced, many of them new versions of old
subjects.   It was as though he could write himself
out on a subject, allow the creative well to refill
itself, and come up with a new version.   Except for
short articles and introductions to books of tricks
he had never produced an elaborate and extensive
history of the subject.   Perhaps the germ of

A.122.   The Master Magicians:
Their Lives and Most Famous Tricks
Garden City, New York: Doubleday and Co., 1966.
xvii, 221p. illus. cloth,

lies in the anecdotes in **Magic Explained (A.54.)** or
as far back as Thurston's autobiography.   Someone
may have just asked him why he didn't write a
history of stage magic.   The book that emerged is
an anecdotal history of the golden age of modern
stage magic (ca. 1845-1948) told through the
stories of nine entertainers: Robert-Houdin,
Professor Anderson, Herrmann, Kellar, Chung Ling
Soo, Thurston, Houdini and his brother Hardeen, and
the Great Raymond.   The book is well-illustrated
with 61 photographs.

Admittedly, the volume is not a scholar's
history, but it is written in a lively style which
conveys the zest of the subject, as well as the
enthusiasm of the author for his topic, in a way
that no scholarly volume could.

Having been ignored in his attempt to revive
The Shadow with a series of new stories, Gibson now
arranged with Grosset and Dunlap to reprint newly
edited and abridged versions of three of the
original novels.

A.123.   Walter Gibson's (alias Maxwell Grant)
The Weird Adventures of The Shadow
New York: Grosset and Dunlap, 1966.
216p. illus. pictorial boards,

collects **Grove of Doom** (September 1, 1933), **Voodoo
Death** (June 1944), and **Murder By Moonlight**
(December 1943), edited to fit the requirements of
the publisher. It is prefaced by a sentimental
memoir of the writing of the pulp series, "Me and
My Shadow." The book appeared during a wave of
nostalgia for things of the 1930s and enjoyed a
well-deserved success. **Grove of Doom** was re-issued
separately as a paperback by Tempo Books in 1969.
For some critical comments on the original version
of this novel contrasted with the abridgement, see
Robert Sampson, "Just a Little Matter of Doom,"
Xenophile, number 4 (June 1974): 7-8.

The revival of The Shadow was accompanied by a
new and thorough revision of one of Gibson's
earliest books, **The Book of** Secrets **(A.7.),** with
new illustrations.

A.124. Secrets of Magic, Ancient and Modern
New York: Grosset and Dunlap, 1966.
147p. illus. pictorial boards,

contains 70 amazing feats of magic explained under
seven headings: Secrets of the Ancients, Magic of
the Middle Ages, Modern Mysteries, Magic of India,
Oriental Magic, Secrets of Stage Magic, and Methods
of Fake Mediums. It was published in England in
1976 by Collins under the title, **Secrets of the
Great Magicians.** There also exists a Japanese
edition.

A.125. Winning the $2 Bet
Garden City, New York: Doubleday and Co., 1967.
146p. paper covers,

was, surprisingly enough, the only wholly new book
Gibson published during that year. Twenty-five ways
to beat the odds in betting on horses are covered
in its pages. It was re-issued in 1975 by the
Gambler's Book Club, Las Vegas, and later by the
Casino Press of New York under the title, **25 Ways
to Beat the Horses** (date not known).

A.126. [Anonymous]
The Key to Hoyle's Games
Owings Mills, Md.: Ottenheimer, 1968.
156p. boards,

was a new version of the **Reference Crammer (A.104.)**
with concise directions for playing more than 100
popular card games, using the official Hoyle rules
and variations.   It was   re-issued   in 1970 as a
paperback by Award Books.

Several of Gibson's early books of mystifying
feats   performed   with   simple,   everyday   objects
contained   material   which   he   now   revised   and
gathered into a single volume as

A.127. Magic With Science
New York: Grosset and Dunlap, 1968.
119p. illus. pictorial boards,

in which the results are obtained through the
application of scientific principles.   It is "magic
made easy" brought up-to-date.

After   several   years   of   seeming   inactivity,
Gibson burst forth in 1969 with several titles,
some of them re-issues of The Shadow's adventures
and some wholly new volumes.   The new works suggest
what had been occupying his thoughts during the
previous two years.

**A.128. The Complete Illustrated Book of
Card Magic**
Garden City, New York:Doubleday and Co., 1969.
xviii, 454p. illus. cloth,

is among the longest books its author ever wrote,
matched only by its companion volume, **The Complete
Illustrated   Book   of   Close-Up   Magic**,   which   was
published a decade later **(A.183.)**.   A comprehensive
and definitive collection of the principles and
techniques   required   for   performing   hundreds   of
tricks,   the   massive   volume   is   organized   under
twelve categories and illustrated with photographs
of its author's hands demonstrating the illusions.
It is enhanced by an elaborate illustrated glossary
and topical index.

In   1969,   Bantam   Books   followed   their
successful reprinting of the Doc Savage pulp novels
by announcing plans to re-issue the Shadow novels,
roughly in their original magazine sequence of
publication, and from the beginning with the first
title.   Their Doc Savage series had been launched
with the first novel, **The Man of Bronze**, but the

ones to follow had been chosen at random.   After
The Living Shadow (A.33.), The Eyes of The Shadow
(A.34.), and The Shadow Laughs (A.35.), they chose
as the fourth novel to be reprinted,

A.129. Maxwell Grant's [Walter B. Gibson]
The Death Tower
New York: Bantam Books, 1969.
138p. paper covers,

which had originally appeared in The Shadow
Detective Monthly for January 1932.   The Shadow
meets a brilliant and diabolical doctor who is
responsible for the deaths of numerous men of
enormous wealth.   The Bantam Books edition was
published in December 1969, but the next book in
the series did not appear for almost a year.

In the meantime, the author published a number
of books under his own name.   He edited a
collection of detective short stories, collaborated
with his wife on a companion volume to their
previous one on the psychic sciences, and turned
out several of the short handbooks on occult topics
for which he had such a talent.

A.130. Dreams
New York: Grosset and Dunlap, 1969.
127p. boards,

is a guide to unravelling the mystery of dreams so
the reader may benefit from their subconscious
messages.   Anecdotes from the past outweigh
contemporary references.   For example, the work
includes common dream patterns and their
interpretations along with a discussion of the
dreams in Lewis Carroll's Alice stories.

A.131. Litzka R. Gibson's and Walter B.
Gibson's
Mystic and Occult Arts: A Guide to Their Use
in Daily Living
New York: Parker Publishing Co., 1969.
224p. cloth,

is a guide to developing ones own psychic or inner
powers to their fullest as related in a series of
anecdotes.   Clairvoyance, precognition, telepathy,
crystal gazing, astral projection, and
reincarnation are covered.   It was re-issued the

following year (1970) by Paperback Library of New
York.

A.132. Rogues' Gallery:
A Variety of Mystery Stories
Garden City, New York: Doubleday and Co., 1969.
398p. illus. cloth,

represents an ambitious undertaking on the part of
Gibson as editor. The introduction to this
anthology of 19 short stories traces the history of
the detective story and states a case for the need
for a broader definition of the form.

Contents: Jacques Futrelle's "The Missing
Necklace," E. W. Hornung's "Nine Points of the
Law," Brett Halliday's "Human Interest Stuff," W.
Somerset Maugham's "The Greek," Agatha Christie's
"At the Stroke of Twelve," Paul Gallico's "Hurry,
Hurry, Hurry!", Raymond Chandler's "Red Wind,"
Vincent Starrett's "The Eleventh Juror," Ellery
Queen's "Bride in Danger," Hugh Pentecost's "Room
Number 23," John D. MacDonald's "Hit and Run,"
Maxey Brook's "Morte d'Alain: An Unrecorded Idyll
of the King," Thomas Walsh's "I Killed John
Harrington," Jacob Hay's "The Belknap Apparatus,"
Stuart Palmer's "Fingerprints Don't Lie," Carter
Dickson's "The Footprint in the Sky," William
Brittain's "Mr. Strang Finds the Answers," Edward
D. Hoch's "The Spy Who Worked for Peace," and
Lawrence Treat's "M as in Mugged." It is an
excellent anthology with few stories with which
readers are likely to be overly familiar.

There were five volumes in 1970 to finish off
the decade (or with which to begin the next one,
depending on your definition), three Shadow novels
were republished and two books on games and
hypnotism appeared.

A.133. Family Games America Plays
Garden City, New York: Doubleday and Co., 1970.
vii, 275p. illus. cloth,

is a book for rainy afternoons with its
instructions for old favorites from 20 Questions to
Charades, Backgammon, Parchesi, Cribbage, Dominoes,
Monopoly, Scrabble, as well as Authors, Rook, and
Old Maid. It was re-issued in 1974 as a Barnes and
Noble paperback.

Similar in scope, if not in content, to his other books, **The Key to Hypnotism** (A.59.) and **Hypnotism Through the Ages** (A.85.),

A.134. Hypnotism
New York: Grosset and Dunlap, 1970.
124p. cloth and paper editions,

is an elementary guide to the history and techniques of the mesmeric art.

A.135. Maxwell Grant's [Walter B. Gibson]
The Ghost Makers
New York: Bantam Books, 1970.
120p. paper covers,

was published in August 1970 as number five in Bantam's Shadow series.   It had been published originally in **The Shadow Magazine** for October 1932, and had been reprinted in the first **Shadow Annual** for 1942 **(A.41.)**.   Murder at a seance leads to The Shadow exposing a ring of crooks which had been squeezing millions from innocent victims.

A.136. Maxwell Grant's [Walter B. Gibson]
Hidden Death
New York: Bantam Books, 1970.
138p. paper covers,

was Bantam's 6th Shadow novel, published in October 1970, and taken from the September 1932 issue of **The Shadow Magazine**.   An inventive genius is murdered at the moment of his greatest success and The Shadow decodes the clues to a bizarre set of serial murders.

The decade (and this chapter) end with Bantam's 7th Shadow novel, issued in December 1970.

A.137.   Maxwell Grant's [Walter B. Gibson]
Gangdom's Doom
New York: Bantam Books, 1970.
166p. paper covers.

Originally published in December 1931 in **The Shadow Magazine**, this is the story of The Shadow's war with Chicago gangland. It is often cited for the historic significance of its tragic episode in which one of The Shadow's agents is killed. It was also the last title in the Bantam series.   For

whatever reasons, poor cover illustrations which
mis-represented the character resulting in
potential readers (old and new) not being drawn to
make a purchase, or poor distribution resulting in
low sales, the series was cancelled. For the time
being, readers in search of more stories about The
Shadow would have to be content to seek back issues
of the original magazines.

Chapter Seven

Later Magic

1971-1979

The decade of the 1970s was almost equally divided between old and new material. The Shadow was revived once again and had a fairly successful run. Gibson's titles on other subjects which were wholly made up of new material were related to his work from the past. Games, memory tricks, the occult, and a final volume about Houdini make up this category.

A.138. Chesley V. Young's [Walter B. Gibson]
The Magic of a Mighty Memory
West Nyack, New York: Parker Publishing Co.,
1971. 249p. cloth,

was almost his last book to appear under a pseudonym or to represent ghosted material. A guide to improving the memory as a tool for success in life and a source of amusement in the hours away from the office, this book was re-issued a decade later in 1981, with a new introduction, signed by Gibson.

While there had never been any great secret about the identity of the writer signing himself Maxwell Grant, Gibson had not devoted much time to defining his own legend. His frequent appearances at collectors' conventions in these years altered that and he found himself telling and re-telling the story of his early years at Street and Smith. He often said he wished he had recorded his best account and had it ready for the next person who stepped up to him and asked "How did you create The Shadow?" A push of the button on a cassette player would have saved his vocal cords. If the

interviews he gave during the last years of his
life all seem to read alike it is because most of
the interviewers tended to ask him the same
questions.

It is surprising that he didn't include the
odds of his being asked how he created The Shadow
in

A.139.   Mel Evans' and Walter Gibson's
What Are the Odds?
New York: Western Publishing Co., 1972.
128p. boards.

This concise collection of data to use as a guide
in making the odds work toward improving one's own
future includes the chances of living to be 100, of
having twins, of breaking the bank at Monte Carlo,
and other topics.   It was part of the "Books 2000"
series of guides for the future issued by Western
Publishing Co.

He collaborated with his wife on a third
volume to stand beside the works on the psychic
sciences and the mystic arts.

A.140.   Walter B. Gibson's and Litzka R.
Gibson's   **The Complete Illustrated Book
of Divination and Prophecy**
Garden City, New York: Doubleday and Co., 1973.
336p. illus. cloth,

contains techniques used for predicting the future,
from palmistry to tea-leaf reading, tarot cards,
and arithmancy.   Indexed, it includes a glossary of
terms.   A British edition was published by Souvenir
Press in 1974; it was followed by a paperback
edition (Signet, 1975) and at least one translation
(Brazil, Editora Pensamento, 1978).

Like the books he wrote on hypnotism, his book
on witchcraft is more anecdotal reportage than a
sustained presentation of a thesis.

A.141.   **Witchcraft**
New York: Grosset and Dunlap, 1973.
149p. boards,

was published in England the same year as
Witchcraft: A History of the Black Art, with

photographic illustrations (London: Arthur Barker, 1973).

The basic concepts and rules of the game of Backgammon are presented with the beginner in mind in

A.142.   Backgammon: The Way to Play and Win
New York: Harper & Row (Barnes & Noble), 1974.
144p. illus. paper covers.

The book was copyrighted by Ottenheimer Publishers in the same year as the Harper edition, but this one has not been seen. It was apparently issued in boards under the title **Backgammon**, by Castle Books of Secaucus, New Jersey, but this edition bears no publication date.

After Bantam Books relinquished the rights to The Shadow as a paperback series, Gibson convinced Pyramid Books to revive the series. With striking covers done by artist Jim Steranko, the series began once more with an edition of **The Living Shadow (A.33.)**, October 1974, but the series continued with material which had never been published as a book.

A.143.   Maxwell Grant's [Walter B. Gibson]
The Black Master
New York: Pyramid Books, 1974.
174p. paper covers,

was issued in October of that year. Originally published in **The Shadow Magazine** for March 1932, it represents one of Gibson's early experiments in mystification over the true identity of The Shadow. The Black Master is the name of the legendary terrorist whom The Shadow meets in this novel. It was one of three Shadow novels reprinted by New English Library, London, 1976.

Gibson revived his collaboration with mentalist Joseph Dunninger at this time for a volume which serves to summarize the man's career and compares to the Blackstone and Houdini collections of tricks of the 1920s and 1930s.   In

A.144. Joseph Dunninger's
Dunninger's Secrets (as told to Walter Gibson)
Secaucus, New Jersey: Lyle Stuart, 1974.
332p. cloth,

he combines biography with a description of the
techniques of the professional mentalist.   In
addition he examines and exposes the tricks of some
famous mystics of history.   Dunninger died the
following year.

A book that is similar in format to
Backgammon: The Way to Play and Win (A.142.),

A.145. **Fell's Guide to Winning Backgammon**
New York: Frederick Fell, 1974.
166p. illus. boards and paper cover editions,

is a basic guide to the game.   It was re-issued as
Winning at Backgammon in 1976 by Horwitz of Hong
Kong.

A.146. **Hoyle's Modern Encyclopedia of Card
Games**
Garden City, New York: Doubleday and Co., 1974.
398p. illus. paper covers,

is truly "a definitive guide to the correct playing
of all known card games."   The entries are arranged
alphabetically by topic, fully cross-referenced,
and enhanced by a glossary-index.

The Shadow returned in a story from **The Shadow
Detective Monthly** of April 1932,

A.147. Maxwell Grant's [Walter B. Gibson]
The Mobsmen on the Spot
New York: Pyramid Books, 1974.
190p. paper covers,

which was issued in December 1974.   The Shadow
exposes the invisible power behind the scenes of a
billion dollar protection racket in volume three of
the Pyramid series.   Again, it was one of three
Shadow novels reprinted by New English Library of
London.

Pinochle and poker are the names of the games
in the aptly titled set of books

A.148. Pinochle is the Name of the Game
New York: Harper & Row, 1974.
143p. paper covers.

A.149. Poker is the Name of the Game
New York: Harper & Row, 1974.
143p. paper covers.

Each contains instructions for the beginner as well
as the expert. Each is copyrighted by Ottenheimer
Publishers and each has an alternatively titled
edition from Castle Books: **Pinochle: How to Play,
How to Win** and **Poker: How to Play, How to Win.**

One of the most comprehensive text books in
magic ever assembled,

A.150. Mark Wilson's
Mark Wilson Course in Magic
(in collaboration with Walter B. Gibson)
North Hollywood, Calif.: Mark Wilson, 1975.
472p. illus. boards,

covers more than 300 tricks from close-up sleight-
of-hand to major stage illusions. Line drawings
illustrate each trick, step by step. Biographical
information on stage and television magician Mark
Wilson and Gibson himself is included. The book
was also published in a spiral bound edition with
black vinyl covers.

Gibson enjoyed convincing publishers (such as
Dover Publications) that there were books worth re-
issuing. He arranged for a number of books basic
to a good magic library to be reprinted in this
way. He also arranged for two stories from the
pages of **The Shadow Magazine** to be collected and
reprinted in facsimile.

A.151. Maxwell Grant's [Walter B. Gibson]
**The Crime Oracle and The Teeth of the Dragon:
Two Adventures of The Shadow**
New York: Dover Publications, 1975.
xxv, 163p. illus. paper covers,

includes fascinating introductions by Gibson and
the editor of **The Shadow Magazine**, John Nanovic.
The two novels were published originally in the
magazine on June 1, 1936, and November 15, 1937,
respectively.

In **The Crime Oracle,** The Shadow faces a seemingly bodiless spectre in a creature known as The Head.   **The Teeth of the Dragon** is one of the popular Chinatown stories and features Myra Reldon as one of The Shadow's agents.

The same year, Gibson arranged for two of his later novels to appear in a collected edition for Doubleday's prestigious Crime Club.

A.152.   The Shadow: The Mask of Mephisto and Murder By Magic, as originally told by Walter Gibson (Alias "Maxwell Grant")
Garden City, New York: Doubleday and Co., 1975.
xi, 179p. boards,

collects two of the shorter novels which had appeared originally in the magazine in July and August 1945.   An introduction and a complete listing of Gibson's Shadow novels were added to these stories of murder at the Mardi Gras and in a magic store.

The paperback series continued with entry number four, issued in January 1975,

A.153. Maxwell Grant's [Walter B. Gibson]
Hands in the Dark
New York: Pyramid Books, 1975.
188p. paper covers.

Originally published in **The Shadow Magazine** for May 1932, it involves a message from a dead man worth a fortune in blood.   The coded message is understood initially only by the man called The Chief, but eventually it is understood by The Shadow.

The books were appearing on a monthly basis by now and

A.154. Maxwell Grant's [Walter B. Gibson]
Double Z
New York: Pyramid Books, 1975.
189p. paper covers,

came out on schedule as volume five, in February 1975.   Notes signed with a "double Z" are received by the future victims of a mysterious killer in a novel which had its original magazine appearance in June 1932.

The March 1975 Shadow novel was number six in the Pyramid series.   It had been the immediate successor to **Double Z** in its original appearance in **The Shadow Magazine** in July 1932.

A.155.   Maxwell Grant's [Walter B. Gibson]
The Crime Cult
New York: Pyramid Books, 1975.
157p. paper covers,

concerns a mystery in which the murder victims are found with a round burn the size of a dime on their foreheads and a thin, white line across their throats.

A.156.   Maxwell Grant's [Walter B. Gibson]
The Red Menace
New York: Pyramid Books, 1975.
176p. paper covers,

deals with a crimson-masked political assassin with roots in the Russian Revolution.   Originally published in **The Shadow Detective Monthly,** November 1931, it was published by Pyramid as number seven in their series in August 1975.

The four-month hiatus between novels six and seven was not repeated between numbers seven and eight.   The next book in the series appeared in September.

A.157.   Maxwell Grant's [Walter B. Gibson]
Mox
New York: Pyramid Books, 1975.
127p. paper covers,

was taken from a later issue of **The Shadow Magazine,** November 1933.   There may have been some concern that the earlier novels, written while Gibson was still developing the character, were not as representative of the series as those from a later date.   Mox is the name of a killer who strikes at midnight, unseen, unfelt, unheard, a killer who strikes by remote control.

Shadow number nine appeared the next month, October 1975, and was another of the earlier novels, published in the magazine, December 1, 1932.

A.158.   Maxwell Grant's [Walter B. Gibson]
The Romanoff Jewels
New York: Pyramid Books, 1975.
143p. paper covers,

takes The Shadow to the Kremlin in Moscow to
prevent Senov from involving America in his plot to
trade the Romanoff jewels for help in restoring the
ancient Russian monarchy.   Of interest to anyone
concerned with the development of The Shadow as a
character is the information it gives us about the
origin of his famed girasol ring.   As a paperback,
The Romanoff Jewels was one of the series which was
re-issued by Jove Books, the successor to Pyramid,
with a new cover illustration (November 1977).   **The
Living Shadow** had been treated to a new printing
and a new cover a month earlier.

A.159.   Maxwell Grant's [Walter B. Gibson]
The Silent Seven
New York: Pyramid Books, 1975.
143p. paper covers,

went back even earlier than **The Romanoff Jewels**, in
order to fill in a gap in the sequence of the
novels.   Issued as number ten in December 1975 it
had been published originally in **The Shadow
Detective Monthly,** February 1932.   The nemesis is a
secret society of hooded criminals who identify
each other by their matching scarab rings.

Gibson cut the cards for another shuffle of
basic tricks (53 in all) which don't require much
intricate sleight of hand, just some practice, in
his next handbook,

A.160.   Card Magic Made Easy
New York: Harper & Row (Barnes & Noble), 1976.
iv, 91p. illus. paper covers.

His next book was longer, but once again proclaimed
itself a work for the novice in its title.

A.161.   Fell's Beginner's Guide to Magic
New York: Frederick Fell, 1976.
170p. illus. boards,

covers over 100 tricks with cards, coins, matches,
and other small apparatus.   It includes a directory

of more than 150 magic dealers in the united
States, Canada, and selected foreign countries.

The renaissance of interest in the lore and
legend of Houdini (as evidenced in E. L. Doctorow's
Ragtime) was met by the man who really knew him in

A.162. The Original Houdini Scrapbook
New York: Corwin, Sterling Publishing Co., 1976.
224p. illus. cloth and paper editions.

Lavishly illustrated with photographs, facsimile
letters, newspaper clippings, magazine articles,
and posters from several private collections
including Gibson's, it is a browser's delight. An
introduction, chronology of Houdini's life, as well
as Gibson's own "Personal Memory" of the man serve
to enhance the value of the volume. Its only flaw
is the lack of an index or table of contents and
there are no citations to indicate the sources of
the many publications represented.

The same criticism can be made of the articles
from Gibson's **Conjurors' Magazine**, reprinted in
facsimile, which appear in

**A.163. Walter Gibson's Encyclopedia of Magic
and Conjuring**
New York: Drake Publishers, Inc., 1976.
x, 213p. illus. cloth and paper editions.

As useful as the collection is for anyone not
fortunate enough to possess a file of the original
magazine, it would be interesting to know just
which issue had contained each article. Of course,
the book was designed more with the casual reader
and browser in mind than the scholar-bibliographer-
collector, but the objection is not entirely
unjustified.

The eleventh volume of the Pyramid Shadow
series was published in February of 1976.

**A.164. Maxwell Grant's [Walter B. Gibson]
Kings of Crime**
New York: Pyramid Books, 1976.
160p. paper covers,

was originally published in **The Shadow Magazine**,
December 15, 1932. As a paperback it was re-

issued, February 1978, by Jove Books, with a new cover illustration. The story concerns a mob of four sleazy crooks who operate in America's most popular resort, Atlantic City.

It was followed the next month, March 1976, by a novel which had been published originally right after it in The Shadow Magazine, January 1, 1933,

A.165. Maxwell Grant's [Walter B. Gibson]
Shadowed Millions
New York: Pyramid Books, 1976.
143p. paper covers.

The paperback was another of those titles in the Pyramid series which Jove Books re-issued with a new cover illustration, April 1978. Ten million dollars is what it will take to give the South American country of Santander its independence. There are American financiers who agree to invest the amount and others who intend that it shall never reach Santander.

With the death of Dunninger in 1975, a young mentalist named Kreskin (born George Kresge, Jr. in 1935) was coming in for a great deal of attention. Arranging with Gibson for a book, he followed the tradition of Blackstone, Houdini, and Thurston. He and Gibson worked on the book at Gibson's home in Eddyville, New York. The resulting volume,

A.166. Kreskin's Mind Power Book
New York: McGraw-Hill, 1977.
xi, 212p. cloth,

contains techniques for tapping the unused powers of the mind with step-by-step directions for harnessing brain-power, quickening mental processes, and achieving the highest levels of mental performance. How much is Kreskin and how much is Gibson is uncertain, but some of the memory tricks in Gibson's earlier books are repeated here.

Having written about The Shadow under the name of Maxwell Grant for half a dozen years, Gibson sought to "legitimize" his claim to priority in use of the name by using it elsewhere. His stories of magician-detective, Norgil, written for Street & Smith's new pulp magazine, Crime Busters, were used to advertise The Shadow and vice versa. The use of the name Maxwell Grant on two series of stories tended to give a reality to the shadowy figure behind the author.

Eight of the stories which had been published originally in **Crime Busters** (November 1937 to June 1938) and in **Street & Smith's Mystery Magazine** (July 1940) were collected in 1977 for

A.167.   Norgil the Magician
New York: The Mysterious Press, 1977.
xv, 209p. frontis. cloth.

Gibson's introduction explains the background of the stories and touches on a theme that was of increasing interest to him, the relationship between magic and mystery fiction. The contents are: "Norgil--Magician," "Ring of Death," "Murderer's Throne," "The Second Double," "Drinks on the House," "Chinaman's Chance," "The Glass box," and "Battle of Magic." The frontispiece and cover by artist Jim Steranko was also made available as an 18 1/4" by 25 3/4" poster.

Pyramid's thirteenth Shadow paperback was published in January 1977.

A.168.   Maxwell Grant's [Walter B. Gibson]
Green Eyes
New York: Pyramid Books, 1977.
159p. paper covers,

had been published originally in **The Shadow Magazine**, October 1, 1932. The mystery: who killed Stephen Laird on the passenger train while everyone slept and what does the message "Green Eyes" mean?

A.169.   Maxwell Grant's [Walter B. Gibson]
The Creeping Death
New York: Pyramid Books, 1977.
144p. paper covers,

concerns the swindle of the century in which the world is threatened by a power-hungry, under-handed financier and his followers as well as by an eccentric inventor. The paperback appeared May 1977 as Shadow number 14. The novel had been published originally in the magazine, January 15, 1933.

Worth Varden escapes the power of a super criminal only to be murdered before he can expose the dope-dealing and blackmail schemes of the crime baron whose story is told in

A.170. Maxwell Grant's [Walter B. Gibson]
Gray Fist
New York: Pyramid Books, 1977.
174p. paper covers.

The novel was published originally in **The Shadow Magazine**, February 15, 1934; here it appears as Shadow number 15 for June 1977.

The following month readers were treated to the story of international criminal Felix Zubian's plan for the perfect crime. With the aid of gunman Gats Hackett he dreamed of a million-dollar robbery in

A.171. Maxwell Grant's [Walter B. Gibson]
The Shadow's Shadow
New York: Pyramid Books, 1977.
174p. paper covers.

Number 16 in The Shadow series (July 1977), it had been published originally on February 1, 1933 in **The Shadow Magazine.**

A publishing merger resulted in Harcourt, Brace, Jovanovich taking over the mass market paperback imprint of Pyramid Books. The new imprint was Jove Books and it continued The Shadow series with number 17, published in September 1977.

A.172. Maxwell Grant's [Walter B. Gibson]
Fingers of Death
New York: Jove Books, 1977.
144p. paper covers,

had its original appearance in **The Shadow Magazine**, March 1, 1933. The title refers to an ingenious and macabre series of murders with weapons which resembled "fingers of death" to the victims.

Jove continued the policy of issuing a Shadow novel each month through the rest of 1977.

A.173.   Maxwell Grant's [Walter B. Gibson]
Murder Trail
New York: Jove Books, 1977.
159p. paper covers,

came out in October as number 18.   It had followed
"Fingers of Death" by only two weeks in 1933,
having been published on March 15, 1933, in **The
Shadow magazine**.   Another master criminal, this one
calling himself "Crix," steals the funds of a
European philanthropist and leaves a trail of
death.

The November novel is perhaps the most
complicated of the entire Shadow canon with the
identity of the Parisian arch-criminal Gaspard
Zemba kept a secret throughout the story in

A.174.   Maxwell Grant's [Walter B. Gibson]
Zemba
New York: Jove Books, 1977.
160p. paper covers.

Number 19 in the series, it was taken from a much
later issue of the magazine than any so far, that
of December 1, 1935.

The next entry (number 20) came from **The
Shadow Magazine** of July 1, 1934.   The gimmick in

A.175.   Maxwell Grant's [Walter B. Gibson]
Charg, Monster
New York: Jove Books, 1977.
158p. paper covers,

revolves around the identity of the mysterious
title character who strikes down the inventor of a
revolutionary new type of engine fuel which means
unlimited power and wealth to its owner.   Gibson
expressed himself as disappointed that so much of
the secret was given away by the cover
illustration.

The second collection of late Shadow novels to
be published by Doubleday's Crime Club,

**A.176. The Shadow: A Quarter of Eight & The
Freak Show Murders**, as originally told by Walter
Gibson (Alias "Maxwell Grant")
Garden City, New York: Doubleday and Co., 1978.
xv, 248p. boards,

was accompanied by an introduction by its author.
The first novel in the title was taken from **The
Shadow Magazine** of October 1945 in which an old
Spanish coin holds the key to the mystery. "The
Freak Show Murders" (**Shadow Magazine**, May 1944) is
set in the gaudy world of the carnival where the
killer is a strange harlequin figure.

Having passed over January in their schedule
of Shadow novels, Jove issued three more at monthly
intervals beginning in February 1978 with

A.177. Maxwell Grant's [Walter B. Gibson]
The Wealth Seeker
New York: Jove Books, 1978.
158p. paper covers,

as number 21, taken from **The Shadow Magazine**,
January 15, 1934. A mysterious philanthropist
named Dorand conceals his identity well, but a
gangster named Pug Hoffler is certain learning
Dorand's identity will make him wealthy. A master
criminal has other ideas about that.

A.178. Maxwell Grant's [Walter B. Gibson]
The Silent Death
New York: Jove Books, 1978.
160p. paper covers,

was originally published in **The Shadow Magazine**,
April 1, 1933. As Jove's Shadow number 22 it was
issued March 1978. Master scientist Professor
Folcroft Ulrich is an unscrupulous killer who has a
method of murder which leaves no trace.

The final volume in the Jove Shadow series
(23) was published in April. Again the theme of
mysterious deaths and a mastermind behind them is
presented. Gibson's fondness for anagrams is
evidenced in the name he gives his villain--Thade,
the Death Giver--in which the name is an anagram
for the word "death."

A.179.   Maxwell Grant's [Walter B. Gibson]
The Death Giver
New York: Jove Books, 1978.
160p. paper covers,

was first published in **The Shadow Magazine**, May 15,
1933. Gibson used the character, Thade, in several
scripts for Shadow Comics as well.

While 23 novels over four years may seem like
a successful venture, the number of copies sold
must have been below that desired by a mass market
publisher. The official reason given by Jove for
suspending the series was that a major motion
picture about The Shadow was in the works and no
paperback books should be published until the film
was released. Perhaps they feared the confusion in
the public mind between The Shadow of the pulps and
The Shadow of the radio. Both Gibson and the most
hard core of Shadow readers disagreed, but to no
purpose. Except for the publication of **The Shadow
Scrapbook** in 1979 **(A.182.)**, Harcourt, Brace,
Jovanovich published no more Shadow titles.

While other publishers would circumvent the
injunction against new Shadow reprints in the near
future, one of them, The Mysterious Press, followed
up its edition of eight Norgil stories with another
collection of eight. Gibson supplied the
introduction to

A.180. **Norgil: More Tales of Prestidigitection**
New York: The Mysterious Press, 1979.
xi, 208p. cloth.

Besides that introduction, the stories that were
preserved were ones about the magician-detective
which had appeared in **Crime Busters** between August
1938 and July 1939. Contents: "The Ghost That Came
Back,"   "The   Silver   Venus,"   "Double-Barreled
Magic," "Magician's Choice," "Old Crime Week,"
"Murder in Wax," "The Mystery of Moloch," and
"$5,000 Reward."   The sub-title is clever, but
proves to be difficult to remember correctly as
well as to spell. It is mis-spelled on the dust
jacket as "Prestigitection." The jacket design is
another effective interpretation of the character
by artist Steranko.

While another seven stories about Norgil were published in the pulps they have not been collected to date. (One has appeared in an anthology.) The publisher felt that there were not enough to make up a third volume and suggested that Gibson write a new story to add to the others. He was willing to do so, but as far as is known, the final Norgil story was never completed. It is too bad for it would have completed the solution to a mystery left by the original stories, Norgil's full name. While it had been revealed that his real name was Loring (an anagram of Norgil) his first name had never been given.

Anyone knowing of the injunction against new editions of The Shadow novels in paperback pending the release of the proposed movie might be excused for puzzlement on seeing the next entry,

A.181. The Shadow: Crime Over Casco and The Mother Goose Murders, as originally told by Walter Gibson (Alias "Maxwell Grant") Garden City, New York: Doubleday and Co., 1979. xiii, 197p. boards.

The reason is simple. The agreement with Harcourt, Brace, Jovanovich apparently covered only the early Shadow novels and only paperback editions. Gibson, shrewdly, had arranged with Doubleday for hardcover editions of the later, and shorter, novels which could be published in collections. To continue to honor this agreement was no breach of the other agreement.

This third Crime Club edition of The Shadow contained "Crime Over Casco," a story set among a group of islands off the coast of Maine (**The Shadow Magazine**, April 1946) and "the Mother Goose Murders," (**The Shadow Magazine**, March 1946), which involved The Shadow with a deadly code made up of Mother Goose rhymes. Once again, Gibson provided an introduction explaining the circumstances under which the stories had been written nearly 35 years before.

Jove Books may have agreed not to publish any Shadow novels in paperback, but there was nothing said against the parent company publishing a book about The Shadow's own history as hero of pulp magazine and radio series.

A.182.   The Shadow Scrapbook
New York: Harcourt, Brace, Jovanovich, 1979.
v, 162p. illus. paper covers,

contains the story of how The Shadow was created
and how the stories were written. This lavishly
illustrated volume includes a list of the novels
from the magazine, a chronology of Shadow radio
broadcasts, stills from The Shadow movies, the
script of the first Shadow broadcast, a previously
unpublished short novel ("The Riddle of the Rangoon
Ruby"), a complete six-week episode of The Shadow
newspaper strip, and much more. The radio script
came from the Street & Smith Archives at Syracuse
University, but their copy lacked the final scene.
Gibson and contributing editor, Anthony G. Tollin,
supplied a new ending.

Among the illustrations are reproductions of
over 48 Shadow covers (25 in full color) and many
of the interior magazine illustrations which
accompanied the original novels, as well as
photographs of the many people, actors, artists,
and writers, who were part of The Shadow story.
Much of the credit for the production of the book
goes to Shadow historian and radio history
authority, Anthony Tollin. The preface was by
Chris Steinbrunner who had written several scripts
for the radio series.

It was an appropriate volume with which to end
the decade of the seventies when Walter Gibson
entered his own eighth decade.

C̲hapter Eight

T̲HE WAND BREAKS

1980-1985

Walter Gibson's last books must have evoked memories for many people. A comprehensive textbook on magic, two Shadow collections, more magic for young people, and two magazine pieces retrieved from "biblivion" (to quote Fred Dannay) make up the titles. More in demand than ever, Gibson gave interviews, made personal appearances at collectors' conventions, and lectured before magicians' groups. A typical weekend might find him in Danbury, Connecticut, for an evening of magic followed by two days at the annual meeting of the Friends of Old Time Radio, before returning to Eddyville for a well-earned rest.

A.183. The Complete Illustrated Book of Close-Up Magic
Garden City, New York: Doubleday and Co., 1980.
xviii, 426p. illus. cloth,

is a companion volume to **The Complete Illustrated Book of Card Magic (A.128.)** and a book that must have been years in preparation. It's an exhaustive and definitive collection of professional techniques for performing magic arranged in seven categories. There are literally hundreds of tricks illustrated with photographs of the hands of the author demonstrating the methods. A glossary-index rounds out the book.

Appropriately enough, Gibson's last book of magic was much like his earliest publications, another collection of easy-to-perform tricks using everyday objects.

85

A.184. Walter Gibson's Big Book of
Magic for All Ages
Garden City, New York: Doubleday and Co., 1980.
vii, 231p. illus. boards.

includes personal anecdotes about Blackstone, T.
Nelson Downs, Houdini, Dunninger, Horace Goldin,
Cardini, The Great Raymond, and Thurston. It was
produced solely for a book club with no trade
edition in the U.S. The British title is Magic For
All Ages.

The following year Doubleday published another
Crime Club edition of Shadow novels in honor of The
Shadow's fiftieth anniversary.

A.185. The Shadow: Jade Dragon and House of
Ghosts, as originally told by Walter Gibson
(Alias "Maxwell Grant")
Garden City, New York: Doubleday and Co., 1981.
ix, 205p. boards.

The first novel was from The Shadow Magazine of
September 1948 and had been the first story Gibson
wrote on his return to the series following the 15
month Bruce Elliot hiatus of 1946 to 1948. "House
of Ghosts" dated from September 1943, just before
the digest-sized format for the magazine had been
introduced. Joseph Dunninger, the mentalist,
appears in the story, one of the few times an
individual from real life was used by Gibson as a
character in his fiction. A brief introduction by
the author is included to set the context for the
stories.

Some of Gibson's short pieces had been
collected in anthologies of his own editing, if not
in books edited by others. The first separate
appearance of his articles from Mystery Digest of
1957 is

A.186. Attic Revivals Presents
Walter Gibson's Magicians
Great Barrington, Mass.: Attic Revivals Press,
1982. 8p. illus. paper covers.

"The Strange Case of Washington Irving Bishop" (a
non-fiction article) and "The Amazing Randi" (a
short story) are accompanied by an introduction and
interview with Gibson conducted by pulp historian

Bernard A. Drew.   The story about magician Randi
(born Randall James Zwinge in Toronto in 1928),
written early in his career, is a minor piece of
the same type as the books and articles Gibson did
to promote Houdini, Blackstone, or Thurston.   The
publication, number four in Drew's series of
reprints of pulp material, is included in the same
"binding" as the next in the series (number five)
which has its own cover and pagination.

The last book of Gibson's to be published in
his lifetime was

A.187.   The Shadow and The Golden Master
New York: The Mysterious Press, 1984.
iv, 130, 114p. illus. cloth.

in which the first two of the Shiwan Khan novels
were reprinted in facsimile in a combined edition
with an introduction written for the book by the
author.   The two novels, "The Golden Master" and
"Shiwan Khan Returns," had been published
originally in **The Shadow Magazine** in September 15
and December 1, 1939, respectively.   The jacket
illustration is by Graves Gladney, taken directly
from the cover of the magazine in which the title
novel first appeared.

Gibson himself hoped that the other two novels
in which The Shadow battled Shiwan Khan ("The
Invincible Shiwan Khan," March 1, 1940; and
"Masters of Death," May 15, 1940) would be
republished in the same format as the first two.
In that he was disappointed, but having his pulp
hero preserved in a sturdy, cloth bound limited
edition (there was both a trade edition and a
limited edition of this title) was no slight
tribute.

Walter Gibson's greatest creation was The Shadow. His adventures appeared in Street & Smith magazines for nearly twenty years. Gibson wrote a total of 283 pulp novels, one paperback original, and two short stories about his hero.

At the peak of his popularity, The Shadow appeared in two versions, the original novels and comic book adaptations. Gibson wrote both.

Three generations of magicians were promoted in books by Walter Gibson to the delight of all ages.

A George Sully edition of a Gibson title. Bindings
were uniform. (See **A.11.**)

This program book was produced to be sold at Blackstone's stage show. (A.44.)

Magic for the masses; the science of illusion.
(A.91.)

During a wave of interest in the occult, Walter Gibson produced a shelf of volumes on the subject.

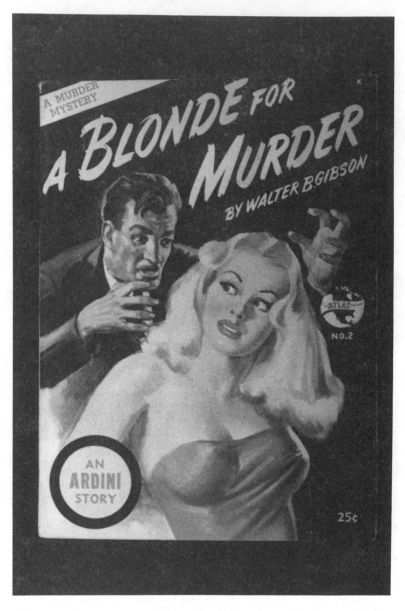

Gibson wrote a handful of mysteries about magician
detectives. A rare paper-covered edition. (A.52.)

B. Contributions to Periodicals ☞

1905

B.1.   "Enigma," **Saint Nicholas**, 31 (October 1905): 1151.

1913

B.2.   "The Hidden Will," **The Wissahickon**, (January 1913): 10-11.
       Short story; Gibson's first published fiction; **The Wissahickon** was the school magazine for Chestnut Hill.

1915

B.3.   "A New Rising Card," **The Sphinx**, 14 (May 1915): 53.

B.4.   "A New Handkerchief Production," **The Sphinx**, 14 (June 1915): 7.

B.5.   "A Wrinkle on the French Drop," **The Sphinx**, 14 (December 1915): 187.

B.6.   "Finger Tip Ball Vanish," **Eagle Magician**, 1 (December 1915): 25.

1916

B.7.   "A New Handkerchief Transposition," **The Sphinx**, 14 (February 1916): 231.

B.8.   "The Two Turned Cards," **Eagle Magician**, 1 (April 1916): 125-126.

B.9.   "The Fingertip Ball Production," **Eagle Magician**, 1 (May 1916): 149.

B.10.   "The Disappearing Die," **Eagle Magician**, 1 (October 1916): 306-307.

B.11.   "Debates on Magic: Should Magic Books Be Placed in Public Libraries?" **Eagle Magician**, 2 (November 1916): 20.

B.12.   "The Mysterious Bowl," **Eagle Magician**, 2 (December 1916): 56.

B.13.   "A New Silk Production," **The Sphinx**, 15 (December 1916): 191.

                              1917

B.14.   "A Few Tips," **The Sphinx**, 15 (January 1917): 215.

B.15.   "The Misdirection Pass," **The Sphinx**, 15 (January 1917): 218.

B.16.   "The Paper and Pan," **Eagle Magician**, 2 (March 1917): 141.

B.17.   "The Card in the Pocket," **The Sphinx**, 16 (March 1917): 9.

B.18.   "The Educated Cards," **The Sphinx**, 16 (March 1917): 13.

B.19.   "Some Thimble Sleights," **The Sphinx**, 16 (June 1917): 54.

B.20.   "The Mysterious Necktie," **The Sphinx**, 16 (June 1917): 74.

B.21.   "Dove Tail False Shuffle," **Eagle Magician**, 2 (July 1917): 266.

B.22.   "The Three Paper Balls," **Eagle Magician**, 2 (September 1917): 345-346.

B.23.   "The Handkerchief Dyeing Tube," **The Sphinx**, 16 (December 1917): 194.

B.24.   "A Mystic Divination," **The Sphinx**, 16 (December 1917): 194.

1918

B.25.   "To the Editor," **Magician**, 14 (February 1918): 45.

B.26.   "Thimble Tricks," **The Sphinx**, 17 (March 1918): 14-15.

B.27.   "A New Card Detection," **The Sphinx**, 17 (May 1918): 52-53.

B.28.   "The 'Three Card' Change," **The Sphinx**, 17 (June 1918): 74-75.

B.29.   "The New Spelling Trick," **Magician**, 14 (July 1918): 106.

B.30.   "An Easy False Shuffle," **The Sphinx**, 17 (July 1918): 83.

B.31.   "The Drum Head Tube," **The Sphinx**, 17 (July 1918): 88.

B.32.   "The Aquatic Thimbles," **The Sphinx**, 17 (July 1918): 89.

B.33.   "Billiard Ball Manipulations," **The Sphinx**, 17 (July 1918): 94-95.

B.34.   "A Startling Appearance," **Magician**, 14 (September 1918): 129.

B.35.   "The Expanding 'Three Card Trick,'" **Magician**, 14 (October 1918): 141.

B.36.   "Up to Date Tricks: The Celluloid Cylinder," **The Sphinx**, 17 (October 1918): 151-152.
     (First of a nine-part series; ends February 1920.)

B.37.   "More Billiard Ball Manipulations," **The Sphinx**, 17 (October 1918): 152.

B.38.   "Up to Date Tricks, part 2: The Chameleon Cards; The Latest Paper Tearing; The Improved Half Pass," **The Sphinx**, 17 (November 1918): 171.

B.39.   "Up to Date Tricks, part 3: More Thimble Moves," **The Sphinx**, 17 (December 1918): 195.

1919

B.40.   "Up to Date Tricks, part 4: Multiplying Billiard Balls; An Easy Color Change; The Slip Back," **The Sphinx**, 17 (January 1919): 216.

B.41.   "Some Good Card Tricks," **The Sphinx**, 17 (February 1919): 232.

B.42.   "The One Hand Palm," **The Sphinx**, 17 (February 1919): 232.

B.43.   "The Roll Vanish," **The Sphinx**, 17 (February 1919): 232.

B.44.   "Up to Date Tricks, part 5: The Latest Four Ace Trick," **The Sphinx**, 17 (February 1919): 236-237.

B.45.   "The New 'Ring on the String,'" **The Sphinx**, 17 (February 1919): 238.

B.46.   "The 'Misdirection' Drop," **The Sphinx**, 17 (February 1919): 239.

B.47.   "Up to Date Tricks, part 6: The Deceptive Dice; The Mysterious Kings," **The Sphinx**, 18 (March 1919): 13.

B.48.   "Up to Date Tricks, part 7: The Three Turned Cards; The 'Top Steal' Color Change," **The Sphinx**, 18 (March 1919): 16.
    We list this as a separate part of the series from the other set of tricks found on page 13 of this issue; there is no indication that the two groups of tricks are to be considered to belong to the same part of the series.

B.49.   "An Easy Card Discovery," **The Sphinx**, 18 (March 1919): 17.

B.50.   "The Whist Trick," **The Sphinx**, 18 (April 1919): 44.

B.51.   "Billiard Ball Novelty," **N.C.A.** (National Conjurors Assoc.), 3 (April 1919): n.p.

B.52.   "The New Spell Trick (Improved)," **Magician**, 15 (May 1919): 72.

B.53.   "The Crystal Cube," by Charles R. Brush [Walter B. Gibson], **The Sphinx**, 18 (May 1919): 67.

B.54.   "Improved 'Latest Rising Cards,'" The **Sphinx**, 18 (May 1919): 68.

B.55.   "A Message from the Spirits," **Magician**, 15 (June 1919): 85.

B.56.   "The Linking Rings: A New Manipulation," The **Magic Wand**, 8 (June 1919): 73.

B.57.   "The Four Heaps," **The** Sphinx, 18 (June 1919): 95.

B.58.   "False Dove Tail," **N.C.A.** Digest, 4 (July 1919): n.p.

B.59.   "To Find a Chosen Card," **The** Sphinx, 18 (July 1919): 107.

B.60.   "Heads or Tails," **The** Sphinx, 18 (July 1919): 107.

B.61.   "The 'Back Palm' Color Change," **The** Sphinx, 18 (July 1919): 117.

B.62.   "Up to Date Tricks, part 8: The Open Hand Vanish; A Novel Card Flourish; The Rising Cards; The Balancing Hat," **The** Sphinx, 18 (July 1919): 118-119.

B.63.   "The Latest Force," **The** Sphinx, 18 (July 1919): 120.

B.64.   "Mystic Circle of Philadelphia (Reports)," **The Sphinx**, 18 (August 1919), 156.

B.65.   "The Mysterious Magazine," **The** Sphinx, 18 (September 1919): 165.

B.66.   "Entre Nous: The Vest Pocket; Billiard Balls; Chosen Card; Aerial Treasury; Vanishing Tumbler," **The Magic Wand**, 8 (October 1919): 160.

B.67.   "The Penetrative Matches," **The** Sphinx, 18 (October 1919): 192.

B.68. "A Changing Card," **N.C.A.** Publication, 4 (November 1919): 6.

B.69. "Philadelphia Magicians' Meeting," The **Sphinx,** 18 (November 1919): 212.

B.70. "A Thimble Vanish," **The Sphinx,** 18 (November 1919): 215.

B.71. "The Penetrative Matches (continued)," The **Sphinx,** 18 (November 1919): 215.

B.72. "The Surprising Shaving Stick," **The Sphinx,** 18 (November 1919): 223.

B.73. "A Second Deal," **The Sphinx,** 18 (December 1919): 239.

1920

B.74. "The Filtering Ink," **The Sphinx,** 18 (January 1920): 281.

B.75. "Philadelphia Assembly: S.A.M. (Society of American Magicians)," **The Sphinx,** 18-20 (January 1920-April 1921).
News notes of the activities of the Philadelphia chapter; individual entries not listed separately in this bibliography.

B.76. "Practical Card Tricks, part 1: Red or Black," **The Magic World,** 3 (January 1920): 118-119.
Series in 14 parts; appeared through March 1921.

B.77. "Up to Date Tricks, part 9: The Appearing Matches; New Thimble Production," **The Sphinx,** 18 (February 1920): 314.

B.78. "Practical Card Tricks, part 2: New Disappearing Spots; A Changing Card," **The Magic World,** 3 (February 1920): 130-131.

B.79. "The Mystic Skull," **The Sphinx,** 19 (March 1920): 14.

B.80. "The Traveling Baseball," **The Sphinx,** 19 (March 1920): 15.

B.81.   "Practical Card Tricks, part 3; Improved Card on Wall; A Card Detection," The Magic World, 3 (March 1920): 142.

B.82.   "The Elusive Die: Another Improvement," The Magic Wand, 9 (March 1920): 5.

B.83.   "The Aerial Treasury," The Magic Wand, 9 (March 1920): 14.

B.84.   "The Vanishing Glass of Water," The Magic Wand, 9 (April 1920): 25.

B.85.   "A Flower Production," The Magic Wand, 9 (April 1920): 28.

B.86.   "A New Department (Editorial Remarks)," The Magic World, 4 (April 1920): 3.

B.87.   "Practical Card Tricks, part 4: A Novel Card Detection; (Two Other Card Detections)," The Magic World, 4 (April 1920): 6-7.

B.88.   "Prohibition," The Magic World, 4 (April 1920): 9.
    Tongue in cheek remarks on the possible use of spirit cabinets to smuggle beer.

B.89.   "Subterfuges," The Magic World, 4 (April 1920): 6.
    Preface to a section of tricks by others.

B.90.   "Practical Card Tricks, part 5: The Peerless Card Detection; A Good Card Discovery; A New Thimble Vanish," The Magic World, 4 (May 1920): 22-23.
    "A New Thimble Vanish" is signed by E. C. Kalbfleisch, i.e. Walter B. Gibson.

B.91.   "Tricks with Matches, part 1: A Matchic Table; The Flying Matches; Card to a Match Box; Upside Down," The Magic World, 4 (May 1920): 24-25.
    Series in 10 parts; ends March 1921.

B.92.   "The Latest Paper Tearing," The Magic Wand, 9 (June 1920): 65.

B.93.   "A New Thimble Vanish," The Sphinx, 19 (July 1920): 131.

B.94.   "O.H. Jensen: An Appreciation," **The Magic World**, 4 (July 1920): 35.
        Biographical sketch signed C. J. Hagen [Walter B. Gibson].

B.95.   "Practical Card Tricks, part 6: The Baffler; Nicking the Edge," **The Magic World**, 4 (July 1920): 38-39.

B.96.   "A Bowl Production," by Weldon the Wizard [Walter B. Gibson], **The Magic World**, 4 (July 1920): 39.

B.97.   "The Philadelphia Assembly S.A.M. Show," **The Magic World**, 4 (July 1920): 39.

B.98.   "Tricks with Matches, part 2: Match Production; Another Match Production," **The Magic World**, 4 (July 1920): 40.

B.99.   "Brema's Vanishing Alarm Clock," by O.H. Jensen [Walter B. Gibson], **The Magic World**, 4 (July 1920): 41.
        Jensen was a contributor to the magazine, but Gibson rewrote his article.

B.100. "My First Performance," **The Sphinx**, 19 (August 1920): 167.

B.101. "A Cigarette Vanish," **Magical Bulletin**, 8 (August 1920): 122.

B.102. "Practical Card Tricks, part 7: The Educated Cards; A Puzzler," **The Magic World**, 4 (August 1920): 54.

B.103. "Prearrangement (Introduction)," **The Magic World**, 4 (August 1920): 54.

B.104. "Tricks with Matches, part 3: The Passe Passe Matches; Lighting a Match," **The Magic World**, 4 (August 1920): 56.

B.105. "The Four Aces," **The Sphinx**, 19 (August 1920): 178.

B.106. "A Tale of Tomorrow," **The Sphinx**, 19 (August 1920): 184-185.
        Short story; Gibson's first professionally published fiction.

B.107. "Mahatma Club Reports (1)," **The Sphinx**, 19 (September 1920): 206.

B.108. "Manipulative Magic, part 1: Match Box Manipulations," **The Sphinx**, 19 (September 1920): 210-211.
   Series in 10 parts; ends August 1921.

B.109. "Quaint Chat from the Quaker City," **Felsman's Magical Review**, 1 (September 1920): 4.

B.110. "Camels and Bull," **Felsman's Magical Review**, 1 (September 1920): 7.

B.111. "Paul, the American Magician," **The Magic World**, 4 (September 1920): 67.

B.112. "Practical Coin Tricks, part 1: New Passe Passe Coins," **The Magic World**, 4 (September 1920): 69.
   Series in 4 parts; ends February 1921.

B.113. "Practical Card Tricks, part 8: The New Spelling Trick," **The Magic World**, 4 (September 1920): 72-73.

B.114. "Regarding 'A Word with Mr. Howard Thurston,'" **The Magic Wand**, 9 (September 1920): 118-119.
   A response to an article in the July issue critical of Thurston's satire on spiritualism, "Unsolved Mysteries of Magic," which had appeared in **People's Home Journal**.

B.115. "Mephisto & Faust," **The Magic Wand**, 9 (September 1920): 111.

B.116. "Editorials," **The Magic World**, 4 (October 1920-April 1921).
   Series of seven articles.

B.117. "Manipulative Magic, part 2: Billiard Ball Moves," **The Sphinx**, 19 (October 1920): 250-251.

B.118. "Special Secrets, part 1: Paul's New Production Box," **The Magic World**, 4 (October 1920): 86.
   Series in 3 parts; ends February 1921.

B.119. "Tricks with Matches, part 4: Moving Matches; The Jumping Heads," **The Magic World,** 4 (October 1920): 85.

B.120. "Practical Card Tricks, part 9: The New Spelling Trick, Simplified Method," **The Magic World,** 4 (October 1920): 88.

B.121. "Gibson's Improved Handkerchief Cassette," **The Magic World,** 4 (October 1920): 90.

B.122. "Arthur Lloyd, the Human Card Index," **The Magic World,** 4 (October 1920): 91.

B.123. "Mahatma Club Reports (2)," **The Sphinx,** 19 (November 1920): 240.

B.124. "Manipulative Magic, part 3: Billiard Ball Manipulation," **The Sphinx,** 19 (November 1920): 294-295.

B.125. "A Novel Card Discovery," by Jack I. Blum [Walter B. Gibson], **The Magic World,** 4 (November 1920): 103.

B.126. "Jack I. Blum," by C. J. Hagen [Walter B. Gibson], **The Magic World,** 4 (November 1920): 103.
    Biographical sketch submitted by Hagen, rewritten by Gibson.

B.127. "Practical Coin Tricks, part 2: Vanishing Dime; Another Dime Vanish," **The Magic World,** 4 (November 1920): 105.

B.128. "Practical Card Tricks, part 10: The Bridge Trick," **The Magic World,** 4 (November 1920): 108-109.

B.129. "A Word to the Wise," **The Sphinx,** 19 (November 1920): 319.

B.130. "Manipulative Magic, part 4: Spool Manipulation," **The Sphinx,** 19 (December 1920): 334.

B.131. "Tricks with Matches, part 5: The Penetrating Matches," **The Magic World,** 4 (December 1920): 121.

B.132. "The Vanishing Handkerchief," by Jack I.
Blum [Walter B. Gibson], **The Magic World**, 4
(December 1920): 123.

B.133.   "Practical Card Tricks, part 11: Number
Nine; A Divination," **The Magic World**, 4 (December
1920): 124-125.

1921

B.134. "Manipulative Magic, part 5: Multiplying
Billiard Balls; Thimble Tricks (part 1)," **The
Sphinx**, 19 (January 1921): 373-374.

B.135. "Subscription Prizes (an article)," **The
Magic World**, 4 (January 1921): 135.

B.136. "Louis Haselmayer," by C.J. Hagen [Walter B.
Gibson], **The Magic World**, 4 (January 1921): 135.
    Biographical.

B.137. "Practical Coin Tricks, part 3: The
Traveling Pennies," **The Magic World**, 4 (January
1921): 137.

B.138. "Practical Card Tricks, part 12: The New
Pocket to Pocket; Card in the Pocket," **The Magic
World**, 4 (January 1921): 140-141.

B.139. "Sleight of Hand Tricks (Introduction)," **The
Magic World**, 4 (January 1921): 140.

B.140. "Special Secrets, part 2: Astral Die," **The
Magic World**, 4 (January 1921): 142.
    Trick invented by Wallace Weldon, alias Weldon
the Wizard, written up by Walter B. Gibson.

B.141. "Manipulative Magic, part 6: Thimble Tricks
(part 2)," **The Sphinx**, 19 (February 1921): 418.

B.142. "The Great Lester (article)," **The Magic
World**, 4 (February 1921): 151.

B.143. "The Vanishing Glass of Water," by Jack I.
Blum [Walter B. Gibson], **The Magic World**, 4
(February 1921): 151.

B.144. "Practical Card Tricks, part 13: The Three Turned Cards; A Practical Shift," **The Magic World,** 4 (February 1921): 153.

B.145. "Special Secrets, part 3: The Aerial Billiard Ball," **The Magic World,** 4 (February 1921): 155.

B.146. "Practical Coin Tricks, part 4: The Han Ping Chien Coin Trick; The Disappearing Dime," **The Magic World,** 4 (February 1921): 156.

B.147. "The Sleeve Swipe," **The Magic World,** 4 (February 1921): 157.

B.148. "The Penetrating Hairpins," **The Magic World,** 4 (February 1921): 157.

B.149. "Manipulative Magic, part 7: Coin Moves; Thimble Moves," **The Sphinx,** 20 (March 1921): 14-15.

B.150. "James C. Wobensmith: a Biography," **The Magic World,** 4 (March 1921): 167.

B.151. "Review: **Miracle Mongers and Their Methods,** by Houdini," **The Magic World,** 4 (March 1921): 167.

B.152. "Practical Card Tricks, part 14: A Practical Palm; Index," **The Magic World,** 4 (March 1921): 169.

B.153. "Tricks with Matches, part 6: Matchless Match Trick," **The Magic World,** 4 (March 1921): 172.

B.154. "Practical Card Tricks, Second Series, part 1: Mechanical Tricks-The Four Aces; The Four Aces (Again)," **The Magic World,** 5 (April 1921): 8-9.
    Series in 6 parts; ends December 1921.

B.155. "Editorial," **The Magic World,** 5 (April 1921): 4-5.

B.156. "Krayak, a Biography," **The Magic World,** 5 (April 1921): 3.

B.157. "Reviews: **The Magic Art,** by Donald Holmes; **The Art of Magic,** by T. Nelson Downs," **The Magic World,** 5 (April 1921): 3.

B.158. "Manipulative Magic, part 8: Moves with Matches," **The Sphinx,** 20 (April 1921): 70-71.

B.159. "Improved Disc Mystery," The Magic World, 5 (May 1921): 23.

B.160. "For Mr. Wise Guy," The Magic World, 5 (May 1921): 23.

B.161. "Practical Card Tricks, Second Series, part 2: The Changing Packs," The Magic World, 5 (May 1921): 24.

B.162. "Manipulative Magic, part 9: Cigarettes and Cigars-Some Cigarette Moves; Cigar Manipulations," The Sphinx, 20 (May 1921): 110-111.

B.163. "Special Secrets-Psycho Secrets, part 1: The Psycho Spirit Message," The Magic World, 5 (May 1921): 26.
    Series in 6 parts; ends November 1921.

B.164. "Special Secrets-Psycho Secrets, part 2: The Psycho Sealed Answer," The Magic World, 5 (June-July 1921):36.

B.165. "Coin Sleights," The Magic Wand, 10 (June-September 1921): 87.

B.166. "Back and Front Move," The Magic Wand, 10 (June-September 1921): 88.

B.167. "Manipulative Magic, part 10: Some Card Sleights," The Sphinx, 20 (August 1921): 210.

B.168. "Special Secrets-Psycho Secrets, part 3: The Psycho Spirit Slates," The Magic World, 5 (August 1921): 51.

B.169. "Carl Brema, a Biography," The Magic World, 5 (September 1921): 67.

B.170. "Book Reviews: Magical Rope Ties and Escapes, by Houdini," The Magic World, 5 (September 1921): 67.

B.171. "Mystic Ring," by Jack I. Blum [Walter B. Gibson], The Magic World, 5 (September 1921): 71.

B.172. "Practical Card Tricks, Second Series, part 3: A New Forcing Pack; Natural Card Tricks-Subterfuges: The Impossible Force," The Magic World, 5 (September 1921): 72-73.

B.173. "Special Secrets-Psycho Secrets, part 4: The Psycho Spirit Smoke," **The Magic World**, 5 (September 1921): 73.

B.174. "Horace Goldin, a Biography," **The Magic World**, 5 (October 1921): 83.

B.175. "Special Secrets-Psycho Secrets, part 5: The Psycho Sealed Reading," **The Magic World**, 5 (October 1921): 86-87.

B.176. "The Jumping Hat," by Jack I. Blum [Walter B. Gibson], **The Magic World**, 5 (October 1921): 87.

B.177."Practical Card Tricks, Second Series, part 4: The Astral Ace; Cigarettes Through Table," **The Magic World**, 5 (October 1921): 88-89.
       Title on article reads: "The Astral Age."

B.178. "Book Reviews: **Patter Paragraphs**, by George Schulte," **The Magic World**, 5 (October 1921): 89.

B.179. "Giant 3 Card Monte," **The Magic Wand**, 10 (October-November 1921): 109.

B.180. "Cunning, the Super-Mind (a Biography)," **The Magic World**, 5 (November 1921): 99.

B.181. "Philadelphia Assembly Notes," **The Magic World**, 5 (November 1921): 99.

B.182. "A Magical Theatre," **The Magic World**, 5 (November 1921): 101.
       Photos and comment on the Kratsky-Baschik Magic Theatre in Vienna.

B.183. "Practical Card Tricks, Second Series, part 5: Super Memory; The One Hand Change Over," **The Magic World**, 5 (November 1921): 102-103.

B.184. "Book Reviews: **Practical Magic**, by Gay K. Austin, **Bargain Magic**, by Magical Ovette, **Conjuring for Conniseurs** (sic), by Bernard Carton," **The Magic World**, 5 (November 1921): 104.

B.185. "Special Secrets-Psycho Secrets, part 6: The Psycho Spirit Ball," **The Magic World**, 5 (November 1921): 105.

B.186. "Magical Tips," The Magic World, 5 (November 1921): 105.

B.187. "Thimble Tips," The Magic World, 5 (December 1921): 122.

B.188. "Practical Card Tricks, Second Series, part 6: A Prediction," The Magic World, 5 (December 1921): 123.

B.189. "False Fingers," The Magic Wand, 10 (December 1921): 184.

B.190. "A Thimble Vanish," by Jack I. Blum [Walter B. Gibson], The Magic Wand, 10 (December 1921): 213.

1922

B.191. "Review: More Exclusive Magical Secrets, by Will Goldston," The Magic World, 5 (January 1922): 135.

B.192. "Book Review: Quality Magic, by Okito [Theo Bamberg], The Magic World, 5 (January 1922): 141.

B.193. "Magic in the Movies," The Magic World, 5 (January 1922): 142-143.

B.194. "Practical Card Tricks, Third Series, part 1: DeLand's Dope Deck," The Magic World, 5 (January 1922): 144.
        Series in 13 parts, including index; ends March 1923.

B.195. "Practical Card Tricks, Third Series, part 2: Sympathetic Connection," The Magic World, 5 (February-March 1922): 155.

B.196. "Practical Card Tricks, Third Series, part 3: Invisible Transposition," The Magic World, 5 (April 1922): 10-11.

B.197. "Practical Card Tricks, Third Series, part 4: The Impromptu Short Card," The Magic World, 6 (May 1922): 22.

B.198. "Magical Tipts (sic)," The Magic World, 6 (May 1922): 22.

B.199. "Practical Card Tricks, Third Series, part 5: New Card Divination," **The Magic World**, 6 (June 1922): 39.

B.200. "Practical Card Tricks, Third Series, part 6: One for the Wise Ones," **The Magic World**, 6 (July 1922): 53.

B.201. "Book Reviews: **New and Original Magic**, by Edward M. Massey; **Revelations of a Spirit Medium**, by Price and Dingwall," **The Magic World**, 6 (August-September 1922): 72.

B.202. "Practical Card Tricks, Third Series, part 7: The Productive Cards," **The Magic World**, 6 (August-September 1922): 78.

B.203. "Jack I. Blum," **The Magic World**, 6 (October 1922): 92.
Biographical sketch.

B.204. "Practical Card Tricks, Third Series, part 8: Hobson's Choice," **The Magic World**, 6 (October 1922): 97.

B.205. "The Thurston Magic Box of Candy," **The Magic World**, 6 (October 1922): 99.

B.206. "Practical Card Tricks, Third Series, part 9: The Mexican Turnover," **The Magic World**, 6 (November 1922): 113.

B.207. "Mystery Hangs Over Shop Where Dark Magic Rules," **The Magic World**, 6 (November 1922): 115.
Reprinted from the **Philadelphia Evening Public Ledger**; about Carl Brema's magic shop. (Original article not seen.)

B.208. "Practical Card Tricks, Third Series, part 10: The Mexican Aces," **The Magic World**, 6 (December 1922): 124.

B.209. "Book Reviews: **Expert Magic**, edited by Percy Naldrett," **The Magic World**, 6 (December 1922): 127.

1923

B.210. "Practical Card Tricks, Third Series, part 11: How It is Done (Method One, Two, Three)," **The Magic World**, 6 (January 1923): 144-145.

B.211. "Two New Books: **Handkerchief Magic**, by Will Blythe and Arthur Ainslee," **The Magic World**, 6 (January 1923): 145.
   Book review. Of the two books mentioned in the article, Gibson reviewed only the one cited.

B.212. "Magical Tip," **The Magic World**, 6 (January 1923): 145.

B.213. "Practical Card Tricks, Third Series, part 12: The 'Change' Four Ace Trick," **The Magic World**, 6 (February 1923): 160.

B.214. "Practical Card Tricks, Third Series, part 13: The Turn-up Card; Index to Third Series," **The Magic World**, 6 (March 1923): 174.

B.215. "Philadelphia Assembly of S.A.M.," **The Magic World**, 7 (May 1923): 4.

B.216. "Practical Card Tricks, Fourth Series, part 1; A Trick of Telepathy," **The Magic World**, 7 (May 1923): 8-9.
   Series in 7 parts; ends February-March 1924.

B.217. "Practical Card Tricks, Fourth Series, part 2: The Clock Trick," **The Magic World**, 7 (June 1923): 27.

B.218. "The Great Blackstone," **The Magic World**, 7 (July 1923): 32-33.

B.219. "Philadelphia Assembly, S.A.M., Annual Banquet," **The Magic World**, 7 (July 1923): 42, 45.

B.220. "Practical Card Tricks, Fourth Series, part 3: The Ever Present Jacks," **The Magic World**, 7 (August 1923): 57.

B.221. "New Tricks: Brema's Four-Ace Trick," **The Magic World**, 7 (September 1923): 65.

B.222. "Practical Card Tricks, Fourth Series, part 4: The X-Ray Card Case," **The Magic World**, 7 (September 1923): 77.

B.223. "The King and Queen," by Harry Blackstone [Walter B. Gibson], **The Magic World**, 7 (September 1923): 72.

B.224. "Where Is It?" by Harry Blackstone [Walter B. Gibson], **The Magic World**, 7 (October–November 1923): 88.

B.225. "Clever Electric Swindle," **Practical Electrics**, 3 (November 1923): 30–31.

B.226. "Trick Shuffleboard," **Practical Electrics**, 3 (December 1923): 53–54.

B.227. "Practical Card Tricks, Fourth Series, part 5: Forty-Nine Cards," **The Magic World**, 7 (December 1923): 103.

B.228. "Philadelphia Assembly, S.A.M.," unsigned [Walter B. Gibson], **The Magic World**, 7 (December 1923): 100.

B.229. "A Page of Puzzles," **The Magic World**, 7 (December 1923): 108.

B.230. "Magicians and Crystal Gazers," **The Magic World**, 7 (December 1923): 110–111.

1924

B.231. "Practical Card Tricks, Fourth Series, part 6: The Simplex Rising Cards; Color Changing Combination," **The Magic World**, 7 (January 1924): 124.

B.232. "The Four Aces, part 1: The Forty-four Aces," **The Magic World**, 7 (January 1924): 126–127. Series in 2 parts.

B.233. "A Page of Puzzles," **The Magic World**, 7 (January 1924): 128.

B.234. "Practical Card Tricks, Fourth Series, part 7: The Extended Card," **The Magic World**, 7 (February–March 1924): 144.

B.235. "The Four Aces, part 2: The Sucker Aces," **The Magic World**, 7 (February–March 1924): 146.

B.236. "Scientific Match Box Puzzles," **Science and Invention**, 11 (February 1924): 994.

B.237. "Coin Tricks Easily Learned," **Science and Invention**, 11 (March 1924): 1114.

B.238. "Easily Performed Match Tricks," Science and Invention, 11 (April 1924): 1223.

B.239. "Dice Tricks Simplified," Science and Invention, 12 (July 1924): 269.

B.240. "Scientific Coin Puzzles," Science and Invention, 12 (August 1924): 365.

B.241. "Scientific Tumbler Tricks," Science and Invention, 12 (October 1924): 370.

1925

B.242. "Stunts for the Smoker," Science and Invention, 12 (February 1925): 999.

B.243. "Handkerchief Tricks," Science and Invention, 12 (March 1925): 1098.

B.244. "Magicians Do Fumble," by Howard Thurston [Walter B. Gibson], Collier's Weekly, 25 (September 19, 1925): 18-19.

1926

B.245. "This Magic Business," by Howard Thurston [Walter B. Gibson], Saturday Evening Post, 198 (March 27, 1926): 25, 124, 128, 133, 135.

B.246. "Trickery in High Places," by Howard Thurston [Walter B. Gibson], Saturday Evening Post, 198 (May 15, 1926): 45, 63, 66, 71.

B.247. "Spirit Tricks," Science and Invention, 14 (September 1926): 407.

1927

B.248. "Magic and How It is Made," by Howard Thurston [Walter B. Gibson], Popular Mechanics, 48 (October 1927): 546-550.

B.249. "Strange Personalities of the Past and Present (1)," by Alfred Maurice [Walter B. Gibson], Tales of Magic and Mystery, 1 (December 1927): 4-5.

B.250. "The Story of the Were-Wolves," unsigned [Walter B. Gibson], **Tales of Magic and Mystery**, 1 (December 1927): 6.

B.251. "The Miracle Man of Benares," by Howard Thurston [Walter B. Gibson], **Tales of Magic and Mystery**, 1 (December 1927): 11-15.

B.252. "Bullet Catching," by Bernard Perry [Walter B. Gibson], **Tales of Magic and Mystery**, 1 (December 1927): 22-26.
    Series in 2 parts.

B.253. "The Ghost Maker," unsigned [Walter B. Gibson], **Tales of Magic and Mystery**, 1 (December 1927): 33.

B.254. "Houdini," **Tales of Magic and Mystery**, 1 (December 1927): 43-48, 64.

B.255. "Houdini in Europe," unsigned [Walter B. Gibson], **Tales of Magic and Mystery**, 1 (December 1927): 49-51.

B.256. "Easy Magic You Can Do," **Tales of Magic and Mystery**, 1 (December 1927-April 1928).
    Series in 5 parts; material from the Ledger Syndicate feature.

                              1928

B.257. "The Temple of Fire," [Walter B. Gibson], **Tales of Magic and Mystery**, 1 (January 1928): 15-16.

B.258. "Strange Personalities (2)," by Alfred Maurice [Walter B. Gibson], **Tales of Magic and Mystery**, 1 (January 1928): 28-29.

B.259. "A Burmese Adventure," by Howard Thurston [Walter B. Gibson], **Tales of Magic and Mystery**, 1 (January 1928): 30-32, 77-78, 80.

B.260. "Number Magic," by Astro [Walter B. Gibson], **Tales of Magic and Mystery**, 1 (January 1928): 37-41.

B.261. "Bullet Catching," by Bernard Perry [Walter B. Gibson], Tales of Magic and Mystery, 1 (January 1928): 42-44.
    Part 2.

B.262. "Houdini in Europe," [Walter B. Gibson], Tales of Magic and Mystery, 1 (January 1928): 49-50.

B.263. "The Story of the Magi," [Walter B. Gibson], Tales of Magic and Mystery, 1 (January 1928): 51.

B.264. "Strange Personalities (3)," by Alfred Maurice [Walter B. Gibson], Tales of Magic and Mystery, 1 (February 1928): 4-5.

B.265. "The Athenian," [Walter B. Gibson], Tales of Magic and Mystery, 1 (February 1928): 16.

B.266. "Further Adventures in India," by Howard Thurston [Walter B. Gibson], Tales of Magic and Mystery, 1 (February 1928): 24-28.

B.267. "Mechanical Men," [Walter B. Gibson], Tales of Magic and Mystery, 1 (February 1928): 33-34.

B.268. "Daring Exploits of Houdini," Tales of Magic and Mystery, 1 (February 1928): 43-47.

B.269. "Strange Personalities (4)," by Alfred Maurice [Walter B. Gibson], Tales of Magic and Mystery, 1 (March 1928): 4-5.

B.270. "Further Famous Escapes of Harry Houdini," Tales of Magic and Mystery, 1 (March 1928): 13-16.

B.271. "Adventures in Mind-Reading," by Bernard Perry [Walter B. Gibson], Tales of Magic and Mystery, 1 (March 1928): 25-28.

B.272. "The Girl Who Was Burned Alive," by Howard Thurston [Walter B. Gibson], Tales of Magic and Mystery, 1 (March 1928): 35-40.

B.273. "Something About Black Cats," [Walter B. Gibson], Tales of Magic and Mystery, 1 (March 1928): 40.

B.274. "The Famous Japanese Decapitation Mystery,"
[Walter B. Gibson], **Tales of Magic and Mystery**, 1
(March 1928): 50.

B.275. "The Evil Eye Superstition," [Walter B.
Gibson], **Tales of Magic and Mystery**, 1 (March
1928): 52.

B.276. "Strange Personalities (5)," by Alfred
Maurice [Walter B. Gibson], **Tales of Magic and
Mystery**, 1 (April 1928): 4-5.

B.277. "Among the Head-Hunters of Java," by Howard
Thurston [Walter B. Gibson], **Tales of Magic and
Mystery**, 1 (April 1928): 33-37.

B.278. "Houdini's Rendition of Mazeppa's Ride,"
Tales of Magic and Mystery, 1 (April 1928): 46-49.

B.279. "The Living Corpse," by Howard Thurston
[Walter B. Gibson], **Tales of Magic and Mystery**, 1
(May 1928).
     Issue announced but never published.

                              1929

B.280. "Making Magic," by Howard Thurston [Walter
B. Gibson], **Youth's Companion**, 103 (February 1929):
85, 107.

B.281. "A Master Magician Makes Magic," by Howard
Thurston and Walter B. Gibson, **Boy's Life**, 19
(February 1929): 36.

B.282."The Witch in the Next Room," **Ghost Stories**,
6 (April 1929): Pages not known.

B.283. "Why I Am Called a Witch," by Madeleine
Grover as told to Walter B. Gibson, **True Strange
Stories**, 1 (May 1929): pages not known.

B.284. "Three Times in the Shadow of the Gallows,"
by Major Robert Brannon [Walter B. Gibson], **True
Strange Stories**, 1 (May 1929): 56-57, 92-94.

B.285. "Nothing Up My Sleeve," by Howard Thurston
[Walter B. Gibson], **Collier's Weekly**, 83 (May
11-June 8, 1929).

Series in 5 parts; the serial version of **My Life of Magic**, A.23; reprinted, 1965-66, in **The Linking Ring**, B.913.

B.286. "Death Valley Scotty's Dash for Fame," **True Strange Stories**, 1 (June 1929): 18-21, 64-69.

B.287. "At the Foot of the Gallows," **True Strange Stories**, 1 (July 1929): 18-19, 66-68, 70.

B.288. "He Squandered His Way Into Fame," **True Strange Stories**, 1 (October 1929): 22-23, 89-92.

1930

B.289. "Measuring Intelligence," **The Thinker**, 1 (January 1930): 14-20.

B.290. "Can a Dog Have a Soul?" by Thomas Windsor as told to Walter B. Gibson, **Ghost Stories**, 8 (June 1930): 98-105.

B.291. "Impromptu Magic," by Harry Blackstone [Walter B. Gibson], **Popular Mechanics**, (1930?): 242-244, 124A.
Cited from clipping found in Gibson's files.

B.292. "Chinese Magic," by Harry Blackstone [Walter B. Gibson], **Popular Mechanics**, (1930?):386-388, 116A.
Cited from clipping found in Gibson's files.

B.293. "Dinner Table Tricks," by Harry Blackstone [Walter B. Gibson], **Popular Mechanics**, (1930?): 546-549, 118A.
Cited from clipping found in Gibson's files.

1931

B.294. "Prizes for Puzzlers, Brain accelerators for every one of Sport Story's readers (1)," conducted by Walter B. Gibson, **Sport Story Magazine**, 30 (1st March issue 1931): 60-62.
This series offered a total of $20 in cash prizes for the correct or most nearly correct answers to both puzzles each month, along with a brief letter explaining how the solutions were arrived at. This episode: "A Baseball Problem," "Golf Acrostics," "Crossword Puzzle."

B.295. "Prizes for Puzzlers-Answers (1)," **Sport Story Magazine**, 30 (2nd March issue, 1931): 43.

B.296. "Prizes for Puzzlers (2)," **Sport Story Magazine**, 31 (1st April issue, 1931): 48-50.
"Cross-Word Puzzle," "Golf With Words."

B.297. "Magical Literature," **The Seven Circles**, 1 (April 1931): 32-33.
The Seven Circles was edited by Gibson.

B.298. "The Living Shadow," by Maxwell Grant [Walter B. Gibson], **The Shadow, A Detective Magazine**, 1 (April-June 1931): 2-113.
The first of Gibson's 283 novels in the series. Originally titled "Murder in the Next Room," it introduces Harry Vincent as the "proxy hero," whose life is saved by a mysterious man in black who requires his complete obedience in return. Reprinted in hardcover by Street & Smith (Ideal Library), included in the first Shadow Annual, and later published in paperback editions by Bantam, Pyramid, Jove, and New English Library.

B.299. "The Green Light," by Walter B. Gibson, **The Shadow, A Detective Magazine**, 1 (April-June 1931): 117-125.

B.300. "Prizes for Puzzlers-Answers (2)," **Sport Story Magazine**, 31 (2nd April issue, 1931): 106-107.
Awards for the winners of the contest in the 1st March issue listed on facing page.

B.301. "Prizes for Puzzlers (3)," **Sport Story Magazine**, 31 (1st May issue, 1931): 118-120.
"Cross-Word Puzzle" and "Golf With Words;" the answers to this and other Cross-Word puzzles involve sports terms.

B.302. "Prizes for Puzzlers-Answers (3)," **Sport Story Magazine**, 31 (2nd May issue, 1931): 28.

B.303. "Sensational Magic: Giant Memory; The Double Bill Tube," **The Seven Circles**, 1 (May 1931): 11-12.
Tricks invented and written up by Gibson.

B.304. "Effective Card Tricks: A Phenomenal Card Mystery," **The Seven Circles**, 1 (May 1931): 16, 21.

Series introduced by Gibson, but not all entries written by him.

B.305. "Sensational Magic: Five and Ten," **The Seven Circles**, 1 (June 1931): 13.

B.306. "Effective Card Tricks: Perfection Speller," **The Seven Circles**, 1 (June 1931): 18.
Trick as performed by Blackstone.

B.307. "Prizes for Puzzlers (4)," **Sport Story Magazine**, 31 (June 10, 1931): 99-101.
"Cross-Word Puzzle;" "Golf With Words;" the magazine continued to publish two issues each month, but dropped the designation of "first issue" and "second issue" in favor of a specific cover date, the 10th and 25th of each month. The text here still refers to the old method of dating; the author may not have caught up with the publisher's decision.

B.308. "Prizes for Puzzlers-Answers (4)," **Sport Story Magazine**, 31 (June 25, 1931): 63.

B.309. "The Eyes of The Shadow," **The Shadow, A Detective Magazine**, 1 (July-September 1931): 2-109.
Lamont Cranston is introduced with the implication that he is the alter ego of The Shadow. Gibson is still developing the character. Reprinted in the Ideal Library and by Bantam Books. We omit the by-line from here on, all Shadow novels in this list were signed by "Maxwell Grant" and written by Walter Gibson. For those by other writers, consult Appendix C.

B.310. "Effective Card Tricks: Surpasso," **The Seven Circles**, 1 (July 1931): 9.

B.311. "Prizes for Puzzlers (5)," **Sport Story Magazine**, 32 (July 10, 1931): 69-71.
Final entry; "Cross-Word Puzzle;" "Word Golf."

B.312. "Prizes for Puzzlers-Answers (5)," **Sport Story Magazine**, 32 (July 25, 1931): 73.

B.313. "The Shadow Laughs," **The Shadow, A Detective Monthly**, 1 (October 1931): 2-95.
End of the initial trilogy; enough doubts are cast on the identity of The Shadow to make him

truly mysterious. Reprinted in the Ideal Library
and by Bantam Books.

B.314. "Effective Card Tricks: The Twenty Card
Trick," **The Seven Circles,** 1 (November 1931): 13.
      As performed at the I.M.C. Convention by
Walter B. Gibson.

B.315. "The Red Menace," **The Shadow, A Detective
Monthly,** 1 (November 1931): 1-110.
      The crimson-masked killer known as The Red
Envoy proclaims himself a revolutionary, but The
Shadow knows better. Reprinted by Pyramid Books,
1975.

B.316. "Sensational Magic: New Black Art Table," by
[Harry] Blackstone [Walter B. Gibson], **The Seven
Circles,** 2 (December 1931): 11.

B.317. "Gangdom's Doom," **The Shadow Detective
Monthly,** 1 (December 1931): 1-102.
      Claude Fellows, one of The Shadow's agents,
tries to negotiate with a Chicago gangster and
loses. The only one of the agents in the series to
be killed. Reprinted by Bantam Books, 1970.

B.318. "Effective Card Tricks: Perfect Card
Location," **The Seven Circles,** 1 (December 1931):
14.

                               1932

B.319. "The Death Tower," **The Shadow Detective
Monthly,** 1 (January 1932): 1-82.
      A mad genius deals death to the unsuspecting
city from a place high above the bright lights.
Reprinted, Bantam Books, 1969.

B.320. "Who Killed Jonathan Adams?" **The Shadow
Detective Monthly,** 1 (January 1932): 126-127.
      A mystery puzzle; solution, signed by "The
Shadow," appeared in the next issue, February 1932,
p. 127.

B.321. "Sensational Magic: Mysterious Flame," **The
Seven Circles,** 2 (January 1932): 7.

B.322. "Effective Card Tricks: Ribboned Card Rise,"
by Harry Blackstone [Walter B. Gibson], **The Seven
Circles**, 2 (January 1932): 8.

B.323.   "Effective   Card   Tricks: Quick   Card
Detection," **The Seven Circles**, 2 (January 1932): 9.

B.324.   "Manipulative   Magic: Checko-Passo,"   The
Seven Circles, 2 (January 1932): 12.

B.325.   "Manipulative   Magic: Traveling   Rice,"   The
Seven Circles, 2 (January 1932): 13.

B.326.   "The Silent Seven," **The Shadow Detective
Monthly**, 2 (February 1932): 1-84.
    The Shadow declares war against the numbers: a
crime budget of <u>millions</u> for <u>50</u> of the Devil's
disciples, lead by <u>seven</u> specialists in crime.
Reprinted, Pyramid Books, 1975.

B.327.   "Sensational   Magic: Checko-Droppo,"   The
Seven Circles, 2 (February 1932): 8.

B.328. "Manipulative Magic: Tearing $ Bill; Ring
Bag; Deceptive Coin Vanish," **The Seven Circles**, 2
(February 1932): 18-20.

B.329. "Manipulative Magic: Novel Black Art Table,"
by Harry Blackstone [Walter B. Gibson], **The Seven
Circles**, 2 (February 1932): 21.

B.330. "The Black Master," **The Shadow Detective
Monthly**, 2 (March 1932): 2-80.
    A   versatile   and   clever   opponent   reveals
another layer of The Shadow's identity. Reprinted,
Pyramid Books, 1974; New English Library, 1976.

B.331. "Who Stole Mrs. Williston's Pearls?" **The
Shadow Detective Monthly**, 2 (March 1932): 126-127.
    Another mystery puzzle; solution, unsigned
this time, appeared in the next issue, April 1932,
p. 128. The promise of a monthly crime problem did
not materialize, this being the final entry.

B.332. "The Passe Passe Bottle," **The Seven Circles**,
2 (March 1932): 5-6.

B.333. "Sensational Magic: The Missing 7," **The
Seven Circles**, 2 (March 1932): 8-9.

B.334. "Manipulative Magic: Gibson's Billiard Ball Roll," The Seven Circles, 2 (March 1932): 19.

B.335. "Manipulative Magic: Cigarette Sleight," by Harry Blackstone [Walter B. Gibson], The Seven Circles, 2 (March 1932): 21.

B.336. "Mobsmen on the Spot," The Shadow Detective Monthly, 2 (April 1932): 1-85.
    A war against organized crime with the entire city as the battleground. Reprinted as The Mobsmen on the Spot, Pyramid Books, 1974; New English Library, 1976.

B.337. "Hands in the Dark," The Shadow Detective Monthly, 2 (May 1932): 1-82.
    A secret code, a series of merciless murders, and the climax to the story aboard a fast train. Reprinted, Pyramid Books, 1975.

B.338. "Double Z," The Shadow Detective Monthly, 2 (June 1932): 2-84.
    A New York judge vanishes, and a cryptic note signed with the last letter of the alphabet is the only warning police and victim are given. Reprinted, Pyramid Books, 1975.

B.339. "The Crime Cult," The Shadow Detective Monthly, 2 (July 1932): 1-85.
    The killer's victims are found with a burn the size of a dime on their foreheads. Reprinted, Pyramid Books, 1975.

B.340. "Mental Magic," by Harry Blackstone [Walter B. Gibson], Popular Mechanics, (July 1932): 45-48.

B.341. "The Blackmail Ring," The Shadow Detective Monthly, 3 (August 1932): 1-89.
    The trail of murder leads The Shadow from Paris to the hills of New England.

B.342. "Hidden Death," The Shadow Detective Monthly, 3 (September 1932): 1-91.
    Both detective Joe Cardona and criminology professor Roger Biscayne are baffled by the series of murders. Reprinted, The Shadow Annual, 1943, and Bantam Books, 1970.

B.343. "Green Eyes," The Shadow Magazine, 3 (October 1, 1932): 1-88.

Is the hypnotic power of Green Eyes greater than the skill of The Shadow? A Chinatown Mystery. The Shadow is now published twice a month and the magazine title has been altered slightly. Reprinted, Pyramid Books, 1977.

B.344. "The Ghost Makers," The Shadow Magazine, 3 (October 15, 1932): 1-91.
A dozen witnesses swear that only a ghost could be the murderer. Reprinted, The Shadow Annual, 1942, and Bantam Books, 1970.

B.345. "The Five Chameleons," The Shadow Magazine, 3 (November 1, 1932): 1-88.
The crime took 10 years to plan, netted loot enough for fifty, but there were only five to divide it.

B.346. "Dead Men Live," The Shadow Magazine, 3 (November 15, 1932): 1-88.
Crime, science, and justice clash when living men die and dead men live.

B.347. "The Romanoff Jewels," The Shadow Magazine, 4 (December 1, 1932): 1-83.
A quest for a king's ransom in jewels is waged beneath the surface of the earth. Reprinted, Pyramid Books, 1975.

B.348. "Kings of Crime," The Shadow Magazine, 4 (December 15, 1932): 1-82.
Community leaders, meeting in secret session, are warned of crimes of the near future. Reprinted, Pyramid Books, 1976.

1933

B.349. "Shadowed Millions," The Shadow Magazine, 4 (January 1, 1933): 2-93.
Is ten million dollars too much of a temptation for the master crook? Reprinted, Pyramid Books, 1976.

B.350. "The Creeping Death," The Shadow Magazine, 4 (January 15, 1933): 1-80.
It's a vendetta against kings and presidents with the only clues a gold coin, a railway ticket, and a feather. Reprinted, Pyramid Books, 1977.

B.351. "The Shadow's Shadow," The Shadow Magazine, 4 (February 1, 1933): 3-91.
It was bound to happen. A master criminal plans a direct assault on The Shadow himself. For once, the master of darkness is on the defense. Reprinted, Pyramid Books, 1977.

B.352. "Six Men of Evil," The Shadow Magazine, 4 (February 15, 1933): 1-86.
Bitter over their treatment by an ancient Indian tribe in Mexico, the six men cross the U.S. Border to commit the perfect crime.

B.353. "Fingers of Death," The Shadow Magazine, 5 (March 1, 1933): 4-85.
Even the police chief, surrounded by guards, cannot escape death delivered by the bony fingers of a skeleton hand. Reprinted, Jove Books, 1977.

B.354. "Murder Trail," The Shadow Magazine, 5 (March 15, 1933): 2-78.
A master criminal steals the philanthropist's fortune, and that incident also explains how a man can disappear from a giant airship in mid-air. Reprinted, Jove Books, 1977.

B.355. "The Silent Death," The Shadow Magazine, 5 (April 1, 1933): 4-84.
Death comes not from bullets or in battle, but swiftly, insidiously, silently, from the invention of a scientist. Reprinted, Jove Books, 1978.

B.356. "The Shadow's Justice," The Shadow Magazine, 5 (April 15, 1933): 2-82.
To test his son's worthiness, the father sends him on a quest with his legacy hidden at the end of it.

B.357. "Artistic Magic," The Seven Circles, 4 (May 1933): 12-13.
Review of the magic act of Roberta and Marion.

B.358. "The Golden Grotto," The Shadow Magazine, 5 (May 1, 1933): 4-91.
Theft on the high seas as a million dollars disappears aboard ship.

B.359. "The Death Giver," The Shadow Magazine, 5 (May 15, 1933): 2-82.

An evil force holds the city, its police, and The Shadow at bay.   Reprinted, Jove Books, 1978.

B.360. "The Red Blot," **The Shadow Magazine**, 6 (June 1, 1933): 4-92.
The city is terrorized, for when the police arrive, the crooks have disappeared, leaving behind them only a red blot.

B.361. "The Ghost of the Manor," **The Shadow Magazine**, 6 (June 15, 1933): 5-89.
A series of sudden deaths at Delthern Manor may have been caused by the family ghost.   Filmed as "The Shadow Strikes," 1937.

B.362. "The Living Joss," **The Shadow Magazine**, 6 (July 1, 1933): 3-84.
The schemes of stock brokers and financiers are controlled by the ancient Chinese god, Kwa. The situation requires an investigation by The Shadow. A Chinatown Mystery.

B.363. "The Silver Scourge," **The Shadow Magazine**, 6 (July 15, 1933): 5-94.
Untold wealth, a crime beyond description, and a trail that leads from the East Side slums to the city of New Avalon.

B.364. "The Black Hush," **The Shadow Magazine**, 6 (August 1, 1933): 3-83.
A scientific device plunges New York City into darkness...a preview of the great blackout of that city some forty years later?   Reprinted, **The Shadow Annual**, 1942.

B.365. "The Isle of Doubt," **The Shadow Magazine**, 6 (August 15, 1933): 3-85.
An island in the Mississippi is the setting for a treasure hunt which leads to crime.

B.366. "The Grove of Doom," **The Shadow Magazine**, 7 (September 1, 1933): 4-87.
What dread secret lies within the grove of copper beeches along the shores of Long Island sound?   Reprinted, abridged, in **The Weird Adventures of The Shadow**, 1966, and by Tempo Books, 1969.

B.367. "Master of Death," **The Shadow Magazine**, 7 (September 15, 1933): 5-85.

Human automatons perform tasks for the man who controls not the living, but the dead.

B.368. "Road of Crime," **The Shadow Magazine**, 7 (October 1, 1933): 4-89.
The innocent find a second chance and learn that real justice can be found along the Road of Crime.

B.369. "The Death Triangle," **The Shadow Magazine**, 7 (October 15, 1933): 9-89.
Murder, complex and mysterious, with the reader invited to solve the mystery along with The Shadow.

B.370. "The Killer," **The Shadow Magazine**, 7 (November 1, 1933): 4-85.
The instrument of death wears a gray fedora.

B.371. "Mox," **The Shadow Magazine**, 7 (November 15, 1933): 10-88.
Who, or what, is the identity of the one named "Mox" and what secret is concealed in the house of death? Reprinted, Pyramid Books, 1975.

B.372. "The Crime Clinic," **The Shadow Magazine**, 8 (December 1, 1933): 5-88.
Is the famous doctor a benefactor of mankind or the master of a strange clinic where more is effected than cures to the ill?

B.373. "Treasures of Death," **The Shadow Magazine**, 8 (December 15, 1933): 9-90.
The missing heir is the beneficiary of a legacy of death.

1934

B.374. "The Embassy Murders," **The Shadow Magazine**, 8 (January 1, 1934): 5-84.
One by one, the members of the United States diplomatic corps disappear from the nation's capital.

B.375. "The Wealth Seeker," **The Shadow Magazine**, 8 (January 15, 1934): 9-89.
Why should philanthropist Dorand go to such lengths just to give away a fortune? Reprinted, Jove Books, 1978.

B.376. "The Black Falcon," **The Shadow Magazine**, 8 (February 1, 1934): 5-85.
The Shadow is unmasked as Lamont Cranston and then kidnapped!

B.377. "Gray Fist," **The Shadow Magazine**, 8 (February 15, 1934): 9-90.
The Shadow is defied by the ruthless criminal known only as Gray Fist. Reprinted, Pyramid Books, 1977.

B.378. "The Circle of Death," **The Shadow Magazine**, 9 (March 1, 1934): 4-81.
Who would suspect that Times Square was a death trap?

B.379. "The Green Box," **The Shadow Magazine**, 9 (March 15, 1934): 9-84.
What connection is there between the dying message and the secret treasure hidden in the green box?

B.380. "The Cobra," **The Shadow Magazine**, 9 (April 1, 1934): 5-80.
The Shadow must save not only his reputation but his life.

B.381. "Crime Circus," **The Shadow Magazine**, 9 (April 15, 1934): 9-96.
Sometimes the bright lights and glamor of the circus conceal the seeds of destruction.

B.382. "Fifth Annual Conclave," **The Seven Circles**, 5 (May 1934): 10.

B.383. "Tower of Death," **The Shadow Magazine**, 9 (May 1, 1934): 5-82.
Why should anyone accept the conditions of this most unusual will?

B.384. "Death Clew," **The Shadow Magazine**, 9 (May 15, 1934): 9-83.
The only clues to the puzzle are the three letters and two numbers on the scrap of paper, but the solution when discovered will save lives.

B.385. "The Key," **The Shadow Magazine**, 10 (June 1, 1934): 5-88.
The only man whose fortune can save the corporation from ruin dies speaking of a key.

B.386. "The Crime Crypt," **The Shadow Magazine,** 10 (June 15, 1934): 9-90.
The perfect crime is planned within the walls of the crypt.

B.387. "Charg, Monster," **The Shadow Magazine,** 10 (July 1, 1934): 4-89.
What sort of a creature is this whom one disobeys at the risk of losing ones life?

B.388. "Chain of Death," **The Shadow Magazine,** 10 (July 15, 1934): 8-97.
Like the Hydra of mythology, every crook whom the police trap is replaced by another just as evil.

B.389. "The Crime Master," **The Shadow Magazine,** 10 (August 1, 1934): 4-86.
He plots his moves and shifts destinies like pawns on a great chess board.

B.390. "Gypsy Vengeance," **The Shadow Magazine,** 10 (August 15, 1934): 7-86.
Gypsy faithfulness and gypsy revenge combine over a stolen treasure.

B.391. "The Spoils of The Shadow," **The Shadow Magazine,** 11 (September 1, 1934): 6-92.
The Shadow's aid is sought...to plan a crime.

B.392. "The Garaucan Swindle," **The Shadow Magazine,** 11 (September 15, 1934): 6-95.
The greatest swindle of the age sends Commissioner Weston to Garauca while The Shadow remains in New York.

B.393. "Murder Marsh," **The Shadow Magazine,** 11 (October 1, 1934): 5-92.
Strange events in the marsh require a strange being like The Shadow to investigate them.

B.394. "The Death Sleep," **The Shadow Magazine,** 11 (October 15, 1934): 8-95.
A game of bridge comes to a halt when the players find they are unable to move their limbs.

B.395. "The Chinese Disks," **The Shadow Magazine,** 11 (November 1, 1934): 6-103.
"Diamond Bert" Farley returns from out of the Shadow's past determined not to be captured a

second time. See "The Living Shadow" for their
first encounter. A Chinatown Mystery.

B.396. "Doom on the Hill," **The Shadow Magazine**, 11
(November 15, 1934): 9-94.
   The body Harry Vincent finds by the roadside
doesn't want to stay put. Does this mean trouble
for Harry?

B.397. "The Unseen Killer," **The Shadow Magazine**, 12
(December 1, 1934): 8-96.
   The master of the shadows meets the invisible
man.

B.398. "Cyro," **The Shadow Magazine**, 12 (December
15, 1934): 9-97.
   The entire globe is the sphere of operations
for The Shadow's latest enemy.

                         1935

B.399. "The Four Signets," **The Shadow Magazine**, 12
(January 1, 1935): 8-93.
   At the core of the secret message of the four
signets is the solution to the mystery.

B.400. "The Blue Sphinx," **The Shadow Magazine**, 12
(January 15, 1935): 11-104.
   The riddle of this sphinx is more puzzling
than that of the original one.

B.401. "The Plot Master," **The Shadow Magazine**, 12
(February 1, 1935): 9-99.
   Not even the highest authorities in
Washington, D.C. can escape the web spun by this
criminal.

B.402. "The Dark Death," **The Shadow Magazine**, 12
(February 15, 1935): 11-94.
   Death from out of the darkness and no one can
tell who may be next.

B.403. "Crooks Go Straight," **The Shadow Magazine**,
13 (March 1, 1935): 9-93.
   When two convicts are released from prison,
how do they meet the test of the outside world?

B.404. "Bells of Doom," **The Shadow Magazine**, 13
(March 15, 1935): 11-97.

Mysterious bells toll the coming of death for someone. Can The Shadow read their warning?

B.405. "Lingo," **The Shadow Magazine**, 13 (April 1, 1935): 9-105.
Can The Shadow prevent Lingo Queed from ruling the whole city? A Chinatown mystery.

B.406. "The Triple Trail," **The Shadow Magazine**, 13 (April 15, 1935): 11-92.
There is no clear trail to the Cellini manuscript. The pathway has three branches which form a triangle.

B.407. "The Golden Quest," **The Shadow Magazine**, 13 (May 1, 1935): 8-92.
A new setting for the master of the night as The Shadow tracks crime into the deep forests of the Michigan lumber company.

B.408. "The Third Skull," **The Shadow Magazine**, 13 (May 15, 1935): 9-100.
Is the third skull real or only an optical illusion?

B.409. "Murder Every Hour," **The Shadow Magazine**, 14 (June 1, 1935): 7-93.
Whenever the police capture one murderer another murder occurs. These are serial murders of a new and frightening kind.

B.410. "The Condor," **The Shadow Magazine**, 14 (June 15, 1935): 7-97.
The master crook's stronghold is so perfect it becomes his greatest weakness. He cannot recognize the members of his own gang.

B.411. "The Fate Joss," **The Shadow Magazine**, 14 (July 1, 1935): 7-103.
Imported from a temple in China, the joss was to be used only against victims from the West. A Chinatown mystery.

B.412. "Atoms of Death," **The Shadow Magazine**, 14 (July 15, 1935): 7-105.
Science and crime are combined in a manner which seems to provide The Shadow's enemies with the perfect advantage against him.

B.413. "The Man from Scotland Yard," The Shadow
Magazine, 14 (August 1, 1935): 7-89.
The Shadow makes an important contact with the
international police when he meets Inspector Eric
Delka, British C.I.D.

B.414. "The Creeper," The Shadow Magazine, 14
(August 15, 1935): 7-103.
Only a ghostly sound reveals the presence of
The Shadow's unseen foe.

B.415. "The Mardi Gras Mystery," The Shadow
Magazine, 15 (September 1, 1935): 7-98.
Beneath the glamor of the New Orleans festival
lie danger and crime.

B.416. "The London Crimes," The Shadow Magazine, 15
(September 15, 1935): 7-96.
The Shadow joins forces with Scotland Yard on
its own territory in an attempt to rid the great
British city of crime.

B.417. "The Ribbon Clues," The Shadow Magazine, 15
(October 1, 1935): 10-97.
What legacy has been left behind that is
marked only by bits of ribbon?

B.418. "The House That Vanished," The Shadow
Magazine, 15 (October 15, 1935): 8-91.
Houdini may have vanished an elephant from the
stage of the Hippodrome, but could even the master
magician have made an entire house disappear?

B.419. "The Chinese Tapestry," The Shadow Magazine,
15 (November 1, 1935): 10-96.
Not worth a fortune in itself, the tapestry is
still the key to a fortune and the means of life
and death.

B.420. "The Python," The Shadow Magazine, 15
(November 15, 1935): 10-97.
Uncoiling his sinuous body, the super-crook
known as the Python winds his coils about a plot to
squeeze a fortune from the unwary.

B.421. "Zemba," The Shadow Magazine, 16 (December
1, 1935): 10-98.
Who is the master criminal known as Zemba?
This is perhaps the most complicated case ever

faced by The Shadow.   International crime centered
in Paris. Reprinted, Jove Books, 1977.

B.422. "The Case of Congressman Coyd," **The Shadow
Magazine,** 16 (December 15, 1935): 9-89.
  The Shadow fights crime within the U.S.
government.

1936

B.423. "The Ghost Murders," **The Shadow Magazine,** 16
(January 1, 1936): 6-91.
  The voice on the telephone sounded like that
of a living person; then how could the caller have
died before placing the call?

B.424. "Castle Doom," **The Shadow Magazine,** 16
(January 15, 1936): 7-92.
  The code of chivalry has been replaced by a
more gruesome tradition when death walks the halls
of the castle.

B.425. "Death Rides the Skyway," **The Shadow
Magazine,** 16 (February 1, 1936): 12-98.
  The Pulaski Skyway has become known as the
greatest highway project in the United States, but
not with death as a commuter.

B.426. "The North Woods Mystery," **The Shadow
Magazine,** 16 (February 15, 1936): 8-87.
  The only clue is a bit of tobacco found at the
scene of the crime, but it leads The Shadow to the
Canadian wilderness to solve the case.

B.427. "The Voodoo Master," **The Shadow Magazine,** 17
(March 1, 1936): 10-94.
  A witch doctor in Times Square may seem a bit
unusual.   The Shadow meets Dr. Rodil Mocquino, but
not for the last time.   Reprinted, **The Shadow
Annual, 1943.**

B.428. "The Third Shadow," **The Shadow Magazine,** 17
(March 15, 1936): 12-100.
  Has The Shadow turned his powers to the
committing of crimes instead of the prevention of
them?

B.429. "The Salamanders," **The Shadow Magazine,** 17
(April 1, 1936): 10-84.

They could survive the flames which would kill anyone else, but could they escape The Shadow?

B.430. "The Man from Shanghai," **The Shadow Magazine**, 17 (April 15, 1936): 10-87.
His identity and purpose were unknown, but death followed his trail. A Chinatown mystery.

B.431. "The Gray Ghost," **The Shadow Magazine**, 17 (May 1, 1936): 8-86.
Bullets cannot hurt him and he cannot be drowned in water. Is he really a ghost? Reprinted, **The Shadow Annual**, 1943.

B.432. "The City of Doom," **The Shadow Magazine**, 17 (May 15, 1936): 6-80.
Dr. Mocquino, "The Voodoo Master," is back and The Shadow knows it!

B.433. "The Crime Oracle," **The Shadow Magazine**, 18 (June 1, 1936): 8-88.
When the talking head spoke, men died! Reprinted, Dover Publications, 1975.

B.434. "Murder Town," **The Shadow Magazine**, 18 (June 15, 1936): 8-89.
No one can predict who will be next to die in this community in which few can stay alive.

B.435. "The Yellow Door," **The Shadow Magazine**, 18 (July 1, 1936): 8-86.
Power, gold, jewels--are these all that lie behind the mysterious yellow door?

B.436. "The Broken Napoleons," **The Shadow Magazine**, 18 (July 15, 1936): 6-84.
The Napoleons were tokens of a broken life and a ruined fortune, but what was the motive for The Vulture's crime?

B.437. "The Sledge-Hammer Crimes," **The Shadow Magazine**, 18 (August 1, 1936): 8-89.
The force of the crimes was stunning to the inhabitants of the city. It was as though they had been hit by a giant sledge-hammer.

B.438. "Terror Island," **The Shadow Magazine**, 18 (August 15, 1936): 5-85.
The crushing waves beat on the shore bringing

danger and death to the group of travelers who
wandered into the den of a master criminal.

B.439. "The Golden Masks," The Shadow Magazine, 19
(September 1, 1936): 10-96.
     The golden masked blackmailers will accept no
less than one million dollars for their silence.

B.440. "Jibaro Death," The Shadow Magazine, 19
(September 15, 1936): 8-93.
     In a teeming modern metropolis, death strikes
from the most unlikely source.

B.441. "City of Crime," The Shadow Magazine, 19
(October 1, 1936): 10-98.
     Not only the highest officials, but the entire
population is gripped by corruption.

B.442. "Death By Proxy," The Shadow Magazine, 19
(October 15, 1936): 8-93.
     One by one, the members of the Lengood family
are visited by death, on a fixed schedule.

B.443. "The Strange Disappearance of Joe Cardona,"
The Shadow Magazine, 19 (November 15, 1936): 14-99.
     Every detective assigned to the mystery of the
purple deaths vanishes--even Inspector Cardona.

B.444. "The Seven Drops of Blood," The Shadow
Magazine, 20 (December 1, 1936): 12-94.
     Seven jewels, pure as fire, disappear only to
re-appear, each in a pool of blood from the veins
of the thief who stole it.

B.445. "Intimidation, Inc.," The Shadow Magazine,
20 (December 15, 1936): 10-88.
     Organized crime strikes at the city with
murder as its goal.

                              1937

B.446. "Vengeance is Mine!" The Shadow Magazine, 20
(January 1, 1937): 10-94.
     Every new task for The Shadow means a new kind
of story. The story for January 15, "Foxhound,"
previewed in the closing paragraphs of this novel,
was written by Theodore Tinsley, not Gibson. (For
a bibliographic citation to "Foxhound" consult
Appendix C.)

B.447. "Loot of Death," **The Shadow Magazine**, 20 (February 1, 1937): 10-94.
What was behind the bank theft?   Who paved the way? Who received the plunder? Could they all be the same man?

B.448. "Quetzal," **The Shadow Magazine**, 20 (February 15, 1937): 12-94.
When a nation lets its vigilance down, the price may be too high to imagine.

B.449. "Death Token," **The Shadow Magazine**, 21 (March 1, 1937): 12-89.
The mark of death, the symbol of the crime, appears as a token of destruction. The Shadow makes clear the meaning of the riddle.

B.450. "Murder House," **The Shadow Magazine**, 21 (March 15, 1937): 12-83.
Outwardly respectable, the country house was the headquarters for a daring gang of thieves and murderers.

B.451. "Washington Crime," **The Shadow Magazine**, 21 (April 1, 1937): 10-88.
Crime rises from the halls of government and threatens the safety of the nation.

B.452. "The Masked Headsman," **The Shadow Magazine**, 21 (April 15, 1937): 10-85.
Has The Shadow met his match in this villain?

B.453. "Test Your Wits!" **Doc Savage Magazine**, 9 (May 1937): 100-101; Answers, p. 127.
First of a series of puzzle columns conducted by Gibson which appeared in this magazine.

B.454. "Treasure Trail," **The Shadow Magazine**, 21 (May 15, 1937): 8-87.
A lost treasure is recovered from the depths of the ocean but the discovery of another map promises greater wealth.

B.455. "Test Your Wits! (2)," **Doc Savage Magazine**, 9 (June 1937): 106-107; Answers, p. 127.

B.456. "Brothers of Doom," **The Shadow Magazine**, 22 (June 1, 1937): 10-89.
Life is so cheap that to the Brothers of Evil a dozen murders are just part of the day's work.

B.457. "The Shadow's Rival," **The Shadow Magazine,** 22 (June 15, 1937): 8-87.
A rival to The Shadow in ability and success against the underworld makes the police wonder if they have at last learned the identity of the crime fighter.

B.458. "Test Your Wits! (3)," **Doc Savage Magazine,** 9 (July 1937): 113-114; Answers, p. 128.

B.459. "Crime, Insured," **The Shadow Magazine,** 22 (July 1, 1937): 8-87.
Up-to-date, efficient, deadly, the newest racket is nearly a trap for The Shadow.

B.460. "House of Silence," **The Shadow Magazine,** 22 (July 15, 1937): 8-85.
A sinister and foreboding structure, the mansion concealed far more than could be imagined.

B.461. "Test Your Wits! (4)," **Doc Savage Magazine,** 9 (August 1937): 106-107; Answers, p. 128.

B.462. "The Shadow Unmasks," **The Shadow Magazine,** 22 (August 1, 1937): 8-87.
A story for which the world is well prepared and for which it has waited for six years, the origin of the master of darkness himself. His true identity is revealed as Kent Allard, aviator. (This explanation is contradicted somewhat in later stories.)

B.463. "The Yellow Band," **The Shadow,** 22 (August 15, 1937): 8-85.
Who and what is The Yellow Band? Is it the equal of The Shadow? (Beginning with this issue and continuing through January 1947, the title of the magazine becomes simply **The Shadow.**)

B.464. "Test Your Wits! (5)," **Doc Savage Magazine,** 10 (September 1937): 120-121; Answers, p. 128.

B.465. "Buried Evidence," **The Shadow,** 23 (September 1, 1937): 8-80.
The past is prologue--even when it is the evil past and the future is the future of crime.

B.466. "The Radium Murders," **The Shadow,** 23 (September 15, 1937): 8-84.

The Shadow faces a unique foe, one who uses radium as a murder weapon.

B.467. "Test Your Wits! (6)," **Doc Savage Magazine**, 10 (October 1937): 118-119; Answers, p. 126.

B.468. "The Keeper's Gold," **The Shadow**, 23 (October 15, 1937): 10-87.
Ill-gotten wealth and the blood of a murderer make a fit breeding ground for crime.

B.469. "Norgil--Magician," by Maxwell Grant [Walter B. Gibson], **Crime Busters**, 1 (November 1937): 74-87.
In which Norgil becomes a target for the protection racket and fights back with more than rabbits from his hat. All of Gibson's stories for **Crime Busters** featured Norgil, magician-detective, and were signed by Maxwell Grant. The series was continued in **Street & Smith's Mystery Magazine** after September 1939.   Reprinted in **Norgil the Magician**, 1977.

B.470. "Test Your Wits! (7)," **Doc Savage Magazine**, 10 (November 1937): 121-122; Answers, p. 127.

B.471. "Death Turrets," **The Shadow**, 23 (November 1, 1937): 12-91.
The reading of the will is followed by the regular demise of each member of the family who remains alive, but the motive of the killer is not greed.

B.472. "Teeth of the Dragon," **The Shadow**, 23 (November 15, 1937): 12-91.
Once again, Ying Ko (The Shadow) battles the forces of the East with the methods of the West. This time he is assisted by a woman known as Ming Dwan, his new agent whose real name is Myra Reldon. A Chinatown mystery.   Reprinted, Dover Publications, 1975.

B.473. "Test Your Wits! (8)," **Doc Savage Magazine**, 10 (December 1937): 121-122; Answers, p. 127.

B.474. "The Sealed Box," **The Shadow**, 24 (December 1, 1937): 14-91.
The secret it contains makes it priceless and worth more than life itself.

B.475. "Racket Town," **The Shadow,** 24 (December 15, 1937): 10-85.
Another city of crime, another murder town, where the leader of the rackets is virtually king.

1938

B.476. "Ring of Death," **Crime Busters,** 1 (January 1938): 30-43.
In which the trick requires Norgil to borrow a ring from someone in the audience, shoot it from a pistol, and return it to its owner. This time the owner vanishes before the ring can be returned. Introduces Miriam Laymond. Reprinted in **Norgil the Magician,** 1977.

B.477. "Test Your Wits! (9)," **Doc Savage Magazine,** 10 (January 1938): 116-117; Answers, p. 126-127.

B.478. "The Crystal Buddha," **The Shadow,** 24 (January 1, 1938): 6-81.
A clear, crystal statuette hides a secret worth a dozen lives.

B.479. "Hills of Death," **The Shadow,** 24 (January 15, 1938); 6-83.
Action, thrills, suspense are promised to Shadow readers in the New Year.

B.480. "Murderer's Throne," **Crime Busters,** 1 (February 1938): 24-37.
In which Norgil baits a gangster with a staged radio announcement, finds a missing murder victim, and provides fitting justice for King Blauden. Reprinted in **Norgil the Magician,** 1977.

B.481. "The Murder Master," **The Shadow,** 24 (February 15, 1938): 6-81.
In which the killer challenges the police and The Shadow as well with warnings about the identity of his next victim.

B.482. "The Second Double," **Crime Busters,** 1 (March 1938): 42-55.
In which the show arrives in town preceded by a well-planned publicity campaign and followed by someone attempting to kill Norgil. Reprinted in **Norgil the Magician,** 1977.

B.483. "Test Your Wits! (10)," **Doc Savage Magazine**, 11 (March 1938): 103-105; Answers, p. 128.

B.484. "The Golden Pagoda," **The Shadow**, 25 (March 1, 1938): 6-84.
He who would be master of the pagoda must pay the price in blood.

B.485. "Face of Doom," **The Shadow**, 25 (March 15, 1938): 6-82.
"Fight and excitement" are promised to the readers of this Shadow novel. Another story in which the editor saw only the title when making up the preview.

B.486. "Drinks on the House," **Crime Busters**, 1 (April 1938): 44-56.
In which Norgil's show is booked into a theatre in a town which may be owned by the king of the rackets. Our magician turns bartender to learn the truth and solve a murder. Reprinted in **Norgil the Magician**, 1977.

B.487. "Serpents of Siva," **The Shadow**, 25 (April 15, 1938): 4-76.
The editors are certain the title alone will sell readers on this novel. (Again, the editors may have seen only the title ahead of time.)

B.488. "Chinaman's Chance," **Crime Busters**, 2 (May 1938): 42-55.
In which Norgil becomes a quick change artist and goes on stage as Chinese magician Ling Ro. Someone else in a dual role means danger for Norgil. Reprinted in **Norgil the Magician**, 1977.

B.489. "Cards of Death," **The Shadow**, 25 (May 1, 1938): 4-78.
In the deadly game of cards, the deadliest card of the pack is dealt by The Shadow.

B.490. "The Hand," **The Shadow**, 25 (May 15, 1938): 4-77.
A new menace: a band of criminals working together and yet each one is independent of the others. The first of a series of six novels on this theme.

B.491. "The Glass Box," **Crime Busters**, 2 (June 1938): 26-39.

In which Norgil stages a buried alive stunt in the waters of the Portville harbor and nearly loses his life when a local hoodlum steps in over a conflict of interest. Reprinted in **Norgil the Magician**, 1977.

B.492. "Voodoo Trail," **The Shadow**, 26 (June 1, 1938): 6-80.
Dr. Rodil Mocquino returns for his third and final encounter with The Shadow.

B.493. "The Rackets King," **The Shadow**, 26 (June 15, 1938): 6-84.
A power struggle for control of New York City with The Shadow against the King of all the rackets. Written earlier than the other novels in "The Hand" series, it is often recommended as comparative reading for its similarity in theme. Thus, we class it as number two of the series.

B.494. "The Mad Magician," **Crime Busters**, 2 (July 1938): 6-20.
In which Professor Caradoc lures Norgil into a dangerous situation with an invitation to examine a collection of rare magic tricks. Reprinted in Otto Penzler's **Whodunit? Houdini?** in 1976, with chapter titles omitted.

B.495. "Murder for Sale," **The Shadow**, 26 (July 1, 1938): 6-78.
There are puns aplenty as the editor describes the return of The Hand which <u>reaches</u> out for The Shadow who must succeed in <u>squeezing</u> crime in his <u>grasp</u>.

B.496. "The Golden Vulture," **The Shadow**, 26 (July 15, 1938): 6-80.
A masked and costumed criminal meets The Shadow. A golden guise versus the dark avenger. Revised from a manuscript by Lester Dent.

B.497. "The Ghost That Came Back," **Crime Busters**, 2 (August 1938): 6-21.
In which Norgil investigates a haunted house and captures a murderer. Reprinted in **Norgil: More Tales of Prestidigitection**, 1979.

B.498. "Death Jewels," **The Shadow**, 26 (August 1, 1938): 8-84.

Is any treasure worth the lives lost to attain this one?

B.499. "The Green Hoods," **The Shadow**, 26 (August 15, 1938): 6-82.
Concealed identities and masked intentions cannot be hidden forever from the master of disguise, The Shadow.

B.500. "The Silver Venus," **Crime Busters**, 2 (September 1938): 41-56.
In which Norgil undertakes to vanish a life-size silver statue and solves the murder of its real-life double. Reprinted in **Norgil**, 1979.

B.501. "Crime Over Boston," **The Shadow**, 27 (September 15, 1938): 6-78.
The authorities think they have the master criminal trapped and rendered harmless, but then he escapes to avenge himself. His first strike is Boston. A Major Cities mystery.

B.502. "The Dead Who Lived," **The Shadow**, 27 (October 1, 1938): 10-85.
Once again, The Shadow has the problem of having to fathom the secrets of the undead.

B.503. "Vanished Treasure," **The Shadow**, 27 (October 15, 1938): 8-81.
A family feud replaces brotherly love and a simple document becomes a death warrant in this search for treasure.

B.504. "Double-Barreled Magic," **Crime Busters**, 3 (November 1938): 44-58.
In which Norgil assists the FBI to find a kidnapped businessman while performing his show at a fairground. Reprinted in **Norgil**, 1979.

B.505. "The Voice," **The Shadow**, 27 (November 1, 1938): 9-82.
The gang leader is not only unknown, but unseen; the underworld only knows what is told it by this disembodied voice.

B.506. "Chicago Crime," **The Shadow**, 27 (November 15, 1938): 9-82.
The Shadow pays a return visit to Chicago to renew his battle with The Hand. Number 4 in The Hand series; a Major Cities mystery.

B.507. "Magician's Choice," **Crime Busters**, 3 (December 1938): 27-42.

In which Norgil uses a trick from Thurston's repertoire to prevent a miscarriage of justice and catch a murderer. Reprinted in **Norgil**, 1979.

B.508. "Shadow Over Alcatraz," **The Shadow**, 28 (December 1, 1938): 9-84.

The pursuit of Zanigew, that Napoleon of crime, leads The Shadow to America's Devil's Island. Is this villain really Professor Moriarty still alive after all these years? The climax is a pastiche of the ending of Conan Doyle's "The Final Problem."

1939

B.509. "Silver Skull," **The Shadow**, 28 (January 1, 1939): 9-80.

The mark of the master mind is a shiny, silver token...of death...shaped liked a skull.

B.510. "Crime Rides the Sea," **The Shadow**, 28 (January 15, 1939): 9-52, 97-130.

Another digit on The Hand is disposed of by The Shadow. No. 5 in The Hand series. From this issue through that dated February 1, 1940, the pagination for the lead novel is not continuous, but interrupted by other features.

B.511. "Old Crime Week," **Crime Busters**, 3 (February 1939): 57-70.

In which Norgil returns to his home town to solve an old family mystery, stays to solve a murder, and reveals to Miriam that his real name is Loring, an anagram of the name Norgil. His first name is never given, although Gibson planned one final story in which it would be revealed that his full name was W. Bates Loring, the "W." standing for Williams. Not William, but Williams, for Williams College. Bates was taken from Bates College and both were institutions which Norgil's family had attended. True to Gibson's love of puzzles and games, the name was also an anagram for his own name. Reprinted in **Norgil**, 1979.

B.512. "Realm of Doom," **The Shadow**, 28 (February 1, 1939): 9-52, 98-129.

A new angle on an old crime and The Shadow's final encounter with the members of The Hand.

B.513. "The Lone Tiger," **The Shadow**, 28 (February 15, 1939): 9-52, 93-125.
The price on his head sets everyone on his trail, including The Shadow.

B.514. "The Vindicator," **The Shadow**, 29 (March 15, 1939): 9-52, 89-125.
Sinner or Saint, no one knows what The Vindicator will do next.

B.515. "Murder in Wax," **Crime Busters**, 3 (April 1939): 9-20, 128-130.
In which a body is discovered in a wax museum and Miriam nearly loses her head to the guillotine. Reprinted in **Norgil**, 1979.

B.516. "Death Ship," **The Shadow**, 29 (April 1, 1939): 9-52, 91-130.
The nations of the world wanted it, provided it would work...and so did the masters of crime.

B.517. "Battle of Greed," **The Shadow**, 29 (April 15, 1939): 9-52, 91-126.
The Shadow's guns must conquer temptation and greed in his opponents...it's a matter of lead against gold.

B.518. "The Three Brothers," **The Shadow**, 29 (May 15, 1939): 9-52, 89-129.
Can brotherly love overcome greed? What evil plot can so victimize others?

B.519. "The Mystery of Moloch," **Crime Busters**, 4 (June 1939): 43-56.
In which Norgil vanishes a lady on the run and produces a diamond necklace to trap a thief. Reprinted in **Norgil**, 1979.

B.520. "Smugglers of Death," **The Shadow**, 30 (June 1, 1939): 9-52, 93-127.
Were they smart enough to by-pass the customs agents or were they only smuggling death into the country?

B.521. "City of Shadows," **The Shadow**, 30 (June 15, 1939): 9-52, 97-129.

From the chambers of government to the dark alleys, crime is a thriving business in the city.

B.522. "$5,000 Reward," **Crime Busters,** 4 (July 1939): 81-92, 94-96.
In which Norgil issues an escape challenge for $5,000 and finds himself faced with an impossible task. Reprinted in **Norgil,** 1979.

B.523. "Death from Nowhere," **The Shadow,** 30 (July 15, 1939): 9-52, 95-129.
Usually there are clues to murder, but this time there are none. And not only is there no clue to the murderer, there is not even a clue to his method!

B.524. "Isle of Gold," **The Shadow,** 30 (August 1, 1939): 9-52, 93-126.
The Shadow knows well that treasure and danger go hand in hand.

B.525. "Wizard of Crime (1)," **The Shadow,** 30 (August 15, 1939): 9-52, 99-128.
Can the trickster of chemistry match the might of The Shadow's automatics? This story is not to be confused with the novel of the same title published in **The Shadow** for February 15, 1943.

B.526. "The Chest of Ching Ling Foo," **Crime Busters,** 4 (September 1939): 25-38.
In which Norgil solves the mystery of a colleague with the aid of a relic from the past. This series was continued in **Street & Smith's Mystery Magazine;** see below.

B.527. "The Crime Ray," **The Shadow,** 31 (September 1, 1939): 9-52, 96-130.
The city is astounded to learn that Lamont Cranston has been accused of being a master criminal.

B.528. "The Golden Master," **The Shadow,** 31 (September 15, 1939): 9-52, 94-130.
The Shadow meets his greatest enemy, the villainous Shiwan Khan. A Chinatown mystery.

B.529. "Castle of Crime," **The Shadow,** 31 (October 1, 1939): 9-52, 95-130.
The citadel on the coast of Maine hides a secret with international ramifications.

B.530. "The Masked Lady," **The Shadow**, 31 (October 15, 1939): 9-52, 91-130.
Her identity was not the only thing concealed by the mask.

B.531. "Ships of Doom," **The Shadow**, 31 (November 1, 1939): 9-52, 88-129.
The series of disasters to American ships was only the first mysterious occurrence.

B.532. "City of Ghosts," **The Shadow**, 31 (November 15, 1939): 9-52, 89-130.
The city dies and The Shadow needs to know the reason.

B.533. "The Blue Pearls," **Street & Smith's Mystery Magazine**, 5 (December 1939): 80-93.
In which Norgil appears to turn a talent for sleights of hand to larceny and Miriam must come to his rescue.

B.534. "Shiwan Khan Returns," **The Shadow**, 32 (December 1, 1939): 9-54, 70-114.
In which that Oriental mastermind has another attempt at conquering the world. A Chinatown mystery.

B.535. "House of Shadows," **The Shadow**, 32 (December 15, 1939): 9-54, 71-111.
There was an old woman who lived alone in the family mansion, her fortune an attraction for a killer.

1940

B.536. "Death's Premium," **The Shadow**, 32 (January 1, 1940): 9-54, 69-108.
The Shadow, in his role of Henry Arnaud, insures the death of Lamont Cranston for a half-million dollars! (We should remember that the author taught himself how to type by writing out insurance policies.)

B.537. "The Hooded Circle," **The Shadow**, 32 (January 15, 1940): 9-54, 69-110.
They meet in the glen of the Druids with their identities concealed by hoods. It is up to The Shadow to penetrate the disguise.

B.538. "The Lady and the Lion," **Street & Smith's Mystery Magazine**, 5 (January 1940): 78-94.
In which a parsimonious theatre owner, a trained lion, and a carnival worker lead Norgil to the man responsible for a crime wave in Westbury.

B.539. "The Getaway Ring," **The Shadow**, 32 (February 1, 1940): 9-54, 71-114.
It is the perfect means of getting away from the scene of a crime, a road map supplied by professional thieves to plot the trail.

B.540. "Voice of Death," **The Shadow**, 32 (February 15, 1940): 9-88.
It is almost a perfect crime, but The Shadow finds the flaw in the Voice announcing death. Reprinted as **The Shadow and the Voice of Murder**, Los Angeles, Bantam Books, 1940.

B.541. "Crime in the Crystal," **Street & Smith's Mystery Magazine**, 5 (March 1940): 57-73.
In which a prophetic swami helps Norgil crack a counterfeiting ring.

B.542. "The Invincible Shiwan Khan," **The Shadow**, 33 (March 1, 1940): 9-91.
The Master Criminal finds a way to make his victims fight against The Shadow. A Chinatown mystery.

B.543. "The Veiled Prophet," **The Shadow**, 33 (March 15, 1940): 9-88.
What face lies behind the gauze-like mask of Mokanna and what is the meaning of his strange emblem? (This character is also used in an early Blackstone story in **Super-Magician Comics**.)

B.544. "The Spy Ring," **The Shadow**, 33 (April 1, 1940): 9-91.
From a position of neutrality, the U.S. is prey to espionage from abroad. Fortunately, The Shadow is in the first line of defence.

B.545. "Too Many Ghosts," **Street & Smith's Mystery Magazine**, 6 (May 1940): 38-54.
In which a latter day Phantom of the Opera stalks the Sherbrook Opera House production of Hamlet and Norgil issues a challenge.

B.546. "Death in the Stars," **The Shadow**, 33 (May 1, 1940): 9-92.
The bearded swami reads the future in the stars and controls his followers by astrology.

B.547. "Masters of Death," **The Shadow**, 33 (May 15, 1940): 9-92.
It was inevitable, another encounter with Shiwan Khan.   Is this to be their battle to the death?   The fourth and final Shiwan Khan story.   A Chinatown mystery.

B.548. "The Scent of Death," **The Shadow**, 34 (June 1, 1940): 9-84.
Death is in the air, bringing a fragrance detectable only to the hawk-like nose of The Shadow.

B.549. "Q," **The Shadow**, 34 (June 15, 1940): 9-90.
A new master of the underworld arises.   He is known only as "Q." Can The Shadow unmask him?

B.550. "Battle of Magic," **Street & Smith's Mystery Magazine**, 6 (July 1940): 39-54.
In which a prize for the most clever magic trick is set at $25,000 and someone tries to take Norgil out of the running permanently.   Reprinted in **Norgil the Magician**, 1977.

B.551. "Gems of Doom," **The Shadow**, 34 (July 15, 1940): 9-89.
Diamonds from South Africa bring intrigue and murder to New York City.

B.552. "Crime at Seven Oaks," **The Shadow**, 34 (August 1, 1940): 9-88.
A banshee interrupts the peacefulness at Seven Oaks and brings danger to the Melridges.

B.553. "The Fifth Face," **The Shadow**, 34 (August 15, 1940): 9-89.
Four crimes, with four faces masking the same criminal...and then he puts on his fifth face.

B.554. "Crime County," **The Shadow**, 35 (September 1, 1940): 9-91.
Overcrowding in the city sends the crooks to the country where they hope to have easy pickings.

B.555. "The Wasp," **The Shadow**, 35 (October 1, 1940): 9-93.
He is an insect in human guise; they call him The Wasp for his sting is death.

B.556. "Tank-Town Tour," **Street & Smith's Mystery Magazine**, 6 (November 1940): 54-70.
In which Norgil is booked on a vaudeville circuit to follow a trained seal act and uncovers a racket in bootleg oil. Norgil has a set of special picklocks once owned by Houdini. (The final Norgil story.)

B.557. "Crime Over Miami," **The Shadow**, 35 (November 1, 1940): 9-95.
A new crime wave strikes in the resort city of Miami, Florida, as an old-fashioned gambling scheme takes root.

B.558. "Xitli, God of Fire," **The Shadow**, 36 (December 1, 1940): 9-94.
New Orleans, a strange place for The Shadow to find the ancient Aztec god of fire.

B.559. "The Shadow, the Hawk, and the Skull," **The Shadow**, 36 (December 15, 1940): 9-91.
Two master criminals for the price of one! Can their combined power overcome The Shadow?

1941

B.560.   "Forgotten Gold," **The Shadow**, 36 (January 1, 1941): 9-94.
If money is the root of all evil, does gold buried for many years sprout tendrils of power?

B.561.   "The Wasp Returns," **The Shadow**, 36 (February 1, 1941): 9-96.
A miniature object, the wing of a wasp, strikes fear in the heart of more than one man, for it means that The Wasp is back for his second, and final, meeting with The Shadow.

B.562.   "The Chinese Primrose," **The Shadow**, 36 (February 15, 1941): 9-93.
A symbol of success or an emblem of failure? The Chinese Primrose can mean life or death.

B.563.   "Mansion of Crime," **The Shadow**, 37 (March 1, 1941): 9-93.
Another stately mansion conceals schemes of robbery and murder.

B.564.   "The Time Master," **The Shadow**, 37 (April 1, 1941): 9-92.
Master of time and master of crime, this villain aspires to be master of The Shadow as well. The first of two 10th anniversary issues of The Shadow as a character and as a magazine.

B.565.   "The House on the Ledge," **The Shadow**, 37 (April 15, 1941): 9-88.
Counterfeit money floods the city and the authorities are helpless to stop it. The second 10th anniversary issue of **The Shadow**.

B.566.   "The League of Death," **The Shadow**, 37 (May 1, 1941): 9-91.
They kill by choice and then take their own lives; their motto is "Achieve and Die!"

B.567.   "Crime Under Cover," **The Shadow**, 38 (June 1, 1941): 9-93.
They speak a strange language which they expect no one to understand, but The Shadow not only understands, he intends to stop their plans of death and warfare. (The language is Esperanto.)

B.568. "The Thunder King," **The Shadow**, 38 (June 15, 1941): 9-89.
As though hurled by the Norse god, Thor, the lightning bolt crashes down, bringing catastrophe. Radio series character, Margo Lane, makes her first appearance in the pulp series in this novel.

B.569. "The Star of Delhi," **The Shadow**, 38 (July 1, 1941): 9-88.
The gem is worth a fortune to the owner or to the criminal who succeeds in stealing it, but it still has the reputation for causing ill fortune. (See also Shadow newspaper strip story, GZ-1 through GZ-18. E.389.)

B.570. "The Blur," **The Shadow**, 38 (July 15, 1941): 9-87.
Not invisibility, but sheer unrecognizability, is the trade-mark of the Blur and his band. What is their secret and where will they strike next?

B.571. "The Shadow Meets the Mask (1)," **The Shadow**, 38 (August 15, 1941): 9-92.
He performs his evil in the glare of the spotlight and in the very presence of the police, his face frozen in a mask. (This story is not to be confused with one of the same title in **The Shadow**, October 1944.)

B.572. "The Devil-Master," **The Shadow**, 39 (September 15, 1941): 9-91.
He has the power to turn people into dolls and neither The Shadow nor Margo Lane are immune.

B.573. "Garden of Death," **The Shadow**, 39 (October 1, 1941): 9-93.
In the quiet of an old home, murder sows seeds to bring forth a garden of evil and death. Death strikes three men at the same time, but from where does it come?

B.574. "Dictator of Crime," **The Shadow**, 39 (October 15, 1941): 9-96.
The leaders of the opposition party in this Central American country are sent to Miami to be killed.

B.575. "The Blackmail King," **The Shadow**, 39 (November 1, 1941): 9-93.

Whether the death is by murder or suicide cannot be determined until The Shadow finds one certain man.

B.576.   "Temple of Crime," **The Shadow**, 39 (November 15, 1941): 9-91.
As gods of ancient Egypt return to their reconstructed temple in the museum, death strikes along the way.

B.577.   "Murder Mansion," **The Shadow**, 40 (December 1, 1941): 9-98.
Only armchair detectives and The Shadow can recognize the guilty party, for the house itself affords no protection from murder.

B.578.   "Crime's Stronghold," **The Shadow**, 40 (December 15, 1941): 9-94.
Just when it seems that Florida is free from crime, a new wave of violence is unleashed like a hurricane on the southern coast.

1942

B.579.   "Pay Off," **The Phoenix**, No. 1 (January 1942): 1-2.
This magical newsletter was edited by Gibson and Bruce Elliot.

B.580.   "Mind Over Money," **The Phoenix**, No. 1 (January 1942): 3.

B.581.   "Alibi Trail (1)," **The Shadow**, 40 (January 1, 1942): 9-94.
The alibi for the first crime only indicates when the next one will happen.   (This novel is not to be confused with the story of the same title from **The Shadow**, June 1946.)

B.582.   "The Book of Death," **The Shadow**, 40 (January 15, 1942): 9-92.
In its pages are recorded the misdeeds of the owners of vast fortunes.   In the hands of a blackmailer it is a deadly weapon.

B.583.   "Death Diamonds," **The Shadow**, 40 (February 1, 1942): 9-94.
Florida: a colony of the wealthy where no one

enters without an invitation...and a fine prospect
for crime.

B.584.   "Lost in the Shuffle," The Phoenix, No. 2
(February 14, 1942): 6-7.

B.585.   "Clip Color," The Phoenix, No. 2
(February 14, 1942): 7.

B.586.   "Vengeance Bay," The Shadow, 41 (March 1,
1942): 9-91.
    Massaquoit Bay, New England...an abandoned
fort and a trail to treasure and death.

B.587.   "Formula for Crime," The Shadow, 41
(March 15, 1942): 9-92.
    Mathematically, he is able to predict when and
where each crime is to occur.

B.588.   "Bull-istics," The Phoenix, No. 3 (March
20, 1942): 13-15.

B.589.   "Room of Doom," The Shadow, 41 (April 1,
1942): 9-93.
    Death in a room from which there can be no
exit. Is it suicide or murder? A locked room
mystery to end all locked room mysteries.

B.590.   "Cut to Measure," The Phoenix, No. 4
(April 3, 1942): 21-22.

B.591.   "The Back Room," The Phoenix, No. 4
(April 3, 1942): 24.
    This was the editorial page. In spite of the
specific dating of each issue, this magazine
usually appeared monthly, not weekly or daily.
Sometimes there were two issues each month, just as
The Shadow was issued twice a month.

B.592.   "The Jade Dragon (1)," The Shadow, 41
(April 15, 1942): 9-97.
    There is a murderer named Shang Chou hiding in
Chinatown, but The Shadow is alerted to the danger.
(This novel is not to be confused with one of
almost the same title, published in The Shadow in
1948.) A Chinatown mystery.

B.593.   "Topper," The Phoenix, No. 7 (April 17,
1942): 27.

B.594.   "The Back Room (2)," **The Phoenix**, No. 7 (April 17, 1942): 28.

B.595.   "The Northdale Mystery," **The Shadow**, 41 (May 1, 1942): 9-96.
A bank robbery in this quiet town is only the first of a series of unexpected crimes.

B.596.   "Soothsayer," **The Phoenix**, No. 8 (May 1, 1942): 31.

B.597.   "The Back Room (3)," **The Phoenix**, No. 8 (May 1, 1942): 32.

B.598.   "Cardee Foolee," by Feng Huang [Walter B. Gibson], **The Phoenix**, No. 9 (May 15, 1942): 33-34.
"Feng Huang" was also the name used for a character in a story in **Shadow Comics**.

B.599.   "Filtration," **The Phoenix**, No. 9 (May 15, 1942): 34.

B.600.   "Twister (After Ching Ling Foo)," **The Phoenix**, No. 9 (May 15, 1942): 34-35.

B.601.   "Confetti of Cathay," by Hee Foo Yuu [Walter B. Gibson], **The Phoenix**, No. 9 (May 15, 1942): 35.

B.602.   "The Back Room (4)," **The Phoenix**, No. 9 (May 15, 1942): 36.

B.603.   "Twins of Crime," **The Shadow**, 42 (June 1, 1942): 9-100.   One man is a respected businessman, a pillar in the community; the other lives by his wits. Noel and Leon Grath are the twins of good and evil whom The Shadow must watch.

B.604.   "The Devil's Feud," **The Shadow**, 42 (June 15, 1942): 9-94.
Foster Granmore is shot dead in the dark with The Shadow looking on. Is this the latest episode in the Granmore-Weldorf feud?

B.605.   "Five Ivory Boxes," **The Shadow**, 42 (July 1, 1942): 9-90.
The contents of the mysterious boxes of ivory mean death. Who is this man who returns to settle an old score with the dead?

B.606.   "Death About Town," **The Shadow**, 42 (July 15, 1942): 9-89.
    Dana Orvill, man about town, is murdered, but his death is only the first in a series.   (The 250th Shadow novel.)

B.607.   "In the Pocket," **The Phoenix**, No. 14 (July 24, 1942): 55-56.

B.608.   "Legacy of Death," **The Shadow**, 42 (August 1, 1942): 9-96.
    The heirs to the Framingham fortune expect wealth, but they soon become heirs to death...strange, unexpected, and swift.

B.609.   "Judge Lawless," **The Shadow**, 42 (August 15, 1942): 9-94.
    He mocks the law by holding court with murderers and crooks as prosecuting attorney, defense attorney, and jury.

B.610.   "The Vampire Murders," **The Shadow**, 43 (September 1, 1942): 9-96.
    Haldrew Hall...a mansion of death that hides a riddle only The Shadow can read.

B.611.   "The Back Room (5)," **The Phoenix**, No. 17 (September 4, 1942): 71-72.

B.612.   "Super Duper Speller," **The Phoenix**, No. 19 (October 2, 1942): 79-80.

B.613.   "Clue for Clue," **The Shadow**, 43 (October 15, 1942): 9-94.
    The crooks are bold enough to plant the clues The Shadow needs to hunt them down, but can he trust them to be more than just red herrings?

B.614.   "DeLand's Floating Smoke," **The Phoenix**, No. 20 (October 16, 1942): 85.

B.615.   "Trail of Vengeance," **The Shadow**, 43 (November 1, 1942): 9-90.
    Bert Glendon swears he will avenge the death of his uncle, old Lionel Glendon, but retribution also sows the seed of crime.

B.616.   "The Murdering Ghost," **The Shadow**, 43 (November 15, 1942): 9-92.

Spiritualism breeds believers and skeptics as well as criminals who take every advantage of their fellow humans.   But is there any defense against ghosts that really kill?

B.617.   "The Hydra," **The Shadow**, 44 (December 1, 1942): 10-96.
He is a master criminal whose agents are replaced two-fold as fast as they are killed or captured.

B.618.   "Voodoo," **The Phoenix**, No. 24 (December 11, 1942): 99-100.

B.619.   "Betcha," **The Phoenix**, No. 24 (December 11, 1942): 101.

B.620.   "The Money Master," **The Shadow**, 44 (December 15, 1942): 10-98.
Elvor Brune's case is only the beginning of The Shadow's quest against a man of genius, a master of wealth and evil.

B.621.   "Getting Away from Card Tricks," **The Phoenix**, No. 25 (December 25, 1942): 105.

1943

B.622.   "The Museum Murders," **The Shadow**, 44 (January 1, 1943): 10-96.
The Shadow was able to succeed in his career by anticipating where crimes would take place. Could he apply this method when the treasures of the Argyle Museum were moved?

B.623.   "Death's Masquerade," **The Shadow**, 44 (January 15, 1943): 10-94.
Industria, the model city which celebrates its progress with an annual show, unwittingly invites the spectre of death to this one.

B.624.   "Count Them Out," **The Phoenix**, No. 27 (January 24, 1943): 112.

B.625.   "The Devil Monsters," **The Shadow**, 44 (February 1, 1943): 10-92.
Castle Chandos is peopled with creatures from hell and presided over by a satanic master of crime.   Are these odds too great for the Shadow?

B.626.   "Billiard Ball Act," The Phoenix, No. 28
(February 5, 1943): 115-117.

B.627.   "Wizard of Crime (2)," The Shadow, 44
(February 15, 1943): 10-90.
     King Kauger, the wizard of finance, is both a
million-dollar swindler and a murderer who sells
his services to the highest bidder in crime.   Not
to be confused with the earlier novel of the same
title.

B.628.   "The Black Dragon," The Shadow, 45 (March
1, 1943): 10-86.
     Behind the tiny dragon token is a sinister
Japanese menace and only The Shadow can save Steve
Trask from death.   A Chinatown mystery.

B.629.   "Peeksie," The Phoenix, No. 31 (March 19,
1943): 129.

B.630.   "Mickey Finn," The Phoenix, No. 34 (April
30, 1943): 140.

B.631.   "The Robot Master," The Shadow, 45 (May
1943): 10-89.
     Robots can free humanity from routine tasks or
turn on the very creatures they are created to
serve.   (The Shadow is now published only once a
month.)

B.632.   "Dunninger Exposes the Supernatural
Racket," by Joseph Dunninger with Walter B. Gibson,
True Detective, 39 (May-August 1943): Series in 4
parts.
     Some of the material in these articles was
used in a different form in Dunninger's Secrets,
1974.

B.633.   "Turnabout," The Phoenix, No. 36 (May 28,
1943): 147-148.

B.634.   "Murder Lake," The Shadow, 45 (June
1943): 10-85.
     An abandoned mining operation leaves gaping
holes which become twin lakes, one that never runs
out of fish and the other which no one can keep
stocked.   A bitter feud divides the community and a
case of murder brings in the Shadow.

B.635.   "Messenger of Death," **The Shadow**, 45 (August 1943): 10-84.
When a secret formula is stolen, divided into four parts, and distributed among four men, it's up to The Shadow to find the four and put the formula together again.

B.636.   "Pick Me Up," **The Phoenix**, No. 41 (August 6, 1943): 169.

B.637.   "House of Ghosts," **The Shadow**, 46 (September 1943): 10-82.
Mentalist Joseph Dunninger offers $25,000 to anyone who can produce a supernatural phenomenon he cannot duplicate, but when he meets the ghosts in Stanbridge Manor he is glad to have the help of The Shadow.   (Reprinted with "The Jade Dragon," Doubleday, 1981.)

B.638.   "King of the Black Market," **The Shadow**, 46 (October 1943): 10-84.
A topical crime story of second World War greed and The Shadow's role in the home defense effort.

B.639.   "91 Cent Miracle," **The Phoenix**, No. 49 (October 24, 1943): 180-181.

B.640.   "The Muggers," **The Shadow**, 46 (November 1943): 10-82.
All the murders appear to be the work of amateurs until The Shadow proves otherwise and stops the knives before they can be used again.

B.641.   "Murder By Moonlight," **The Shadow**, 46 (December 1943): 8-102.
A series of murders, a mad doctor, an insane asylum, and a mysterious house on the hill, all are classic gothic story ingredients with The Shadow as the catalyst who brings the mix to a boil.   (The first of the digest-sized issues of **The Shadow** as a magazine.   Reprinted, abridged, in **The Weird Adventures of The Shadow**, 1966.)

B.642.   "80 Seconds to Solve It (1)," **The Shadow**, 46 (December 1943): 103-104.
The murder of Wayne Pennington.   Find the clues and solve the mystery; solution on page 130 of the same issue.

B.643.   "Deferred Coincidence," The Phoenix, No.
50 (December 17, 1943): 206.

                          1944

B.644.   "The Crystal Skull," The Shadow, 46
(January 1944): 8-84.
     Even Lamont Cranston is unable to look upon
the talisman and not be captured by its hypnotic
power, but The Shadow may have better luck.

B.645.   "80 Seconds to Solve It (2)," The Shadow,
46 (January 1944): 85, 122; solution, p. 130.
     The murder of Ray Larraby.

B.646.   "Yankee Vase," The Phoenix, No. 52
(January 21, 1944): 213.

B.647.   "'Free' French Drop," The Phoenix, No. 52
(January 21, 1944): 213.

B.648.   "On and Off," The Phoenix, No. 52
(January 21, 1944): 214.

B.649.   "Syndicate of Death," The Shadow, 46
(February 1944): 6-78.
     Thinking it is part of the play, the audience
is not startled when an actor is shot during the
performance on stage, but this is only the first
step in a criminal scheme.

B.650.   "80 Seconds to Solve It (3)," The Shadow,
46 (February 1944): 112; solution on p. 130.
     Table of contents errs in listing this as
appearing on p. 79.

B.651.   "The Toll of Death," The Shadow, 47
(March 1944): 6-83.
     Black Arthur returns to Long Valley in
fulfillment of the ancient legend as the tolling of
the death bell is heard. (Reprinted, The Shadow
Annual, 1947.)

B.652.   "80 Seconds to Solve It (4)," The Shadow,
47 (March 1944): 84-85; solution on p. 103.
     The theft of Martin Mayland's $10,000.

B.653.   "Super Magic Blackstone," The Phoenix,
No. 55 (March 3, 1944): 224-225.

B.654.   "Crime Caravan," **The Shadow**, 47 (April 1944): 5-80.

Wholesale murders and the sudden disappearance of large numbers of used cars en route to the Pacific Coast from New York reveal a new kind of racket to The Shadow.

B.655.   "80 Seconds to Solve It (5)," **The Shadow**, 47 (April 1944): 125-127; solution, p. 130.

Who was the accomplice in the Horton robbery?

B.656.   "Gold Seal Mystery," by Walter B. Gibson and Bruce Elliot, **The Phoenix**, No. 59 (April 28, 1944): 240-241.

B.657.   "The Freak Show Murders," **The Shadow**, 47 (May 1944): 5-77.

A killer dressed as Harlequin follows the travelling carnivals to find his victims. (Reprinted with "A Quarter of Eight," Doubleday, 1978.)

B.658.   "Voodoo Death," **The Shadow**, 47 (June 1944): 5-75.

The secrets of the Tarn Emerald are deep and unfathomable to everyone but The Shadow. By accident, Walter Gibson's own name appears as author on the first page of the novel. (Reprinted, abridged, in **The Weird Adventures of The Shadow**, 1966.)

B.659.   "80 Seconds to Solve It (6)," **The Shadow**, 47 (June 1944): 106; solution on p. 129.

The body on the avenue mystery.

B.660.   "Seers and Suckers: An Expose of the Spiritualist Racket," by Joseph Dunninger [Walter B. Gibson], **The American Weekly**, (June 18, 1944): 6-7.

Series in 5 parts; part 1; concludes with **B.668.**

B.661.   "(Well I'll be--) Switched," **The Phoenix**, No. 63 (June 23, 1944): 258.

B.662.   "The Back Room (6)," **The Phoenix**, No. 63 (June 23, 1944): 259, 257.

Continued on an earlier page than the one on which it began.

B.663.   "Seers and Suckers: Racketeers Turn to
Science," by Joseph Dunninger [Walter B. Gibson],
The American Weekly, (June 25, 1944): 6-7.

B.664.   "Town of Hate," The Shadow, 47 (July
1944): 5-79.
     The sleeping town awakes when a villain who
controls the elements strikes with his own brand of
lightning and a local feud runs its course.

B.665.   "80 Seconds to Solve It (7)," The Shadow,
47 (July 1944): 130; solution, p. 130.
     The murder of Craig Muir in the Club Rocco.
Solution printed upside down on the same page as
the mystery.

B.666.   "Seers and Suckers: Racketeers Control
Spooks," by Joseph Dunninger [Walter B. Gibson],
The American Weekly, (July 2, 1944): 4-5.

B.667.   "Seers and Suckers: Martian Cults
Exploited," by Joseph Dunninger [Walter B. Gibson],
The American Weekly, (July 9, 1944): 22-23.

B.668.   "Seers and Suckers: Spirit Photography,"
by Joseph Dunninger [Walter B. Gibson], The
American Weekly, (July 16, 1944): 4-5.

B.669.   "Death in the Crystal," The Shadow, 47
(August 1944): 5-77.
     Mahatma Xanadu, demon of mystery, conjures up
some unbelievable images which become real.

B.670.   "Release from Reason," by Walter B.
Gibson and L. Vasburgh Lyons, The Phoenix, No. 66
(August 4, 1944): 268-269.

B.671.   "The Chest of Chu-Chan," The Shadow, 48
(September 1944): 5-79.
     The Shadow and Margo find the secret contents
of Chu-Chan's chest are curios and corpses--and the
murder suspect is a statue of a beautiful Burmese
dancer. (Fred Cook)

B.672.   "80 Seconds to Solve It (8)," The Shadow,
48 (September 1944): 124-125.
     The National Bank holdup. Solution printed
upside down on page 125.

B.673. "The Shadow Meets the Mask (2)," **The Shadow**, 48 (October 1944): 5-79.

A mystery criminal commits fabulous robberies while being denounced on the air by a radio commentator. (This novel is not to be confused with the novel of the same title in **The Shadow** for August 15, 1941.)

B.674. "80 Seconds to Solve It (9)," **The Shadow**, 48 (October 1944): 80.

Who passed the counterfeit $20 bills? Solution printed on same page as mystery, but not upside down.

B.675. "Fountain of Death," **The Shadow**, 48 (November 1944): 5-83.

A rest home is a strange setting for this tale of stolen gems and a killer only Lamont Cranston (not The Shadow) can beat.

B.676. "80 Seconds to Solve It (10)," **The Shadow**, 48 (November 1944): 130.

The Stewart Craven murder. Solution printed on same page, but not upside down.

B.677. "No Time for Murder," **The Shadow**, 48 (December 1944): 5-79.

A sealed room mystery created by the craft of a Houdini, the only witness to the crime is a century-old grandfather clock. (Reprinted, **The Shadow Annual**, 1947.)

B.678. "Tom, Dick & How Many," **The Phoenix**, No. 74 (December 8, 1944): 302.

B.679. "The Back Room (WBG Bows Out)," **The Phoenix**, No. 74 (December 8, 1944): 303.

The last issue of **The Phoenix** under the joint editorial guidance of Gibson and Elliot. Bruce Elliot continued as editor until the magazine ceased.

1945

B.680. "Guardian of Death," **The Shadow**, 48 (January 1945): 5-78.

A winged statue, created to guard a sealed crypt, hides a mystery only The Shadow can solve.

B.681.   "80 Seconds to Solve It (11)," The
Shadow, 48 (January 1945): 95.
     The Frank Greer case. Solution on same page,
but not printed upside down.

B.682.   "Merry Mrs. Macbeth," The Shadow, 48
(February 1945): 5-78.
     Another murder committed on stage by a
sinister figure waiting in the wings, watched over
only by The Shadow.

B.683.   "80 Seconds to Solve It (12)," The
Shadow, 48 (February 1945): 118.
     The movie theatre robbery. Solution given on
the same page, but not printed upside down.

B.684.   "Tomorrow's Tricks: Clear Through
(invented by Edward Massey); The Magic Port-hole;
Raymode's Paddle," The Conjuror's Magazine, 1
(February 1945): 8-10.
     Gibson left The Phoenix to found a more
elaborate magical magazine, named for the famous
one edited by Houdini.

B.685.   "Howard Thurston's Magic Lessons (1),"
The Conjuror's Magazine, 1 (February 1945): 38-39.
     First Lesson--Impromptu Magic. Series in 5
parts; reprints the book of the same title,
ghost-written by Gibson in 1928; parts 2-5 listed
below. See also A.19.

B.686.   "Five Keys to Crime," The Shadow, 49
(March 1945): 5-80.
     Larry returns from overseas to collect his
inheritance by solving the mystery of the five
keys.

B.687.   "Sextuple Stranger Than Hallucination,"
The Phoenix, No. 80 (March 23, 1945): 325.

B.688.   "The Amazing Creations of Theodore
DeLand," The Conjuror's Magazine, 1 (March 1945):
24-26, 31.

B.689.   "Howard Thurston's Magic Lessons (2),"
The Conjuror's Magazine, 1 (March 1945): 36-37.
     Second Lesson--The Cut and Restored String;
Third Lesson--Card Tricks.

B.690.   "Death Has Grey Eyes," The Shadow, 49
(April 1945): 51-130.
    Our hero can't escape the feeling he is being
stared at. The grey eyes haunt him as a symbol of
his buried past. Then The Shadow steps in to help
him.

B.691.   "More Amazing Creations of Theodore
DeLand," The Conjuror's Magazine, 1 (April 1945):
12-13.

B.692.   "A Great Book: Magic Without Apparatus,
by Camille Gautier," The Conjuror's Magazine, 1
(April 1945): 19.
    Book review.

B.693.   "Howard Thurston's Magic Lessons (3),"
The Conjuror's Magazine, 1 (April 1945): 40-41.
    Card Effect (cont.); Third (i.e. Fourth)
Lesson--A Complete Mind Reading Act.

B.694.   "Teardrops of Buddha," The Shadow, 49
(May 1945): 49-130.
    A stage production doomed to failure may yet
be saved through The Shadow's knowledge of the
mysterious East. A Chinatown mystery.

B.695.   "Two Book Reviews," The Conjuror's
Magazine, 1 (May 1945): 20.
    Gibson's contribution is a review of
Heineman's Original Magic.

B.696.   "DeLand's Marked Card Creations," The
Conjuror's Magazine, 1 (May 1945): 32-35.

B.697.   "Howard Thurston's Magic Lessons (4),"
The Conjuror's Magazine, 1 (May 1945): 36-37.
    Fifth Lesson--A Complete Magic Act.

B.698.   "Three Stamps of Death," The Shadow, 49
(June 1945): 53-130.
    Why should someone he never heard of keep
writing to him, and why should the orange postage
stamps signify death?

B.699.   "More DeLand Creations," The Conjuror's
Magazine, 1 (June 1945): 31-32.

B.700.   "Howard Thurston's Magic Lessons (5),"
The Conjuror's Magazine, 1 (June 1945): 28-29.

Sixth Lesson--A Complete Magic Act (cont.);
Seventh Lesson--A Handkerchief Act. Final part of
series.

B.701. "The Mask of Mephisto," **The Shadow**, 49
(July 1945): 52-130.
Mardi Gras! Gaiety! Laughter! Masked Figures!
Murder! (Reprinted, with "Murder By Magic,"
Doubleday, 1975.)

B.702. The Hardeen Memorial Issue, **The
Conjuror's Magazine**, 1 (July 1945): contents not
analyzed.
As editor, Gibson may have contributed most of
the unsigned articles.

B.703. "Murder By Magic," **The Shadow**, 49 (August
1945): 51-130.
The body may be hidden in the prop for the
famous Chinese Pagoda Trick, but the crown jewels
of the Sultan are somewhere else. (Reprinted, with
"The Mask of Mephisto," Doubleday, 1975.)

B.704. "More Miracles by Theodore L. DeLand,"
The Conjuror's Magazine, 1 (August 1945): 20-23.

B.705. "The Taiwan Joss," **The Shadow**, 50
(September 1945): 45-130.
A trail of blood leads the way to the location
of the famed Taiwan Joss!

B.706. "Houdini's Secrets Lost Forever?" **The
American Weekly**, (September 2, 1945): 10.

B.707. "DeLand's Special Packs," **The Conjuror's
Magazine**, 1 (September 1945): 12-14.

B.708. "A Quarter of Eight," **The Shadow**, 50
(October 1945): 48-130.
Claire Winslow inherits one fourth of a coin
that is the clue to the location of a treasure.
Finding the missing parts of that "piece of eight"
is the most dangerous task. (Reprinted, with "The
Freak Show Murders," Doubleday, 1978.)

B.709. "DeLand's Ever-Ready Card Tricks," **The
Conjuror's Magazine**, 1 (October 1945): 28-29, 36.

B.710. "The White Skulls," **The Shadow**, 50
(November 1945): 46-129.

The killer's face is that of a skull and his followers resemble him closely in this and other aspects.   He sets a riddle of life and death for The Shadow to solve.

B.711.   "DeLand's Greatest Card Creation," **The Conjuror's Magazine**, 1 (November 1945): 36-38, 58.

B.712.   "Neff Show Review," **The Conjuror's Magazine**, 1 (November 1945): 23.

B.713.   "The Stars Promise Death," **The Shadow**, 50 (December 1945): 44-130.
Margo and The Shadow visit Seaview City's Boardwalk out of season and find fake mediums and a fake sand-dune. (Fred Cook)

B.714.   "DeLand's Changing Cards," **The Conjuror's Magazine**, 1 (December 1945): 31-34.

1946

B.715.   "The Banshee Murders," **The Shadow**, 50 (January 1946): 49-130.
Lost treasure, a kidnapping and a murder, and a ghost haunting Central Park: all in a day's work for The Shadow.

B.716.   "More DeLand Card Effects," **The Conjuror's Magazine**, 1 (January 1946): 20-23.

B.717.   "1945-The Passing Parade-1946," **The Conjuror's Magazine**, 1 (January 1946): 10.

B.718.   "Crime Out of Mind," **The Shadow**, 50 (February 1946): 51-130.
The Shadow meets The Great Planchini, a stage magician; Gibson exposes stage tricks and even exposes The Shadow masquerading as Planchini! (Fred Cook)

B.719.   "Magic Tricks," **Calling All Boys**, No. 2 (February-March 1946): 29.

B.720.   "The Mother Goose Murders," **The Shadow**, 51 (March 1946): 6-83.
Reading between the lines of the childhood verses, The Shadow can see the source of the crimes, but can the riddle be read in time to save

lives? (Reprinted, with "Crime Over Casco," Doubleday, 1979.)

B.721.   "More DeLand Card Effects," The Conjuror's Magazine, 2 (March 1946): 33-34.

B.722.   "Crime Over Casco," The Shadow, 51 (April 1946): 6-86.
    A map, a group of islands off Maine's rocky coast, and a forgotten crime...a new adventure. (Reprinted, with "The Mother Goose Murders," Doubleday, 1979.)

B.723.   "Double 'A' Production Cabinet," The Conjuror's Magazine, 2 (April 1946): 26-27.

B.724.   "The Curse of Thoth," The Shadow, 51 (May 1946): 6-83.
    A papyrus manuscript contains a secret formula for which men are prepared to fight and die. What secret lies within the violated Egyptian tomb?

B.725.   "Magic Tricks," Calling All Boys, No. 4 (May 1946): 48.

B.726.   "Trick Stuff," Ethyl News, (May 1946): 14-17.

B.727.   "DeLand's Mental Mysteries," The Conjuror's Magazine, 2 (May 1946): 22-23.

B.728.   "Alibi Trail (2)," The Shadow, 51 (June 1946): 5-79.
    The clues to the mystery are scattered along the path: a playing card, a baggage check, a torn bank check, and a photograph. All suggest a solution revealing deceit at the end of the road. (Not to be confused with the story of the same title from January 1, 1942.)

B.729.   "Special DeLand Effects," The Conjuror's Magazine, 2 (June 1946): 20-21.

B.730.   "What's New in Books," The Conjuror's Magazine, 2 (June 1946): 36.

B.731.   "Malmordo," The Shadow, 51 (July 1946): 6-89.
    Human rats are the strange cargo of the steamship Santander, but the most dreaded of all is

their evil master, Malmordo. (Gibson did not write another Shadow novel for two years; in the interval, Bruce Elliot contributed 15 stories to the series. See Appendix C.)

B.732.   "Silk, Tubes and Glass...Herman Hanson's Version," **The Conjuror's Magazine**, 2 (July 1946): 18-19.
     Unsigned, attributed to Gibson on being reprinted in **The Magic Magazine**, April 1977.

B.733.   "Trick Stuff," **The Bat**, No. 33 (September 1946): 180-182.

B.734.   "Blackstone Reveals," by Blackstone the Great [Walter B. Gibson], **Sensation**, 3 (September 1946): 20-23, 68, 70.

B.735.   "Joe Miller--Myth of Mirth," **Sensation**, 3 (September 1946): 24-25, 73-75.

B.736.   "DeLand's Floating Skeleton," **The Conjuror's Magazine**, 2 (October 1946): 11.

B.737.   "Open Season on Saps," **Sensation**, 3 (October 1946): 26-27, 68, 70, 72.

B.738.   "Along With Blackstone," **The Conjuror's Magazine**, 2-3 (December 1946-Aug, Dec 1947).
     A series of reports concerning events during Blackstone's tour in the 1946-1947 season.

B.739.   "Walter B. Gibson Says: 'It Can't Be Wrong,'" **The Conjuror's Magazine**, 2 (December 1946): 30.

B.740.   "Benny the Character," by Carter Johnson [Walter B. Gibson], **Sensation**, 3 (December 1946): 16-17, 92-94, 96.
     An account of some of the more colorful aspects of Benjamin Franklin's life.

B.741.   "Magic's Greatest Riddle," **Sensation**, 3 (December 1946): 50-53, 90-92.

                         1947

B.742.   "Thirty-Nine Steps," **The Conjuror's Magazine**, 2 (January 1947): 23.

B.743.   "New Mental Card Chart," The Conjuror's Magazine, 2 (February 1947): 19.

B.744.   "Dissolving Cigarette Pack," The Conjuror's Magazine, 3 (April 1947): 18-19.

B.745.   "Ideas in Brief...Heard on the Road," The Conjuror's Magazine, 3 (June 1947): 13.

B.746.   "Convention Magic," The Conjuror's Magazine, 3 (June 1947): 22-23.

B.747.   "Notes on Sleeving," The Conjuror's Magazine, 3 (July 1947): 10-11.

B.748.   "Tut, Tut, Abracadabra," The Conjuror's Magazine, 3 (August 1947): 6.

B.749.   "The Self Stacking Pack," The Conjuror's Magazine, 3 (September 1947): 14-15.

B.750.   "Perfect Nested Chests," The Conjuror's Magazine, 3 (October 1947): 9, 11.

B.751.   "Double Bill Tube," The Conjuror's Magazine, 3 (November 1947): 13.

B.752.   **"Magic With Small Apparatus, by Dhotel,"** The Conjuror's Magazine, 3 (November 1947): 18.
    Book review.

B.753.   "The Card Tells," The Conjuror's Magazine, 3 (November 1947): 42.

B.754.   "Houdini Lives Again," The Conjuror's Magazine, 3 (December 1947): 23.

                          1948

B.755.   "In Memory of My Friend 'The Great Raymond," The Conjuror's Magazine, 3 (February 1948): 10.

B.756.   "Neff and His Great Show," The Conjuror's Magazine, 3 (February 1948): 12-13, 20.

B.757.   "Thurston's Comedy Hat Routine," The Conjuror's Magazine, 3 (February 1948): 41.

B.758.   "A Nifty," The Conjuror's Magazine, 4
(Match 1948): 42.

B.759.   "Silk from Cigarette," The Conjuror's
Magazine, 4 (April 1948): 39.

B.760.   "Magic Sets the Fashion," The Conjuror's
Magazine, 4 (July 1948): 9.

B.761.   "Joker Interlude," The Conjuror's
Magazine, 4 (July 1948): 11.

B.762.   "Jade Dragon (2)," Shadow Mystery,   54
(August-September 1948): 7-120.
      In pursuit of a band of jade smugglers, The
Shadow finds a deadly talisman, the touch of which
means death.   Not to be confused with the novel of
a similar title, "The Jade Dragon," The Shadow,
April 15, 1942.   In 1947, The Shadow had merged
with Street & Smith's Mystery Magazine to form
Shadow Mystery.   (Reprinted with "House of Ghosts,"
Doubleday, 1981.)

B.763.   "Dead Man's Chest," The Shadow, 54 (Fall
1948): 6-95.
      On the trail of ancient gold, Doug Lawton
finds a number of dead men and leads The Shadow and
his agents into a skirmish with modern-day pirates.
The magazine was restored to its pre-war size (and
title) with this and the next three issues.

B.764.   "Improved Nickels and Dimes," The
Conjuror's Magazine, 4 (October 1948): 18.
      Trick invented by Walter Gibson.

B.765.   "On the Magic Bookshelf: 'Workability' of
Kaplan Effects Scored," The Conjuror's Magazine, 4
(November 1948): 16.
      Book review of The Fine Art of Magic by George
G. Kaplan.

                          1949

B.766. "The Magigals Mystery," The Shadow, 54
(Winter 1949): 8-95.
      The scene is Chicago and a convention of
female magicians.   The crime is a series of
suicides of men who carry magical devices on their
persons.   (Gibson is mentioned in the story as

editor of **Conjuror's Magazine.** Litzka Raymond has
been erroneously referred to as being a member of
the Magigals, but they were a group of amateur
magicians and she was a professional.)

B.767. "Twice Around the Clock," **The Conjuror's
Magazine,** 4 (January 1949): 13, 21.

B.768. "Card Magic: The Card Tells," **The Conjuror's
Magazine,** 4 (February 1949): 10.

B.769. "Here, There & Everywhere," **The Conjuror's
Magazine,** 4 (February 1949): 15.
      A report on the current Shadow novel, "The
Magigals Mystery."

B.770. "Side Lights," **The Conjuror's Magazine,** 4
(February 1949): 26-27.

B.771. "The Black Circle," **The Shadow,** 54 (Spring
1949): 6-87.
      A group of crooks all carry identifying
tokens and serve an unknown leader named The Voice.

B.772. "Gabbatha," **The Conjuror's Magazine,** 5
(March 1949): 15-18.
      A "magazine within a magazine", as declared
and edited by Walter B. Gibson; by actual count his
7th magical magazine; includes "Match Trick
Encore," "The Spirit Cardigram;" "Over the Years;"
and "Jinxiana."

B.773. "Gabbatha and Jinxiana," **The Conjuror's
Magazine,** 5 (April 1949): 15-18.
      Includes "Check Payer;" "A Bargain in Needle
Tricks;" "Queries and Answers;" "Superphonic
Telepathy;" and "Brema's Newspaper Coin Fold."

B.774. "Jinxiana (1)," **The Conjuror's Magazine,** 5
(May 1949): 15-18.
      Another "magazine within a magazine;" includes
"Watch for This One;" "The Five key Code;" "The
World's Greatest Forcing Pack;" ["News and Notes"].

B.775. "The Whispering Eyes," **The Shadow,** 55
(Summer 1949): 6-83.
      A master hypnotist terrorizes New York until
The Shadow stops him with the aid of a Persian cat
named Washington Mews. The final novel and the
final issue of **The Shadow.**

B.776. "Jinxiana (2)," **The Conjuror's Magazine,** 5
(June 1949): 15-18.
"The Five Key Code;" News and notes section
includes a rebuttal to the criticism that Gibson's
Professional Magic for Amateurs was merely a
reworking of old tricks.

B.777. "Jinxiana (3)," **The Conjuror's Magazine,** 5
(July 1949): 15-18.
"The Elusive Dollar;" "Kiddingram;" and News
and Notes.

B.778. "Jinxiana (4)," **The Conjuror's Magazine,** 5
(August 1949): 15-18.
"The Floating Candle;" "The Nerve Test;" News
and Notes and a section of "Thurstoniana."

B.779. "Jinxiana (5)," **The Conjuror's Magazine,** 5
(September 1949): 13-16.
The final appearance of this section and the
final issue of the magazine.

1950

B.780. "Tobacco Magic," **The American Smoker,** 5
(July 1950): 44-52.

B.781. "Tobacco Trickery," **The American Smoker,** 5
(August 1950): 32-42.

1951

B.782. "Magician in the Mint," **True Police Cases,** 3
(January 1951): pp. not known.
The earliest recorded true crime article. Not
seen.

B.783. "Mind Over Motor," **True Police Cases,** 3
(January 1951): 3.
Not seen.

B.784. "Crime's Prime Minister," by Martin Donohue
[Walter B. Gibson], **True Police Cases,** 3 (September
1951): 4.
Not seen.

B.785. "Assignment Mousetrap." by Henry (Hank) Rodney and Walter B. Gibson, **True Police Cases**, 3 (September 1951): 18.
Not seen.

B.786. "The Seven Year Alibi," by John Ellert [Walter B. Gibson], **The Big Story**, 1 (October 1951): 2-25.
A reporter from the Evansville, Indiana, **Press** finds the evidence to free Eddie Bannon from prison and the sentence for murder, September 8, 1942.

B.787. "Lonely Hearts Lured to Doom," by Charles Russell [Walter B. Gibson], **The Big Story**, 1 (October 1951): 26-51.
The reporter on the **Seattle Post-Intelligencer** gets the goods on a modern day Bluebeard.

B.788. "The Strange Case of the Murderer's Double," by Julian Houseman [Walter B. Gibson], **The Big Story**, 1 (October 1951): 105-126.
"How a mother's plea, a reporter's hunch and a scrap of handwriting reversed the sworn testimony of a dozen witnesses." The reporter was from the Richmond, Virginia, **News-Leader**.

B.789. "Shadow and Substance," **Daring Detective**, 19 (November 1951): 28.
Ohio, 1936; Margaret Perryman gets a life sentence for murder.

B.790. "Blood Under the Palms," by Wesley Chalk [Walter B. Gibson], **The Big Story**, 1 (November 1951): 19-43.
"A three-day hunt solves the riddle of the woman in red." Chalk was with the Pensacola, Florida, **News-Journal**.

B.791. "Java 972," by Herbert Mayer [Walter B. Gibson], **The Big Story**, 1 (November 1951): 44-67.
"When a body floated to the surface in New Orleans harbor, a reporter (with the **New Orleans Item**) had to invade the French Quarter to find the killer."

B.792. "The Girl with the Photographic Mind," by Harry Friedenberg [Walter B. Gibson], **The Big Story**, 1 (November 1951): 104-127.
A reporter with the **Boston Traveler** solves the mystery of the blazing automobile.

B.793. "Which Murder Do You Want Me For?" **True Detective**, 57 (December 1951): 36.
     Not seen.

B.794. "The Blubbering Boy Bandits," by Edward Griffin [Walter B. Gibson], **The Big Story**, 1 (December 1951): 2-21.
     "They thought the teller was reaching for a gun, but he was only tuning his hearing aid." The reporter was with the Syracuse, New York, **Herald-Journal**.

B.795. "Siren Lure Traps Missing Killer," by Ray Girardin [Walter B. Gibson], **The Big Story**, 1 (December 1951): 43-63.
     "What was the secret of the mysterious blonde whose chance trail offered the only key to crime?" Reporter for the **Detroit Times** solves the case.

B.796. "Dame Rumor--Criminal!" by George Goodwin [Walter B. Gibson], **The Big Story**, 1 (December 1951): 82-103.
     "A stranger in a strange land finds himself the victim of a prejudice that only a courageous reporter (from the **Atlanta Journal**) dares to combat."

                          1952

B.797. "She Framed a Man for Murder," by Martin Donohue [Walter B. Gibson], **True Police Cases**, 4 (January 1952): 22-   .
     Willimantic, Connecticut. January 29, 1929. Murder of W. E. Jackson by Gertrude Jackson. Not seen; notes supplied by Litzka Gibson, identified hereafter by LRG.

B.798. "Crazy Quilt Guilt," **True Police Cases**, 4 (March 1952): 4.
     Hull, Massachusetts. The murder of Frank Cusumano by Lana Cusumano and Enrico Mascioli. Not seen. (LRG)

B.799. "Counterfeit Alibi," by Martin Donohue [Walter B. Gibson], **True Police Cases**, 4 (March 1952): 39-   .
     Martin Crayle and the counterfeit hundred dollar bills. A 15 year sentence. Not seen. (LRG)

B.800. "The Girl Decoy of Death," **Daring Detective,** 20 (July 1952): 6-9, 68-72.
Philadelphia, 1920.   The murder of Henry T. Pierce.

B.801. "The Day New York Ended," **Fantastic Science Fiction,** 1 (August 1952): 4-19.
Edited by Gibson with contributions primarily by Ed Burkholter and himself, this magazine lasted only two issues.

B.802. "The Black Planet," by G. A. Lacksey [Walter B. Gibson], **Fantastic Science Fiction,** 1 (August 1952): 42-47.

B.803. "The Secret of the Locked Laboratory," by Bruce Crandall [Walter B. Gibson?], **Fantastic Science Fiction,** 1 (August 1952): 20-25.
The style of this story suggests it may be Gibson's work.

B.804. "Alias the Shadow," **Daring Detective,** 20 (September 1952): 24-   .
Indian River, Florida, 1934.   The murder of Ethel Allen by Willard Barton.   Not seen in this edition.   (Reprinted in **True Police Year Book,** No. 5, 1956.)

B.805. ["New York Night Court,"] **Timely Detective Cases,** 5 (October 1952): 30.
Not seen.   Title supplied from LRG notes.

B.806. ["New York's Finest,"] **Authentic Detective Police Cases,** 5 (November 1952): 24.
"Harry Gross story" (LRG)

B.807. "The Poison Death of the Yielding Widow," **Daring Detective,** 20 (November 1952): 22-   .
Ladysmith, Wisconsin, 1915. Jennie McCormick is murdered by her second husband.   New evidence convicts him in 1924.   Not seen in this edition. Notes taken from reprint.   (Reprinted as "The Ghost from the Grave" in **The Fine Art of Murder,** 1965.)

B.808. "Killer's Bait," **True Police Cases,** 4 (November 1952): 32.
High Spring, Florida. January 1, 1936. Murder of Lee Walker by Arty Burton who received a life sentence. Not seen. (LRG)

B.809. "The War of the Moons," **Fantastic** Science **Fiction,** 1 (December 1952): 4-22.
Second and final issue; Litzka Raymond, listed as associate editor, contributed the book review feature, "Science Fiction on Parade."

B.810. "Spiderman and the Cakes," by Bruce Crandall [Walter B. Gibson?], **Fantastic** Science **Fiction,** 1 (December 1952): 23-27.
Style and plot suggest this may be Gibson's work.

B.811. ["New York Felony Court,"] **Timely** Detective **Cases,** 5 (December 1952): 30.
Not seen. (LRG)

                            1953

B.812. "Two Girl Victims for the Rapist Killer," **Startling** Detective, 44 (January 1953): 6-9, 71-74.
Washington, D.C., 1944. The murder of Margaret Fitzwater and Dorothy Berrum by Joseph Medley and Earl McFarland, alias John Dills.

B.813. "Penny Postage Solution," by Russ T. Creighton [Walter B. Gibson], **True Police Cases,** 5 (January 1953): 39.
Nineteenth Century. Richard Canning served a life term for a crime he never committed, but had his name cleared by a clue in a letter found a century later.

B.814. "Omen of Death," **Daring Detective,** 21 (March 1953): 6-9, 68-71.
The Grand Hotel, New York City, 1928. Murder of Mrs. Cecil Clyde Campbell by her husband.

B.815. "Do Vice Raids Increase Sex Crimes?" by Thomas McClary and Walter B. Gibson, **Authentic Detective Cases,** 6 (March 1953): 24-27, 75-78.
"Wide publicity attending current vice investigations is believed by some authorities to have inflammatory effect on first offenders, for crime statistics show a rising graph in sex offenses for first half of year 1952." (Publisher's blurb.)

B.816. "Facts Are Stranger Than Fiction," **Timely Detective Cases,** 6 (April 1953): 70-76.

Anecdotes involving President Garfield, Lincoln, John Wilkes Booth, Lewis J. Valentine, Roman coins, P. T. Barnum, and other topics.

B.817. "The Girl in Room 15," **Daring Detective**, 21 (May 1953): 26-29, 74-77.
Lebanon, Pennsylvania, 1952. The murder of Irene Krochell by Harold Donough.

B.818. "Strangled Nude in the Palmettos," **True Police Cases**, 5 (May 1953): 3, 53-56.
Miami, 1952. The death of Ruby Colvin.

B.819. "The Sometimes Deadly Spirits," **True Police Cases**, 5 (September 1953): 33, 43-45.
Anecdotes about ghosts linked with murders from the 19th century to the 1950s.

B.820. "Monster of Carpenter Hall," **Startling Detective**, 44 (September 1953): 16-19, 48-50.
Chestnut Hill, Pa., December 1937. The murder of Wilma Carpenter. "In a quiet house of elegance, a murdering rapist suddenly appeared, and just as silently vanished from the scene of his crimes." (Publisher's blurb) (Reprinted, as by Martin Donohue, **True Police Year Book**, No. 5, 1956.)

B.821. "Dreams and Their Meanings," **Foto-Rama**, 1 (September 1953): 13-19.

B.822. "Who Killed Three Hunters on Gaspe?" **Official Detective Stories**, 23 (November 1953): 20-
Not seen. (LRG)

B.823. "Too Many Books," by Gene W. Byrnes [Walter B. Gibson], **Startling Detective**, 44 (November 1953): 4.
England, World War I. Percy Willingdon, bookseller, billed deceased clergy for pornography for which the heirs were glad to pay to keep the matter hushed up. He was exposed when it was learned that one of his "customers" was not only blind, but paralyzed, and could not have frequented the shop.

B.824. "The Gay Divorcee and the Lover's Lane Slayer," **True Police Cases**, 5 (December 1953): 20-22, 43-46.
Tampa, Florida, 1940. The murder of Mrs. Ethel Wigington by Charles Oliver.

1954

B.825. "John Christie and His House of Death," by John Abbington [Walter B. Gibson], **Crime Case Book Magazine**, 1 (January 1954): 1-118.
"The fantastic story of the meek little man who lured and wantonly murdered seven women." (Publisher) Gibson contributed the majority of the material used in this short-lived magazine.

B.826. "Murder from Nowhere," by Rufus Perry [Walter B. Gibson], **Crime Case Book Magazine**, 1 (January 1954): 119-122.
"Old Phil Peters kept hearing those creepy sounds day after day, until he met his macabre pursuer face to face." (Publisher)

B.827. "The Unseen Witness," by David Gray [Walter B. Gibson], **Crime Case Book Magazine**, 1 (January 1954): 123-126.
"An inheritance case that was decided by the testimony of a ghost." (Publisher)

B.828. "Monte Carlo Incident," by Gautier Lebrun [Walter B. Gibson], **Crime Case Book Magazine**, 1 (January 1954): 126-127.
"The man who devised a 'system' to beat the Monte Carlo gaming tables." (Publisher)

B.829. "Lizzie Borden Baked a Cake," by Warren Palmer [Walter B. Gibson], **Crime Case Book Magazine**, 1 (January 1954): 128.
"What advice did a mother give a child in order not to eat a cake baked by infamous Lizzie Borden?" (Publisher)

B.830. "Murder of the Carnival Buccaneer," **Startling Detective**, 45 (January 1954): 32-33, 53-56.
Tampa, Florida, January 1931. The murder of wealthy Joe B. Johnson by three men, all who paid for their crime in a triple execution.

B.831. "Two Girls Meet the Hatchet Man," **True Detective**, 60 (January 1954): 16-19, 85-87.
Twickenham, England, 1953. The murders of Barbara Songhurst and Christine Reed.

B.832. "Miami Where Sin is Hotter Than Sunshine,"
by Earl J. Abbott [Walter B. Gibson], **True Police
Cases,** 6 (February 1954): 4-7, 74-77.
   "The investigator-author is not a weather
forecaster, but he does predict a hurricane of
crime and trouble for the Winter resort capital."
(Publisher)

B.833. "The Castle of Horrors," **Crime Case Book
Magazine,** 1 (March 1954): 1-79.
   The true story of the murders in Chicago by H.
H. Holmes.

B.834. "To the Last Drop..." [Walter B. Gibson],
Crime Case Book Magazine, 1 (March 1954): 79.
   Myths about execution methods. For example,
there are not always 13 steps to the gallows.

B.835. "The Case of the Vanished Bride," by David
Woodsman [Walter B. Gibson], **Crime Case Book
Magazine,** 1 (March 1954): 92-105.
   The disappearance, and murder, of Mildred
Williams, Atlanta, 1941.

B.836. "Death in the Duffel-Bag," by Neil Michaels
[Walter B. Gibson], **Crime Case Book Magazine,** 1
(March 1954): 106-119.
   Wichita, Kansas, 1952. Death of Mary Brady.

B.837. "Death Dealt Double," [Walter B. Gibson],
Crime Case Book Magazine, 1 (March 1954): 119.
   Wilmington, Delaware, a strange suicide. A man
took poison, but was shot as well when the rigor
mortis made his trigger finger tighten.

B.838. "A Question of Evidence," by Warren Palmer
[Walter B. Gibson], **Crime Case Book Magazine,** 1
(March 1954): 124-125.
   The case of William Shaw, Leith, Scotland,
hanged for a crime he never committed.

B.839. "Page Mr. Bertillon," by Jess Nichols
[Walter B. Gibson], **Crime Case Book Magazine,** 1
(March 1954): 126-127.
   Controversy over the Bertillon system of
identification.

B.840. "The Man Who Couldn't Lose," [Walter B.
Gibson], **Crime Case Book Magazine,** 1 (March 1954):
128.

How Gaston Morceau changed the policy of using gold coins at Monte Carlo.

B.841. "The Strange Case of the Armchair Detective," **Foto-Rama**, 2 (March 1954): 68-72.

B.842. "Nude on the Green," by Martin Donohue [Walter B. Gibson], **Startling Detective**, 45 (March 1954): 10-13, 50-53.
Tazewell, Virginia, 1946. The murder of Aileen Lockhart at the Tazewell Country Club by Harold Beavers.

B.843. "Sin Secret of the Murdering Mistress," **Startling Detective**, 45 (March 1954): 24-25, 43-44, 46-50.
Chattanooga, Tenn., 1937. The murder of Jimmie Revels.

B.844. "In a Mask He Couldn't Take Off," by C. B. Crowe [Walter B. Gibson], **Official Detective Stories**, 24 (April 1954): 14.
"January 13, 1954. Mary Phelen of Blanchard." (LRG) Not seen; C. B. Crowe was an in-joke with Gibson; his wife, Litzka Raymond, once used a rooster named Chinaboy in her magic act.

B.845. "With Not a Cop in Town," **Official Detective Stories**, 24 (April 1954): 37.
Not seen. (LRG)

B.846. "Doom Tide at Ocean Point," **True Police Cases**, 6 (April 1954): 12-15, 66-68.
Maine, 1936. The murder of Dolda Brewer.

B.847. "Murder Was the Keystone of His Career," by Martin Donohue [Walter B. Gibson], **True Police Cases**, 6 (April 1954): 10-11, 73-77.
Denver, 1953. Murder of Army Captain Lloyd Larson.

B.848. "The Coronation Murders," by P. L. Raymond [Walter B. Gibson], **Crime Case Book Magazine,** 1 (May 1954): 2-97.
Dark deeds mark the Coronation Celebration in England. (Note this passage on page 97... 'initials...carved by a <u>living shadow</u> that lurks there no more,"[my underlining])

B.849. "The Honor of Armand Peltzer," by Edward S, Sullivan [Walter B. Gibson], **Crime Case Book Magazine**, 1 (May 1954): 114-122.
   The disappearance of a young, wealthy attorney in Belgium becomes a cause celebre.

B.850. "The Vanished Victim," **Crime Case Book Magazine**, 1 (May 1954): 123-128.
   Berkeley, California, 1925.   The strange dual life of Howard Warren.

B.851. "Are You a Sucker for Marked Cards?" by Sidney H. Radner [Walter B. Gibson], **Foto-Rama**, 2 (May 1954): 65-70.

B.852. "You Won't Live to Tell It," **Official Detective Stories**, 24 (May 1954): 40.
   "Blackmail." (LRG)   Not seen.

B.853. "Clue of the Reptile Witness," **Startling Detective**, 45 (May 1954): 4-5, 76-80.
   Mohawk, Florida, 1929.   The murder of Angie Gillis and Levi Allen by J. C. Pike.   A life sentence.

B.854. "Mystery of the Secret Burials," by M. I. Donohue [Walter B. Gibson], **Startling Detective**, 45 (May 1954): 32-33, 54-57.
   Llanginning, Wales, October 1953.   The murder of Phoebe and John Harries by Ronald Harries.

B.855. "The Willing Killer," by Don Monroe [Walter B. Gibson], **Startling Detective**, 45 (May 1954): 62.
   1953. Derek Wright tries to hire someone to kill his former wife's lover.

B.856. "Welcome from a Smothered Woman," **Official Detective Stories**, 24 (June 1954): 28.
   "Hosmer," (LRG).   Not seen.

B.857. "Sergeant Bond," by C. B. Crowe [Walter B. Gibson], **Official Detective Stories**, 24 (June 1954): 30.
   Not seen.

B.858. "Among Only 5,000 Witnesses," **Official Detective Stories**, 24 (July 1954): 24.
   "Durham, N.H.   Robbery," (LRG)   Not seen.

B.859. "Four-Forty in Holyoke's Holocaust,"
Official Detective Stories, 24 (August 1954): 12.
    "Arson," (LRG). Not seen.

B.860. "If This Social Set Hadn't Swapped
Husbands," Official Detective Stories, 24
(September 1954): 8.
    "Clark Amesbury," (LRG). Not seen.

B.861. "Merchants of Murder," Startling Detective,
45 (September 1954): 28-31, 51-54.
    Philadelphia, 1930s. A notorious murder ring
which still remains mysterious.

B.862. "One Date Mary Didn't Want," by Gilbert Kay
[Walter B. Gibson], Official Detective Stories, 24
(December 1954): pp. not known.
    "Mary Bartlett, Lynn Ann Smith, Springfield,
Mass, Bob Litten," (LRG). Not seen.

B.863. "The Sitter, the Baby and the Nice Boy Down
the Street," Official Detective Stories, 24
(December 1954): pages not known.
    Not seen.

B.864. "Fate Saves a Witness," by David Atkins
[Walter B. Gibson], Real Police Stories, 23
(December 1954): 58.
    "Trial of mail robbers, England," (LRG). Not
seen.

B.865. "Grim Stranger of Mansion House," Real
Police Stories, 23 (December 1954): 18-19, 50-54.
    Bucks County, Pa., 1954.   The murder of a
young insurance executive, Anthony C. Lankford, by
William Wolf, Jr.

                        1955

B.866. "Who Broke the Teenage Curfew?" Official
Detective Stories, 25 (January 1955): 14.
    "Norwalk, Mass.   Geraldine Annese," (LRG).
Not seen.

B.867. "Did They Kill Nick Flash Too?" Official
Detective Stories, 25 (March 1955): 28.
    "Nat? George, by Donick?" (LRG) Not seen.

B.868. "The Florentine Masks," **The Saint Detective Magazine**, 3 (March 1955): 65-85.
In which an old acquaintance calls on the Great Gerard, magician, for help in post-war Europe. The first of two stories about Gerard Whitestone. (Reprinted in **Sleight of Crime**, 1977)

B.869. "Three Women in the Life of Claude," **Startling Detective**, 46 (March 1955): 28-29, 54-58.
Dearborn, Mich., 1954. Claude Morse murders his wife.

B.870. "Journey Into Nowhere," **Foto-Rama**, 3 (April 1955): 12-17.
The story of John Wise's trans-Atlantic balloon trip in 1859.

B.871. "Rape Slaying of the Blonde Beauty," **Startling Detective**, 46 (July 1955): 3, 56-60.
Panama City, Florida, 1955. The murder of Lou Ellen Jones.

B.872. "Magic Tricks You Can Perform," **Foto-Rama**, 3 (August 1955): 120-125.

B.873. "Mad at the World," **Real Police Stories**, 24 (August 1955): 30-33, 39-45.
Hayward, Wisconsin, 1955. The death of Emil and Clara Salzman, shot by their son, Eugene, a deadly marksman.

B.874. "Out of the Dusk," by Richard Mullen [Walter B. Gibson], **Real Police Stories**, 24 (August 1955): 40.
England. An historical story in which Harry Hilliard saws his wife in two.

B.875. "Body in the Woods," **Real Police Stories**, 24 (October 1955): 3, 36-38.
Maine, 1952. The murder of Mary Petley by Joseph Camuso, alias John Burzillo.

B.876. "One Night in Paris," **The Saint Detective Magazine**, 4 (November 1955): 91-119.
In which a man is found murdered in his own treasure room. The second story about the Great Gerard. (Reprinted in **Whodunit? Houdini?**, 1976 and **Houdini's Magic Magazine**, 1977.)

1956

B.877. "Double Murder Starts the Day," **Startling Detective**, 47 (January 1956): 4, 78-80.
    Columbus, Ohio, 1955. The murder of Gomer and Betty Thomas by her son.

B.878. "Rape Murder of the Co-Ed," **Startling Detective**, 47 (February 1956): 30-31, 68-70.
    Kalamazoo, Michigan, 1950. The murder of Carolyn Downs.

B.879. "Time Out for Murder," by Martin Donohue [Walter B. Gibson], **Startling Detective**, 47 (February 1956): 32-33, 70-73.
    St. Johnsbury, Vermont, 1955. The murder of Archie Webber, Jr., by Lionel Goyet.

B.880. "Red Trail of the Bludgeon Killer," by Morton Faber [Walter B. Gibson], **Startling Detective**, 47 (February 1956): 46, 93-96.
    Bordentown, New Jersey, 1955. The murder of John Hornyak, the owner of Flo's Delicatessen, by John Denn.

B.881. "Branded," by Peter Darrington [Walter B. Gibson], **Startling Detective**, 47 (February 1956): 54.
    Las Vegas, 1955. Science identifies a robber by his tools.

B.882. "Strangling of the Gay Widow," **Startling Detective**, 47 (March 1956): 44-47, 74-77.
    Philadelphia, 1955. The murder of Mrs. Lulubel Rossman by Frank Ellsworth and Raymond Wilson.

B.883. "We Smashed the Philadelphia Dope Menace," by Lieut. Thomas McDermot [Walter B. Gibson], **Startling Detective**, 47 (April 1956): 4.
    Not seen.

B.884. "$1,500,000 Phantom Firebug," **Startling Detective**, 47 (May 1956): 8-10, 76-79.
    Lowell, Mass., 1955. Walter M. Jean is indicted on 3 counts of arson, including the setting of a fire at the Medical Arts Building.

B.885. "Flaming Alibi That Backfired," **Startling Detective**, 47 (May 1956): 31-33, 86-88.

Ossipee, New Hampshire, 1916. The murder (by fire) of Arlene Small by her husband, Frederick Small. (The table of contents lists "Martin Donoghue" as author, but first page of story credits Gibson.)

B.886. "When the Hunter Becomes the Prey," **Startling Detective**, 47 (August 1956): 4-6, 65-68.
Shepherd's Pass, Mexico, 1956. The murder of Pauline and Everett Kennison by Shelton and O'Brien.

B.887. "Passion Slaying of Dana Marie," by Jack C. Peters [Walter B. Gibson], **Startling Detective**, 47 (August 1956): 10-13, 46-47.
Roanoke, Virginia, 1949. The murder of Dana Marie Weaver by Lee Scott, who could be paroled in 12 years.

B.888. "She Saw Her Father Murdered," by Martin Donoghue [Walter B. Gibson], **Startling Detective**, 47 (August 1956): 24-25, 74-77.
Pejepscot, Maine, 1956. The murder of Wilfred J. Blair by Richard Woods. (This spelling of the pseudonym was used only two times.)

B.889. "Flaming Death for Four," **Startling Detective**, 47 (September 1956): 10-13, 46.
Holyoke, Mass., 1956. A case of arson and murder.

B.890. "Roadside Strangler and His Nude Lust Victim," **Startling Detective**, 47 (December 1956): 20-23, 48-49.
Fayette City, Pa., 1945. The murder of Anna Dreyer by Frederick Hauser.

B.891. "Bludgeoned Teenager," by Martin Donohue [Walter B. Gibson], **Startling Detective**, 47 (December 1956): 36-37, 77-80.
Boston, 1956. The murder of Diane Ferriani by Robert Carney.

B.892. "Monster of Carpenter Hall," by Martin Donohue [Walter B. Gibson], **True Police Year Book**, No. 5 (1956): 15-17, 68-70.
(Reprinted from **Startling Detective**, September 1953.)

B.893. "Alias 'the Shadow'," True Police Year Book,
No. 5 (1956): 44-47, 54-57.
   (Reprinted from Daring Detective, September
1952.)

1957

B.894. "The Bullet Clue to Murder," by Martin
Donohue [Walter B. Gibson], Startling Detective, 48
(February 1957): 13-   .
   Hartland, Maine, 1956.   The murder of Clarence
Towle by Louis Thursby, Jr.   (LRG)   Not seen.

B.895. "Catherine Had a Date with Murder,"
Startling Detective, 48 (February 1957): 16-   .
   Lowell, Mass., 1946.   The murder of Catherine
Nordlie by Rosario Milinazzo. (LRG)   Not seen.

B.896. "The Strange Case of Washington Irving
Bishop," Mystery Digest, 1 (May 1957): 27-29.
   The life and times of a nineteenth century
mind reader.   (Reprinted in Attic Revivals Presents
Walter Gibson's Magicians, 1982.)

B.897. "Lover's Lane Murder Tryst and the Nude
Corpse," Startling Detective, 48 (June 1957):
29-31, 41-47.

B.898. "Red Light Vengeance," by Martin Donohue
[Walter B. Gibson], Startling Detective, 48 (June
1957): 34-35, 41-47.

B.899. "The Amazing Randi," Mystery Digest, 1 (July
1957): 109-120.
   In which a gang of robbers kidnap real life
magician, Randi, to have him open a safe for them.
(Reprinted in Attic Revivals Presents Walter
Gibson's Magicians, 1982.)

B.900. "Lifer Sees Light of Freedom," Startling
Detective, 48 (July 1957): 24-25, 71-73.
   Springfield, Mass., 1954.   The murder of
Mildred Hismer.

B.901. "Lust Slaying of the Roving Redhead," by
Martin Donohue   [Walter B. Gibson], Startling
Detective, 48 (July 1957): 34-35, 54-56.
   Boston, 1948.   The murder of Dorothy Brennan.

B.902. "The Positive Power of Hypnotism," **Popular Medicine**, 2 (October 1957): 11-23.

1958

B.903. "Nude Corpse in Lover's Lane," **Startling Detective**, 49 (January 1958): 40-41, 58-60.

B.904. "Bridge of Doom," by Martin Donohue [Walter B. Gibson], **Startling Detective**, 49 (January 1958): 48-49, 66-68.

B.905. "Yoga, to Keep Young and Healthy," **Popular Medicine**, 2 (July 1958): 30-37.

B.906. "Truth About Royal Jelly," by Robert Russell Smith [Walter B. Gibson], **Popular Medicine**, 3 (November 1958): 19-28.

B.907. "Hypnotism Can Cure," **Popular Medicine**, 3 (November 1958): 45-52.

1959

B.908. "Is There Life After Death?" by Adolph Toman [Walter B. Gibson], **Popular Medicine**, 3 (March 1959): 41-50.

B.909. "Don't Be Afraid of Hypnotism," by Auguste Forel, M.D. with Alfred Toman [Walter B. Gibson], **Popular Medicine**, 3 (November 1959): 34-43.

B.910. "Can Astrology Help Your Health?" by Gautier LeBlun [sic] [Walter B. Gibson], **Popular Medicine**, 3 (November 1959): 44-51.

1961

B.911. "The Unwanted Evidence," **Analog Science Fact & Fiction**, 67 (August 1961): 108-119.
    A discussion of what constitutes evidence in investigations of psychic phenomena.

1963

B.912. "Betting and Bluffing in Poker," by Sidney H. Radner [Walter B. Gibson], **Foto-Rama**, 20 (September 1963): 80-87.

1965

B.913. "Nothing Up My Sleeve," by Howard Thurston
[Walter B. Gibson], **The Linking Ring**, 45-46 (June
1965-August 1966).
     (Reprinted   from   the   series   in   **Collier's**
Weekly, 1929.)

1971

B.914. "Ashes of the Phoenix," [Walter B. Gibson],
Magick, No. 16 (February 12, 1971): 77-78, 80.
     Material in this and the two articles below
appears to have been adapted from earlier articles
written by Gibson or from information supplied the
magazine by him. Sources have not been traced.

B.915. "Three Card Mental Repeat," [Walter B.
Gibson], **Magick**, No. 25 (June 18, 1971): 121-122,
124.

B.916. "Triple Mental Repeat," [Walter B. Gibson],
Magick, No. 28 (July 23, 1971): 137-138, 140.

1972

B.917. "Harry Houdini: Magician or Psychic?" **Beyond**
Reality, 1 (December 1972): 16-20, 42.

1973

B.918. "The House in Berkeley Square," **Beyond**
Reality, 1 (March 1973): 58-60, 62.
     Bulwer Lytton's story, "The Haunted and the
Haunters", had a basis in fact as well as fancy.

B.919. "Time Will Tell," by [Joseph] Dunninger and
Walter B. Gibson, **Magick**, No. 90 (December 14,
1973): 447-448, 450.
     Both this and the following item are possibly
reprints, but the sources have not been traced.

1974

B.920. "The Spaced-Out Card," by [Joseph] Dunninger
and Walter B. Gibson, **Magick**, No. 107 (August 9,
1974)ı 531-532, 534.

1975

B.921. "Dunninger on Mindreading," by Joseph
Dunninger and Walter B. Gibson, The Magic Magazine,
2 (April 1975): 14-15, 35-41, 44-45, 47-49
     (Excerpted from Dunninger's Secrets, 1974.)

B.922. "Herrmann the Great," The Magic Magazine, 2
(April 1975): 29-34.
     (Excerpted from The Master Magicians, 1966.)

B.923. "Secrets of Magic Mysteries: How to Walk
Under Water," The Magic Magazine, 2 (April 1975):
27-28.
     (Reprinted from The Book of Secrets, 1927, and
Secrets of Magic, 1966.)

B.924. "Secrets of Magic: Burning Alive," The Magic
Magazine, 2 (April 1975): 28.
     (Reprinted from The Book of Secrets and
Secrets of Magic.)

B.925. "It's Magic," Child Life, 54 (June-July
1975): 11.
     Material for this and the three subsequent
articles in this series was adapted from
Professional Magic for Amateurs.

B.926. "It's Magic! Three Tricky Tumblers," Child
Life, 54 (August-September 1975): 96-97.

B.927. "It's Magic! Find the Blue," Child Life, 54
(October 1975): 50.

B.928. "It's Magic! The Dissolving Coin," Child
Life, 54 (November 1975): 22-23.

1976

B.929. "The Mark Wilson Course in Magic," Genii:
The International Conjuror's Magazine, 40 (March
1976): 164-165.
     A review of the comprehensive course and
manual of magic by one of the collaborators.

B.930. "Date Sense," [Walter Gibson], Magick, No.
161 (September 3, 1976): 802, 804.
     Reprint?

B.931. "The Amazing Creations of Theodore DeLand,"
The Magic Magazine, 3 (November 1976): 12-13,
42-43.
(Reprinted from **Conjuror's Magazine**, March
1945.)

1977

B.932. "DeLand's Special Packs," **The Magic
Magazine**, 3 (February 1977): 48-50.
(Reprinted from **Conjuror's Magazine**, September
1945.)

B.933. "DeLand's Ever-Ready Trick Cards," **The Magic
Magazine**, 3 (March 1977): 17-19, 60, 63.
(Reprinted from **Conjuror's Magazine**, October
1945.)

B.934. "Silk, Tubes and Glass: Herman Hanson's
Version," **The Magic Magazine**, 4 (April 1977):
51-52, 54.
(Reprinted from **Conjuror's Magazine**, July
1946.)

B.935. "More DeLand Card Effects," **The Magic
Magazine**, 4 (April 1977): 17-20, 54.
(Reprinted from **Conjuror's Magazine**, June
1946.)

B.936. "Howard Thurston's Magic Lessons (1)," **The
Magic Magazine**, 4 (May 1977): 37, 40-41, 48.
(Reprinted from **Conjuror's Magazine**,
February-June 1945, and **The Thurston Magic Lessons**,
1928. **A.19.**)

B.937. "Cut-and-Paste Magic: Hardin's Magic Cards,"
The Magic Magazine, 4 (May 1977): 29-30, 32-33.
Probably a reprint from **Conjuror's Magazine**;
source not traced.

B.938. "DeLand's Changing Cards," **The Magic
Magazine**, 4 (May 1977): 18-24.
(Reprinted from **Conjuror's Magazine**, December
1945.)

B.939. "DeLand Card Effects," **The Magic Magazine**, 4
(August-September 1977): 10-11.
Probably a reprint from **Conjuror's Magazine**;
source not traced.

B.940. "Howard Thurston's Magic Lessons (2)," **The Magic Magazine**, 4 (August-September 1977): 20-21, 58-59.
(Reprinted from **Conjuror's Magazine**, February-June 1945, and **The Thurston Magic Lessons**, 1928.)

B.941. "Hardin's Miracles and Explanation," **The Magic Magazine**, 4 (August-September 1977): 14-15, 58.
Source not traced; probably **Conjuror's Magazine.**

B.942. "One Night in Paris," Houdini's **Magic Magazine**, 1 (October 1977): 38-39, 78, 82-88, 90-93.
(Reprinted from **The Saint Detective Magazine**, November 1955.)

1978

B.943. "Presenting Harry Kellar," **Houdini's Magic Magazine**, 2 (January 1978): 34-39, 59-61.
(Reprinted from **The Master Magicians**, 1966.)

1979

B.944. "Cards: The Quarter Crimp and the Baffled Burglars," **Hocus Pocus**, 1 (July-August 1979): 35-37.
Probably a reprint; source not traced.

1980

B.945. "Memoirs," **M-U-M (Magic-Unity-Might)**, 71 (July-August 1980).
Two parts of anecdotal reminiscences for the autobiography which Gibson never completed.

1983

B.946. "Revealed: How Top Magicians Fool the World," **National Examiner**, 20 (April 5, 1983): 14-15.
(Reprints, with the original illustrations, "The Secret of the Burning Oven," "Catching a

Cannonball," and "Spirit Raps" from **The** Book of **Secrets,** 1927.)

B.947. "Secrets of the Mystery Men of Magic," **National Examiner,** 20 (April 12, 1983): 14-15.
    (Reprints, with the original illustrations, "Fire Eating," "The Man of Iron," and "The Indian Rope Trick," from **The Book of Secrets.)**

B.948. "Secrets of the Sorcerers," **National Examiner,** 20 (April 19, 1983): 30-31.
    (Reprints, with the original illustrations, "Snake Charming," "Buried Alive," and "Walking Through Fire" from **The Book of Secrets.)**

                              1984

B.949. "A Look at the Real Miss America," **National Examiner,** 21 (October 9, 1984): 17.
    An original article, not a reprint.

B.950.   "The Mystery of the 60-foot Phantom," **National Examiner,** 21 (October 16, 1984): 38.
    An original article, not a reprint.

When **The Shadow Magazine** ceased publication, Gibson turned to the True Crime field.

C. Contributions to Books and Pamphlets by Other Writers ☞

C.1. Secret Writing: An Introduction to Cryptograms, Ciphers and Codes, by Henry Lysing [John L. Nanovic]. New York: David Kemp & Co., 1936. x, 117.
Much, if not all, of this was actually written by Gibson. See in particular, chapter ix, "The Shadow's Codes." Nanovic was the editor of **The Shadow** and Henry Lysing was the name used on the codes section in the magazine. (Reprinted in facsimile, Dover Publications, 1974.)

C.2. "Foreword," by Walter B. Gibson to **The Great Houdini, Magician Extraordinary**, by Beryl Williams and Samuel Epstein. New York: Julian Messner, 1950.

C.3. "Foreword," by Walter B. Gibson to **Cups and Balls Magic: Manipulation and Routines**, by Tom Osbourne. Philadelphia: Kanter's Magic Shop, 1955.
Re-issue of a 1937 pamphlet.

C.4. "The Riddle of Devil's Mountain," by Helen Wells [Walter B.Gibson] in **Cherry Ames Girls' Annual**. Manchester, England: World Distributors, 1964. pp. 81-100.

C.5. "The Ghost from the Grave," by Walter B. Gibson in **The Fine Art of Murder**, edited by Walter B. Gibson. New York: Grosset & Dunlap, 1965. pp. 163-185. (Reprinted from **Daring Detective Magazine**, November, 1952. See B.807.)

C.6. "Introduction," by Walter B. Gibson in **Dunninger's Monument to Magic**, by Joseph Dunninger. Secaucus, New Jersey: Lyle Stuart, 1974. pp. 11-14.
Re-issued as **Dunninger's Book of Magic** (New York: Bonanza Books, 1979) with re-set type and only pages 1-115 of the original 222 pages; omitted are pages of facsimile letters and photos.

C.7. "The Shadow," by Maxwell Grant [Walter B. Gibson] in **Pages, the World of Books, Writers, and Writing**, edited by Matthew J. Bruccoli and C. E. Frazer Clark, Jr. Detroit: Gale Research Co., 1976. pp. 263-267.
Reprinted in **The Great Detective**, edited by Otto Penzler (Boston: Little, Brown, 1978), pp.205-216.

C.8. "The Mad Magician," by Maxwell Grant [Walter B. Gibson] in **Whodunit? Houdini?**, edited by Otto Penzler.New York: Harper & Row, 1976. pp. 150-169.

C.9. "One Night in Paris," by Walter B. Gibson in **Whodunit? Houdini?**, edited by Otto Penzler. New York: Harper & Row, 1976. pp. 171-202.

C.10. "The Man of Mystery," by Walter B. Gibson in **Sleight of Crime**, edited by Cedric E. Clute, Jr. and Nicholas Lewin. Chicago: Henry Regnery Co., 1977. pp. 91-98.

C.11. "The Florentine Masks," by Walter B. Gibson in **Sleight of Crime**, edited by Cedric E. Clute, Jr. and Nicholas Lewin. Chicago: Henry Regnery Co., 1977. pp. 223-250.

C.12. "Introduction," by Walter B. Gibson to **Death from a Top Hat**, by Clayton Rawson. Boston: Gregg Press, 1979. pp. v-x.

C.13. "Magician's Paraphernalia: Tricks, Effects and Evocations," by Walter B. Gibson in **The Encyclopedia of Collectibles: Lalique to Marbles**. Alexandria, Va.: Time-Life Books, 1979. pp. 90-103.

C.14. "Introduction," by Walter B. Gibson to **The Best Dam Tricks**, by Magic (Ian), pseud. Middletown, New York: Ian Sutz, 1980.

C.15. "Blackmail Bay," by Walter B. Gibson in **The Duende History of The Shadow Magazine**, edited by Will Murray. Greenwood, Mass.: Odyssey Publications, 1980. pp. 103-112.
A new Shadow story, written for a syndicated series, but published for the first time here.

C.16. **Magic Secrets from The Seven Circles**, compiled by Walter B.Graham. Omaha: Modern Litho, Inc., nd.

Magic tricks reproduced in facsimile from the pages of The Seven Circles magazine.   Includes two signed articles by Gibson, "A Phenomenal Card Mystery" and "Perfect Card Location" as well as the trick, "Giant Memory," invented by him.   Since Gibson was the editor of the magazine, much of the rest, unsigned, may be his work as well.

Credit goes where credit is due.   Other names are on the cover, but this is still a Gibson title. (A.50.)

D. Syndicated
Features ☞

      For two decades (1921--1943) Gibson wrote thousands of short articles which were distributed to newspapers through the services of the Philadelphia Public Ledger and other syndicates. Below are those which have been identified as his work, arranged alphabetically by series title. Inclusive dates and the number of entries have been given if known followed by a brief description of content.

D.1. "After Dinner Tricks," [Walter B. Gibson]. Ledger Syndicate. 1921-March 7, 1925. 1,080 numbers.
      Daily feature consisting of about 75 words of text describing a simple magic trick, illustrated with a line drawing. Expected to run a few weeks at most, this series ran for nearly 5 years. The concept was used with variations in other Gibson features such as "Easy Magic." Selected tricks collected under the title **After Dinner Tricks (A.1.).**

D.2. "Blackstone Magic," [Walter B. Gibson]. Dell Publishing. 1930. 9 numbers.
      Instructions for performing simple magic tricks. Part One was two pages in length with black and white illustrations as part of a Sunday feature called "The Funnies." The remaining 8 numbers were one page each and illustrated in color.

D.3. "Brain Tests," [Walter B. Gibson]. Public Ledger, Inc. ca 1928. 1,920 numbers.
      A series of brief intelligence tests requiring ingenuity, accuracy, speed, judgment, observation, as well as a knowledge of history, literature, and mathematics. Answers to each test were given the same day as the question. Also called **Your Brains**

If Any. 150 collected in book form (A.25.). Nos
1-554 copyrighted, New York Evening Post, Inc.

D.4.   "Bunco Games to Beware Of," [Walter B.
Gibson]. Ledger Syndicate. 1923-24. 50 numbers.
    Short illustrated articles describing games of
skill used at carnivals and how they can be rigged
to favor the operator of the game.   Revised and
collected as **The Bunco Book (A.8.).**

D.5.   "Clue Mysteries," [Walter B. Gibson]. Ledger
Syndicate. ca 1941. 8 numbers.
    Solve it yourself mysteries published in
serial form; each began on Monday and concluded on
Saturday.   Clues were contained in the
illustrations as well as in the stories.   (Titles:
Who Killed Robert Burrick? The Diamond Robbery,
The Murdered Hermit, Hotel Room Secret, Counterfeit
Trail, The Kidnapped Proxy, Clock-Dial Message, The
Stolen Portrait.)

D.6.   "Daily Crossword Puzzle," [Walter B. Gibson].
Ledger Syndicate. October 1, 1924- ?   2,000
numbers?
    The crossword puzzle was so new when Gibson
began creating them that instructions for working
one were necessary.   During the height of the
craze, he produced 14 each week for a period of
about two years and followed that with 8 each week.
Examples preserved in his scrapbooks include some
contributed by his brother.

D.7.   "Easy Magic You Can Do," [Walter B. Gibson].
Ledger Syndicate. 1922. 20 numbers.
    A weekly feature describing the secrets behind
simple magic tricks slightly more complicated than
the **After Dinner Tricks** series, but in a similar
format.   Often there would be two tricks each week.
Text revised and abridged for **The Book of Secrets
(A.7.)** using the same illustrations.

D.8.   "Human Enigmas, Who Still Keep the World
Guessing," [Walter B. Gibson]. Ledger Syndicate.
1924. 16 parts.
    Articles on psychics, wizards, and mediums,
past and present, from Daniel Douglas Home and
Madame Blavatsky, to Cagliostro and the Eddy
Brothers.   Sub-title varies: with number 7, it
became "That Still Keep the World Guessing."

D.9.   "Intelligence Tests," [Walter B. Gibson]. Public Ledger, Inc. 1920s? 240 numbers.

A feature similar to the **Brain Tests** series with a problem relating to an illustration or diagram which depends on logic and not guesswork for its solution. The answer accompanies each puzzle.

D.10.   "Lessons in Magic," by Howard Thurston [Walter B. Gibson]. Ledger Syndicate. 1923-24. 50 lessons.

This series originally appeared in the **Thurston Magic Box of Candy** (see Section F). The tricks were chosen by Gibson and magician John Mulholland (1898-1970), but written up by Gibson. They were lengthened for the newspaper series. Most of the material appeared in Thurston's **Book of Magic (A.13.).** Two columns wide, illustrated, with photo of Thurston.

D.11.   "Magic Made Easy," [Walter B. Gibson]. Public Ledger, Inc. late 1920s. 1,770 numbers.

Illustrated directions for simple magic tricks, in comic strip format, with 3 pictures and captions per trick. Over 200 collected in the book of the same name **(A.30).**

D.12.   "Master Mysteries of Magic," [Walter B. Gibson]. Ledger Syndicate. 1927-28. 26 parts.

Brief, illustrated stories, similar in content and format to those in **Miracles--Ancient and Modern.**

D.13.   "Mind Reading," by Joseph Dunninger [Walter B. Gibson]. Ledger Syndicate. ca 1943. 24 parts.

"A series of twenty-four easy lessons in mental telepathy, one of the most discussed subjects of the day." (Publisher's statement.) Collected, revised, and published as **What's On Your Mind (A.43.).**

D.14.   "Miracles--Ancient and Modern," [Walter B. Gibson]. Ledger Syndicate. 1922. 50 parts.

Brief, illustrated stories explaining the secrets behind some of the most famous feats of magic, such as sawing a woman in half and the hindu rope trick. The same illustrations were used in **The Book of Secrets (A.7.),** but the text was rewritten.

D.15. "Numerology: The Prophetic Science of Numbers," [Walter B. Gibson]. Ledger Syndicate. ca 1926. Number of parts not known.

Comprehensive daily series includes material on how events have been and can be predicted through numbers, what the birth numbers of famous people mean, and how to interpret your own name according to numerology. Similar in format to **After Dinner Tricks,** but not illustrated.

D.16. "Nuts to Crack: The Best Puzzles of the Month," [Walter B. Gibson], **Youth's Companion;** date not known (1920s?), no. of parts unknown. Not a syndicated feature as such. Appeared monthly in the magazine. Selected examples found in Gibson's scrapbooks. Sub-title varies ("A Corner for Busy Minds"), with enigmas, charades, word-squares, anagrams, and other word games. The solutions appeared in the following issue of the magazine.

D.17. "Intelligent People Are More Easily Fooled," by Howard Thurston [Walter B. Gibson], **Philadelphia Sunday Ledger Magazine,** (March 1, 1925). pages not known.

These occasional articles on a variety of topics appeared between 1925 and 1931. Dates given are for the appearances in the feature magazine section of the **Ledger,** appearances in other newspapers may have carried other dates.

D.18. "If You Can't Find Your Freak, Make It," by Walter B. Gibson, **Philadelphia Sunday Ledger Magazine,** (April 26, 1925).

D.19. "Look Out for the 'Short-Changer!'" by Walter B. Gibson, **Philadelphia Sunday Ledger Magazine,** (May 17, 1925).

D.20. "Revealing the Mysteries of Magic," by Howard Thurston [Walter B. Gibson], **Philadelphia Sunday Ledger Magazine,** (January 3, 1926).

D.21. "You Can't Fool the Monte Man," by Walter B. Gibson, **Philadelphia Sunday Ledger Magazine,** (May 23, 1926).

D.22. "One of the Games You Cannot Win," by Walter B. Gibson, **Philadelphia Sunday Ledger Magazine,** (August 22, 1926).

D.23.   "Mysteries of Hindu 'Magic' Revealed," by
Walter B. Gibson, **Philadelphia Sunday Ledger
Magazine,** (September 19, 1926).

D.24.   "Houdini's Last Interview Revealed His
Narrow Escapes," by Walter B. Gibson, **Philadelphia
Sunday Ledger Magazine,** (December 5, 1926).

D.25.   "Look Out for No. 1--in 1927!" by Walter B.
Gibson, **Philadelphia Sunday Ledger Magazine,**
(January 2, 1927).

D.26.   "'Age of Torture' in Vogue Again," by Walter
B. Gibson, **Philadelphia Sunday Ledger Magazine,**
(January 22, 1928).

D.27.   "Escape from 'Living Burials,'" by Howard
Thurston [Walter B. Gibson], **Philadelphia Sunday
Ledger Magazine,** (April 1, 1928).

D.28.   "'Powwow' to Defeat Black Magic," by Walter
B. Gibson, **Philadelphia Sunday Ledger Magazine,**
(January 13, 1929).

D.29.   "Thrilling Feats of an Escape Artist," by
Harry Blackstone [Walter B. Gibson], **Philadelphia
Sunday Ledger Magazine,** (October 20, 1929).

D.30.   "Which Rules the World--Blond or Brunette?"
by Walter B. Gibson, **Philadelphia Sunday Ledger
Magazine,** (December 1, 1929).

D.31.   "Teeth: An Index to Temperament," by Walter
B. Gibson, **Philadelphia Sunday Ledger Magazine,**
(April 20, 1930).

D.32.   "'Flivver Blimp' New Baby in Aviation," by
Walter B. Gibson, **Philadelphia Sunday Ledger
Magazine,** (August 3, 1930).

D.33.   "Will Sherlock Holmes Return from the
Grave?" by Walter B. Gibson, **Philadelphia Sunday
Ledger Magazine,** (August 10, 1930).

D.34.   "America Goes Endurance Crazy," by Walter B.
Gibson. **Philadelphia Sunday Ledger Magazine,**
(August 24, 1930).

D.35.   "Science Battles Menace of the Earthquake,"
by Walter B. Gibson, **Philadelphia Sunday Ledger
Magazine**, (August 31, 1930).

D.36.   "Revealing the Trickery of Fake Hypnotists,"
by Harry Blackstone [Walter B. Gibson],
Philadelphia Sunday Ledger Magazine, (September 14,
1930).

D.37.   "Putting Your Lazy Hand to Work," by Walter
B. Gibson, **Philadelphia Sunday Ledger Magazine**,
(September 28, 1930).

D.38.   "High in the Sky to Map the World," by
Walter B. Gibson, **Philadelphia Sunday Ledger
Magazine**, (November 23, 1930).

D.39.   "Back to Backgammon and the
Checkerboard," by Walter B. Gibson, **Philadelphia
Sunday Ledger Magazine**, (March 1, 1931).

D.40.   "A Puzzle a Day," [Walter B. Gibson]. Ledger
Syndicate. 1922-23. 940 numbers.
     A variation of the **Brain Tests** series.
Observation and logic were required to solve these
puzzles whose solutions were supplied the following
day.   Line drawings illustrate up to 150 words of
text.   Example: 6 volumes of a set of books are out
of order and can be arranged correctly in no more
than 3 moves by moving 2 books at a time.

D.41.   "Science Questions," [Walter B. Gibson].
     Not examined.   Perhaps a variant title for
"Why Is It?" (See **D.47**.)

D.42.   "Teasers," [Walter B. Gibson].   Public
Ledger, Inc. 1923-25. about 600 numbers.
     A variation on the "Puzzle a Day" series; 508
have been preserved in Gibson's scrapbooks.   Memory
tests, spelling quizzes, making as many words as
possible from a given series of letters.   Line
drawings accompany about 120 words of text with
answers provided in the following number.

D.43.   "Thurston's Page of Magic," by Howard
Thurston [Walter B. Gibson]. Ledger Syndicate. May
10-June 21, 1925.
     A rival feature to Houdini's "Red Magic"
newspaper series.   8 to 10 simple magic tricks
explained.   Illustrated.

D.44. "A Trick a Day," by Ponjay Harah [Walter B. Gibson]. Public Ledger, Inc. ca 1930. At least 204 numbers.
A variation on the "After Dinner Tricks" series; illustrated. Over 200 numbers preserved in Gibson's scrapbooks.

D.45. "Tricks You Can Do," by Howard Thurston [Walter B. Gibson]. Ledger Syndicate. ca 1925-26. About 50 numbers.
A daily series in two-column format. Three or four cartoon panels illustrate the presentation of each trick which uses 75-100 words of text.

D.46. "Who's Guilty?" [Walter B. Gibson]. Ledger Syndicate. Date not known, at least 60 numbers.
The "minute mystery" formula designed to appeal to those "readers of thrill stories who are able to pick the guilty person in the early paragraphs of any mystery." Approximately 300 words (including solution) in each day's feature.

D.47. "Why Is It?" [Walter B. Gibson]. Ledger Syndicate. 1924. At least 18 numbers.
Puzzles requiring some knowledge of basic science for their solution. Why is the sky blue? What makes the bumble bee hum? Why does the giraffe have such a long neck? About 150 words of text (including solution to previous day's question) with line drawing. Possible variant title for "Science Questions" **(D.41.)**   18 in Gibson files.

D.48. "Word Building," [Walter B. Gibson]. Ledger Syndicate. Late 1920s, at least 36 numbers.
Each day's puzzle is made up of blocks or squares in the shape of a "building" in which one or more letters must be fitted. Definitions are given for each "story" of the building and each succeeding word uses an additional letter to the one below it (O; PO; POE; POSE; POSER, etc.).

E. Comic Books & Newspaper Comic Strips ☞

Walter Gibson was a pioneer in the field of comic books. While his name and contributions may not rank at the top, his work deserves future study. He recycled many of his Shadow plots and several pulp novels have their counterparts in **Shadow Comics**. From trying to adapt a novel to fit 10 pages of comic book format he developed into a writer who considered the visual impact of the stories he told. He was unfortunate in his choice of artists to illustrate his scripts by choosing ones he had known from the Philadelphia Ledger or with whom he "hit it off", as he frequently phrased it. Some of the artists from the Jack Binder shop (noted below by the name "Jack Binder") were excellent draughtsmen, but other artists were not as talented. (All work signed "Jack Binder" is not in the same style, so it is assumed that this is the work of his "shop" and not his personal work.) Only the work of Bob Powell has left any artistic impact, but he illustrated few of Gibson's scripts. (For a list of Powell's work on The Shadow in comics see Appendix C.)

The material below is arranged according to individual comic book title, the most significant preceding the lesser known titles. Following that, the sequence is issue by issue. Story titles have been supplied for those which did not have titles in the actual comics. These are enclosed in brackets []. Walter Gibson's name appears in brackets as well unless a pen name ("Maxwell Grant") actually appears on the story. The name after Gibson's is that of the artist. It appears in brackets if the story was not signed and the name has had to be supplied. The identification of artist is based largely on a study of the style since no records remain in the Street & Smith Archives.

199

Most individual comic book stories have an individual pagination which is independent of the pagination on other stories in the same issue. For this bibliography, the pagination given covers the entire issue and not merely the specific story listed. Except in rare instances the front cover and inside front cover are considered as pages 1 and 2. Early issues of Street & Smith comics had page numbers printed in the upper corner margin of each page; this number has been retained for the entries from those issues, otherwise new numbering has been supplied. Where a story begins on page 2 (or 4) of an issue, that means that page 1 (as given by the publisher) or 3 (as supplied by the bibliographer) is an advertising page which had no connection to the story which followed. The Street & Smith comics were identified by volume number and issue number within each volume, as well as by date. Whole numbers for the series were not used. In each entry below the volume and issue numbers are given thus: 1.2 (that is, volume one, number two).

Shadow Comics

E.1. ["Gem Robberies"], [Walter B. Gibson], **Shadow Comics**, 1.2 (April 1940): 2-6.
In which The Shadow undertakes the protection of a delivery of gems and saves one million dollars in cash as well.

E.2. "Norgil the Magician Magic Square," [Walter B. Gibson], **Shadow Comics**, 1.2 (April 1940): front cover verso.
Mathematical trick. Magician tells someone the total of the numbers he/she has covered with a coin or match stick. Answers on last page of issue.

E.3. ["Silk Tabor"], [Walter B. Gibson], **Shadow Comics**, 1.3 (May 1940): 1-6.
In which The Shadow defends his reputation against an imposter and saves Horace Lybolt's million dollar bonds.

E.4. "Norgil: [The Bannishaw Pearls]," [Walter B. Gibson], **Shadow Comics**, 1.3 (May 1940): 41-45.
In which Norgil is hired to try to steal some pearls at a party. Suggested by "The Blue Pearls"

in **Street & Smith's Mystery Magazine,** December
1939.   Includes three simple magic tricks.

E.5.   ["More Gem Robberies"], [Walter B. Gibson],
Shadow Comics, 1.4 (June 1940): 1-8.
   In which a talking, bodiless head gives
directions to a gang of thieves. Suggested by "The
Crime Oracle" from **The Shadow,** June 1, 1936. Uses
the original pulp cover illustration on this issue.

E.6.   ["Arson"], [Walter B. Gibson], **Shadow Comics,**
1.5 (July 1940): 1-8.
   In which a gang of thieves uses fire to mask
their deeds. Suggested by "The Salamanders," **The
Shadow,** April 1, 1936.

E.7.   ["Czar of Crime"], [Walter B. Gibson], **Shadow
Comics,** 1.6 (August 1940): 1-7.
   In which Lingo Queed tries to take over Rook
Hollister's gang and The Shadow moves in to mop up.
Suggested by "Lingo," **The Shadow,** April 1, 1935.

E.8.   "The Shadow and The Creeping Death," [Walter
B. Gibson], **Shadow Comics,** 1.7 (November 1940):
1-12.
   In which The Shadow encounters an
international counterfeiting scheme and a strangler
who cannot be seen. Suggested by "The Creeping
Death," **The Shadow,** January 15, 1933.

E.9.   "Charg, The Murder Monster," [Walter B.
Gibson], **Shadow Comics,** 1.8 (January 1941): 3-22.
   In which a mechanical killer seeks the formula
for a new motor fuel while The Shadow seeks the
human brain behind the robot named Charg.
Suggested by "Charg, Monster," **The Shadow,** July 1,
1934.

E.10.   "The Mystery of the Sealed Box," [Walter B.
Gibson]: Vernon Greene, **Shadow Comics,** 1.9 (March
1941): 3-35.
   In which the evidence of graft in local
politics contained in Mayor Dyken's sealed box is
the object of much interest for both crooks and The
Shadow. Suggested by "The Sealed Box," **The Shadow,**
December 1, 1937. (Reprints Shadow newspaper strip
nos. 1-48; reprinted in **The Shadow Scrapbook.**)

E.11.   ["Old Home Week in Westbury"], [Walter B.
Gibson], **Shadow Comics,** 1.9 (March 1941): 48-53.

In which Norgil returns home to solve a family mystery.   Suggested by "Old Crime Week," **Crime Busters,** February 1939.

E.12.   "The Shadow Matches Wits with Hoang Hu," [Walter B. Gibson]: Vernon Greene, **Shadow Comics,** 1.10 (May 1941): 3-27.
In which the dread leader of the Wing Fan and keeper of the Fate Joss finds The Shadow more than a worthy opponent.   Suggested by "The Fate Joss," **The Shadow,** July 1, 1935. (Reprints Shadow newspaper strips nos. B1-B36.)

E.13.   "The Leopard Strikes," [Walter B. Gibson]: Vernon Greene, **Shadow Comics,** 1.11 (July 1941): 3-15.
In which a mysterious killer strikes down people in the park near the zoo and The Shadow discovers a leopard cult in New York City. Possibly suggested by "The Leopard Strikes," a Shadow radio script, Mutual Network, January 5, 1941.

E.14.   "The Shadow Meets 'The Dagger,'" [Walter B. Gibson]: Vernon Greene, **Shadow Comics,** 1.12 (September 1941): 3-30.
In which The Shadow joins the prisoners of Shark Island and saves a United States defense base from a human dagger and his convict band. (Reprints Shadow newspaper strip nos. C1-C72.)

E.15.   "The Shadow Battles the Bund," [Walter B. Gibson]: Vernon Greene, **Shadow Comics,** 2.1 (November 1941): 3-28.
In which Kurt Schorn and his gang of saboteurs attempt to convert lacquer into high explosives for an attack on U.S. defense plants until The Shadow and Margo Lane interfere.   (Reprints Shadow newspaper strip nos. D1-D36.)

E.16.   "The Devil Master," [Walter B. Gibson]: Vernon Greene, **Shadow Comics,** 2.2 (January 1942): 3-12.
In which Professor Su Yeng captures American inventors in order to defeat U.S. plans to aid the Chinese government while The Shadow works to prevent him from succeeding.   Suggested by "The Devil-Master," **The Shadow,** September 15, 1941.

E.17. "The Masked Lady," [Walter B. Gibson]: Vernon Greene, **Shadow Comics,** 2.2 (January 1942): 25-34.

In which a lady in a mask wages a one-woman war against crooked gamblers and helps The Shadow catch a murderer. Suggested by "The Masked Lady," **The Shadow,** October 15, 1939.

E.18. "The Shadow versus Doctor Mocquino," [Walter B. Gibson], **Shadow Comics,** 2.2 (January 1942): 57-63.

In which the leader of a voodoo cult uses his powers in the city of New York and The Shadow needs a new way to become invisible. Suggested by "The Voodoo Master," **The Shadow,** March 1, 1936.

E.19. "The Shadow Protects His Country Against the Evil Plots of the Bund on the Ghost Fleet!" [Walter B. Gibson]: Vernon Greene, **Shadow Comics,** 2.3 (March 1942): 3-27.

In which Kurt Schorn returns to prevent a fleet of re-conditioned ships from delivering its vital cargo. (Reprints Shadow newspaper strips nos. D37-D72.)

E.20. "I Am Shiwan Khan the Golden Master!...And I Am The Shadow," [Walter B. Gibson]: Vernon Greene, **Shadow Comics,** 2.4 (May 1942): 3-23.

In which the oriental mastermind uses hypnotic power, establishes a base in New York to buy airplanes for his plot to rule the world from Asia. Suggested by "The Golden Master," **The Shadow,** September 15, 1939. (Reprints Shadow newspaper strips nos. E1-E84.)

E.21. "The Shadow and the Adventure of the Mayan Museum," [Walter B. Gibson]: William Smith, **Shadow Comics,** 2.4 (May 1942): 53-62.

In which Lamont Cranston traces the source of a series of murders to a New Orleans museum and an ancient cult. Suggested by "Xitli, God of Fire," **The Shadow,** December 1, 1940.

E.22. "The Shadow Fights The Ghost Faker," [Walter B. Gibson]: [Vernon Greene?], **Shadow Comics,** 2.5 (July 1942): 3-13.

In which a series of jewel robberies at the Summer colony of Lake Calada are solved through a seance interrupted by The Shadow. (Redrawn from Shadow newspaper strips nos. G37-G54.)

E.23. "The Shadow Unmasks a Fraud," [Walter B. Gibson]: Vernon Greene, **Shadow Comics,** 2.5 (July 1942): 51-64.

In which The Shadow saves the Darvin fortune from falling into the wrong hands and reveals the identity of another mastermind of crime. (Reprints Shadow newspaper strips nos. F1-F66.)

E.24. "The Shadow and the Ghosts of the Malden Manse," [Walter B. Gibson]: Jack Binder, **Shadow Comics,** 2.6 (September 1942): 3-10.

In which no one can inherit the mansion who cannot spend a night in the tower room and The Shadow has to find the key to a locked door. Introduces Skeet Harley, the young friend of Cranston and Margo, to the comic book. He also appears in the newspaper strip, see below.

E.25. "The Shadow Nips the Nipponese," [Walter B. Gibson]: Jack Binder, **Shadow Comics,** 2.6 (September 1942): 11-20. In which The Shadow stops the secret agents who try to halt the synthetic rubber industry. Includes Skeet Harley, Margo Lane, and Valda Rune.

E.26. "The Shadow Traps the Society Swindlers," [Walter B. Gibson]: Jack Binder, **Shadow Comics,** 2.6 (September 1942): 21-24.

In which Lamont Cranston plays Swami to help The Shadow catch the swindlers.

E.27. "The Shadow and the Two Gray Ghosts," [Walter B. Gibson]: Vernon Greene, **Shadow Comics,** 2.6 (September 1942): 52-62.

In which the Debrossler jewels are protected from the Gray Ghost by the invisible Shadow. Suggested by "The Gray Ghost," **The Shadow,** May 1, 1936. (Abridged from Shadow newspaper strips nos. GX1-GX24.)

E.28. "Blackstone World's Greatest Magician," [Walter B. Gibson], **Shadow Comics,** 2.6 (September 1942): 63-66.

In which Blackstone demonstrates a sword trick for Rhoda on the island of Salamba to advertise his latest adventure in **Super-Magician Comics.**

E.29. "The Shadow Snares the White Dragon," [Walter B. Gibson]: Vernon Greene, **Shadow Comics,** 2.7 (October 1942): 3-12.

In which The Shadow solves the mystery of the vanishing Chinese jewel thieves and unmasks a two-faced artist.

E.30.   "The Shadow Again Meets the Incredible Shiwan Khan," [Walter B. Gibson]: Jack Binder, **Shadow Comics**, 2.7 (October 1942): 13-20.
In which personality changes in some friends of Lamont Cranston lead The Shadow into the web spun by the Golden Master. Suggested by "Shiwan Khan Returns," **The Shadow**, December 1, 1939.

E.31.   "The Shadow: The Dead Return," [Walter B. Gibson]: Jack Binder, **Shadow Comics**, 2.7 (October 1942): 38-47.
In which the Master of Doom and the Master of Darkness meet to do battle in an abandoned graveyard. Possibly suggested by "The Master of Death," **The Shadow**, September 15, 1933.

E.32.   "A Plea," [Walter B. Gibson?], **Shadow Comics**, 2.7 (October 1942): 65-66.
In which it is explained how The Shadow gained "the ability to cloud men's minds so that, to all intents and purposes, he becomes invisible." (Text feature, not illustrated.)

E.33.   "The Shadow Saves the Game," [Walter B. Gibson?]: Jack Binder, **Shadow Comics**, 2.7 (October 1942): inside back cover.
Advertisement for the code department in **The Shadow Magazine**.

E.34.   "Horror House," [Walter B. Gibson], **Shadow Comics**, 2.8 (November 1942): 5-14.
In which The Shadow solves the mystery of the murdered inventors and the death-dealing python plant.

E.35.   "Giant's Garden," [Walter B. Gibson]: Jack Binder, **Shadow Comics**, 2.8 (November 1942): 15-22.
In which Margo and Skeet are trapped in a garden of giant flowers and The Shadow once again faces Shiwan Khan.

E.36.   "The Shadow: The Haunted Mill," [Walter B. Gibson]: Jack Binder, **Shadow Comics**, 2.8 (November 1942): 23-34. In which a band of counterfeiters with a base in the mountains is not clever enough to fool The Shadow.

E.37. "The Shadow and the Hand of Death," [Walter B. Gibson], **Shadow Comics**, 2.9 (December 1942): 3-12.

In which death threats are carried out by a giant skeleton hand until The Shadow locates the arm attached to it. Possibly suggested by "Fingers of Death," **The Shadow**, March 1, 1933.

E.38. "The Mystery of the Goona Goona Fan," [Walter B. Gibson]: Vernon Greene, **Shadow Comics**, 2.9 (December 1942): 21-28.

In which a murder is committed in a locked office and The Shadow finds a clue in the sound of an electric fan.

E.39. "The Shadow and the Chinese Torture Cage," [Walter B. Gibson]: Jack Binder, **Shadow Comics**, 2.9 (December 1942): 53-60.

In which Shiwan Khan obtains a stolen invention and tries to use it to capture The Shadow, but is stopped by modern science.

E.40. "The Shadow and the 'Silver Skull,'" [Walter B. Gibson]: Jack Binder, **Shadow Comics**, 2.10 (January 1943): 3-12.

In which wealthy men disappear or are found dead. Beside each dead man is found a small death token in the form of a silver skull. Suggested by "The Silver Skull," **The Shadow**, January 1, 1939.

E.41. "The Shadow and the Spotted Death," [Walter B. Gibson]: Jack Binder, **Shadow Comics**, 2.10 (January 1943): 21-28.

In which an ocelot appears to be the cause of many deaths in Westbury until The Shadow shows how a beast can change its spots.

E.42. "The Shadow Encounters 'Dr. Satani,'" [Walter B. Gibson]: Jack Binder, **Shadow Comics**, 2.10 (January 1943): 49-56.

In which The Shadow meets a man who has been dead for years, but kept alive by hypnotism. (Possibly suggested by Edgar Allan Poe's short story "The Facts in the Case of M. Valdemar.")

E.43. "The Shadow Solves 'The Museum Murders,'" [Walter B. Gibson?]: Jack Binder, **Shadow Comics**, 2.10 (January 1943): 61-62.

Advertisement for the January 1943 issue of **The Shadow Magazine**.

E.44. "The Shadow versus Devil Kyoti," [Walter B. Gibson]: Jack Binder, **Shadow Comics**, 2.11 (February 1943): 3-20.

In which The Shadow encounters a supernatural saboteur whose power comes from the flames and whose only weakness is a fear of ice. A text section, pp. 65-66, "Who is Devil Kyoti?" links him to Shintoism.

E.45. "For the First Time--The Shadow As He Appears on the Radio--Presented in the Comics," [Walter B. Gibson?], **Shadow Comics**, 2.11 (February 1943): 21-24.

An advertisement for The Shadow radio show when Bill Johnstone and Marjorie Anderson portrayed Lamont Cranston and Margo Lane.

E.46. "The Hand of The Shadow," [Walter B. Gibson]: Jack
Binder, **Shadow Comics**, 2.11 (February 1943): 57-64.

In which Shiwan Khan tries to steal the secrets of Titus Renfrew's experimental rocket.

E.47. "The Shadow and Devil Kyoti Returns," by Maxwell Grant [Walter B. Gibson]: Jack Binder, **Shadow Comics**, 2.12 (March 1943): 5-22.

In which the strange saboteur, agent of the Black Dragon, returns through the molten iron of a steel plant, but The Shadow gives him an even warmer reception.

E.48. "The Green Hoods," [Walter B. Gibson]: Vernon Greene, **Shadow Comics**, 2.12 (March 1943): 58-65.

In which a group known as The Green Hoods invites Lamont Cranston to join them as their 13th member, thus arousing The Shadow's suspicions about their motives. Suggested by "The Green Hoods," **The Shadow**, August 15, 1938.

E.49. "The Shadow: The Trail of Devil Kyoti," [Walter B. Gibson], **Shadow Comics**, 3.1 (April 1943): 5-22.

In which The Black Dragon sends Devil Kyoti to destroy Victory City on the Russian-Chinese border until The Shadow sends him back to Fujiyama.

E.50. "The Shadow in the Voodoo Trail," by Maxwell Grant [Walter B. Gibson]: Jack Binder, **Shadow Comics**, 3.1 (April 1943): 58-65.

In which wealthy New Yorkers vanish to become Dr. Mocquino's zombies until The Shadow breaks their trance. (Dr. Mocquino appears in the pulp novels as well.)

E.51. "The Shadow and The Black Ray," [Walter B. Gibson]: Vernon Greene. **Shadow Comics,** 3.2 (May 1943): 5-14.
In which Valda Rune goes undercover in a cat costume to learn more about Althor's invention to stifle gunfire. (Redrawn from Shadow newspaper strips nos. I-1 to I-48.)

E.52. "The Shadow Invades Tokyo to Meet Devil Kyoti!" [Walter B. Gibson], **Shadow Comics,** 3.2 (May 1943): 15-32.
In which the Shinto Wizards of The Black Dragon bind Devil Kyoti to a sacred mirror to force him to perform what has to be a suicide mission. (Part 1 of 2 parts.)

E.53. "The Shadow Meets Monstrodamus," by Maxwell Grant [Walter B. Gibson]: Jack Binder, **Shadow Comics,** 3.3 (June 1943): 5-20.
In which The Shadow uses his power of invisibility to conquer Monstrodamus, master of past and future, whose elixir of life renders him immune to death. Suggested by "The Devil Monsters," **The Shadow,** February 1, 1943.

E.54. "Crime Strikes The Shadow," by Maxwell Grant [Walter B. Gibson]: Jack Binder, **Shadow Comics,** 3.3 (June 1943): 21-28.
In which Dr. Zee's ultra-violet ray nullifies The Shadow's Powers of invisibility until an infra-red bulb casts a neutralizing beam.

E.55. "The Shadow Traps Devil Kyoti," by Maxwell Grant [Walter B. Gibson]: Jack Binder, **Shadow Comics,** 3.3 (June 1943): 51-58.
In which The Shadow imprisons Devil Kyoti in a glacier and the Japanese must accept the demon as only a frozen asset. (Part 2 of 2 parts.)

E.56. "The Shadow in Monstrodamus Returns," [Walter B. Gibson]: [Jack Binder?], **Shadow Comics,** 3.4 (July 1943): 4-21.
In which Monstrodamus restores a mummified Egyptian princess to life in his quest for power and riches.

E.57.   "The Shadow in Vampire Hall," by Maxwell
Grant [Walter B. Gibson]: Jack Binder, **Shadow
Comics,** 3.4 (July 1943): 23-30.
   In which the heir to the Halldrew fortune
spends the night in the haunted mansion and puts
the family vampire to rest. Gibson names his
vampire for the character in the old Gothic tale,
Varney the Vampire.   (Suggested by "The Vampire
Murders," **The Shadow,** September 1, 1942.)

E.58.   "The Shadow and The Crime Wizard," [Walter
B. Gibson]: Al Bare, **Shadow Comics,** 3.4 (July
1943): 58-65.
   In which The Shadow is stopped by The Crime
Wizard's "hypnograph" until Valda Rune's color
blindness proves an adequate defense.

E.59.   "The Shadow Again Meets Monstrodamus in
Treasure Bay," by Maxwell Grant [Walter B. Gibson]:
Jack Binder, **Shadow Comics,** 3.5 (August 1943):
5-20.
   In which Monstrodamus manufactures gold to buy
monsters from the past with which to shape the
future. (Introduces Mojo, the giant mole.)

E.60.   "The Shadow at Ghost Manor," [Walter B.
Gibson]: Al Bare, **Shadow Comics,** 3.5 (August 1943):
21-30.
   In which Skeet and Valda search for the loot
of Dorthon in his old headquarters and encounter a
live ghost.

E.61.   "The Shadow Meets the Spy Master," [Walter
B. Gibson]: Al Bare, **Shadow Comics,** 3.5 (August
1943): 58-65.
   In which The Shadow is trapped by Loxol, the
spymaster, and is rescued by Valda, Skeet, and
Margo.

E.62.   "The Shadow Encounters Monstrodamus and His
Devils of the Deep," [Walter B. Gibson]: [Jack
Binder?], **Shadow Comics,** 3.6 (September 1943):
5-20.
   In which Monstrodamus hatches a dinosaur and
The Shadow has to battle with an octopus to prove
the threat from the master of the past is a real
one.

E.63. "The Shadow: The Crime Wizard Returns,"
[Walter B. Gibson]: [Charles Coll?], **Shadow Comics**,
3.6 (September 1943): 21-28.
    In which The Crime Wizard uses his
"hypnograph" to escape from prison and attempts to
wreck the fast freight carrying war materials.

E.64. "The Shadow in Terror Inn," by Maxwell Grant
[Walter B. Gibson], **Shadow Comics**, 3.6 (September
1943): 57-66.
    In which people who visit Vacation Inn
disappear and The Shadow, Margo, Skeet, and Valda
find a familiar face behind the whiskers of the
proprietor.

E.65. "The Shadow Encounters Monstrodamus and His
Flying Serpents," [Walter B. Gibson]: W. Dar,
Shadow Comics, 3.7 (October 1943): 5-20.
    In which Monstrodamus finds an antidote for
Princess Theba's boredom, sends winged serpents on
a mission of destruction, but forgets some of the
most important parts of the legend of the sacred
Ibis.

E.66. "The Shadow Finds Too Many Ghosts," [Walter
B. Gibson]: Al Bare, **Shadow Comics**, 3.7 (October
1943): 21-30.
    In which Lamont Cranston is asked to coax old
man Keene out of his beloved haunted house while
The Shadow unmasks a crooked swami.

E.67. "The Shadow Versus The Money Master," by
Maxwell Grant [Walter B. Gibson]: Charles Coll,
Shadow Comics, 3.7 (October 1943): 55-62.
    In which Eric Zorva controls enough wealth to
make his own currency good, but lets the gold go to
his head until he is brought to earth by The
Shadow.   Suggested by "The Money Master," **The
Shadow**, December 15, 1942.

E.68. "The Shadow Encounters Monstrodamus and His
Creatures of Fable," by Maxwell Grant [Walter B.
Gibson]: Charles Coll, **Shadow Comics**, 3.8 (November
1943): 4-19.
    In which The Shadow and Jerry Craig use the
Umbrette (also known as a Shadow Bird) against the
Gryphon, Cockatrice, Dragon, and Wyvern of
Monstrodamus, until the Sphinx of Princess Theba
turns all the creatures to stone.

E.69.   "The Shadow Defies the Monster of Murder Mansion," by Maxwell Grant [Walter B. Gibson]: Charles Coll, **Shadow Comics**, 3.8 (November 1943): 21-30.
In which each member of the Granmore family elects to sleep in the mansion in the hope that the ghost will reveal where the family wealth is buried and The Shadow discovers the secret of the sealed room.   Suggested by "Murder Mansion," **The Shadow**, December 1, 1941.

E.70.   "The Shadow Defeats Thor, King of Thunder," [Walter B. Gibson], **Shadow Comics**, 3.8 (November 1943): 59-66.
In which Blaine Thordon's artificial lightning machine is turned against him when he tries to use it on The Shadow.   Suggested by "The Thunder King," **The Shadow**, June 15, 1941.

E.71.   "The Shadow and Monstrodamus Seek the 'Pearls of Cleopatra,'" by Maxwell Grant [Walter B. Gibson]: Charles Coll, **Shadow Comics**, 3.9 (December 1943): 3-18.   In which Monstrodamus seeks to replenish his supply of the elixir of life and Princess Theba once again animates the Sphinx.

E.72.   "The Shadow at Murder Circus," [Walter B. Gibson]: Al Bare, **Shadow Comics**, 3.9 (December 1943): 19-28.
In which The Shadow solves the mystery of the murdered circus owner by unmasking an imposter.

E.73.   "The Shadow Invades the Stolen Light House!" by Maxwell Grant [Walter B. Gibson]: Charles Coll, **Shadow Comics**, 3.9 (December 1943): 51-58.
In which Japanese invaders plan to use an abandoned light house to guide their submarines to the American coast.

E.74.   "The Shadow and Monstrodamus Learn the Riddle of the Sphinx," by Maxwell Grant [Walter B. Gibson]: Charles Coll, **Shadow Comics**, 3.10 (January 1944): 3-16.
In which Monstrodamus revives the ancient Egyptian gods in his battle with The Shadow and Princess Theba returns to her past.   (Last of the Monstrodamus series.)

E.75. "The Shadow: Red Mask," [Walter B. Gibson]: Al Bare, **Shadow Comics,** 3.10 (January 1944): 17-26.
In which a robber at a costume party is unmasked by The Shadow.

E.76. "The Seven Shadows," Maxwell Grant [Walter B. Gibson]: Charles Coll, **Shadow Comics,** 3.10 (January 1944): 51-58.
In which Professor Remic's "Shadow projector" proves confusing to both police and crooks until Lamont Cranston takes control of the switch.

E.77. "The Shadow Meets the Death Master," [Walter B. Gibson]: [Charles Coll], **Shadow Comics,** 3.11 (February 1944): 3-16.
In which Thade, whose very name spells death, uses living skeletons as weapons of murder until he is stopped by The Shadow's science. Suggested by "The Master of Death," The Shadow, September 15, 1933.

E.78. "The Shadow Solves the Riddle of Seven Towers," [Walter B. Gibson]: [Charles Coll], **Shadow Comics,** 3.11 (February 1944): 49-56.
In which members of the Arlington family disappear, then are found murdered, and The Shadow discovers the mystery of the extra room.

E.79. "The Shadow in 'Double or Nothing,'" [Walter B. Gibson]: [Charles Coll], **Shadow Comics,** 3.11 (February 1944): 49-56.
In which The Shadow rolls dice with a killer and finds the missing Carlisle rubies.

E.80. "The Shadow and the Valley of Sleep," by Maxwell Grant [Walter B. Gibson]: Charles Coll, **Shadow Comics,** 3.12 (March 1944): 3-16.
In which Thade steals Professor Marland's tornado-breaker, but The Shadow steals his thunder.

E.81. "The Shadow Faces Death by Degrees," [Walter B. Gibson]: [Charles Coll?], **Shadow Comics,** 3.12 (March 1944): 17-26.
In which The Shadow solves the murders at the logging camp and puts some killers on ice.

E.82. "The Shadow: Calling Nick Carter," [Walter B. Gibson]: [Charles Coll?], **Shadow Comics,** 3.12 (March 1944): 51-58.

In which Nick Carter is hired to find the criminal named Vox, but needs The Shadow's help to reveal his identity. Suggested by "The Voice," **The Shadow**, November 1, 1938.

E.83.   "The Shadow Encounters the Ghost Machine," by Maxwell Grant [Walter B. Gibson]: [Charles Coll], **Shadow Comics**, 4.1 (April 1944): 3-14.
In which Thade invents a three-dimensional projector and The Shadow makes the ghost go west.

E.84.   "The Four Porcelain Dragons," [Walter B. Gibson]: [Charles Coll], **Shadow Comics**, 4.1 (April 1944): 15-24.
In which a porcelain dragon gains a new value and The Shadow teaches a collector an impressive lesson.

E.85.   "The Shadow and the Riddle of the Astral Bells," by Maxwell Grant [Walter B. Gibson]: Charles Coll, **Shadow Comics**, 4.1 (April 1944): 49-56.
In which bells which no one but Gilbert Gately can hear are a clue to a criminal plot.

E.86.   "The Shadow Meets the 'Brain of Nippon,'" by Maxwell Grant [Walter B. Gibson]: Charles Coll, **Shadow Comics**, 4.2 (May 1944): 3-16.
In which the bodiless, but living, head of a warlord, killed two centuries ago, seeks to rule the world.

E.87.   "The Shadow in the Museum Mystery," [Walter B. Gibson]: Al Bare, **Shadow Comics**, 4.2 (May 1944): 17-26.
In which a murder in an Egyptian museum leads to the discovery of a fortune in jewels. Suggested by "The Museum Murders," **The Shadow**, January 1, 1943.

E.88.   "The Shadow Again Meets The Terrible Three," [Walter B. Gibson]: [Charles Coll], **Shadow Comics**, 4.2 (May 1944): 51-58.
In which the murderer is described by a witness as a pair of white spiders and The Shadow knows he must deal once again with Thade, Adrem, and Durrem.

E.89. "The Shadow Seeks Solarus, the Space Master," by Maxwell Grant [Walter B. Gibson]: Charles Coll, **Shadow Comics,** 4.3 (June 1944): 3-16.
    In which a mad scientist shrinks Margo, Valda, and himself and sends them by rocket to the planet Venus. (Part 1 of 3 parts.)

E.90. "The Shadow: Seven Drops of Blood," [Walter B. Gibson]: Al Bare, **Shadow Comics,** 4.3 (June 1944): 17-26.
    In which Lamont Cranston demonstrates how a man can be killed by an experiment with a knife, an apple, and a bottle of ink. Suggested by "The Seven Drops of Blood," **The Shadow,** December 1, 1936.

E.91. "The Shadow Meets the Green Ghoul and the Red Roamer," [Walter B. Gibson], **Shadow Comics,** 4.3 (June 1944): 51-58.
    In which The Shadow demonstrates how two men can be in one place at the same time, yet not appear to be together.

E.92. "The Shadow Again Meets Solarus on the Planet Venus," by Maxwell Grant [Walter B. Gibson]: Charles Coll, **Shadow Comics,** 4.4 (July 1944): 3-16.
    In which The Shadow follows Solarus to Venus and saves his friends from the Venusians who seem glad to be rid of them. (The Venusians refer to Earth as Mars since the name means "war" and war rules on Earth.) (Part 2 of 3.)

E.93. "The Shadow Baffles Berlin," [Walter B. Gibson]: [Charles Coll], **Shadow Comics,** 4.4 (July 1944): 25-34.
    In which the image of a man in cloak and slouch hat is used in Berlin as a symbol of the underground resistance.

E.94. "The Shadow Brings Terror to Tokio," [Walter B. Gibson]: [Charles Coll], **Shadow Comics,** 4.5 (August 1944): 3-16.
    In which The Shadow uses his own mirror image to help the Japanese underground resistance group known as the Kura.

E.95. "The Shadow and the Coils of The Python," [Walter B. Gibson]: [Charles Coll], **Shadow Comics,** 4.5 (August 1944): 51-58.

In which The Python traps The Shadow at the bottom of the sea until a knowledge of natural forces turns the tide against the criminals. Suggested by "The Python," **The Shadow**, November 15, 1935.

E.96.   "The Shadow and the Vanishing Prisoners," [Walter B. Gibson]: [Charles Coll], **Shadow Comics**, 4.6 (September 1944): 3-16.
In which The Shadow frees prisoners of the Japanese by application of a mathematical illusion and comes to the aid of the Kura again.   (More of a dramatization of a classic illusion than story.)

E.97.   "The Shadow Meets The Tarantula," [Walter B. Gibson]: [Charles Coll], **Shadow Comics**, 4.6 (September 1944): 51-58.
In which The Shadow solves the mystery of the destruction to the airliners and captures a human spider who spins a web of alloy.

E.98.   "The Shadow Finds the Crypt of the Seven Skulls," [Walter B. Gibson]: [Charles Coll], **Shadow Comics**, 4.7 (October 1944): 3-16.
In which the dead try to preserve the secret of Hogart Hall until The Shadow proves that one against seven are better odds than might be imagined.

E.99.   "The Shadow: Solarus Returns," [Walter B. Gibson]: [Charles Coll], **Shadow Comics**, 4.7 (October 1944): 51-58.
In which the men Solarus sent to Venus in part one return to Earth to help The Shadow stop a bank robbery.   (Part 3 of 3 parts.)

E.100.   "The Shadow Smashes Murderer's Row," [Walter B. Gibson]: [Charles Coll], **Shadow Comics**, 4.8 (November 1944): 3-16.
In which Lamont Cranston's deductions save a friend from being a murder suspect, allowing The Shadow to capture the Indigo Mob.

E.101.   "The Shadow Visits The House in the Marsh," by Maxwell Grant [Walter B. Gibson]: Hoae, **Shadow Comics**, 4.8 (November 1944): 51-58.
In which the ghosts of Kenbury are laid to rest by The Shadow.   (Artist's signature nearly unreadable.)

E.102. "The Shadow and the Haunted Glen," [Walter B. Gibson]: [Charles Coll], **Shadow Comics,** 4.9 (December 1944): 3-14.
    In which a friend of Lamont Cranston's is accused of murder and The Shadow must unmask a ghost to prove him innocent.

E.103. "The Shadow Meets the Mad Inventor," by Maxwell Grant [Walter B. Gibson]: Hoae, **Shadow Comics,** 4.9 (December 1944): 43-50.
    In which a new super explosive is demonstrated by its inventor, but The Shadow discovers a deception.

E.104. "The Shadow Conquers The Hydra," [Walter B. Gibson]: [Charles Coll], **Shadow Comics,** 4.10 (January 1945): 3-16.
    In which an organization of master criminals doubles its members whenever one is destroyed. Suggested by "The Hydra," **The Shadow,** December 1, 1942.

E.105. "The Shadow and The Riddle of the 'Hanging Skeleton'," [Walter B. Gibson]: [Charles Coll], **Shadow Comics,** 4.10 (January 1945): 43-50.
    In which the missing Homer Craxton returns to unlock a door that has not been opened for twenty years and The Shadow literally finds a skeleton in a closet.

E.106. "The Shadow Meets The Seven Sinners," [Walter B. Gibson]: [Charles Coll], **Shadow Comics,** 4.11 (February 1945): 3-16.
    In which seven paintings by Jeno Caldore are stolen yet not removed from the premises.

E.107. "The Shadow Visits...The Haunted Island," [Walter B. Gibson]: [Charles Coll], **Shadow Comics,** 4.11 (February 1945): 43-52.
    In which the ghost of Tom Harbelow haunts Holiday Island until The Shadow proves that the ghost is solid, if not real.

E.108. "The Shadow Invades The Castle of Death," [Walter B. Gibson]: [Charles Coll], **Shadow Comics,** 4.12 (March 1945): 3-16.
    In which the stakes are high and deadly on the roulette wheel of Maitre Lamorte until The Shadow changes the odds.

E.109.   "The Shadow Battles the Robot Master,"
[Walter B. Gibson]: [Charles Coll], **Shadow Comics,**
4.12 (March 1945): 39-48.
In which a music box tune is the key to the
control of a giant robot created for crime.

E.110.   "The Shadow and the Coins of Feng Huang,"
[Walter B. Gibson]: [Charles Coll], **Shadow Comics,**
5.1 (April 1945): 3-16.
In which a blackmail scheme proves to be a
cover-up for another plot entirely and some Chinese
laundry tickets take on a new significance. (The
message of the laundry tickets was suggested by
"The Chinese Disks," **The Shadow,** November 1, 1934.)

E.111.   "The Shadow Solves The Hampshire Horror,"
[Walter B. Gibson]: [Charles Coll], **Shadow Comics,**
5.1 (April 1945): 43-50.
In which the ghost of the mansion is summoned
to prove the heir to the estate is not a vampire.

E.112.   "The Shadow and the Bells of Doom," [Walter
B. Gibson]: Charles Coll, **Shadow Comics,** 5.2 (May
1945): 3-16.
In which the bells in a haunted tower predict
death and a murderer cannot even hang himself with
his own rope. Suggested by "The Bells of Doom,"
The Shadow, March 15, 1935.

E.113.   "The Shadow Finds 'The Pink Lady,'" [Walter
B. Gibson]: Charles Coll, **Shadow Comics,** 5.2 (May
1945): 43-50.
In which the person responsible for half a
dozen robberies cannot be identified by even the
most competent of police observers until Lamont
Cranston proves retired officer Riley's color
blindness is an asset.

E.114.   "The Shadow Invades The Circle of Death,"
[Walter B. Gibson]: [Charles Coll], **Shadow Comics,**
5.3 (June 1945): 3-16.
In which a series of "accidents" in a certain
section of the city are proved by Lamont Cranston
to be murders.

E.115.   "The Shadow and The Crystal Skull," [Walter
B. Gibson]: [Charles Coll], **Shadow Comics,** 5.4
(July 1945): 3-16.
In which the murder victims are found, each
clutching a tiny crystal skull, the token of a

secret group. Suggested by "The Crystal Skull,"
The Shadow, January 1944.

E.116. "The Shadow Invades The Tower of Death,"
[Walter B. Gibson], **Shadow Comics,** 5.4 (July 1945):
43-50.
     In which the signals mean piracy until The
Shadow cracks the code.

E.117. "The Shadow Meets Damon the Nomad and His
Unseen Horrors!!!" [Walter B. Gibson], **Shadow
Comics,** 5.5 (August 1945): 3-16.
     In which Damon, the Nomad, proves master of
the life symbol, the Monad, and harnesses the
lightning to create invisible monsters. (Gibson's
love of anagrams is evident here.)

E.118. "The Shadow Fights Piracy Among the Golden
Isles," [Walter B. Gibson]: Charles Coll, **Shadow
Comics,** 5.6 (September 1945): 3-16.
     In which modern pirates prey on the yachting
crowd in the swamp lands until The Shadow makes
Blackbeard himself walk the plank.

E.119. "The Shadow Encounters The Death Master's
Vengeance," [Walter B. Gibson]: Charles Coll,
Shadow Comics, 5.6 (September 1945): 43-50.
     In which Maitre Lamorte, the Death Master,
sets a trap for The Shadow using Margo Lane as
bait, but finds his castle has not been built on as
solid a rock as he had thought.

E.120. "The Shadow Visits The Crime Museum,"
[Walter B. Gibson]: [Charles Coll], **Shadow Comics,**
5.7 (October 1945): 3-16.
     In which Professor Malbona's museum of the
history of crime attracts a new master criminal
known as The Talon.

E.121. "The Shadow Finds The Talon," [Walter B.
Gibson]: [Charles Coll], **Shadow Comics,** 5.8
(November 1945): 3-16.
     In which The Hag leaves the employ of
Professor Malbona to join The Talon when he steals
not one, but an entire collection of valuable
paintings.

E.122. "The Shadow Meets The Wodahs," [Walter B.
Gibson]: [Charles Coll], **Shadow Comics,** 5.8
(November 1945): 43-50.

In which ghostly figures scare people from a mansion built directly on the state line until The Shadow realizes the name they call themselves is his own spelled backwards.

E.123. "The Shadow Takes Up the Trail of the Talon," [Walter B. Gibson]: [Charles Coll], **Shadow Comics,** 5.9 (December 1945): 3-16.
In which The Talon and The Hag steal Simon Solo's super-explosive, Blexine, in their pursuit of the wealth of the world.

E.124. "The Shadow and the 'Hands of Doom,'"[Walter B. Gibson]: [Charles Coll], **Shadow Comics,** 5.9 (December 1945): 43-50.
In which the path to Hiram Maytree's wealth means learning who or what or where "Clujin" may be.

E.125. "The Shadow Meets The Crime Master," [Walter B. Gibson]: Charles Coll, **Shadow Comics,** 5.10 (January 1946): 3-16.
In which a master criminal plays a deadly game of chess with human lives until The Shadow can checkmate his game. Suggested by "The Crime Master", **The Shadow,** August 1, 1934.

E.126. "The Shadow Uncovers the Invisible Killer, " [Walter B. Gibson]: [Charles Coll], **Shadow Comics,** 5.10 (January 1946): 43-50.
In which unseen hands from nowhere strangle victims on the street until The Shadow finds that the size of their neckwear is the clue to the mystery.

E.127. "The Shadow Defies the Clutch of The Talon," [Walter B. Gibson]: [Charles Coll], **Shadow Comics,** 5.11 (February 1946): 3-16.
In which The Talon and The Hag enlarge their circle of crime and try to rid the world of The Shadow.

E.128. "The Shadow Meets the Black Swami," [Walter B. Gibson]: [Charles Coll], **Shadow Comics,** 5.12 (March 1946): 3-10.
In which Lamont Cranston demonstrates the use of a black blotter for recording messages and signatures in a blackmail scheme and The Shadow Rescues Margo from the Swami's throne.

E.129. "The Shadow: Trapped by The Talon," [Walter B. Gibson]: [Charles Coll], **Shadow Comics,** 5.12 (March 1946): 43-50.
In which The Talon tries to capture The Shadow in Professor Koma's compression chamber.

E.130. "The Shadow Meets Double Z," Maxwell Grant [Walter B. Gibson]: Charles Coll, **Shadow Comics,** 6.1 (April 1946): 3-10.
In which a series of bombings are believed to be the work of a hooded criminal who leaves the sign of the double "Z" at his crimes. Suggested by "Double Z," **The Shadow,** June 1932.

E.131. "The Shadow and the Message of Death," [Walter B. Gibson]: [Charles Coll], **Shadow Comics,** 6.1 (April 1946): 19-26.
In which an inventor's canary is not affected by the gas which kills its master.

E.132. "The Shadow Solves the Riddle of Professor Mentalo," [Walter B. Gibson]: [Charles Coll], **Shadow Comics,** 6.2 (May 1946): 3-10.
In which a mentalist leaves town too suddenly and Lamont Cranston goes into the stock broker business to find a match for the serial numbers on a series of ten dollar bills.

E.133. "The Shadow Foils The Talon's Trap," [Walter B. Gibson]: [Charles Coll], **Shadow Comics,** 6.2 (May 1946): 23-30.
In which Margo falls into the trap set by The Talon and The Hag and The Shadow saves her with the help of Pietro, his hurdy gurdy, and his monkey.

E.134. "The Shadow--Convicts Judge Lawless," [Walter B. Gibson]: [Charles Coll], **Shadow Comics,** 6.3 (June 1946): 3-10.
In which The Shadow's justice prevails over Judge Lawless's court of injustice to save the Marmaduke treasure. Suggested by "Judge Lawless," **The Shadow,** August 15, 1942.

E.135. "The Shadow Fights Crime at Thunder Lake," [Walter B. Gibson]: [Charles Coll], **Shadow Comics,** 6.3 (June 1946): 29-36.
In which Lamont Cranston's nautical knowledge proves time-saving in a race to stop the masked marauders at Lakeview Lodge.

E.136.   "The Shadow Sees...'Death in the Crystal,'"
[Walter B. Gibson]: [Charles Coll], **Shadow Comics,**
6.4 (July 1946): 3-10.
   In which Doctor Zenith predicts future events
and arranges for them to come true.   The title
suggests a connection to the story in **The Shadow,**
August 1944, but this may be only coincidental.

E.137.   "The Shadow Meets The Blur," [Walter B.
Gibson]: [Charles Coll], **Shadow Comics,** 6.4 (July
1946): 17-24.
   In which a burglar whose features are a blur
can be stopped only by The Shadow whose features
are invisible.   Suggested by "The Blur," **The
Shadow,** July 15, 1941.

E.138.   "The Shadow Sets a Trap for Crime," [Walter
B. Gibson], **Shadow Comics,** 6.4 (July 1946): 43-50.
   In which an old Spanish treasure baits a trap
for some modern crooks.

E.139.   "The Shadow Uncovers The Harlequin,"
[Walter B. Gibson]: [Charles Coll], **Shadow Comics,**
6.5 (August 1946): 3-10.
   In which The Shadow solves a carnival mystery
by a trick with mirrors.   Suggested by "The Freak
Show Murders," **The Shadow,** May 1944.

E.140.   "The Shadow Battles The Cloudmaster,"
[Walter B. Gibson]: [Charles Coll], **Shadow Comics,**
6.5 (August 1946): 12-19.
   In which a gang of crooks specializes in
looting skyscrapers until The Shadow demonstrates
how fog can cover a trail of crime.

E.141.   "The Shadow Investigates Midnight Murder,"
[Walter B. Gibson], **Shadow Comics,** 6.5 (August
1946): 42-49.
   In which the heirs to the Kirkland estate
discover how dangerous it is to turn twenty-one at
midnight.

E.142.   "The Shadow Invades the Crucible of Death
to Conquer Crime," [Walter B. Gibson]: [Charles
Coll], **Shadow Comics,** 6.6 (September 1946): 3-16.
   In which The Shadow guesses the riddle of
Professor Seba who wants to become the master of
the future by controlling the volcanic island of
Ovoxovo. (The name is a palindrome.)

E.143. "The Shadow Jolts Landlubber's Haven, The Ship That Stays on Shore," [Walter B. Gibson]: [Charles Coll?], **Shadow Comics**, 6.6 (September 1946): 43-50.

In which The Shadow rounds up the smugglers who operate just out of range of the authorities from their seashore resort rendezvous.

E.144. "The Shadow Conquers Crime in Centralba," [Walter B. Gibson]: [Charles Coll], **Shadow Comics**, 6.7 (October 1946): 3-16.

In which The Shadow arranges an honest election in a central American country. Possibly suggested by "Dictator of Crime," **The Shadow**, October 15, 1941.

E.145. "The Shadow Battles Crime Among the Aztecs," [Walter B. Gibson]: [Charles Coll], **Shadow Comics**. 6.8 (November 1946): 3-16.

In which The Shadow finds war criminals who use an ancient Aztec city, Zentoma, as a refuge from justice. Possibly suggested by "Quetzal," **The Shadow**, February 15, 1937.

E.146. "The Shadow Follows The Talon Along the Trail of Gold," [Walter B. Gibson]: [Charles Coll], **Shadow Comics**, 6.8 (November 1946): 43-50.

In which a treasure in gold coins proves to be the undoing of The Shadow's old foes, The Talon and The Hag. (Stylistic evidence of two artists' work on this story, perhaps begun by Coll, but finished by someone else.) Interviews with Gibson suggest this was his last regular script contributed to the series.

E.147. "The Shadow Solves the Riddle of the Black Pagoda," [Walter B. Gibson]: [Charles Coll?], **Shadow Comics**, 6.11 (February 1947): 3-16.

In which The Shadow frees a post-war Tibet from the power of a would-be dictator. (Internal evidence suggests this and the following two stories were in Gibson's inventory when he quit writing the series.)

E.148. "The Shadow Cracks the Riddle of The Yellow Band," [Walter B. Gibson]: [Charles Coll], **Shadow Comics**, 7.1 (April 1947): 3-16.

In which the correct definition for "yellow band" is a clue to an international mystery.

Suggested by "The Yellow Band," **The Shadow,** August 15, 1937.

E.149. "The Shadow Proves That Dead Men Live," [Walter B. Gibson]: [Charles Coll], **Shadow Comics,** 7.2 (May 1947): 3-16.
    In which crooks who think they have escaped the law live to pay the penalty they deserve. Suggested by "Dead Men Live," **The Shadow,** November 15, 1932.

Super-Magic Comics

The character of Harry Blackstone was used by Gibson to promote the real magician's stage show. Copies of his comic book adventures were given out at performances. While it is recorded that he did not have an assistant whose name was Rhoda, followers of his fictional career would never have believed it.

E.150. "Blackstone the Magician and the Thugees of Kali," [Walter B. Gibson], **Super-Magic Comics,** 1.1 (May 1941): 4-40.
    In search of the secret of the hindu rope trick, Blackstone becomes involved in a matter of international intrigue and rescues an American damsel in distress.

E.151. "A Personal Message from Blackstone the Magician: [Walter B. Gibson], **Super-Magic Comics,** 1.1 (May 1941): 41-47.
    Elementary magic tricks explained and illustrated with some backstage talk by Blackstone. This feature appeared under various titles in each issue of the comic. Subsequent installments will not be entered individually below. With the next issue, **Super-Magic Comics** changed its title to **Super-Magician Comics.**

Super-Magician Comics

E.152. "Blackstone the Magician Matches Black Magic with the Wild Tribes of Africa," [Walter B. Gibson], **Super-Magician Comics,** 1.2 (September 1941): 4-42.
    On a successful engagement to South Africa, Blackstone is hired to find Professor Cedric Trent.

Only a magician can get past the witch doctor who
stands in their way.

E.153. "Blackstone the Magician: [His Egyptian
Adventure]," [Walter B. Gibson]: Jack Binder,
Super-Magician Comics, 1.3 (December 1941): 4-40.
    In which Blackstone visits Egypt to learn the
secret of Mokanna, the veiled prophet, and put an
end to his cult. See also "The Veiled Prophet,"
The Shadow, March 15, 1940.

E.154. "Blackstone the Magician Matches Magic with
Quetzal the Mayan Master," [Walter B. Gibson]: Jack
Binder, **Super-Magician Comics,** 1.4 (March 1942):
6-38.
    In which Blackstone finds a lost civilization
in Yucatan and prevents a new Mexican revolution.

E.155. "Blackstone and the Penang Rubies," [Walter
B. Gibson]: Jack Binder, **Super-Magician Comics,** 1.5
(May 1942): 6-36.
    In which Blackstone goes into the interior of
Malaya to seek the answer to the riddle of the
rubies which are used as payment for stolen
munitions. Introduces Blackstone's assistant and
girl Friday, Rhoda Brent, whom he finds in Malaya.

E.156. "Blackstone Meets the Shinto Wizards,"
[Walter B. Gibson], **Super-Magician Comics,** 1.6
(July 1942): 3-36.
    In which the magician and Rhoda use magic to
help the military governor of the island of Tongu
outwit an ancient Japanese cult.

E.157. "Blackstone Among the Head Hunters,"
[Walter B. Gibson]: Jack Binder, **Super-Magician
Comics,** 1.7 (September 1942): 3-36.
    In which Blackstone and Rhoda use the headless
lady illusion to discourage the custom of head
hunting on the island of Salamba.

E.158. "Blackstone Fights the Voodoo Hoodoos,"
[Walter B. Gibson]: Jack Binder, **Super-Magician
Comics,** 1.8 (November 1942): 3-36.
    In which the magician overthrows the voodoo
king of Tortilla and makes the island safe as a
military base.

E.159. "Blackstone: [His Panama Adventures]," [Walter B. Gibson]: Jack Binder, **Super-Magician Comics,** 1.9 (January 1943): 3-36.

In which Rhoda plays sun-goddess among the Jibaros while Blackstone searches for the lost expeditions along the Amazon and halts the cataract of the Ijinoco in mid-flow!

E.160. "Blackstone Matches Magic with the Pirates of the Sargasso Sea," [Walter B. Gibson]: Jack Binder, **Super-Magician Comics,** 1.10 (February 1943): 3-36.

In which Blackstone carries secret papers past enemy submarines while Rhoda becomes a mermaid to tempt a pirate crew.

E.161. "Blackstone Conquers the Fire Wizards," [Walter B. Gibson]: Jack Binder, **Super-Magician Comics,** 1.11 (March 1943): 5-37.

In which Blackstone and Rhoda travel to the Middle East to present some fire tricks and secure a contract for the U.S. for the oil deposits there.

E.162. "Blackstone at Baalbek," [Walter B. Gibson]: Jack Binder, **Super-Magician Comics,** 1.12 (April 1943): 5-37.   In the Middle East, Blackstone and Rhoda divert the plans for conquest of Arabia by Nazi plotters. (Artistic rendition of Blackstone is very realistic; he resembles the real magician more accurately than in previous issues.)

E.163. "Blackstone: The White Lama," [Walter B. Gibson], **Super-Magician Comics,** 2.1 (May 1943): 5-37.

In which Blackstone and Rhoda go to the Himalayas to combat the Axis wizards for the secret of the White Lama's mental power.

E.164. "The Shadow and the Masked Headsman," [Walter B. Gibson?]: Jack Binder, **Super-Magician Comics,** 2.1 (May 1943): 56-65.

In which Verdugo, the masked headsman, seeks a treasure by killing off everyone who may be its keeper. (Uncertain this is Gibson's work, but included for the record.)

E.165. "Blackstone in the Adventure of 'the Jade Idol,'" by Maxwell Grant [Walter B. Gibson]: Jack Binder, **Super-Magician Comics,** 2.2 (June 1943): 5-38.

In which Blackstone, disguised as a Chinese
magician, and Rhoda, disguised as a jade idol,
expose a Japanese stronghold along the Great Wall
of China.

E.166.   "Blackstone on Skull Island," by Maxwell
Grant   [Walter   B.   Gibson]:   Jack   Binder,
Super-Magician Comics, 2.3 (July 1943): 5-38, 61.
In which a duel of magic saves Blackstone's
head and traps a Japanese magician.

E.167.   "Blackstone   on   Incredible   Island,"   by
Maxwell Grant [Walter B. Gibson]: Jack Binder,
Super-Magician Comics, 2.4 (August 1943): 5-38.
In which Blackstone's magic helps him defeat
the cannibals and save the missing explorers on the
floating island.

E.168.   "Blackstone Discovers the Lost Land of
Lemuria,"   [Walter   B.   Gibson],   **Super-Magician
Comics,** 2.5 (September 1943): 5-38.
In which the floating island washes up on the
shores of Lemuria and Blackstone must animate some
of the island's fabulous statues before he and
Rhoda are rescued by a passing ship.

E.169.   "Blackstone Finds the Treasure of Golden
Valley,"   [Walter   B.   Gibson]:   James   Hammon,
Super-Magician Comics, 2.6 (October 1943): 5-38.
In which Blackstone discovers Incas in the
Antarctic and defeats Death Carver and his crew in
their search for gold.

E.170.   "Blackstone Discovers the Greatest of All
Spanish   Treasure,"   [Walter   B.   Gibson]:   James
Hammon, **Super-Magician Comics,** 2.7 (November 1943):
3-30.
In   which   Blackstone   sets   ancient   pirates
against modern ones in the quest for the treasure
of Bobadilla and the fountain of youth.

E.171.   "Blackstone Among the Marabouts," [Walter
B. Gibson]: James Hammon, **Super-Magician Comics,**
2.8 (December 1943): 3-18.
In which Blackstone meets the challenge of the
Marabouts with some "flashy" magic.

E.172.   "Blackstone Meets the Algerian Assassins,"
[Walter B. Gibson]: [James Hammon], **Super-Magician
Comics,** 2.8 (December 1943): 45-54.

In which being an escape artist helps
Blackstone save his own life and ends the reign of
terror of Sidi Sadu.

E.173.   "Blackstone: 'Sahara Trail,'" [Walter B.
Gibson]: [James Hammon], **Super-Magician Comics**, 2.9
(January 1944): 3-16.
In which Blackstone vanishes a camel and
defeats Annu Ated's plans for a desert rebellion.

E.174.   "Blackstone and the Wizards of
Kilimanjaro," [Walter B. Gibson]: James Hammon,
Super-Magician Comics, 2.9 (January 1944): 17-26.
In which Blackstone discovers a lost city in
the crater of an extinct volcano in Africa and
unmasks the wizards to stop an Axis plot.

E.175.   "Blackstone Does White Magic," [Walter B.
Gibson]: James Hammon, **Super-Magician Comics**, 2.9
(January 1944): 49-56.
In which Blackstone's magic defeats the Oolgi
and restores the rightful leaders to the Eskimos.

E.176.   "Blackstone Foils the Fakirs of Foolu,"
[Walter B. Gibson]: [James Hammon], **Super-Magician
Comics**, 2.10 (February 1944): 3-16.
In which Blackstone proves himself a better
magician than the fakirs and saves the Rajah from
Amu Zam's kidnap plot. (Blackstone's real life
brother, Pete, makes an unannounced cameo
appearance.)

E.177.   "Blackstone Battles the Demon of the Deep,"
[Walter B. Gibson]: James Hammon, **Super-Magician
Comics**, 2.10 (February 1944): 17-26.
On Celu, isle of pearls, off the coast of
Central America, Blackstone discovers the reason
for the disappearance of the native pearl divers as
he battles some giant sea creatures.

E.178.   "Blackstone Haunts Pirate's Cove," [Walter
B. Gibson]: [James Hammon], **Super-Magician Comics**,
2.11 (March 1944): 3-12.
In which Blackstone is hired to chase the
ghosts from the old tin mines at Port-au-Port,
capital of the Starboard Islands.

E.179.   "Blackstone Visits Pelican Island," [Walter
B. Gibson]: James Hammon, **Super-Magician Comics**,
2.11 (March 1944): 21-34.

In which Blackstone re-conquers a potential military base, meets a modern-day Merlin who is working for the Japanese wizard, Ichi, and arranges an honest election for governor of the island.

E.180. "Blackstone in Voodoo Valley," [Walter B. Gibson]: James Hammon, **Super-Magician** Comics, 2.11 (March 1944): 47-54.
In which Blackstone's magic defeats the voodoo magic used to halt construction along the Pan-American highway.

E.181. "Blackstone Discovers Indigo Island," [Walter B. Gibson]: James Hammon, **Super-Magician** Comics, 2.12 (April 1944): 3-16.
In which a canoe trip from Pelican Island is interrupted by a typhoon landing Blackstone and Rhoda on Indigo Island and a meeting with a Nazi named Ogidni and his invisible men.

E.182. "Blackstone Meets the Wizard of Wanga," [Walter B. Gibson]: [James Hammon], **Super-Magician** Comics, 2.12 (April 1944): 25-34.
On a U.S.O. tour, Blackstone arrives in Alaska and searches for the lost engineers on the island of Wanga.

E.183. "Blackstone and the Gold of Amu Zam," [Walter B. Gibson]: [James Hammon], **Super-Magician** Comics, 2.12 (April 1944): 43-50.
In which Blackstone and Rhoda return to Gwalapore and another battle of magic with Amu Zam (whose name is "mazuma" spelled backwards). Gibson has forgotten that he gave this land another name in the previous story.

E.184. "Blackstone Defies the Hand of Glory," [Walter B. Gibson]: James Hammon, **Super-Magician** Comics, 3.1 (May 1944): 3-16.
In which Blackstone's "rapping hand" trick leads to the discovery of black magic practiced in America by Wilfred the Warlock. (The Hand of Glory was used in one of the Blackstone radio shows as well.)

E.185. "Blackstone Meets the Lady or the Tiger," [Walter B. Gibson]: [James Hammon], **Super-Magician** Comics, 3.1 (May 1944): 25-34.
In which a magic lantern brought to a South Seas island by a missionary gives a young princess

ideas for re-enacting an old story to gain Blackstone as a husband.

E.186.   "Blackstone Defies The Druids of Land's End," [Walter B. Gibson]: [James Hammon], Super-Magician Comics, 3.2 (June 1944): 3-16.
In which a secret group plans revolt in England under the guise of a Druidic cult, but Blackstone settles matters as the oldest Druid of all.

E.187.   "Blackstone and the Valley of Thunder," [Walter B. Gibson]: [James Hammon], Super-Magician Comics, 3.2 (June 1944): 25-32.
In which Blackstone challenges the leader of a fanatic faction to a duel using a magic scimitar, but needs to rescue his friend, Malef Bey, governor of an Arabian province, from the Valley of Thunder when he faces the Djinoon.

E.188.   "Blackstone Among the Magonians," [Walter B. Gibson]: [James Hammon], Super-Magician Comics, 3.2 (June 1944): 39-46.
In which Blackstone prevents the Magonians from selling the secret of their skyship to Japan by a "lightning" maneuver.

E.189.   "Blackstone Finds the Enchanted Garden," [Walter B. Gibson]: [James Hammon], Super-Magician Comics, 3.3 (July 1944): 3-16.
In which Blackstone tours England for the U.S.O. and lays the ghost of Playfair Castle. The "Enchanted Garden" was one of the most elaborate and colorful illusions in his show, one which Blackstone, Jr., still performs.

E.190.   "Blackstone Duels with The Wizard of the North," [Walter B. Gibson]: [James Hammon], Super-Magician Comics, 3.3 (July 1944): 25-34.
In which Blackstone visits the Wapitimagami trading post to match wits with Ulaluma, Wizard of the North, and brings peace to the wilderness.

E.191.   "Blackstone Meets the Mad Magician," [Walter B. Gibson]: [James Hammon], Super-Magician Comics, 3.3 (July 1944): 51-58.
In which Magnus, the Mad Magician, tries to depose Blackstone who must save Rhoda's life from the Super-Guillotine illusion.

E.192.   "Blackstone Finds the Aztec Treasure,"
[Walter B. Gibson]: [James Hammon], **Super-Magician Comics,** 3.4 (August 1944): 3-16.
    In which Blackstone revives an Aztec legend to
reclaim a treasure.

E.193.   "Blackstone Visits the Haunted Mesa,"
[Walter B. Gibson]: [James Hammon], **Super-Magician Comics,** 3.4 (August 1944): 17-24.
    In which Blackstone reveals the secrets of
"reel" magic and lays the ghosts to restore the
Southwest territory to its rightful residents.

E.194.   "Blackstone Meets Swami Simla, the Mystic
Seer," [Walter B. Gibson]: [James Hammon],
Super-Magician Comics, 3.4 (August 1944): 51-58.
    In which Blackstone uses the Swami's turban to
escape from his tower prison and exposes another
fraudulent medium.

E.195.   "Blackstone Crosses the River of Fear,"
[Walter B. Gibson], **Super-Magician Comics,** 3.5
(September 1944): 3-10.
    In which Blackstone must solve the mystery of
what lies beyond the river in deepest Africa so
that an essential rail-line may be laid through the
jungle. (A fair imitation of Hammon's art.)

E.196.   "Blackstone and the Buried Fakir," [Walter
B. Gibson]: [James Hammon], **Super-Magician Comics,**
3.5 (September 1944): 11-18.
    In which Blackstone once again combats the
magic of Amu Zam who has buried himself alive to
protest the Maharajah's rule.   (The burial trick
was also used in a story on the Blackstone radio
show.)

E.197.   "Blackstone Meets the Pirates of Twin
Island," [Walter B. Gibson]: [James Hammon],
Super-Magician Comics, 3.6 (October 1944): 3-16.
    In which modern pirates rob the residents of
Twin island until Blackstone confronts them with
some pirates of old. (Some of the tricks
demonstrated in this story will be found in the
Blackstone radio show as well.)

E.198.   "Blackstone Banishes the Banshee," [Walter
B. Gibson]: [James Hammon], **Super-Magician Comics,**
3.6 (October 1944): 20-27.

In which Blackstone lays the ghost of the
castle and increases the value of the building as
real estate.

E.199.   "Blackstone Finds the Weird Waterfall,"
[Walter B. Gibson]: James Hammon, **Super-Magician
Comics,** 3.6 (October 1944): 51-58.
In which Blackstone traps the corn gods and
puts a Yucatan mine back into production.

E.200.   "Blackstone Uncovers Guy Fawkes and the
Gunpowder Plot," [Walter B. Gibson]: [James
Hammon], **Super-Magician Comics,** 3.7 (November
1944): 3-16.
In which Blackstone and Rhoda both vanish
through a stage trap and become involved with some
remnants of the original followers of Guy Fawkes.

E.201.   "Blackstone Uncovers Smuggler's Cove,"
[Walter B. Gibson]: James Hammon, **Super-Magician
Comics,** 3.7 (November 1944): 43-50.
In which some enemy smugglers in the Caribbean
find some opposition from Blackstone and Rhoda.

E.202.   "Blackstone Exposes Professor Nizam, the
Spook-Maker," [Walter B. Gibson]: James Hammon,
Super-Magician Comics, 3.8 (December 1944): 3-16.
In which a phony spiritualist finds new
trouble when Blackstone becomes an acting sheriff.

E.203.   "Blackstone and the Devil's Chimney,"
[Walter B. Gibson], **Super-Magician Comics,** 3.8
(December 1944): 43-50.
In which Blackstone exposes the trickery
behind a legend in Nicador, Central America, and
allows a highway to be built to gain access to the
area of rubber plantations. (Another imitation of
Hammon's art.)

E.204.   "Blackstone Defeats the Jungle Jugglers,"
[Walter B. Gibson]: [James Hammon], **Super-Magician
Comics,** 3.9 (January 1945): 3-16.
In which Blackstone and Rhoda make a trip up
the Amazon to see what's stopping the rubber
production and use a tidal wave against some enemy
agents.

E.205.   "Blackstone and the Missing Ghost," [Walter
B. Gibson]: [James Hammon], **Super-Magician Comics,**
3.9 (January 1945): 43-50.

In which Blackstone is hired to de-haunt a house and restore the family mansion, even if it is the ancestral ghost which is causing trouble.

E.206. "Blackstone Meets the Water Wizards," [Walter B. Gibson]: [James Hammon], **Super-Magician Comics,** 3.10 (February 1945): 3-16.
In which Blackstone solves the mystery of the missing munitions of Castle Laguna in Central America while Rhoda imitates a water lily.

E.207. "Blackstone Meets Malbini, the Millionaire Mystic," [Walter B. Gibson], **Super-Magician Comics,** 3.10 (February 1945): 43-50.
In which Blackstone encounters an old foe, but is lent a "hand" in defeating his sabotage trickery. (Hammon's imitator again.)

E.208. "Blackstone Grapples the Green Goliath," [Walter B. Gibson]: [James Hammon], **Super-Magician Comics,** 3.11 (March 1945): 3-16.
In which Blackstone visits the Andes mountains and helps defeat the giant wizard who prevents anyone from approaching the lost emerald mine of the Incas.

E.209. "Blackstone Meets the Zombi Master," [Walter B. Gibson]: [James Hammon], **Super-Magician Comics,** 3.11 (March 1945): 43-50.
In which Count Diablo's zombies are defeated by Blackstone's drum which won't stop beating. (This plot device was also used in "The Riddle of the Seven Zombies" on the Blackstone radio show.)

E.210. "Blackstone Invades Cagliostro's Castle," [Walter B. Gibson]: [James Hammon], **Super-Magician Comics,** 3.12 (April 1945): 3-16.
In which Rhoda disappears beneath the waters of the Hidden Glade and Blackstone shows a modern-day Cagliostro something about the transmuting of precious metal.

E.211. "Blackstone Thwarts Crime in the Stars," [Walter B. Gibson]: [James Hammon], **Super-Magician Comics,** 3.12 (April 1944): 43-50.
In which Blackstone and Rhoda set a trap for an astrology faker named Professor Codini with the help of some false whiskers.

E.212.   "Blackstone Uncovers a Carnival of Crime,"
[Walter B. Gibson]: [James Hammon], **Super-Magician
Comics**, 4.1 (May 1945): 3-16.
    In which Rhoda goes underwater as a mermaid
and Blackstone does some sharpshooting to learn why
the carnival is always accompanied by its own crime
wave.

E.213.   "Blackstone Finds the Fairfax Fiend,"
[Walter B. Gibson]: [James Hammon], **Super-Magician
Comics**, 4.1 (May 1945): 43-50.
    In which Blackstone finds clues to the
identity of a mystery robber when he examines a
sack with holes in it and a single black silk
stocking.

E.214.   "Blackstone Conquers the Invisible Men,"
[Walter B. Gibson]: [James Hammon], **Super-Magician
Comics**, 4.2 (June 1945): 3-16.
    In which an Algerian castle is being haunted
by Conte Diavolo and Rhoda sheds some light on the
theory of invisibility.

E.215.   "Blackstone Conquers King Neptune," [Walter
B. Gibson]: [James Hammon], **Super-Magician Comics**,
4.2 (June 1945): 43-50.
    In which Commodore Neptune King turns pirate
(and reverses the order of his names) to try
something new by way of ransoms.

E.216.   "Blackstone Defies the River Demons,"
[Walter B. Gibson]: [James Hammon], **Super-Magician
Comics**, 4.3 (July 1945): 3-16.
    In which Blackstone defeats the Fire Demons to
open up the lost gold mines of the Golden River.

E.217.   "Blackstone: Ghost Meets Ghost," [Walter B.
Gibson]: [James Hammon], **Super-Magician Comics**, 4.3
(July 1945): 43-50.
    In which Blackstone is hired to prove Thornley
Manor is not haunted, even when the present
occupant doesn't wish him to succeed.

E.218.   "Blackstone Battles Doctor Zero," [Walter
B. Gibson]: [James Hammon], **Super-Magician Comics**,
4.4 (August 1945): 3-16.
    Guest or prisoner?   Those who visit Doctor
Zero have a habit of disappearing--until Blackstone
investigates the impossible and adds a new meaning
to the word "inflation."

E.219.   "Blackstone Solves the Riddle of the
Rajpoot Ruby," [Walter B. Gibson]: [James Hammon],
Super-Magician Comics, 4.4 (August 1945): 43-50.
    In which Blackstone is hired to give a magic
show in order to prevent a ruby from being stolen.

E.220.   "Blackstone Defies the Masked Miller,"
[Walter B. Gibson]: [James Hammon], **Super-Magician
Comics**, 4.5 (September 1945): 3-16.
    In which Blackstone sets a decoy to bait a
trap for a crook and prevents a disaster to the
town by some sleight of hand at the dam.

E.221.   "Blackstone Outwits Dalban the Dervish,"
[Walter B. Gibson]: [James Hammon], **Super-Magician
Comics**, 4.5 (September 1945): 43-50.
    In which Rhoda seems to desert Blackstone when
she takes a job with another magician, and learns
just how fast stolen goods may be recovered.

E.222.   "Blackstone Uses the Invisible Ray Against
the Wreckers of Sea Breeze Beach," [Walter B.
Gibson]: [James Hammon], **Super-Magician Comics**, 4.6
(October 1945): 3-16.
    In which Rhoda's invisible ray helps
Blackstone net some smugglers at a once-thriving
seaside resort.

E.223.   "Blackstone Meets the Unlucky Seven,"
[Walter B. Gibson]: [James Hammon], **Super-Magician
Comics**, 4.6 (October 1945): 43-50.
    In which Blackstone unmasks the animal-headed
crooks behind the Interstate Fair robberies.

E.224.   "Blackstone Presents Sawing a Woman in Half
in the Haunted Theatre!" [Walter B. Gibson]: [James
Hammon], **Super-Magician Comics**, 4.7 (November
1945): 3-17.
    In which Blackstone de-haunts a theatre and
captures a peddler of Japanese silk named Professor
Phanterio by means of some of his most famous stage
illusions. (Text page 17 explaining how the trick
is done is illustrated by Charles Coll.)

E.225.   "Blackstone and the Whispering Ghost,"
[Walter B. Gibson]: [James Hammon], **Super-Magician
Comics**, 4.7 (November 1945): 43-50.
    In which Blackstone is hired by a millionaire
to perform only the vanishing watch illusion and
discovers a double game in progress.

E.226. "Blackstone Unmasks the Night Riders with the Mystery of the Vanishing Horse," [Walter B. Gibson]: [James Hammon], **Super-Magician Comics**, 4.8 (December 1945): 3-16, 22.
In which prosperity follows the new power project in Mountain City and Blackstone unmasks the chief of the Night Riders when the Vanishing Horse illusion shows him how. (Page 22 explains how the trick was done.)

E.227. "Blackstone Encounters Kalunga, the Marsh Master," [Walter B. Gibson]: [James Hammon], **Super-Magician Comics**, 4.8 (December 1945): 43-50.
In which crime is rampant in Bauxite City while Blackstone finds the clue in an old magic book and the oracle speaks on stage.

E.228. "Blackstone and the Golden Pool," [Walter B. Gibson]: [James Hammon], **Super-Magician Comics**, 4.9 (January 1946): 3-16.
In which someone has been robbing all the resort towns in Florida and Blackstone finds a new use for a stuffed alligator to bag the robbers at the Golden Pool.

E.229. "The Floating Light: Blackstone's Greatest Illusion," [Walter B. Gibson], **Super-Magician Comics**, 4.9 (January 1946): 24.
Text page describing the illusion without giving away its secret.

E.230. "Blackstone Invades Crooks' Jungle," [Walter B. Gibson]: [James Hammon], **Super-Magician Comics**, 4.9 (January 1946): 43-50.
In which the vanishing bank robbers are found hiding in Jungle Land and Rhoda takes a dancing lesson.

E.231. "Blackstone Visits the Isle of Doom," [Walter B. Gibson]: [James Hammon], **Super-Magician Comics**, 4.10 (February 1946): 3-16.
When wealthy people disappear with all their cash, Blackstone investigates Swami Mango at the Happy Hunting Ground at Doubling River and learns how waves can turn back on themselves.

E.232. "Blackstone Outwits the Secret Six," [Walter B. Gibson]: [James Hammon], **Super-Magician Comics**, 4.10 (February 1946): 43-50.

When the numeral or word "six" is found
scrawled all over the theatre lobby where
Blackstone's show is appearing it's a signal for
crime until Blackstone marks the crooks for
identification by the police. (Last Blackstone
story in Super-Magician.)

E.233. "Magic in Shangri-La," [Walter B. Gibson]:
[James Hammon], **Super-Magician Comics,** 4.11 (March
1946): 3-16.
When Nigel Elliman (magician-hero of this new
series which replaces the Blackstone stories) is
asked to promote peace in New Guinea, he re-creates
an old legend. The character of Blackstone,
originally drawn for this story, has been touched
up and given dark hair. The magic tricks in the
issue are now presented by Elliman.

E.234. "Introducing Nigel Elliman, Ace of Magic,"
[Walter B. Gibson]: [James Hammon], **Super-Magician
Comics,** 4.12 (April 1946): 3-16.
In which Nigel Elliman, Lorna Doane, and the
Chinese juggler, Ling Foo, make their official
arrival in the pages of **Super-Magician** in time to
save the royal jewels of the Sultan of Kudu from
vanishing into the hands of some crooks. (Cover
signed by Charles Coll.)

E.235. "Elliman Invades the House of Spooks,"
[Walter B. Gibson]: [Charles Coll], **Super-Magician
Comics,** 4.12 (April 1946): 43-50.
In which Elliman is hired to expose a fake
ghost and discovers a tricky relative on the
Clavistock family tree.

E.236. "Elliman, Ace of Magic, Meets the Wizard of
the Everglades," [Walter B. Gibson]: [James
Hammon], **Super-Magician Comics,** 5.1 (May 1946):
3-16.
In which voodoo magic leads to buried Spanish
gold in the Everglades and Elliman shows how easy
it is to hypnotize an alligator.

E.237. "Elliman, Ace of Magic, Solves the Riddle
of the Fifth Crook," [Walter B. Gibson]: [James
Hammon], **Super-Magician Comics,** 5.1 (May 1946):
43-50.
In which Elliman's magic show at the mansion
of Nine Oaks helps narrow down the number of crooks
on the guest list.

E.238. "Elliman, Ace of Magic, Finds the Spanish Treasure," [Walter B. Gibson]: [James Hammon], **Super-Magician Comics,** 5.2 (June 1946): 3-16.
In which the regular appearance of old Spanish coins in Miami leads Elliman to dive near a Spanish galleon in search of more.

E.239. "Elliman, Ace of Magic, and the Mysterious Sharpshooter," [Walter B. Gibson]: [James Hammon], **Super-Magician Comics,** 5.2 (June 1946): 43-50.
In which Carbino, the trick sharpshooter, fires his way into a place on the bill next to Elliman, and the magician must vanish to prevent a robbery and murder in response to another sort of firing.

E.240. "Elliman, Ace of Magic, Battles 'Triple Crime,'" [Walter B. Gibson], **Super-Magician Comics,** 5.3 (July 1946): 3-16.
In which three crooks borrow some ideas from Elliman's show for the Bankers' Club, but end up without the loot or the secrets behind the tricks.

E.241. "Elliman Solves 'The Riddle of the Pyramid,'" [Walter B. Gibson], **Super-Magician Comics,** 5.3 (July 1946): 43-50.
In which Elliman learns how valuables can be stolen from high places during the course of a charity bazaar.

E.242. "Elliman, Ace of Magic, Exposes The Invisible Monster," [Walter B. Gibson], **Super-Magician Comics,** 5.4 (August 1946): 3-16.
In which Elliman advises a scientist on his invention while Lorna solves a mystery by a quick trip to the cellar.

E.243. "Elliman, Ace of Magic, Tricks the Crooks of Glenwood," [Walter B. Gibson], **Super-Magician Comics,** 5.4 (August 1946): 39-46.
In which Elliman demonstrates how magic can put the finger on the man who stole Judge Falkenrod's paintings.

E.244. "Elliman's Magic Baffles the Natives of The Twin Pools," [Walter B. Gibson], **Super-Magician Comics,** 5.5 (September 1946): 3-16.
In which Elliman uses magic to make peace between two tribes and cements another link in the Pan American highway.

E.245. "Elliman and the Baffled Burglars," [Walter B. Gibson], **Super-Magician Comics,** 5.6 (October-November 1946): 12-19.
In which Lorna overhears a crime plotted, but manages to pass the clue to Elliman.

E.246. "Magic Battles Crime Back Stage," [Walter B. Gibson], **Super-Magician Comics,** 5.6 (October-November 1946): 43-50.
In which the strong man's secret is a clue for Elliman to the culprits in a robbery. Appears to have been originally drawn for the Blackstone series. Possibly in Gibson's inventory of unpublished material used during his hiatus from employment at Street & Smith.

E.247. "Elliman, Ace of Magic, Meets the Wizards of the North," [Walter B. Gibson], **Super-Magician Comics,** 5.7 (December-January 1947): 37-50.
In which Elliman discovers a new set of "Northern Lights" and breaks up a gang of renegade trappers. This is not the same story that appeared in Super-Magician, July 1944; may have been originally a Blackstone story, but redrawn.

E.248. "Elliman Solves the Riddle of the Rockies," [Walter B. Gibson], **Super-Magician Comics,** 5.8 (February-March 1947): 36-49.
In which Elliman, Lorna, and Ling Foo become involved with Outlaws, Corn Spirits, and Vigilantes to learn what lies hidden in Happy Valley. The last issue of **Super-Magician;** as with many other stories in previous issues, this is a variant on an old Blackstone plot.

Blackstone, Master Magician Comics

E.249. "Blackstone Presents 'From Film to Life,'"[Walter B. Gibson], **Blackstone, Master Magician Comics,** No. 1 (March-April 1946): 26p.
When Street & Smith failed to renew their contract with Harry Blackstone to publish the stories of his "adventures" in **Super-Magician Comics,** Gibson took the idea to Vital Publications who issued three numbers.

E.250. "Blackstone and His Super Magic," [Walter B. Gibson], **Blackstone, Master Magician Comics,** No. 1 (March-April 1946): 4p.

E.251.   "Blackstone Solves the Sealed Vault
Mystery," [Walter B. Gibson]: Charles Coll,
Blackstone, Master Magician Comics, No. 1
(March-April 1946): 14p.

E.252.   "Blackstone Does Magic That You Too Can
Do," [Walter B. Gibson], Blackstone, Master
Magician Comics, No. 1 (March-April 1946): 4p.

E.253.   "Blackstone Invades the Castle of Doom!!!"
[Walter B. Gibson]: E. C. Stoner, Blackstone,
Master Magician Comics, No. 2 (May-June 1946): 26p.

E.254.   "Blackstone Talks About Magic," [Walter B.
Gibson], Blackstone, Master Magician Comics, No. 2
(May-June 1946): 4p.
    Text article, no illustrations.

E.255.   "Blackstone Shows You How to Do Magic,"
[Walter B. Gibson], Blackstone, Master Magician
Comics, No. 2 (May-June 1946): 4p.

E.256.   "Blackstone Defies El Devi and the Desert
Dervishes," [Walter B. Gibson], Blackstone, Master
Magician Comics, No. 2 (May-June 1946): 14p.

E.257.   "Blackstone and the Mystery of 'The
Midnight Express,'" [Walter B. Gibson], Blackstone,
Master Magician Comics, No. 3 (July-August 1946):
14p.

E.258.   "Blackstone Solves the Riddle of the
Vanishing Mummies," [Walter B. Gibson], Blackstone,
Master Magician Comics, No. 3 (July-August 1946):
14p.

E.259.   "Blackstone Battles the Fog Monsters,"
[Walter B. Gibson], Blackstone, Master Magician
Comics, No. 3 (July-August 1946): 14p.

E.260.   "Blackstone's Multiplying Money Trick,"
[Walter B. Gibson], Blackstone, Master Magician
Comics, No. 3 (July-August 1946): 3p.

                  Blackstone the Magician

E.261.   "Blackstone: Costumed for Crime," [Walter
B. Gibson], Blackstone the Magician, No. 2 (May
1948): 9p.

A continuation of the comic book series,
Blackstone the Magician Detective Fights Crime (No.
1, March 1948), which has not been examined. With
No. 3, the title became **Blackstone the Magician
Detective.**

E.262.   "Rhoda: Sleepytime Pal!" [Walter B.
Gibson], **Blackstone the Magician,** No. 2 (May 1948):
2p.
        The solo adventures of Blackstone's girl
Friday.

E.263.   "Blackstone: Murder at Eight!" [Walter B.
Gibson], **Blackstone the Magician,** No. 2 (May 1948):
9p.

E.264.   "Blackstone: Riddle of the Third Face!"
[Walter B. Gibson], **Blackstone the Magician
Detective,** No. 3 (July 1948): 8p.
        The title of this comic book series now
reflects that of the radio series from 1944,
"Blackstone the Magic Detective."

E.265.   "Blackstone: The Isle of Doom," [Walter B.
Gibson], **Blackstone the Magician Detective,** No. 3
(July 1948): 7p.

E.266.   "Blackstone: Mystery of the Rajah's Ruby,"
[Walter B. Gibson], **Blackstone the Magician
Detective,** No. 3 (July 1948): 5p.
        A fourth issue was published, dated September
1948. This has not been examined.

Blackstone the Magician Detective Fights Crime
(See entry E.261. above)
Ghost Breakers

E.267.   "Dr. Neff Chases the Jinx from Hoodoo
City," [Walter B. Gibson]: Bob Powell, **Ghost
Breakers,** 1.1 (September 1948): 3-16.
        In which Dr. Neff exposes a man-made
superstition in a town where the citizens believe
bad luck is the norm. Real life magician, Bill
Neff, with his "Madhouse of Mystery" appears in
this series. See also stories in **Red Dragon Comics**
and **Racket Squad in Action.**

E.268.   "Dr. Neff Confronts the Hang-Kow Demons,"
[Walter B. Gibson]: Bob Powell, **Ghost Breakers**, 1.1
(September 1948): 17-24.
    In which Dr. Neff must make the demons of
Chinatown into laughing stocks.

E.269.   "Neff Trix," [Walter B. Gibson?]:   Bob
Powell, **Ghost Breakers**, 1.1 (September 1948): 25-
28.
    In which Dr. Neff explains the tricks of
spiritualists.

E.270.   "Dr. Neff Cracks the Menace of the
Vanishing Ghosts," [Walter B. Gibson]: Bob Powell,
Ghost Breakers, 1.1 (September 1948): 29-42.
    In which Dr. Neff uses a scientific experiment
in reflex images to scatter a crowd of fake
spirits.

E.271.   "Ghostly Bottles," [Walter B. Gibson?]: Joe
Maneely, **Ghost Breakers**, 1.1 (September 1948): 44-
45.
    A trick explained.

E.272.   "Believe in Ghosts?" [Walter B. Gibson?],
Ghost Breakers, 1.1 (September 1948): 46-47.
    Text article.

E.273.   "Ghost Breakers (Letter Column)," [Walter
B. Gibson?], **Ghost Breakers**, 1.1 (September 1948):
48.

E.274.   "Dr. Neff Blasts the Voodoo Hoodoo,"
[Walter B. Gibson]: Bob Powell, **Ghost Breakers**, 1.2
(December 1948): 3-16.
    In which Papa Bazan and his voodoo racket are
no match for Dr. Neff, the original ghost-breaker.

E.275.   "Django Jinks, Ghost Chaser: 'The Ghost of
Devon,'" [Walter B. Gibson?]: Joe Maneely, **Ghost
Breakers**, 1.2 (December 1948): 17-24.
    In which the young magician defies the local
ghosts to raise money for charity.   Uncertain if
this is the work of Gibson.

E.276.   "The Ghost of the Pyramid Priest," [Walter
B. Gibson?]: Zangerle, **Ghost Breakers**, 1.2
(December 1948): 25-31.
    In which a university professor travels back

in time to solve the mystery of the agate rings of Merdok.

E.277.   "Tao Anwar, Boy Magician: 'Tao's Televised Trickery,'" [Walter B. Gibson?]: Joe Maneely, **Ghost Breakers,** 1.2 (December 1948): 32-39.
     In which the young magician astounds the producer of his own television show. Tao Anwar appeared in other Street & Smith comics as well; it is possible that the stories were the work of Bruce Elliot and not Gibson.

E.278.   "Ghost Breakers: One Hundred Years of Spooks and Spoof," by Dr. Bill Neff [Walter B. Gibson], **Ghost Breakers,** 1.2 (December 1948): 40-41.
     Text article.

E.279.   "The Chateau of Shadows: A Dr. Neff Mystery of the 'Other' World," [Walter B. Gibson]: Bob Powell, **Ghost Breakers,** 1.2 (December 1948): 42-49.
     In which a ghost from the past reaches out a deadly hand to the present.

Red Dragon Comics

E.280.   "Behind the Eight Ball," [Walter B. Gibson?]: Edd Cartier, **Red Dragon Comics** (2d Series), 1.1 (November 1947): 17-24.
     In which Lorna is taken along on a burglary, but Elliman manages to get the message. (Not certain this is Gibson's work; a story that may have been intended for **Super-Magician** which had ceased publication earlier in 1947.)

E.281.   "Doctor Neff the Ghost Breaker Battles Professor Drade [Walter B. Gibson]: Bob Powell, **Red Dragon Comics** (2d Series), 1.3 (May 1948): 3-14.
     In which Bill Neff is hired to debunk the ghosts of Mallory Mansion and uncovers some real horrors. (Gibson's use of anagrams to name his characters is evident here.)

E.282.   "Bill (Dr.) Neff," [Walter B. Gibson], **Red Dragon Comics** (2d Series), 1.3 (May 1948): 17.
     A background article introducing Bill Neff to the readers. Neff was a high school classmate of actor Jimmy Stewart in Indiana, Pa.

E.283. "Elliman Does Magic in Miami," [Walter B. Gibson]: [James Hammon], **Red Dragon Comics** (2d Series), 1.3 (May 1948): 26-39.
    In which Elliman's magic is a match for a band of jewel thieves. "The Crystal Packet" is promised for the following issue, but never appeared.

Crime and Punishment

E.284. "Match Your Wits With Private Detective Selton in 'The Case of the Expectant Heirs,'" [Walter B. Gibson]: Fred Guardineer, **Crime and Punishment**, No. 27 (June 1950): 9p.
    Title of series varies, but all are on the "minute mystery" or "solve it yourself" theme. The titles say it all.

E.285. "Who Dunnit? Can You Solve 'The Case of the Inquisitive Photographer?'" [Walter B. Gibson]: Fred Guardineer, **Crime and Punishment**, No. 28 (July 1950): 6p.

E.286. "Can You Solve 'The Mystery of Who Killed Luigi?'" [Walter B. Gibson]: Fred Guardineer, **Crime and Punishment**, No. 29 (August 1950): 7p.

E.287. "Who Dunnit? 'Death Takes a Ride,'" [Walter B. Gibson]: Fred Guardineer, **Crime and Punishment**, No. 30 (September 1950): 6p.

E.288. "Who Dunnit? 'Death Rides the 5:15,'" [Walter B. Gibson]: Fred Guardineer, **Crime and Punishment**, No. 31 (October 1950): 6p.

E.289. "Who Dunnit? Can You Solve 'The Mystery of Death from the Fairway?'" [Walter B. Gibson]: Fred Guardineer, **Crime and Punishment**, No. 32 (November 1950): 6p.

E.290. "Can You Solve 'the Puzzle of the Rocky Gorge Murder?'" [Walter B. Gibson]: Fred Guardineer, **Crime and Punishment**, No. 33 (December 1950): 6p.

E.291. "How Good a Detective Are You? 'The Poison Dart Murder Case,'" [Walter B. Gibson]: Fred Guardineer, **Crime and Punishment**, No. 34 (January 1951): 6p.
    Match wits with Special Agent Alan Kent.

E.292.   "Who Dunnit? 'The Case of the
Orange-Pickers' Payroll,'" [Walter B. Gibson]: Fred
Guardineer, **Crime and Punishment,** No. 35 (February
1951): 6p.

E.293.   "Who Dunnit? 'Death Comes for the
Double-Crosser,'" [Walter B. Gibson]: Fred
Guardineer, **Crime and Punishment,** No. 36 (March
1951): 7p.
        Can you solve the puzzling case of Richard
Thull?

E.294. "How Good a Detective Are You? 'The Beauty
Contest Murder Case,'" [Walter B. Gibson]: Fred
Guardineer, **Crime and Punishment,** No. 37 (April
1951): 6p.
        "Can you judge a Clue as well as a Cutie? Can
you pick the loser [in this contest?]"

E.295. "Who Dunnit? 'The Shakedown Murder Case,'"
[Walter B. Gibson]: Fred Guardineer, **Crime and
Punishment,** No. 38 (May 1951): 6p.

E.296.   "Who Dunnit? 'Death Goes to College,"
[Walter B. Gibson]: Fred Guardineer, **Crime and
Punishment,** No. 39 (June 1951): 6p.

E.297.   "Who Dunnit?   'The Death of the Private
Eye,'" [Walter B. Gibson]: Fred Guardineer, **Crime
and Punishment,** No. 40 (July 1951): 6p.

E.298.   "Who Dunnit?   'The Case of the Elusive
Go-Between,'" [Walter B. Gibson]: Fred Guardineer,
Crime and Punishment, No. 41 (August 1951): 6p.

E.299.   "Who Dunnit? 'Death at Gray Gables,'"
[Walter B. Gibson]: Fred Guardineer, **Crime and
Punishment,** No.42 (September 1951): 6p.

E.300.   "Who Dunnit? 'The Moosehorn River
Mystery,'" [Walter B. Gibson]: Fred Guardineer,
Crime and Punishment, No. 43 (October 1951): 6p.

E.301. "Who Dunnit? 'The Bull's-Eye Murder Case,'"
[Walter B. Gibson]: Fred Guardineer, **Crime and
Punishment,** No. 44 (November 1951): 5p.

Crime Does Not Pay

E.302. "Chip Gardner, Private Eye: The Rock-a-Bye Baby Murder," [Walter B. Gibson]: George Tuska, **Crime Does Not Pay,** No. 87 (May 1950): 13p.
The notes to each story are taken from the individual splash pages. No further annotations are necessary!

E.303. "Chip Gardner: The Case of the Substitute Nephew," [Walter B. Gibson]: Robert Fujitani, **Crime Does Not Pay,** No. 88 (June 1950): 13p.
Chip Gardner, Private Eye, stops wise-cracking when he sees that death carries a torch.

E.304. "Chip Gardner: The Escort Murder Case," [Walter B. Gibson]: Robert Fujitani, **Crime Does Not Pay,** No. 89 (July 1950): 13p.
Chip Gardner, Private Eye, finds himself on a one-way road to the hot seat.

E.305. "Chip Gardner: The Case of the Losing Winners," [Walter B. Gibson]: Robert Fujitani, **Crime Does Not Pay,** No. 90 (August 1950): 13p.
Chip Gardner, Private Eye, shrugs off an anti-gambling crusade until it leads to the Alhambra Club Murders.

E.306. "Chip Gardner: The Case of the King-Sized Miracle," [Walter B. Gibson]: Robert Fujitani, **Crime Does Not Pay,** No. 91 (September 1950): 13p.
Chip Gardner, Private Eye, works in the dark while death watches the clock.

E.307. "Chip Gardner: The Payroll Bonus Murders & The Case of the Insistent Sister," [Walter B. Gibson]: Robert Fujitani, **Crime Does Not Pay,** No. 92, (October 1950): 13p.
Chip Gardner, Private Eye, walks into one case and falls into another.

E.308. "Chip Gardner: The Ostrich Murder Case," [Walter B. Gibson]: Robert Fujitani, **Crime Does Not Pay,** No. 93 (November 1950): 13p.
Chip Gardner, Private Eye, lured by Florida sunshine and a fat fee, tangles with a mob that plays for keeps, mixing larceny with murder and abduction.

E.309. "Chip Gardner: The Case of the Vanishing Beauty Shops," [Walter B. Gibson]: Robert Fujitani, **Crime Does Not Pay,** No. 94 (December 1950): 13p.
     Chip Gardner, private Eye, lands a free-spending client, only to learn that money can be a source of evil.

E.310. "Chip Gardner: The Case of the Buffalo Nickels," [Walter B. Gibson]: Robert Fujitani, **Crime Does Not Pay,** No. 95 (February 1951): 13p.
     Chip Gardner, Private Eye, on a routine "missing persons" mission, walks into a mysterious house in suburban Buffalo, seeking life but finding death in the back room.

E.311. "Chip Gardner: The Case of the Movie Star's Double," [Walter B. Gibson]: Robert Fujitani, **Crime Does Not Pay,** No. 96 (March 1951): 13p.
     Chip Gardner, Private Eye, rides the rails with death as he cracks an alibi for murder.

E.312. "Chip Gardner: Death on the Run or The Case of the Darling Daughter," [Walter B. Gibson]: Robert Fujitani, **Crime Does Not Pay,** No. 97 (April 1951): 13p.
     Chip Gardner, Private Eye, gets squeezed between a murderous pair who knew too much and the police who hadn't learned enough.

E.313. "Chip Gardner: The Case of the Ring That Cracked Itself," [Walter B. Gibson]: Robert Fujitani, **Crime Does Not Pay,** No. 98 (May 1951): 13p.
     Chip Gardner, Private Eye, follows a frantic call for help into the wildest caper of his career! He's a set up for murder.

E.314. "Chip Gardner: The Case of the Death's Head Ruby," [Walter B. Gibson]: Robert Fujitani, **Crime Does Not Pay,** No. 99 (June 1951): 13p.
     Chip Gardner, Private Eye, tangles with greed, cunning and sudden death on the twelfth-floor girders of an unfinished skyscraper, while farther uptown the head of the mob executes a neat double-cross.

E.315. "Chip Gardner: The Case of the Jittery Patient," [Walter B. Gibson]: Robert Fujitani, **Crime Does Not Pay,** No. 100 (July 1951): 13p.

Chip Gardner, Private Eye, with an assist from Wendy, solves two murders for the price of one.

E.316. "Chip Gardner: The Case of the Crooked Politician," [Walter B. Gibson]: Robert Fujitani, **Crime Does Not Pay,** No. 101 (August 1951): 9p.
A mug, three dames and a hundred thousand bucks! Add a robbery of incriminating documents, scramble with greed, hate and murder, and you come up with this case from the files of Chip Gardner, Private Eye. (The Chip Gardner story is no longer the lead story in the magazine.)

E.317. "Chip Gardner: You'll Never Live to Tell," [Walter B. Gibson]: Robert Fujitani, **Crime Does Not Pay,** No. 102 (September 1951): 9p.
Chip Gardner, Private Eye, thought he'd get a vacation from crime when he accepted the job as temporary warden at the State Pen! He didn't know that somewhere within the confines of the great stone walls a hand would circle a neck, a voice would hiss ...'You'll Never Live to Tell' and a murder that shocked a nation would explode in his face.

E.318.   "Chip Gardner: The Rabbit-Punch Murder Case," [Walter B. Gibson]: Robert Fujitani, **Crime Does Not Pay,** No. 103 (October 1951): 9p.
The last Chip Gardner story.

E.319.   "Who Dunnit?   Riddle of Blackbeard's Treasure," [Walter B. Gibson]: Fred Guardineer, **Crime Does Not Pay,** No. 104 (November 1951): 6p.
This story really belongs to the series from **Crime and Punishment.**

Detective Comics

E.320.   "The Batman Encounters Gray Face," Walter B. Gibson: Tom Yeates, **Detective Comics,** No. 500 (March 1981): 43-50.
An illustrated text story, much in the style of The Shadow. It is believed that Gibson scripted several Batman comic book stories in the 1950s, but the titles do not appear to be on record at the publishing company, DC comics.

Racket Squad in Action

E.321.   "Gamblers Won't Gamble," [Walter B. Gibson]: Tyler & Dick Giordano, **Racket Squad in Action,** 1.1 (May-June 1952); 12-16.
The gambler prefers a "sure thing" until it catches up with him. Features real life gambling expert, Sidney H. Radner, who tells a story of one of his recent experiences with a crooked card player.

E.322.   "Gamblers Won't Gamble, But Sometimes They Will Take a Chance," [Walter B. Gibson]: Tyler, **Racket Squad in Action,** 1.2 (July-August 1952): 27-30.
In which Sid Radner proves sometimes you can lose even when you have a pair of straight dice.

E.323.   "Hook, Line and Sucker!" [Walter B. Gibson], **Racket Squad in Action,** 1.3 (September-October 1952): 23-27.
In which Sid Radner shows how some crooked gamblers can even work the racket in bowling. (This story was re-printed in issue number 18, September 1955.)

E.324.   "Dr. Neff in 'Smashing the Spook Racket,'" [Walter B. Gibson], **Racket Squad in Action,** 1.3 (September-October 1952): 28-34.
In which the original "ghost-breaker" teams with Inspector O'Malley (series character in this comic) to crack down on Professor Lorenzo and his spook racket.

E.325.   "Gamblers Never Gamble, They Just Put the Game on Ice..." [Walter B. Gibson]: Dick Giordano, **Racket Squad in Action,** 1.4 (December 1952): 12-15.
In which Sid Radner demonstrates the use of the "Cold Deck."

E.326.   "Dr. Neff Debunks the Spirit Photo Racket," [Walter B. Gibson]: Frank Frollo, **Racket Squad in Action,** 1.4 (December 1952): 23-29.
In which Neff, the original ghost-breaker, and O'Malley expose a racket using spirit photos to defraud the heir to the Hargrave fortune.

E.327.   "Dr.   Neff...Uncovers   the   Spirit   Post Office," [Walter B. Gibson]: Frank Frollo, **Racket Squad in Action,** 1.5 (February 1953): 3-7.
In which Neff exposes the racket where letters written from the spirit world are sold to the living for high prices.

E.328.   "Shake Well Before Choosing," [Walter B. Gibson], **Racket Squad in Action,** 1.5 (February 1953): 23-24.
In which Sid Radner explains a racket using a supposedly empty match box.

E.329.   "Sid Radner Says...When Odds Are Even It's Time to be Wary!" [Walter B. Gibson]: Dick Giordano and Al Fago, **Racket Squad in Action,** 1.6 (April 1953): 2p.

E.330.   "Dr. Neff: When Spooks Begin to Ask for Cash..It's Time to Watch Out," [Walter B. Gibson]: Frank Frollo, **Racket Squad in Action,** 1.6 (April 1953): 4p.

E.331.   "Bet the Pot," [Walter B. Gibson]: Dick Giordano and Al Fago, **Racket Squad in Action,** 1.6 (April 1953): 2p.

E.332.   "The Shiner," [Walter B. Gibson]: John Belfi, **Racket Squad in Action,** 1.7 (June 1953): 3p.
A Sidney Radner story.

Space Western

We are not certain Gibson wrote everything for this title, but it is possible.

E.333.   "Migration   to   the   Moon," [Walter B. Gibson], **Space Western,** No. 40 (October 1952): inside front cover.
Compares pioneer travel in the Old West to space travel.

E.334.   "The Saucer Men," [Walter B. Gibson]: John Belfi, **Space Western,** No. 40 (October 1952): 8p.
Spurs   Jackson   and   his   Space   Vigilantes. Formerly **Cowboy Western Comics** (Nos. 1-39) and continues under that title with No. 46

E.335.   "The Outlaws of the Desert," [Walter B. Gibson]: John Belfi, **Space Western**, No. 40 (October 1952): 5p.
A Hank Roper story.

E.336.   "Incident at Powder River," [Walter B. Gibson]: Lou Morales, **Space Western**, No. 40 (October 1952): 2p.
A Jesse James story.

E.337.   "The Moon Monsters," [Walter B. Gibson], **Space Western**, No. 40 (October 1952): 2p.
Text story, no illustrations.

E.338.   "Spurs Jackson: Death from U-235," [Walter B. Gibson], **Space Western**, No. 40 (October 1952): 7p.

E.339.   "The Mystery of the Indian Hills," [Walter B. Gibson], **Space Western**, No. 40 (October 1952): 8p.
A Strong Bow story.

E.340.   "How a Visitor from Space Won the Great West for America," [Walter B. Gibson], **Space Western**, No. 40 (October 1952): inside back cover.
The date is 1811 and the visitor is a comet sighted by Tecumseh.

E.341.   "Spurs Jackson and his Space Vigilantes Battle the Green Men of Venus," [Walter B. Gibson]: Stan Campbell, **Space Western**, No. 41 (November-December 1952): 8p.

E.342.   "Jinx of Black Ridge Ranch," [Walter B. Gibson]: Stan Campbell, **Space Western**, No. 41 (November-December 1952): 7p.

E.343.   "The Red Men from Mars," [Walter B. Gibson], **Space Western**, No. 41 (November-December 1952): 2p.
Text story, no illustrations.

E.344.   "Spurs Jackson and his Space Vigilantes Deal with Danger Below," [Walter B. Gibson]: Stan Campbell, **Space Western**, No. 41 (November-December 1952): 8p.

E.345.   "Strong   Bow   Uncovers   the   Phantom
Highjackers," [Walter B. Gibson], **Space Western,**
No. 41 (November-December 1952): 7p.

E.346.   "Spurs Jackson and his Space Vigilantes
Meet the Sun Masters," [Walter B. Gibson]: Stan
Campbell, **Space Western,** No. 42 (February 1953):
8p.

E.347.   "The Return of the Aztecs," [Walter B.
Gibson]: John Belfi, **Space Western,** No. 42
(February 1953): 7p.
     Strong Bow and His Warriors.

E.348.   "The Space Bronco," [Walter B. Gibson],
Space Western, No. 42 (February 1953): 2p.
     Text story.

E.349.   "Spurs Jackson and his Space Vigilantes
Tangle with the Outlaws of Mars," [Walter B.
Gibson]: Stan Campbell, **Space Western,** No. 42
(February 1953): 8p.

E.350.   "An Amazing Space Journey: A Tale of the
Canadian West," [Walter B. Gibson], **Space Western,**
No. 42 (February 1953): 1p.

E.351.   "Hank Roper and the Riddle of Skull
Valley," [Walter B. Gibson], **Space Western,** No. 42
(February 1953): 6p.

E.352.   "Spurs Jackson and his Space Vigilantes
Face the Menace of the Meteor Men," [Walter B.
Gibson]: Stan Campbell, **Space Western,** No. 43
(April 1953): 8p.

E.353.   "The Battle of Spaceman's Gulch, Featuring
Hank Roper," [Walter B. Gibson], **Space Western,** No.
43 (April 1953): 6p.

E.354.   "Visit Spurs Jackson at His Spaceranch in
Spaceman's Gulch," [Walter B. Gibson], **Space
Western,** No. 43 (April 1953): 1p.
     How Spurs brings back creatures, like the
Saturlope, from outer space to dig gold and pull
the ore carts.

E.355.   "Spurs Jackson and the Vanishing Water,"
[Walter B. Gibson], **Space Western,** No. 43 (April
1953): 2p.

Text story, no illustrations.

E.356. "Spurs Jackson and his Space Vigilantes Battle the Red Menace Beyond the Moon," [Walter B. Gibson]: Stan Campbell, **Space Western,** No. 43 (April 1953): 8p.

E.357. "Space Prospectors," [Walter B. Gibson], **Space Western,** No. 43 (April 1953): 1p.
Science feature.

E.358. "Trip to Mercury," [Walter B. Gibson], **Space Western,** No. 43 (April 1953): 6p.
A Strong Bow story.

E.359. "Spurs Jackson and the Madman of Mars (Part 1)," [Walter B. Gibson]: Stan Campbell, **Space Western,** No. 44 (June 1953): 8p.
Continued in No. 44 which has not been examined.

E.360. "Spurs Jackson: Spurs Sees Red!" [Walter B. Gibson]: John Belfi, **Space Western,** No. 44 (June 1953): 6p.

E.361. "Visit Spurs Jackson in Spaceman's Gulch," [Walter B. Gibson], **Space Western,** No. 44 (June 1953): 1p.
This month, the habits of the Jovian Bandersnatch.

E.362. "Spurs Jackson and the Selenites," [Walter B. Gibson], **Space Western,** No. 44 (June 1953): 2p.
Text story.

E.363. "Strong Bow Meets the Stone Men from Space," [Walter B. Gibson]: John Belfi, **Space Western,** No. 44 (June 1953): 6p.

E.364. "Spurs Jackson and his Space Vigilantes Meet the Menace of Comet 'X'," [Walter B. Gibson]: John Belfi, **Space Western,** No. 44 (June 1953): 8p.

Strange Adventures

E.365. "The Hands from Nowhere," Walter B. Gibson: Bob Oksner and Bernard Sachs, **Strange Adventures,** No. 229 (March-April 1971): 6p.

Reprinted from **Mystery in Space,** ca 1952. This earlier edition has not been seen.

Commercial Comics

E.366. [Commercial Comics] (First Series), [Walter B. Gibson], 1946-1960. 7 1/2" x 10 1/4"; 8 to 24p. (varies)
Comic book format used to promote products which were either incorporated into the story line or their titles printed in a space provided on the cover. Savings & Loan institutions, political parties, General Mills, and Chevrolet were among the companies involved. At least 32 titles appeared in this format.

E.367.   [Commercial Comics] (Second Series), [Walter B. Gibson], 1946-1960. 3 1/2" x 7 1/4"; 8 to 24 pp. (varies)
This series was half the over-all size of the one described in E.366. There were at least 3 titles: "Bottle Patrol" (a collection of games), "1001 Hours of Fun", and "A Trip Through Space with Elsie the Cow." The last promoted the Borden milk products.

E.368.   **Jim Solar, Space Sheriff,** [Walter B. Gibson], 1958 to 1961. 3 1/2" x 7 1/4"; 16p.
At least 19 titles have been recorded (**Overstreet Comic Book Price Guide,** 1987) In some stories, Solar is assisted by Dara Starr and her Spacettes.

E.369. **Captain Fortune Series,** [Walter B. Gibson], 1955-1959. 3 1/2" x 7 1/4"; 16p.
Historical adventure stories told through the eyes of Captain Fortune who meets Robin Hood, Buffalo Bill, Daniel Boone, and Garibaldi, among others. At least 24 titles (Publisher's promotion catalog; **Overstreet Comic Book Price Guide,** 1987).

E.370. **The "Funline" Series,** [Walter B. Gibson], 1955. 3 1/2" x 7 1/4"; 16p.
At least 5 titles ("Indoor-Outdoor Game Book", "Magic for Everyone", "Magic Tricks You Can Do", "Secrets of Magic", and "When School is Out") have been examined. Publishing imprint varied on the "Commercial Comics", either William C. Popper or Vital Publications (Julian Proskauer's firm).

E.371.   Carnation Series, [Walter B. Gibson], 1948.
3 1/2" x 7 1/4"; 16p.
     A set of six comics sold for 10 cents and a
label from Carnation Malted Milk.   Only 4 were by
Gibson: "China Boy in 'A Trip to the Zoo,'"
"Blackstone and the Gold Medal Mystery," "Johnny
Starboard and the Underseas Pirates," and "The
Return of the Phantom."   (The joke in this last
story was that it was a sequel to a story that
never existed.)

**E.372.   Finer Points of Baseball for Everyone
Series,** [Walter B. Gibson], 1961-1966.   3 3/8" x 4
3/4"; 16p.
     There were 12 titles in this series of
miniature comic books.   Topics covered: Batting,
pitching, catching, playing all three bases,
shortstop, outfield, how to run bases, use baseball
signals, how to umpire, and a general "Finer Points
for Everyone."   Gibson was a life-long baseball
fan.

E.373.   How to Play Better Basketball Series,
[Walter B. Gibson], nd.   3 3/8" x 4 3/4"; 16p.
     At least 5 titles appeared in this series.

E.374.   Football Pointers Series, [Walter B.
Gibson], 1962.   3 3/8" x 4 3/4"; 16p.   A   t
least 3 titles; the only one seen is No. 3, "How to
Kick and Return Punts."

E.375.   Playing Better Hockey Series, [Walter B.
Gibson], nd.   3 3/8" x 4 3/4"; 16p.
     At least 11 titles have been recorded.

E.376.   Freedom's Trail Series, [Walter B. Gibson],
1958-1960.   3 3/8" x 4 3/4"; 16p.
     At least 12 titles from "A Message to Garcia"
and "The Mayflower Compact" to "The Story of the
Star Spangled Banner" and "The Declaration of
Independence."   Publisher's imprint varies; some
indicate Vital Publications, an off-shoot of
Popper.

E.377.   [Books of the States] Series, [Walter B.
Gibson], 1954.   3 3/8" x 4 3/4"; 16p.
     25 titles in this series, each describing two
of the 48 states, Alaska and Hawaii.

E.378. [Miscellaneous] Series, [Walter B. Gibson],
1958. Page count varies.
     To this series we have assigned a 5 5/8" x 8
1/2" booklet of 12 pages called "Cattle Brands You
Should Know!" and an 8 page newspaper fold-out
supplement coloring book called "Nancy Nurse Doll
Coloring Newspaper." There may be others we have
not located.

Newspaper Comic Strips

The Shadow

Distributed by the Philadelphia Public Ledger
Syndicate. Most of the stories were reprinted or
redrawn for use in Street & Smith's **Shadow Comics.**

E.379. "The Mystery of the Sealed Box," [Walter B.
Gibson]: Vernon Greene. (June 17-August 1940):
Strip nos 1-48.
     The mayor dies, leaving a box containing
evidence to convict the brains behind the local
graft ring...and then the box is stolen! Reprinted
in **Shadow Comics** (March 1941) and in **The Shadow
Scrapbook** (A.182.).

E.380.   "The Shadow in His Sanctum," [Walter B.
Gibson]: Vernon Greene. (August 12-September 21,
1940): Strip nos. A.1-A.36.
     In which a mystery-crook named Kalgar seeks
the formula for Professor Garth's sleeping gas and
the plans for Craig North's new plane.   Not
reprinted.

E.381.   "The Shadow versus Hoang Hu," [Walter B.
Gibson]: Vernon Greene.   (September 23-November 2,
1940): Strip nos. B.1-B.36.
     In which The Shadow seeks the mysterious idol
known as "The Fate Joss" and must find it before it
can be seized by Hoang Hu, ruler of the Wing Fan.
Reprinted in **Shadow Comics,** May 1941.

E.382.   ["The Shadow on Shark Island"], [Walter B.
Gibson]: Vernon Greene. (November 4, 1940-January
25, 1941): Strip nos. C.1-C.72.
     In which The Shadow, disguised as a captured
spy, goes to Shark Island to thwart the plot to

destroy the U. S. defense bases in the Caribbean.
Reprinted in **Shadow Comics,** September 1941.

E.383. ["The Shadow versus The Bund"], [Walter B.
Gibson]: Vernon Greene. (January 27-April 19,
1941): Strip nos. D.1-D.72.
   In which The Shadow does his patriotic duty
against the leaders of the Nazi bund, Kurt Schorn
and Freda Luhn. First half reprinted in **Shadow
Comics,** November 1941; second half in **Shadow
Comics,** March 1942; first appearance of Margo Lane
in the newspaper strip.

E.384. "The Shadow versus Shiwan Khan," [Walter B.
Gibson]: Vernon Greene. (April 21-July 26, 1941):
Strip nos. E.1-E.84.
   In which West meets East as the champion of
justice encounters a master of intrigue. Reprinted
in **Shadow Comics,** May 1942.

E.385.   ["The Shadow and the Darvin Fortune"],
[Walter B. Gibson]: Vernon Greene. (July 28-October
11, 1941): Strip nos. F.1-F.66.
   In which Lamont Cranston and Margo Lane
conduct a campaign against the swindlers who seek
Roy Darvin's legacy. Reprinted in **Shadow Comics,**
July 1942.

E.386. ["The Shadow and the Adele Varne Mystery"],
[Walter B. Gibson]: Vernon Greene. (October
13-November 22, 1941): Strip nos. G.1-G.36.
   In which The Shadow goes to the aid of Adele
Varne to save her fortune. See following story for
the continuation of strip numbering sequence. Not
reprinted.

E.387.   ["The Shadow and Professor Scorpio"],
[Walter B. Gibson]: Vernon Greene. (November
24-December 13, 1941): Strip nos. G.37-G.54.
   In which The Shadow investigates robberies at
Lake Calada and becomes suspicious of an astrologer
named Scorpio. While the numbering continues that
of the previous story, there appear to be two
distinct plots here. Reprinted in **Shadow Comics,**
July 1942.

E.388. "The Shadow and the Gray Ghost," [Walter B.
Gibson]: Vernon Greene. (December 15, 1941-January
10,1942): Strip nos. GX.1-GX.24.

In which The Shadow pretends to be his own
antagonist in order to unmask a criminal known as
the Gray Ghost. Reprinted in **Shadow Comics**,
September 1942.

E.389.   ["The Shadow and the Star of Delhi,"]
[Walter B. Gibson]: Vernon Greene. (January 12-31,
1942): Strip nos. GZ.1-GZ.18.
    In which The Shadow sends Margo to a
masquerade as a Hindu princess named Iliona to
learn who stole the famous sapphire, "The Star of
Delhi." The Shadow is referred to as being
invisible although the drawings do nothing to
indicate this. Suggested by the novel of the same
title in **The Shadow**, July 1, 1941. Not reprinted.

E.390.   ["The Shadow and the Earthquake Machines,"]
[Walter B. Gibson] Vernon Greene. (February 2-March
28, 1942): Strip nos. H.1-H.48.
    In which the villain known as Althor,
operating from his domain underground at Mt.
Tonnere to gain dominion over the cities with man-
made lightning and earthquakes, is thwarted by not
only The Shadow, but one of his own followers.
Introduces Skeet Harley and Valda Rune to the comic
strip. Possibly suggested by "The Thunder King,"
The Shadow, June 15, 1941. The name of the villain
suggests the thunder god, "Al-Thor," being
Norwegian for "All Thor." The Shadow is drawn to
appear transparent (or invisible) for the first
time in the strip. Not reprinted.

E.391.   ["The Shadow and the Return of Althor,"]
[Walter B. Gibson] Vernon Greene. (March 30-May 23,
1942): Strip nos. I.1-I.48.
    Althor returns for another engagement with The
Shadow, this time he is armed with a black ray
which nullifies the guns of the master of darkness.
Valda dresses as a panther. but there is a real
jungle cat, Nagu, to watch out for as well.
According to The Shadow, invisibility depends on
making one's mind a perfect blank. Redrawn for
Shadow Comics, May 1943.

E.392.   ["The Shadow and the Cliff Castle
Mystery,"] [Walter B. Gibson]: Vernon Greene. (May
25-June 13, 1942): Strip nos. J.1-J.18.
    In which The Shadow investigates the murders
of wealthy refugees by calling on Professor
Demester in his Cliff Castle on the Hudson. Story

incomplete when strip was cancelled, leaving Valda and Skeet trapped in the castle and The Shadow still looking for a way in. Not reprinted.

Other Newspaper Strips

E.393.   Arrow: The Family Comic Weekly. [Walter B. Gibson]. September 7-December 17, 1953. 8p. newspaper section.
     Publisher claimed this syndicated feature appeared in 200 papers. Gibson recalled it lasted only 6 weeks, but copies examined disprove this. Gibson scripts for "Bruce Gentry", "Straight Arrow", "Captain Galaxy", and "Debbie Dean" (from #2 on) were all written for older titles which were revived for this syndication. Strips which were published in the supplement, other than those listed here, were not written by Gibson.

E.394.   Rick Kane, Space Marshall. [Walter B. Gibson]: Elmer Stoner, 1952.
     Syndicated newspaper strip; number of episodes not recorded. Not seen.

F. Radio Scripts and Miscellaneous Works ☞

During his long career, Walter Gibson wrote or contributed to many radio series. We have included those we have been able to identify as well as some series with which he had some connection. They are arranged, alphabetically by series title, and then chronologically within each series. Following this section is a short list of material which could not be fitted into any of the other categories in this Bibliography.

The Avenger (First Series)

There is no indication that Gibson had anything to do with this series, but it has been included to avoid possible confusion with the Avenger series for which he did write scripts.

F.1. "The Hate Master," [Walter B. Gibson?] July 25, 1941. 21p.
The Avenger radio series (1); based on "The Hate Master," by Kenneth Robeson (Paul Ernst), **The Avenger Magazine**, May 1941. Script in Street & Smith Archives gives broadcast time of Friday, 9:00-9:30 p.m. The Avenger is not named, but the field operators and Inner Circle of Justice, Inc. are present. No author on script.

F.2. "Tear Drop Tank," [Walter B. Gibson?] August 1, 1941. 22p.
The Avenger radio series (1); based on characters in **The Avenger Magazine**. Avenger still not named. Script in Street & Smith Archives.

F.3. "River of Ice," [Walter B. Gibson?] August 15, 1941. 22p.
The Avenger radio series (1); based on "The River of Ice," **The Avenger Magazine**, July 1940. Features Justice, Inc., but The Avenger is not named. Broadcast time appears to be constant,

Fridays 9:00-9:30 p.m. No signature on script in Street & Smith Archives.

F.4.   "Three Gold Coins," [Walter B. Gibson?] August 22, 1941. 24p.
    The Avenger radio series (1); based on "The Three Gold Coins," **The Avenger Magazine,** January 1941. Richard Benson, Chief of Justice, Inc. opens script with "Enemies of Justice! This is the Avenger! You who operate beyond the law...you who seek to wreck the peace of America...Beware!...I shall crush your power...destroy the vultures who prey upon the innocent and the unsuspecting!...I am...The Avenger!"

F.5.   "Blood Ring," [Walter B. Gibson?] August 29, 1941. 20p.   The Avenger radio series (1); based on "The Blood Ring," **The Avenger Magazine,** March 1940.   Richard Benson named as character.   No author given on script in Street & Smith Archives.

F.6.   "The Devil's Horns," [Walter B. Gibson?] September 2, 1941. 21p.
    The Avenger radio series (1); based on "The Devil's Horns," **The Avenger Magazine,** December 1939. Richard Benson named in script. No author on script in Street & Smith Archives.

F.7.   "The Avenger," [Walter B. Gibson?] September 9, 1941. 20p.
    The Avenger radio series (1); based on characters in **The Avenger Magazine.** Richard Benson named in script; no author given.

The Avenger (Second Series)

    The Avenger in this series is Jim Brandon, a famous bio-chemist, who uses the telepathic indicator and the diffusion capsule (which makes him invisible) in his fight against crime. Assisted by Fern Collyer, Brandon is very much in the image of the radio Shadow.   According to scripts in the Street & Smith Archives, Brandon was played by James Monks, Fern Collyer by Helene Adamson, Allyn Edwards was the announcer, and Doc Whipple was the organist.   Others listed on the cast sheet include James La Curto who once portrayed The Shadow on the air. Scripts for the 26 episodes listed here are in the Street & Smith

Archives.   Audio recordings exist for the first 24 episodes.

F.8.   "The High-Tide Murders," [Walter B. Gibson with Ruth and Gilbert Braun]. No. 1. 23p.

F.9.   "The Mystery of the Giant Brain," [Walter B. Gibson with Ruth and Gilbert Braun]. No. 2. 23p.

F.10.   "Rendezvous with Murder," [Walter B. Gibson with Ruth and Gilbert Braun]. No. 3. 21p.

F.11.   "The Eyes of Shiva," [Walter B. Gibson with Ruth and Gilbert Braun]. No. 4. 22p.

F.12.   "The Coins of Death," [Walter B. Gibson with Ruth and Gilbert Braun]. No. 5. 21p.

F.13.   "The Mystery of Dead Man's Rock," [Walter B. Gibson with Ruth and Gilbert Braun]. No. 6. 20p.

F.14.   "The Tunnel of Disaster," [Walter B. Gibson with Ruth and Gilbert Braun]. No. 7. 21p.

F.15.   "The Crypt of Thoth," [Walter B. Gibson with Ruth and Gilbert Braun]. No. 8. 20p.

F.16.   "The Melody of Murder," [Walter B. Gibson with Ruth and Gilbert Braun]. No. 9. 19p.

F.17.   "The Fiery Deaths," [Walter B. Gibson with Ruth and Gilbert Braun]. No. 10. 20p.

F.18.   "The Ghost Murder," [Walter B. Gibson with Ruth and Gilbert Braun]. No. 11. 22p.

F.19.   "The Blue Pearls," [Walter B. Gibson with Ruth and Gilbert Braun]. No. 12. 21p.

F.20.   "The Wingate Heirs," [Walter B. Gibson with Ruth and Gilbert Braun]. No. 13. 19p.

F.21.   "The Thoroughbred Murder," [Walter B. Gibson with Ruth and Gilbert Braun]. No. 14. 20p.

F.22.   "The Department of Death," [Walter B. Gibson with Ruth and Gilbert Braun]. No. 15. 20p.

F.23.   "The Keys to the City," [Walter B. Gibson with Ruth and Gilbert Braun]. No. 16. 21p.

F.24. "Death in Mid-Air," [Walter B. Gibson with Ruth and Gilbert Braun]. No. 17. 20p.

F.25. "The Hooded Circle," [Walter B. Gibson with Ruth and Gilbert Braun]. No. 18. 20p.

F.26. "Death Rings the Bell," [Walter B. Gibson with Ruth and Gilbert Braun]. No. 19. 21p.

F.27. "The Subway Ghost," [Walter B. Gibson with Ruth and Gilbert Braun]. No. 20. 20p.

F.28. "The Cradle of Doom," [Walter B. Gibson with Ruth and Gilbert Braun]. No. 21. 20p.

F.29. "Death Meets the Boat," [Walter B. Gibson with Ruth and Gilbert Braun]. No. 22. 19p.

F.30. "Murder Hits the Jackpot," [Walter B. Gibson with Ruth and Gilbert Braun]. No. 23. 19p.

F.31. "The Diploma of Death," [Walter B. Gibson with Ruth and Gilbert Braun]. No. 24. 18p.

F.32. "Shot in the Dark," [Walter B. Gibson with Ruth and Gilbert Braun]. No. 25. 19p. Exists as script only; no audio recording known.

F.33. "Death Counts Ten," [Walter B. Gibson with Ruth and Gilbert Braun]. No. 26. 20p. Exists as script only; no audio recording known.

Blackstone, the Magic Detective

Harry Blackstone solved mysteries with the aid of magic in this series of 15 minute episodes. Sources differ, but the date appears to have been 1944. Each story was accompanied by the explanation by Blackstone of a simple magic trick to the incredulous announcer and Blackstone's "girl Friday", Rhoda Brent. Fran Carlon portrayed Rhoda, Ed Jerome played Blackstone, and Ted Osborne was a regular part of the cast. The announcers were Alan Kent and Don Hancock. The annotations on the first 14 episodes come from a typescript found in Gibson's files. Audio recordings for most episodes extant.

F.34.   "The Ghost That Trapped a Killer," by Nancy Webb [with Walter B. Gibson]. No. 1.

"Dead men tell no tales--but perhaps their ghosts can!   That was what Parker Harley thought when he came to steal the money of the man that he had murdered.   He didn't know that Blackstone the magician was around, manufacturing ghosts on order, to bring out the truth concerning crime!" Blackstone explains: "The Match in the Glass."

F.35.   "The Reluctant Buzz Saw," by Nancy Webb [with Walter B. Gibson], No. 2.

"When Blackstone's beautiful assistant Rhoda Brent spotted the crooks who staged a bank robbery, they decided to do away with her.   They found the very instrument they wanted: a buzz-saw. Their game was to saw through Rhoda, but Blackstone saw through their game.   Even the buzz-saw became reluctant under the spell of Blackstone's magic!" Blackstone explains "Three Coins Worth 35 Cents and Six Glasses in a Row."

F.36.   "The Emerald in the Fish Bowl," by Nancy Webb [with Walter B. Gibson], No. 3.

"The Van Layden emerald was safer than in a bank vault.   It lay in a fish-bowl along with the colored pebbles, where anyone who tried to steal it would get his hands wet and thus prove his crime. Yet the emerald disappeared and the thief thought he had staged the perfect crime until Blackstone the Magician matched him trick for trick and placed the guilt where it belonged!"   Blackstone explains "The Dry Hand Trick."

F.37.   "The Maharajah's Gold," by Nancy Webb [with Walter B. Gibson], No. 4.

"The Maharajah of Calgore found something to amaze even the Great Blackstone.   A Swami from Benares was producing gold from nowhere and giving it to the poor of the realm. Generous indeed, but being a magician, Blackstone knew that the gold must come from somewhere and the man who had the most was the Maharajah himself.   That was the clue that set Blackstone on the trail of the biggest fakir in all India!   Blackstone explains "Transportation of Coins."

F.38.   "The Educated Dummy," by Nancy Webb [with Walter B. Gibson], No. 5.

"The charity show was over and the cash was
all ready to be counted--except that it was gone!
Suspicion fell upon none other than Blackstone the
Magician, for everyone else had a perfect alibi,
including Voxola, the Ventriloquist. But Voxola
had a dummy that was smarter than its master.
Being still smarter, Blackstone called upon the
Educated Dummy to name the guilty party!"
Blackstone explains "The Seven Pile."

F.39. "The Riddle of the Talking Skull," by Nancy
Webb [with Walter B. Gibson], No. 6.
"When the Talking Skull spoke, it delivered
the death sentence to all who heard its voice.
Blackstone the Magician and Rhoda Brent, his chic
assistant, were the two who heard those words of
doom.   Locked in a vault with bronze doors that
allowed no escape, Blackstone and Rhoda were facing
their last dilemma until Blackstone solved the
riddle of the Skull and used it to defy the death
threat!"   Blackstone explains: "Mental Spelling
Trick."

F.40. "The Whispering Buddha," by Nancy Webb [with
Walter B. Gibson], No. 7.
"Blackstone the Magician was a prisoner, bound
and helpless under the close watch of desperate
men.   Pretty Rhoda Brent was a captive too, but for
her escape was possible if only Blackstone could
tell her how.   Only a magician could have figured
how to send that message and magic was Blackstone's
trade.   Before the criminals could even suspect the
wizardry at work, Blackstone and his magic had
scored another triumph!" Blackstone explains: "The
Magic Lie Detector."

F.41.   "The Organ Murder," by Nancy Webb [with
Walter B. Gibson], No. 8.
"Helen Wesley said she heard the shot that
killed her husband.   No one doubted that part of
her story because all the evidence indicated that
she herself had fired the death-shot. Blackstone
the Magician listened to Helen's claim of
innocence, because he had a sensitive ear.   The
magic ear was geared to music too. Magic and music
solved the mystery of murder!"   Blackstone
explains: "The Vibrating Fork."

F.42. "The Ghost That Wasn't," by Nancy Webb [with
Walter B. Gibson], No. 9.

"Only a ghost could have killed Clarence
Weldon when he fell screaming to his death from the
tower of the family mansion. Blackstone the
Magician didn't believe in ghosts, but Rhoda Brent
did when she visited the same haunted tower. Even
the grandfather's clock stopped in horror during
those chilling minutes while Blackstone was saving
Rhoda from a ghastly fate. For years that clock
had tolled the hours; that night it told all to
Blackstone the Magician!" Blackstone explains:
"Balancing Bottles and a Dollar Bill."

F.43. "The Icy Touch," by Nancy Webb [with Walter
B. Gibson], No. 10.
"The gold Greek medal was valued at fifty
thousand dollars. Blackstone suspected that
someone would try to steal it and Blackstone's
guess was right. When the medal suddenly vanished
they couldn't blame it on Blackstone's magic, for
he was tied to a chair when the medal disappeared.
Yet Blackstone's magic was at work, placing the
guilt upon a man who thought he could out-trick the
master!" Blackstone explains: "A Dozen Pennies."

F.44. "The Underwater Death," by Nancy Webb [with
Walter B. Gibson], No. 11.
"This was a crime that crooks were sure would
pay. With Blackstone nailed in a packing box and
dropped to the bottom of a river, the master
magician could not hope to halt crime's progress.
Nor could Rhoda Brent, for she was bound and
helpless. But Blackstone's magic could still move
faster than crime, even when he was faced by
underwater death!" Blackstone explains: "Throwing
Cards Into a Hat."

F.45. "The Coins of Confucius," by Nancy Webb
[with Walter B. Gibson], No. 12.
"When the Chinese necklace disappeared from
the museum, Blackstone found a way to uncover the
thief. He distributed the Coins of Confucius among
the suspects, for tradition claimed that these
coins would force a thief to declare himself. But
the real secret was Blackstone's magic. It was the
method behind the ancient legend and it caused the
thief to trick himself!" Blackstone explains: "Odd
or Even Coins."

F.46. "Murder on Stage," by Nancy Webb [with
Walter B. Gibson], No. 13.

"Blackstone the Magician, bound hand and foot in a glass tank filled with water, ready to attempt a daring escape where failure would mean death! A thousand witnesses were watching such a drama when murder began on stage, with Blackstone powerless to prevent it! But Blackstone's magic held the answer, with a thrilling climax that turned an audience's horror to applause!" Blackstone explains: "Table Knife and a Deck of Cards."

F.47. "The Midway Robberies," by Nancy Webb [with Walter B. Gibson], No. 14.
"Meet Ajab the automatic chess player and Madame La Belle, the gypsy fortune teller. Blackstone the Magician met them, when he and lovely Rhoda Brent went to the Midway to investigate the series of robberies that were driving away the customers. Jed Traymore, the Midway owner, didn't want a scandal but Blackstone wouldn't listen to his pleas. For Blackstone was using his inside knowledge of magic to beat a daring criminal at his own game!" Blackstone explains: "Match and Handkerchief."

F.48. "The Frozen Lady," by Nancy Webb [with Walter B. Gibson], No. 15.
Blackstone explains: "Two Hats and a Deck of Cards."

F.49. "The Hooded Rider," by Nancy Webb [with Walter B. Gibson], No. 16.
Blackstone explains: "Knot in a Handkerchief."

F.50. "The Phantom Intermezzo," by Nancy Webb [with Walter B. Gibson], No. 17.
Blackstone explains: "Selecting One Out of Three in a Hat."

F.51. "The Vanishing Pearls," by Nancy Webb [with Walter B. Gibson], No. 18.
Blackstone explains: "Ice Cube on a String."

F.52. "The Curse of the Yogi," by Nancy Webb [with Walter B. Gibson], No. 19.
Blackstone explains how "A Cigarette Floats in a Bottle."

F.53. "The Coin of Cleopatra," by Nancy Webb [with Walter B. Gibson], No. 20.
Blackstone explains: "The Magnetic Matches."

F.54. "The Hand of Cagliostro," by Nancy Webb [with Walter B. Gibson], No. 21.
Blackstone explains: "A One Deck, Two Card Location."

F.55. "The Message from Nowhere," by Nancy Webb [with Walter B. Gibson], No. 22.
Blackstone explains: "Locating Five Different Cigarette Brands in a Hat."

F.56. "The Riddle of the Red Rose," by Nancy Webb [with Walter B. Gibson], No. 23.
Blackstone explains: "Mentally Selected Cards." Script extant in Gibson files.

F.57. "The Aztec Fire God," by Nancy Webb [with Walter B. Gibson], No. 24.
Blackstone explains: "Mental Telepathy."

F.58. "The MIssing Palmist," by Nancy Webb [with Walter B. Gibson], No. 25.
Blackstone explains: "Coin and Handkerchief."

F.59. "The Ladder of Wealth," by Nancy Webb [with Walter B. Gibson], No. 26.
Blackstone explains: "Nickel, Quarter and Penny."

F.60. "The Locked Book," by Nancy Webb [with Walter B. Gibson], No. 27.
Blackstone explains: "Anti-gravity."

F.61. "The Deathless Shots," by Nancy Webb [with Walter B. Gibson], No. 28.
Blackstone explains: "The Turnover Bill."

F.62. "The Riddle of the Other Eight Ball," by Nancy Webb [with Walter B. Gibson], No. 29.
Blackstone explains: "The Disappearing Half."

F.63. "The Cellini Statuette," by Nancy Webb [with Walter B. Gibson], No. 30.
Blackstone explains: "Balancing an Egg."

F.64. "The Curse of Kali," by Nancy Webb [with Walter B. Gibson], No. 31.
Blackstone explains: "Dollar Bill Serial Number."

F.65.   "Footsteps in the Night," by Nancy Webb
[with Walter B. Gibson], No. 32.
    Blackstone explains: "Spectator Names Card."

F.66.   "The Voodoo Treasure," by Nancy Webb [with
Walter B. Gibson], No. 33.
    Blackstone explains: "The Walking Hairpin."

F.67.   "The Four Keys to Crime," by Nancy Webb
[with Walter B. Gibson], No. 34.
    Blackstone explains: "A Bottle, Match and
Coin."

F.68.   "The Knife from the Dark," by Nancy Webb
[with Walter B. Gibson], No. 35.
    Blackstone explains: "Two Thieves and Five
Sheep."

F.69.   "Death in the Crystal," by Nancy Webb [with
Walter B. Gibson], No. 36.
    Blackstone explains: "Cut and Restored
String."

F.70.   "The Hindu Sword Cabinet," by Nancy Webb
[with Walter B. Gibson], No. 37.
    Blackstone explains: "The Whispering Queen."

F.71.   "The Face of Death," by Nancy Webb [with
Walter B. Gibson], No. 38.
    Blackstone explains: "Divining a Match Pack."

F.72.   "The Voice from the Void," by Nancy Webb
[with Walter B. Gibson], No. 39.
    Blackstone explains: "The Prediction of Three
Equal Piles."

F.73.   "The Bird of Doom," by Nancy Webb [with
Walter B. Gibson], No. 40.
    Blackstone explains: "The Rising Cigarette."

F.74.   "The Phantom Detective," by Nancy Webb [with
Walter B. Gibson], No. 41.
    Blackstone explains: "A Glass, a Coin, and a
Dollar Bill."

F.75.   "The Riddle of the Seven Zombies," by Nancy
Webb [with Walter B. Gibson], No. 42.
    Blackstone explains: "Match Box Anti-Gravity."

F.76. "Crime in the Stars," by Nancy Webb [with Walter B. Gibson], No. 43.
Blackstone explains: "The Ghost Trick."

F.77. "The Devil's Cauldron," by Nancy Webb [with Walter B. Gibson], No. 44.
Blackstone explains: "Picking Up Seven Matches with One."

F.78. "The Ghost in the Crypt," by Nancy Webb [with Walter B. Gibson], No. 45.
Blackstone explains: "Two Fists and Hypnotism."

F.79. "The Accusing Corpse," by Nancy Webb [with Walter B. Gibson], No. 46.
Blackstone explains: "The Riddle of the Three Jacks."

F.80. "Death Defying Death," by Nancy Webb [with Walter B. Gibson], No. 47.
Blackstone explains: "Balancing a Glass on a Dollar Bill."

F.81. "The Criminal Who Caught Himself," by Nancy Webb [with Walter B. Gibson], No. 48.
Blackstone explains: "The Disappearing Dime."

F.82. "The Vanishing Brooch," by Nancy Webb [with Walter B. Gibson], No. 49.
Blackstone explains: "'Yankee Doodle' Card Trick."

F.83. "Crimes on a Merry-Go-Round," by Nancy Webb [with Walter B. Gibson], No. 50.
Blackstone explains: "Gravity Defied."

F.84. "The Magic Writing," by Nancy Webb [with Walter B. Gibson], No. 51.
Blackstone explains: "Mind Over Matter with a Match."

F.85. "The Men from Mecca," by Nancy Webb [with Walter B. Gibson], No. 52.
Program title is all that survives; script and audio recording not extant; name of trick not known. Program title, trick, and any recording of Program #53 as well have not been located.

F.86. "The Mark of Crime," by Nancy Webb [with Walter B. Gibson], No. 54.
    Blackstone explains: "Card Selection in a Handkerchief."

F.87. "The Creeping Death," by Nancy Webb [with Walter B. Gibson], No. 55.
    Blackstone explains: "Floating Lump of Sugar." Programs #55 through #77 have not been located.

F.88. "The Gory Goldfish," by Nancy Webb [with Walter B. Gibson], No. 78.
    Blackstone explains: "The Half-Dollar Trick." Final program in series; as Blackstone said at the end of each show: "I hope you liked that trick, ladies and gentlemen; and until next time, this is Blackstone saying, Good Magic and Good Bye!"

Chick Carter, Boy Detective

    Mutual Broadcasting Network. Daytime serial, Monday-Friday, 5:15-5:30 p.m. Starred Billy Lipton and Leon Janney. Chick Carter was Nick Carter's foster son on radio, Nick Carter's first assistant in the dime novels and pulps. First 20 episodes credited to Ed Gruskin alone in the Copyright Office records, but credited to Gibson as well on the scripts. Complete file of scripts in the Street & Smith Archives.

F.89. "Chick Carter, Boy Detective, [Meets The Rattler]," by Walter B. Gibson and Edward Gruskin. July 2-September 2, 1943. Episodes 1-44.

F.90. "Chick Carter: The Rattler and the Life-line of Oil," by Walter B. Gibson and Edward Gruskin. September 3-27, 1943. Episodes 45-61.

F.91. "Chick Carter [Meets The Bat]," by Walter B. Gibson and Edward Gruskin. September 28-December 8, 1943. Episodes 62-113.

F.92. "Chick Carter and the Shalimar Diamond," by Walter B. Gibson and Edward Gruskin. December 9, 1943-January 20, 1944. Episodes 114-144.

F.93. "Chick Carter [and The Octopus]," by Walter B. Gibson and Edward Gruskin. January 21-March 21, 1944. Episodes 145-187.

The last script credited to Gibson and Gruskin was #162, February 15, 1944. Nancy and Jean Webb took over the writing of the series with #163. The serial ended with script #524, Friday, July 6, 1945.

Frank Merriwell

F.94.   Frank Merriwell, by Ruth and Gilbert Braun [with Walter B. Gibson], 1946-1949.
NBC radio network weekly adventure radio series based on the stories by Gilbert Patten writing as Burt L. Standish.   Gibson recalls plotting one in which a student at Yale who came from Australia demonstrated his ability with the boomerang.   An episode titled "Boomerang Pitch" exists, but has not been examined.

The Return of Nick Carter

Based on the old dime novel and pulp series, the radio show featured a modern day detective whose secretary and girl Friday was named Patsy Bowen. Another regular in the series was Inspector Matthewson ("Matty") of the New York Police Department.   Lon Clark played Nick, Charlotte Manson played Patsy.   It was one of the longer running detective series on radio and one of the last to leave the air in the 1950s.

F.95.   "The Strange Dr. Devolo," by Walter B. Gibson and Edward Gruskin. No. 1. April 11, 1943.
Mutual   Broadcasting System. Thirty minute weekly episodes. Gibson shared credit with Gruskin for the first 16 episodes, wrote nos. 17-21 by himself, and shared credit with Jean and Nancy Webb for no. 22.

F.96.   "The Voice of Crime," by Walter B. Gibson and Edward Gruskin. No. 2. April 18, 1943.

F.97.   "Nick Carter and the Mystery of the Indian Idols; or, The Curse of the Astral Bells," by Walter B. Gibson and Edward Gruskin. No. 3. April 27, 1943.

F.98. "The Mystery of the Old Red Mill; or, Nick Carter and the Underground River," by Walter B. Gibson and Edward Gruskin. No. 4. May 4, 1943.

F.99. "Seven Drops of Blood," by Walter B. Gibson and Edward Gruskin. No. 5. May 11, 1943.

F.100. "Three Blind Mice; or, Nick Carter and the Mystery of the Secret Formula," by Walter B. Gibson and Edward Gruskin. No. 6. May 18, 1943.

F.101. "The Skeleton in the Closet; or, Nick Carter Settles an Old Score," by Walter B. Gibson and Edward Gruskin. No. 7. May 25, 1943.

F.102. "The Purloined Portraits; or, Nick Carter and the Riddle of the Seven Sinners," by Walter B. Gibson and Edward Gruskin. No. 8. June 1, 1943.
This plot and title were also used in the Blackstone comic book series in **Super-Magician Comics.**

F.103. "Murder in Bronze; or, Nick Carter and the Rogue's Gallery Mystery," by Walter B. Gibson and Edward Gruskin. No. 9. June 8, 1943.

F.104. "Insured for Death; or, Nick Carter Takes a Premium on Life," by Walter B. Gibson and Edward Gruskin. No. 10. June 15, 1943.
This has echoes of one of The Shadow pulp novels of the same period with a similar title.

F.105. "The Forgotten Alibi; or, Nick Carter Solves a Perfect Crime," by Walter B. Gibson and Edward Gruskin. No. 11. June 22, 1943.

F.106. "Endowment for Murder; or, Nick Carter Finds the Coin of Death," by Walter B. Gibson and Edward Gruskin. No. 12. June 29, 1943.

F.107. "The Echo of Death; or, Nick Carter and the Phantom Clue," by Walter B. Gibson and Edward Gruskin. No. 13. July 6, 1943.

F.108. "Death Across the Tracks; or, Nick Carter and the Mystery of the Night Freight," by Walter B. Gibson and Edward Gruskin. No. 14. July 12, 1943.
The day of the week for the broadcast has been moved up one, thus explaining this being dated only 6 days following the previous script.

F.109.   "Death's Double Deal; or, Nick Carter Held for Murder," by Walter B. Gibson and Edward Gruskin. No. 15. July 19, 1943.

F.110.   "The Haunted Glen; or, Nick Carter and the Mystery of the Devil's Treasure," by Walter B. Gibson and Edward Gruskin. No. 16. July 26, 1943.

F.111.   "Murder in the Crypt; or, Nick Carter and the Jackal God," by Walter B. Gibson. No. 17. August 2, 1943.

F.112.   "Murder on Skull Island; or, Nick Carter and the Mystery of the Sea Serpent," by Walter B. Gibson. No. 18. August 9, 1943.

F.113.   "Carnival of Death; or, Nick Carter and the Game of Death," by Walter B. Gibson. No. 19. August 16, 1943.

F.114.   "Dead Man's Reef; or, Nick Carter and the Mystery of the Abandoned Lighthouse," by Walter B. Gibson. No. 20. August 23, 1943.

F.115.   "The Ragoff Brooch; or, Nick Carter and the Mystery of the Murdered Bandit," by Walter B. Gibson. No. 21. August 30, 1943.

F.116.   "The Tattooed Twin; or, Nick Carter and the Mystery of the Threatening Voice," by Walter B. Gibson with Jean and Nancy Webb. No. 22. September 6, 1943.

Strange

ABC radio series.   Forty 15 minute episodes broadcast during the Summer of 1955.   Written and narrated by Gibson himself.   Scripts for all episodes have not been found, but may exist in Gibson's files.   Audio recordings of only four episodes extant.

F.117.   "The Ghost of La Chatraine," by Walter B. Gibson. 1955.
    Extant script in Gibson files.

F.118.   "The Percy Castle Ghost," by Walter B. Gibson. 1955.
    Extant script in Gibson files.

F.119. "Lightening a Ghost House," by Walter B. Gibson. 1955.
    Extant script in Gibson files.

F.120. "Killed by a Ghost in a Taxi," by Walter B. Gibson. 1955.
    Extant script in Gibson files.

F.121. "Washington Irving Bishop," by Walter B. Gibson. 1955.
    Extant script in Gibson files.

F.122. "The Ghost Train," by Walter B. Gibson. 1955.
    Extant audio recording.

F.123. "Deadman's Reef," by Walter B. Gibson. 1955.
    Extant audio recording.

F.124. "Greenwood Acres," by Walter B. Gibson. 1955.
    Extant audio recording.

F.125. "The Flying Dutchman," by Walter B. Gibson. 1955.
    Extant audio recording.

Manuscripts and Miscellaneous Publications

F.126. **The Astrologer's Almanac and Occult Miscellany,** edited by Litzka R. and Walter B. Gibson. New York: Pyramid Publications, 1975. 96p. paper covers.
    1975 Aries to 1976 Pisces. Contains much unsigned and reprinted material in public domain. Includes "The Remarkable Prophecies of Mother Shipton" and "'The Centuries' of Nostradamus."

F.127. **The Astrologer's Almanac and Occult Miscellany,** edited by Litzka R. and Walter B. Gibson. New York: Pyramid Publications, 1976. 96p. paper covers.
    1976 Aries to Pisces 1977. Includes "The Inside Story of The Shadow" and "The Ghost of Gay Street" by Gibson.

F.128. The Astrologer's Almanac and Occult Miscellany, edited by Litzka R. and Walter B. Gibson. New York: Pyramid Publications, 1977. 96p. paper covers.

1977 Aries to Pisces 1978. Includes "The Insights of Edgar Cayce," "The Strange Dream of Lemuel Orton," and "The Werewolf: Fact or Fantasy."

F.129. The Astrologer's Almanac and Occult Miscellany, edited by Litzka R. and Walter B. Gibson. New York: Everbe Press, 1978. 96p. paper covers.

1978 Aries to Pisces 1979. Includes "The Seer of Poughkeepsie" and "Stranger Than Fiction" (about Daniel Home).

F.130. The Astrologer's Almanac and Occult Miscellany, edited by Litzka R. and Walter B. Gibson. New York: Everbe Press, 1979. 96p. paper covers.

1979 Aries to Pisces 1980. Includes "The Presidential Jinx" and "1980 Potential Presidential Candidates." The final issue of this annual to be compiled by the Gibsons.

F.131. "Adventures of an Escape Artist." by Harry Blackstone [Walter B. Gibson]. 14p.

Undated typescript found in Gibson files.

F.132. "The Han Ping Chien Coin Trick." by Walter B. Gibson. 1957. 7p.

Typescript found in Gibson files of a trick "as performed by Paul Rosini...Descriptions by Walter B. Gibson."

F.133. "Harley Strand, Ghost Breaker," by Walter B. Gibson: Birmingham [artist].

Unpublished newspaper comic strip. 12 daily episodes extant in Gibson files.

F.134. How to Do Magic, by Walter B. Gibson. 23p.

Typescript outline for a book on magic which would be illustrated with photographs demonstrating the techniques involved with each trick. Possibly a forerunner of The Complete Illustrated Book of Close-Up Magic.

F.135. The Interlocked Back-and-Front-Hand Card Production, by Walter B. Gibson. Philadelphia: [Mitchell] Kanter's Magic Shop, 1958. 7p.

Illustrates three methods, including moves employed by Channing Pollock, using drawings and descriptions from **The Phoenix**; alternative method by Walter B. Gibson.

F.136.   Master Mental, by Walter B. Gibson. The Magic Art Studio.   Undated. Cards and instructions for performing the trick, contained in a business size envelope illustrated with a drawing of Gibson. "Another amazing effect from the mind of Walter Gibson."

Nick Carter Revisions

F.137.   Empire of Crime, by Nicholas Carter [Richard Wormser]. New York: Vital Publications, 1945. 128p. paper covers.
Originally published as "Crooks' Empire," **Nick Carter Magazine**, April 1933. Revised and edited by Gibson for book publication.

F.138.   Murder Unlimited, by Nicholas Carter [Richard Wormser]. New York: Vital Publications, 1945. 128p. paper covers.
Originally published as "Bid for a Railroad," **Nick Carter Magazine**, January 1934.   Revised and edited (with new chapter titles) by Gibson for book publication.

F.139.   Death Has Green Eyes, by Nicholas Carter [Richard Wormser]. New York: Vital Publications, 1946. 128p. paper covers.
Originally published under the same title in **Nick Carter Magazine**, May 1934. Revised and edited for book publication by Gibson.

F.140.   Park Avenue Murder, by Nicholas Carter [Richard Wormser]. New York: Vital Publications, 1946. 128p. paper covers.
Originally published as "Death on Park Avenue," **Nick Carter Magazine**, July 1934. Revised and edited for book publication by Gibson.

F.141.   The Yellow Disc Murder Case, by Nicholas Carter [Thomas Calvert McClary]. New York: Vital Publications, 1948. 128p. paper covers.
Originally published as "Power," **Nick Carter Magazine**, August 1934. Revised and edited for book publication by Gibson.

F.142.   Rendezvous with Dead Men, by Nicholas Carter [John Chambliss]. New York: Vital Publications, 1948. 128p. paper covers.
Originally published as "Murder on Skull Island," **Nick Carter Magazine,** September 1934. Revised and edited for book publication by Gibson.

Other Works

F.143.   Repeat Reverso, by Walter B. Gibson. The Magic Art Studio.
Undated apparatus and instructions for the trick, packed in a business size envelope labelled "Another amazing effect from the mind of Walter Gibson."

F.144.   Simplified Mind Reading, by Walter B. Gibson. 6p.
Typescript of a two person routine compiled by Walter B. Gibson and copyrighted by Mitchell Kanter.

F.145.   "They'll Do It Every Time." by Dunn and Scadutz. King Features Syndicate, November 13, 1978.
Syndicated newspaper cartoon panel originated by Jimmy Hatlo. Topic suggested by Gibson and credited to him: "Tuning in on the family's hypochondriac."

F.146.   Thurston's Course in Magic, by Howard Thurston [Walter B. Gibson]. New York: Thurston, the Magician & Assoc., nd. 47p.
Illustrated text of Thurston's Personal Course-By-Mail in Home Entertaining with Magic. Each trick includes the effect, the method of performing it, and suggested patter.

F.147.   Thurston's Magic Box of Candy, by Howard Thurston [Walter B. Gibson], 1922.
A series of 50 numbered tricks which can be performed with ordinary articles or small pieces of special apparatus, distributed in boxes of candy. Each box was numbered for ease in collecting. The tricks also formed the basis for **Thurston's Lessons in Magic (D.11.).**

A fine tribute to the master. This was the official badge at Pulpcon XV in 1986. (Courtesy of Frank Hamilton)

Appendix ☜

Appendix A

"Walter Gibson, Writing as. . ."

Pseudonyms and Ghosts: Gibson's many pen names are listed below in alphabetical order by their last names. All names which are not fictitious, but represent real people with whom he collaborated or for whom he served as ghost writer, are marked *. (We apologize to any person, living or dead, who has been mis-represented.)

John Abbington; Andrew Abbott; Earl J. Abbott; Andy Adams; Astro; David Atkins; "The Author of Cherry Ames"; Bill Barnum; Ishi Black; Harry Blackstone;* Jack I. Blum;* Douglas Brown; Major Robert Brannon;* Charles R. Brush;* Gene W. Byrnes; Wesley Chalk;* Bruce Crandall; Russ T. Creighton; C. B. Crowe (this name was taken from the rooster mascot, China Boy, used by Litzka Raymond in her magic act); Peter Darrington; Martin Donohue (also spelled "Donoghue" at least once); Joseph Dunninger;* John Ellert;* Morton Faber; Felix Fairfax; Harry Friedenberg;* Wilber Gaston; Ray Girardin;* Walter Glass; George Goodwin;* Maxwell Grant; Edward Griffin;* Madeleine Grover;* C. J. Hagen;* Ponjay Harah; Harry Hershfield;* Julian Houseman;* David Hoy;* Feng Huang; O. H. Jensen;* Carter Johnson; E. C. Kalbfleisch;* Gilbert Kay; Maborushi Kineji; Kreskin [George Kresge];* G. A. Lacksey; Gautier LeBrun (also spelled LeBlun); Thomas McClary;* Lieut. Thomas McDermot; Roy Masters [there was a real "Roy Masters", but Gibson did not use his name intentionally]; Alfred Maurice; Herbert Mayer;* Neil Michaels; Don Monroe; Richard Mullen; Theodore (Teddy) Nadler;* Jess Nichols; Warren Palmer; Bernard Perry; Rufus Perry; Jack C.

Peters; Julian J. Proskauer;* Sidney H. Radner;*
P. L. Raymond;*   Henry [Hank] Rodney;*   Charles
Russell;*   Sy Seidman;   Prof. Alfred Francis
Seward; Robert Russell Smith; Edward S. Sullivan;
Howard Thurston;*   Alfred Toman;   Wallace Weldon
[Weldon the Wizard];* Helen Wells;* Mark Wilson;*
Thomas Windsor;*   David Woodsman;   Chesley V.
Young;* Hee Foo Yuu.

Who would guess the master of magic and mystery
would try historical fiction? (A.90.)

Appendix B

A Library of Magazines

Gibson contributed material to, or edited, or had his work published or reprinted in, dozens of periodicals. Below we list those consulted in preparing this bibliography. We include comic books and indicate variant titles where applicable. The list is as complete as human frailty can achieve.

The American Smoker; The American Weekly; Analog Science Fact & Fiction; Authentic Detective/Police Cases; The Bat [magical magazine]; Batman [comic]; Beyond Reality; The Big Story; Blackstone, Master Magician [comic]; Blackstone the Magician [comic]; Blackstone the Magician Detective [comic]; Blackstone the Magician Detective Fights Crime [comic]; Boys' Life; Calling All Boys [comic]; Child Life; Collier's Weekly; The Conjuror's Magazine; Crime and Punishment [comic]; Crime Busters; Crime Case Book Magazine; Crime Does Not Pay [comic]; Daring Detective; Detective Comics; Doc Savage; Eagle Magician; Ethyl News; Fantastic Science Fiction; Felsman's Magical Review; Fotorama; Genii [magical magazine]; Ghost Breakers [comic]; Ghost Stories; Hocus Pocus; Houdini's Magic Magazine; The Linking Ring [magical magazine]; M-U-M [magical magazine]; The Magic Magazine; The Magic Wand; The Magic World; Magical Bulletin; Magician; Magick; Mystery Digest; Mystery in Space [comic]; N. C. A. Digest [magical magazine]; N. C. A. Publication [magical magazine]; National Examiner; Official Detective; The Phoenix; Popular Mechanics; Popular Medicine; Popular Science Monthly; Practical Electrics; Racket Squad in Action [comic]; Real Police Stories; Red Dragon Comics; The Saint Detective Magazine; Saint Nicholas; Saturday Evening Post; Science and Invention; Sensation; The Seven Circles; The Shadow [pulp] (title varies); Shadow Comics; Space Western Comics; The Sphinx; Startling Detective; Strange Adventures [comic]; Street & Smith's Mystery Magazine; Street & Smith's Sport Story Magazine; Super-Magic Comics; Super-Magician Comics; Tales of Magic and Mystery; The Thinker; Timely Detective; True Detective; True

Police Cases; True Police Year-Book; True Strange
Stories; Youth's Companion.

Among the many magazines with which Gibson was
associated, this was his short-lived science
fiction series. (B.801.)

Appendix C

The Other Maxwell Grants

Street and Smith used the name "Maxwell Grant" as the signature on several stories which Gibson did not write. By implication, the name has been applied to over 50 scripts for **Shadow Comics** which were the work of others. A discussion of the adaptations of the character of The Shadow to media other than print has been saved for Appendix D. Comic book adaptations other than those published by Street & Smith will be discussed there as well.

Theodore Tinsley (1894-1979) contributed 27 novels to the series for **The Shadow Magazine**. None seem to have been reprinted in book form, or in any of the **Shadow Annuals,** although several were revised and appeared in the British periodical, **The Thriller.**

"Partners in Peril," **The Shadow Magazine,** 19 (November 1, 1936): 14-98.

"Foxhound," **The Shadow Magazine,** 20 (January 15, 1937): 8-92. (According to Anthony Tollin in **The Shadow** Scrapbook, this novel served as the basis for the film, **International Crime,** 1938. See Appendix D.)

"The Cup of Confucius," **The Shadow Magazine,** 21 (May 1, 1937): 8-83.

"The Pooltex Tangle," **The Shadow Magazine,** 23 (October 1, 1937): 8-92.

"The Fifth Napoleon," **The Shadow,** 24 (February 1, 1938): 6-81.

"The Crimson Phoenix," **The Shadow,** 25 (April 1, 1938): 6-81.

"The Golden Dog Murders," **The Shadow,** 27 (September 1, 1938): 6-87.

"Double Death," **The Shadow,** 28 (December 15, 1938): 9-84.

"River of Death," **The Shadow,** 29 (March 1, 1939): 9-52, 93-128.

"Death's Harlequin," **The Shadow**, 29 (May 1, 1939): 9-52, 90-129.

"Noose of Death," **The Shadow**, 30 (July 1, 1939): 9-52, 89-127.

"Prince of Evil," **The Shadow**, 33 (April 15, 1940): 9-96.

"Murder Genius," **The Shadow**, 34 (July 1, 1940): 9-92.

"The Man Who Died Twice," **The Shadow**, 35 (September 15, 1940): 9-90.

"City of Fear," **The Shadow**, 35 (October 15, 1940): 9-92.

"The Devil's Paymaster," **The Shadow**, 35 (November 15, 1940): 9-95.

"The Green Terror," **The Shadow**, 36 (January 15, 1941): 9-89.

"The White Column," **The Shadow**, 37 (March 15, 1941): 9-88.

"Master of Flame," **The Shadow**, 37 (May 15, 1941): 9-91.

"The Crimson Death," **The Shadow**, 38 (August 1, 1940): 9-94.

"Gems of Jeopardy," **The Shadow**, 39 (September 1, 1941): 9-91.

"Blue Face," **The Shadow**, 40 (February 15, 1942): 9-99.

"Death's Bright Finger," **The Shadow**, 41 (May 15, 1942): 9-94.

"Syndicate of Sin," **The Shadow**, 43 (September 15, 1942): 9-89.

"The Devil's Partner," **The Shadow**, 43 (October 1, 1942): 9-90.

"Young Men of Death," **The Shadow**, 45 (April 1943): 10-105.

"The Golden Doom," **The Shadow**, 45 (July 1943): 10-87.

* * *

Following a contract dispute between Gibson and Street and Smith, Bruce Elliot (1917-1973) contributed 15 novels to the series while Gibson worked on some of his other projects. Like Gibson, Elliot was a magician, an author of several magic books, and an editor of a magical magazine. His Shadow novels were shorter than Gibson's and gave greater emphasis to the persona of Lamont Cranston.

"The Blackest Mail," **The Shadow**, 51 (August 1946): 6-89.

"Happy Death Day," **The Shadow**, 52 (September 1946): 4-83.

"The Seven Deadly Arts," **The Shadow**, 52 (October 1946): 4-84.

"No Safety in Numbers," **The Shadow**, 52 (November 1946): 6-83.

"Death on Ice," **The Shadow**, 52 (December 1946): 7-66.

"Death Stalks the U.N.," **The Shadow**, 52 (January 1947): 6-84.

"Murder in White," **Shadow Mystery**, 52 (February-March 1947): 6-43.

"Room 1313," **Shadow Mystery**, 53 (April-May 1947): 6-54.

"Model Murder," **Shadow Mystery**, 53 (June-July 1947): 7-58.

"Svengali Kill," **Shadow Mystery**, 53 (August-September 1947): 6-53.

"Jabberwocky Thrust," **Shadow Mystery**, 53 (October-November 1947): 7-46.

"Ten Glass Eyes," **Shadow Mystery**, 53 (December-January 1948): 7-62.

"The Television Murders," **Shadow Mystery**, 53 (February-March 1948): 7-62.

"Murder on Main Street," **Shadow Mystery**, 54 (April-May 1948): 7-56.

"Reign of Terror,"` **Shadow Mystery**, 54 (June-July 1948): 7-64.

* * *

In order to maintain the pretense of "Maxwell Grant" as a distinct entity and real person and not a "house name," Street and Smith used the name on several stories outside the mystery field. The records in the Street and Smith Archives do not identify all of these "other" Maxwell Grants.

Maxwell Grant, "He Hated Baseball," **Street & Smith's College Stories**, 23 (September 1931): 62-72.

Maxwell Grant, "Bald-Pate," **Street & Smith's College Stories**, 23 (October 1931): 72-81.

Maxwell Grant, "Voice of Victory," **Street & Smith's College Stories**, 23 (November 1931): 38-48.

Maxwell Grant [Arthur Mann], "Is Wrestling On the Level?" **Sport Story Magazine**, 33 (December 25, 1931): 15-24.

Maxwell Grant [Tom Lewis], "Doubling for Dynamite," **Street & Smith's Sport Story Magazine**, 34 (February 10, 1932): 124-144. (Rewritten by Lon Murray)

Maxwell Grant [J.P.Olsen], "Confidence Plus," **Street & Smith's Sport Story Magazine**, 34 (March 10, 1932): 74-79.

* * *

Although comic book stories in the 1940s were not signed as a rule, the name "Maxwell Grant" was so much a part of The Shadow tradition that we have included a list of the scripts from **Shadow Comics** which Gibson does not appear to have written himself. He once admitted he didn't write the script for the first issue and relinquished the

series in 1946 during his break with Street and
Smith. Where the artist's name is known, it
precedes each story title.

["Sabotage"], **Shadow Comics**, 1.1 (March 1940):
2-7.

[Charles] Coll, "One Small Bier," **Shadow
Comics**, 6.9 (December 1946): 3-16.

[Charles Coll], "The Winged Dagger," **Shadow
Comics**, 6.9 (December 1946): 41-47, 50.
The Shadow takes an assistant, a boy who can
become invisible.

[Charles Coll], "The Shadow Battles Crime at
Devil's Passage," **Shadow Comics**, 6.10 (January
1947): 3-16.

[Charles Coll], "The Shadow Ends the Voodoo
Hoodoo," **Shadow Comics**, 6.10 (January 1947): 42-49.

[Charles Coll], "The Shadow Meets the Subway
Ghost," **Shadow Comics**, 6.11 (February 1947): 43-50.

[Bob] Powell, "The Shadow Solves the Mystery
of the Missing Uranium," **Shadow Comics**, 6.12 (March
1947): 3-15.

[Bob] Powell, "The Shadow Proves That Truth
Will Out," **Shadow Comics**, 6.12 (March 1947): 43-50.

"The Shadow: Crime Off Shore," **Shadow Comics**,
7.1 (April 1947): 43-50.

"Shadow, Jr.: The Steal Mill," **Shadow Comics**,
7.2 (May 1947): 43-50. (The adventures of Donny
Dart)

[Bob] Powell, "The Shadow Unearths Crime Under
the Border," **Shadow Comics**, 7.3 (June 1947): 3-16.

[Bob] Powell, "The Shadow and the Mystery of
One Tree Island," **Shadow Comics**, 7.4 (July 1947):
3-17.

[Charles] Coll, "The Six Fingers of Death,"
Shadow Comics, 7.5 (August 1947): 3-16.

[Charles] Coll, "Shadow, Jr. Meets Snake Eyes," **Shadow Comics**, 7.5 (August 1947): 42-49.

[Bob] Powell, "The Shadow Saves The Sacred Sword of Sanjorjo," **Shadow Comics**, 7.6 (September 1947): 3-15.
Contest for best solution to how The Shadow knew the real sword; title spelled "Sanjorojo" on cover.

[Charles Coll], "The Shadow Defies The Flames of Death," **Shadow Comics**, 7.6 (September 1947): 40-47.

[Charles] Coll, "Crime K.O.," **Shadow Comics**, 7.7 (October 1947): 3-16.

[Charles Coll], "The Shadow Uncovers Links of Crime," **Shadow Comics**, 7.7 (October 1947): 42-49.

[Charles] Coll, "The Shadow Raids Crime Harbor," **Shadow Comics**, 7.8 (November 1947): 3-16.

[Bob Powell], "Dolls of Death," **Shadow Comics**, 7.8 (November1947): 42-49.

[Bob] Powell, "Kilroy Was Here," **Shadow Comics**, 7.9 (December 1947): 3-16.

[Charles Coll], "Time for Crime," **Shadow Comics**, 7.9 (December 1947): 36-49.

[Bob] Powell, "The Riddle of the Flying Saucers," **Shadow Comics**, 7.10 (January 1948): 3-16.

[Bob Powell], "The Solution of the Mystery of The Shadow and the Sacred Sword of Sanjorjo," **Shadow Comics**, 7.10 (January 1948): 49-50.

[Bob] Powell, "The Hiss of Death," **Shadow Comics**, 7.11 (February 1948): 3-16.

[Bob] Powell, "Murder in the Carnival," **Shadow Comics**, 7.11 (February 1948): 35-46.

[Bob] Powell, "Back from the Grave," **Shadow Comics**, 7.12 (March 1948): 3-16.

[Charles] Coll, "The Red Death," **Shadow Comics**, 7.12 (March 1948): 36-49.

[Bob] Powell, "The Curse of the Cat," Shadow Comics, 8.1 (April 1948): 3-16.

[Charles] Coll, "The Shadow and the Treasure Chest of Death," Shadow Comics, 8.1 (April 1948): 35-48.

[Bob] Powell, "Terror in the Bayou," Shadow Comics, 8.2 (May 1948): 3-14. (Radio adaptation)

[Charles] Coll, "Three False Crimes," Shadow Comics, 8.2 (May 1948): 29-42.

[Bob] Powell, "Spider Boy," Shadow Comics, 8.3 (June 1948): 3-16. (Radio adaptation)

[Bob] Powell, "The League of Smiling Men," Shadow Comics, 8.3 (June 1948): 33-46.

[Bob] Powell, "Death Rises Out of the Sea," Shadow Comics, 8.4 (July 1948): 3-16.

"The Shadow Fights Crime in the Cave of the Thousand Buddhas," Shadow Comics, 8.4 (July 1948): 33-46.

[Bob] Powell, "The Jekyll-Hyde Murders," Shadow Comics, 8.5 (August 1948): 3-16. (Radio adaptation)

[Charles Coll], "The Shadow Solves the Fifth Ace Murders," Shadow Comics, 8.5 (August 1948): 36-49.

[Bob] Powell, "The Secret of Valhalla Hall," Shadow Comics, 8.6 (September 1948): 3-16.

[Bob] Powell, "The Man Who Could Not Die," Shadow Comics, 8.6 (September 1948): 42-49.

[Bob] Powell, "The Shadow in Danger!" Shadow Comics, 8.7 (October 1948): 3-16.

[Bob] Powell, "The Dream of Death," Shadow Comics, 8.7 (October 1948): 39-46.

[Bob] Powell, "The Four Giants of Amsterdam," Shadow Comics, 8.8 (November 1948): 3-16.

"From The Shadow's Crime File," **Shadow Comics**, 8.8 (November 1948): 31-33. (How thieves work)

[Bob] Powell, "The Spotlight on the Duchess," **Shadow Comics**, 8.8 (November 1948): 34-47.

[Bob] Powell, "I Must Never Sleep Again," **Shadow Comics**, 8.9 (December 1948): 3-14.

[Bob] Powell, "Relax...and Murder!" **Shadow Comics**, 8.9 (December 1948): 41-46, 48-49.

[Bob] Powell, "This'll Kill You," **Shadow Comics**, 8.10 (January 1949): 3-16.

[Bob] Powell, "From The Shadow's Crime File," **Shadow Comics**, 8.10 (January 1949): 27-28. (Coins and Disappearing Ink)

[Bob] Powell, "The Shadow Solves the Riddle of Desert City," **Shadow Comics**, 8.10 (January 1949): 39-46.

[Bob] Powell, "The Turban Top Mystery," **Shadow Comics**, 8.11 (February 1949): 3-16.

[Bob Powell], "From The Shadow's Crime File," **Shadow Comics**, 8.11 (February 1949): 27-29. (Tricks of con men explained)

[Bob] Powell, "Murder Can't Be Logical," **Shadow Comics**, 8.11 (February 1949): 42-49.

[Bob] Powell, "Three Curious Clues," **Shadow Comics**, 8.12 (March 1949): 3-16.

[Bob] Powell, "Your Number's Up!" **Shadow Comics**, 9.1 (April 1949): 3-16.

[Bob] Powell, "The Deadly Isle," **Shadow Comics**, 9.2 (May 1949): 3-16.

[Bob] Powell, "The Shadow's Shadow," **Shadow Comics**, 9.3 (June 1949): 3-16.

[Bob] Powell, "Murder Through the Looking Glass," **Shadow Comics**, 9.4 (July 1949): 3-16.

[Bob] Powell, "Death in the Stars," **Shadow Comics**, 9.5 (August-September 1949): 3-16.

* * *

Edward Gruskin collaborated with Gibson on a number of occasions, specifically the early Nick Carter and Chick Carter radio scripts. He wrote a series of stories for **Shadow Comics** about a jungle boy named Beebo, some of which were illustrated by August Froehlich. As a curiosity, we include the four stories in which The Shadow is cast up on the jungle island.

[Ed Gruskin]. "Beebo in Knife in the Back," **Shadow Comics**, 3.6 (September 1943): 37-44.

[Ed Gruskin]. "Beebo of Jungle Isle and His Wonder Horse, Fleet, in 'Revenge'," **Shadow Comics**, 3.7 (October 1943): 31-38.

[Ed Gruskin]. "Death Under the Sea," **Shadow Comics**, 3.8 (November 1943): 31-38.

[Ed Gruskin]. "Beebo of Jungle Isle and His Wonder Horse, Fleet," **Shadow Comics**, 3.9 (December 1943): 37-44.

* * *

Some readers and collectors have assumed that Gibson himself wrote the scripts for the three Better Little Books (also referred to, generically, as Big Little Books, a variant series title). In later years Gibson expressed some irritation that he had not been asked to write them. Will Murray has noted there are many "Gibsonisms" in the books, particularly in the use of names of characters which are in the Gibson manner found in the pulps. The books did not make use of the newspaper strip he and Vernon Greene produced for the Philadelphia Public Ledger Syndicate. All three were signed "Maxwell Grant"; illustrations for the first two are signed by Erwin L. Hess, the third by Erwin L. Darwin. The second and third contain drawings that give the illusion of movement when the pages are flipped.

The Shadow and the Living Death. Racine, Wisc.: Whitman Publishing Co., 1940. illus. 425p.

The Shadow and the Master of Evil. Racine, Wisc.: Whitman Publishing Co., 1941. illus. 425p.

The Shadow and the Ghost Makers. Racine, Wisc.: Whitman Publishing Co., 1942. illus. 425p. (Cover signed by John Coleman Burroughs)

In spite of not being able to claim authorship, Gibson signed dozens of copies over the years for fans who didn't mind the discrepancy. The Shadow was still his creation.

*   *   *

Dennis Lynds (1924-   ) replaced Walter B. Gibson on the series from Belmont Books in 1964. He wrote 8 novels signed "Maxwell Grant" which were produced by Lyle Kenyon Engel with permission from Conde Nast Publications who had bought the Street and Smith properties. While the books have their adherents, they are nearly as controversial among Shadow purists as the DC comic book of the 1980s. (See Appendix D.) Contemporaneous with the time during which they were written, Lynds' novels feature The Shadow's battle against a "globe-strangling network of evil" called C.Y.P.H.E.R. Gibson himself did not approve of them and was known to surreptitiously rip pages from copies he found on newsstands. (My own set, shelved near my collection of Gibson Shadow paperbacks, was once sprayed by one of my cats who somehow missed desecrating the authentic works.)

The Shadow Strikes. New York: Belmont Books, [October] 1964.

Shadow Beware. New York: Belmont Books, [January] 1965.

Cry Shadow! New York: Belmont Books, [April] 1965.

The Shadow's Revenge. New York: Belmont Books, [October] 1965.

Mark of The Shadow. New York: Belmont Books, [May] 1966.

Shadow--Go Mad! New York: Belmont Books, [September] 1966.

The Night of the Shadow. New York: Belmont Books, [November] 1966.

The Shadow: Destination Moon. New York: Belmont Books, [March] 1967.

* * *

And then there is the curious phenomenon of the Australian romance novelist whose real name seems to be Maxwell Grant. To date he has published two novels, one of which has been attributed to Walter Gibson, erroneously.

Inherit the Sun. New York: Coward McCann & Geoghegan, 1981.

Blood Red Rose. New York: Macmillan, 1986.

Appendix D

Casting Pale Shadows

This is a brief account of some of those adaptations of Walter Gibson's creation that have presented alternative and often controversial versions of The Shadow. Contrary to what is often believed, Gibson had little to do with the radio Shadow. The man who could "cloud men's minds so that others could not see him" was not the version which his creator would have preferred to linger in the public mind. To chronicle the radio show in any detail is beyond the scope of this book. We leave that to Shadow collector and historian, Anthony G. Tollin, who is preparing the definitive work on the radio series. We will concern ourselves here with three comic book series and a half dozen movies.

*   *   *

Comic Books

During the super hero renaissance of the 1960s, Radio Comics, Inc. published 8 issues of a Shadow comic book in their Archie Series (August 1964--September 1965). In this version, The Shadow was a masked, caped, costumed super hero with few of the characteristics, beyond a skill in hypnotism, of the Gibson version. The artist has not been identified, but students of graphic art may be able to supply the name for themselves.

"The Shadow vs. The RXG Spymaster," **The Shadow** (Archie Series), No. 1 (August 1964): 3-8, 10-11, 13-14.

"The Shadow's Doom," **The Shadow** (Archie), No. 1 (August 1964): 15-24.
Part 2 of story listed above.

"The Adventures of The Shadow," **The Shadow** (Archie), Nos. 1-8 (August 1964-September 1965).
Serialized text story, left incomplete in issue no. 8.

"The Eyes of the Tiger," **The Shadow** (Archie), No. 1 (August 1964): 29-33.

"Shiwan Khan's Murderous Master-Plan," **The Shadow** (Archie), No. 2 (September 1964): 3-8, 10-11, 13-14.

"The Triangle of Terror," **The Shadow** (Archie), No. 2 (September 1964): 15-24.
Part 2 of Shiwan Khan story in this issue.

"Margo Lane's Honeymoon," **The Shadow** (Archie), No. 2 (September 1964): 29-33.

"Shiwan Khan's House of Horrors," **The Shadow** (Archie), No. 3 (November 1964): 3-8, 10-11, 13-24.
The Shadow's costume includes purple tights and a green cape!

"The Princess of Death," **The Shadow** (Archie), No. 3 (November 1964): 29-33.

"The Diabolical Dr. Demon," **The Shadow** (Archie), No. 4 (January 1965): 3-8, 10-11, 13-24.

"The Human Bomb," **The Shadow** (Archie), No. 4 (January 1965): 29-33.

"The Menace of Radiation Rogue," **The Shadow** (Archie), No. 5 (March 1965): 3-8, 10-11, 13-24, 29-33.

"The Incredible Alliance of Shiwan Khan and Attila The Hunter," **The Shadow** (Archie), No. 6 (May 1965): 3-8, 10-11, 13-24, 29-33.

"The Shadow Battles the Brute," **The Shadow** (Archie), No. 7 (July 1965): 3-8, 10-11, 13-24, 29-33.

"The Game of Death," **The Shadow** (Archie), No. 8 (September 1965): 3-8, 10-11, 13-18, 20-24, 26, 29-33.

* * *

Nearly a decade later, DC Comics published 12 issues of a Shadow comic book. The stories were set in the 1930s and were faithful to their original source with a number of "in-jokes" for those who knew the background of The Shadow. There was even a cross-over in which The Shadow made an appearance in **The Batman** series ["Who Knows What

Evil?", **Batman**, 253 (November 1973)]. This was appropriate since The Shadow had been an influence on the creator of The Batman. Writers' and artists' names precede the title of each story below.

Denny O'Neil: M.W. Kaluta. "The Doom Puzzle!" **The Shadow** (DC), 1.1 (October-November 1973): 3-6, 9-12, 15-18, 21-22, 25-28, 31-32.

Denny O'Neil: M.W. Kaluta. "The Freak Show Murders," **The Shadow** (DC), 1.2 (December-January 1974): 3-6, 9-12, 15-17, 21-22, 24-28, 31-32.

Denny O'Neil: Michael Wm. Kaluta and Berni Wrightson. "The Kingdom of the Cobra," **The Shadow** (DC), 1.3 (February-March 1974): 3-6, 9-12, 15-16, 20-22, 24-28, 31-32.

Denny O'Neil and Len Wein: Michael Wm. Kaluta. "Death is Bliss!" **The Shadow** (DC), 2.4 (April-May 1974): 3-6, 9-12, 15-17, 20-22, 25-28, 31-32.

Denny O'Neil: Frank Robbins. "Night of Neptune's Death," **The Shadow** (DC), 2.5 (June-July 1974): 3-6, 9-12, 15-17, 20-22, 25-28, 31-32.
The titles with "Night" in them may have been inspired by the traditional episode titles for the television series, **Wild Wild West**.

Denny O'Neil: Michael Wm. Kaluta. "Night of the Ninja," **The Shadow** (DC), 2.6 (August-September 1974): 3-6, 9-12, 15-17, 20-22, 25-28, 31-32.

Denny O'Neil: Frank Robbins. "The Night of the Beast," **The Shadow** (DC), 2.7 (October-November 1974): 3-6, 9-12, 15-17, 20-22, 25-28, 31-32.

Denny O'Neil: Frank Robbins. "The Night of the Mummy," **The Shadow** (DC), 2.8 (December-January 1975): 3-6, 9-12, 15-17, 20-22, 25-28, 31-32.

Michael Uslan: Frank Robbins and Frank McLaughlin. "The Night of the Falling Death," **The Shadow** (DC), 3.9 (February-March 1975): 3-6, 9-12, 15-17, 20-22, 25-28.

Anthony Tollin. "The Shadow: A Dossier," **The Shadow** (DC), 3.9 (February-March 1975): 32-33.

Denny O'Neil: E.R. Cruz. "The Night of the Killers," **The Shadow** (DC), 3.10 (April–May 1975): 3-6, 9-12, 15-16, 21-22, 25-28, 31-32.

Michael Uslan: E.R. Cruz. "The Night of the Avenger!" **The Shadow** (DC), 3.11 (June–July 1975): 3-6, 9-12, 15-16, 21-22, 25-28, 31-32.

Denny O'Neil: E.R. Cruz. "Night of the Damned!" **The Shadow** (DC), 3.12 (August–September 1975): 3-6, 9-12, 15-16, 21-22, 25-28, 31-32.

* * *

More controversial is the 4 issue mini-series by Howard Chaykin and its sequel by Andrew Helfer with art by Sienkewicz, Orlando, Rogers, and Baker. It can only be termed a "revisionist" version. The stories are full of graphic violence and present a darker, more cynical Shadow. Set in the 1980s, the stories reveal how The Shadow has remained young while his agents have aged, died, or have been murdered.

Howard Chaykin. "Blood and Judgment," **The Shadow** (DC mini-series), 1 (May 1986): 3-30.
Includes "The Shadow's Agents," pp. 31-33, and "The Man Who Created The Shadow," p. 34, both by Anthony Tollin.

Howard Chaykin. "Crime and Punishment," **The Shadow** (DC mini-series), 2 (June 1986): 3-17, 20-32.
Includes "The Story of The Shadow," pp. 33-34, by Anthony Tollin.

Howard Chaykin. "Syndicate of Fear," **The Shadow** (DC mini-series), 3 (July 1986): 3-30.

Howard Chaykin. "Brothers in Blood," **The Shadow** (DC mini-series), 4 (August 1986): 3-30.
Includes "Voices from The Shadows," p. 31-33, by Anthony Tollin.

Howard Chaykin. **The Shadow: Blood and Judgment**. New York: DC Comics, 1987. 128p.
Collects the four issues of the mini-series, with an introduction, by Anthony Tollin ("Shades of The Shadow" and an interview with Howard Chaykin by Joe Orlando, "The Light Behind The Shadow." (The

DC edition was distributed through comic shops; there was another trade edition with the Warner Books imprint for distribution through book stores.)

Andrew Helfer: Bill Sienkewicz. "Shadows and Light: Hat Trick," The Shadow (DC Second Series), 1 (August 1987): 3-30.

Andrew Helfer: Bill Sienkewicz. "Shadows and Light: The Cool Kill," The Shadow (DC Second Series), 2 (September 1987): 3-30.

Andrew Helfer: Bill Sienkewicz. "Shadows and Light: Blazing Apostles," The Shadow (DC Second Series), 3 (October 1987): 3-29.

Andrew Helfer: Bill Sienkewicz. "Shadows and Light: Balance of Power," The Shadow (DC Second Series), 4 (November 1987): 3-29.

Andrew Helfer: Bill Sienkewicz. "Shadows and Light: Saving Grace," The Shadow (DC Second Series), 5 (December 1987): 3-11, 13-31.

Andrew Helfer: Bill Sienkewicz, "Shadows and Light: Passion Play," The Shadow (DC Second Series), 6 (January 1988): 3-30. (Conclusion to the story begun in issue 1.)

Andrew Helfer: Marshal Rogers. "Harold Goes to Washington," The Shadow (DC Second Series), 7 (February 1988): 3-29.

Andrew Helfer: Kyle Baker. "Seven Deadly Finns: Seeing Red," The Shadow (DC Second Series), 8 (March 1988): 3-29. (First of a multi-part series. See below for details.)

Andrew Helfer: Kyle Baker. "Seven Deadly Finns: Fool for a Client," The Shadow (DC Second Series), 9 (April 1988): 3-10, 12-17, 20-25, 27-33.

Andrew Helfer: Kyle Baker. "Seven Deadly Finns: Fool's Parade," The Shadow (DC Second Series), 10 (May 1988): 3-10, 12-14, 16-21, 23-25, 27-33.

Andrew Helfer: Kyle Baker. "Seven Deadly

Finns: Prime Time," **The Shadow** (DC Second Series),
11 (June 1988): 3-10, 12-14, 16-21, 23-25, 27-33.

Andrew Helfer: Kyle Baker.   "Seven Deadly
Finns: Dark Shadows," **The Shadow** (DC Second
Series), 12 (July 1988): 3-10, 12-14, 16-21, 23-25,
27-33.

Andrew Helfer: Kyle Baker.   "Seven Deadly
Finns: [Untitled Story]," **The Shadow** (DC Second
Series), 13 (August 1988): 3-10, 12-14, 16-21, 23-
25, 27-34.   (The Shadow dies[?] in this story, but
the series continues into the sequence which begins
in the next issue.)

Andrew Helfer: Kyle Baker.   "Body and Soul:
Eulogy," **The Shadow** (DC Second Series), 14
(September 1988): 3-10, 12-14, 16-21, 23-25, 27-33.
(With The Shadow lying dead, his agents continue
the fight. The first of a multi-part series.)

Andrew Helfer: Joe Orlando.   "Shadows and
Light, Prolog: Fragment of the Sun," **The Shadow
Annual** (DC Second Series), 1 (1987): 3-45.

Denny O'Neil: Michael Kaluta, Russ Heath. **The
Shadow: Hitler's Astrologer.**   New York: Marvel
Entertainment Group, 1988. 62 pages. (A graphic
novel, in the style of the first DC Series, set in
the 1940s.)

* * *

Motion Pictures

The Shadow hasn't fared too well in having
his adventures adapted to motion pictures. Hastily
made films in the past have not encouraged optimism
on the part of viewers about future efforts. While
not representing The Shadow's persona or exploits
accurately, the films do remain as representing the
style and mood of the crime or mystery film of
their day. In most of them the hero could just as
well have been Ellery Queen or Boston Blackie.
However, watching Victor Jory portray Lamont
Cranston portraying a telephone repairman in
chapter 9 of the movie serial (1940) has its own
peculiar entertainment value.

The Shadow Strikes

(Grand National, 1937. 61 min. black and white.)
Rod La Rocque (Lamont Granston) [sic], Lynn Anders
(Marcia Delthern), James Blakely (Jasper Delthern),
Walter McGrail (Winstead Comstock), Bill Kellogg
(Humphrey Comstock), Cy Kendall (Brossett), Kenneth
Harlan (Captain Breen), Norman Ainsley (Hendricks),
John St. Polis (Mr. Delthern), Wilson Benge
(Wellington), John Carnivale (Warren Berringer).

Producer, Max Alexander, Arthur Alexander.
Director, Lynn Shores. Screenplay by Al Martin,
based on "The Ghost of the Manor," by Maxwell Grant
[Walter B. Gibson]. Cinematographer, Marcel Picard.
Film editor, Charles Henkel.

The deviation from the original inspiration
begins with renaming the hero Lamont Granston and
continues from there. Granston is a lawyer whose
father's legal career was ended by racketeers, so
that his motive for being The Shadow and tracking
down criminals is personal revenge. By the end of
the film he has identified the killer of his father
(through ballistics) and terminated his reason to
be The Shadow, but decides to keep the cloak around
just in case it may be needed in the future. A
slow moving film starring a matinee idol of the
silent films, it has little of the real Shadow
about it. La Rocque spends most of the film
impersonating another lawyer named Chester Randall
so that knowing who is who does require a score
card. It has been suggested that making this a
film about The Shadow was an afterthought on the
part of the studio.

International Crime

(Grand National, 1938. 64 min. black and white.)
Rod La Rocque (Lamont Cranston), Astrid Allwyn
(Phoebe Lane), Thomas Jackson (Commissioner
Weston), Oscar O'Shea (Heath), Lew Hearn (Moe
[Shrevnitz]), William Von Brinken (Flowtow), Tenen
Holtz (Starkhov), William Pawley (Honest John),
William Moore ([Clyde] Burke), John St. Polis
(Roger Morton), Jack Baxley (Mathews), Walter Bonn
(Stefan), Harry Bradley (Barrows), also Lloyd
Whitlock.

Producer, Max and Arthur Alexander. Director,
Charles Lamont. Screenplay by Jack Natteford based
on "Foxhound" by Maxwell Grant [Theodore Tinsley].
Assoc. Prod. Alfred Stern. Cinematographer, Marcel
Le Picard. Film editor, Charles Henkel. Music
Director, Dr. Edward Kileyni. Art Director, Ralph
Berger.

It is 8:00 by the clock on the radio building
as the **Daily Classic** radio show presents Lamont
Cranston aka The Shadow as a radio crime reporter
with a story about Honest John, a safe cracker just
out of prison. Listeners are enthralled by his
stories and children take down the license number
of a stolen car to report to him. Everyone knows
that The Shadow and Lamont Cranston are one and the
same and he also writes a newspaper column ("The
Shadow Says...") which uses the picture of The
Shadow in its headline. On the wall of the radio
studio is a framed portrait of The Shadow from the
pulps. Phoebe (not Margo) Lane is the niece of the
owner of the newspaper (also the **Daily Classic**) and
a college journalism student who hands Lamont a tip
about a robbery while he is on the air. (Possibly
the name "Margo" suggests a sophisticated person
while Astrid Allwyn's portrayal is of someone more
suitably named "Phoebe.") The main plot involves
international loans and foreign agents (hence the
title).

There is a bit of internal advertising in the
scene where Lamont visits the Metropolitan Theatre
to prevent it from being robbed. A theatre poster
announces "Here's Flash Casey" with Eric Linden,
another Grand National film. The movie is based on
George Harmon Coxe's character from **Black Mask**
magazine.

The Shadow

(Columbia Pictures Serial in 15 Chapters, 1940,
black and white.) Victor Jory (The Shadow, Lin
Chang, Lamont Cranston), Veda Ann Borg (Margot
[Lane]), Roger Moore ([Harry] Vincent), Robert
Fiske (Marshall), J. Paul Jones (Turner), Jack
Ingram (Flint), Charles Hamilton (Roberts), Edward
Peil Sr. ([Inspector] Cardona), Frank Larue
([Commissioner] Weston), ? ? ? (The Black Tiger).

Producer, (not given). Director, James W. Horne. Screenplay by Joseph Poland, Ned Dandy, and Joseph O'Donnell, "based upon stories published in 'The Shadow' Magazine."

"The economic life of the city is threatened by a well organized criminal body headed by a mysterious figure known as The Black Tiger, whose mad ambition is to acquire supreme financial power. Industrial leaders prevail upon Lamont Cranston, noted scientist and criminologist, to combat this menace. Cranston frequently works in disguise as The Shadow, a character of his own creation, who is a feared enemy of the underworld, but the police have come to believe that The Shadow and The Black Tiger are one and the same person."

With these words to set the scene, each chapter of this serial begins, followed by a paragraph to describe the cliffhanger situation at the end of the previous chapter. The film was far more faithful to Gibson's creation than the previous features, but still fell short of its potential. Jory looked the part of Lamont Cranston and gave such a good interpretation to the role that it is to be regretted that he wasn't allowed to appear in a sequel which had a larger budget and better writers.

Chapter One: "The Doomed City."

Cliffhanger: The Shadow, giving warning of the danger from The Black Tiger who plans to destroy an exhibition of the new medium of television, is trapped when the machinery explodes.

Chapter Two: "The Shadow Attacks."

Resolution: Falling beams protect The Shadow from receiving the full brunt of the collapsing ceiling.

Cliffhanger: A gasoline truck is sent on a suicide mission to blow up the powder house at a telephone station with The Shadow a doomed passenger.

Chapter Three: "The Shadow's Peril."

Resolution:.The Shadow throws himself clear of the truck just before it hits the powder house.

Cliffhanger: The Shadow battles the men of The Black Tiger in the basement of a house when the flames trigger an explosion.

Chapter Four: "In The Tiger's Lair."

Resolution: Everyone escapes from the house. What we did not notice before is that The Shadow, having recovered in time, escaped from the room before the explosion occurred.

Cliffhanger: The Shadow pursues one of The Black Tiger's men into the house which serves as the gang's headquarters and falls through a trap door into a cellar room which then explodes.

Chapter Five: "Danger Above."

Resolution: Debris which falls from the cellar roof shields The Shadow from the effects of the explosion and gives him a ladder with which to climb out of the dungeon.

Cliffhanger: The Black Tiger's men turn the secret airplane engine nullifying ray on The Shadow. Escaping that danger he pursues them by car, leaping from his own car (driven by Harry Vincent) into the open car of The Black Tiger's men. The car veers off toward an electric dynamo and an explosion results.

Chapter Six: "The Shadow's Trap."

Resolution: Still clutching the nullifying ray gun, The Shadow leaps from the moving car just before it crashes.

Cliffhanger: Trapped by Flint and The Black Tiger's men, Margot Lane falls into the basement level elevator shaft, after which the elevator is sent down the shaft towards her!

Chapter Seven: "Where Horror Waits."

Resolution: The Shadow arrives in time to pull Margot out before the elevator reaches the bottom of the shaft.

304

MAN OF MAGIC AND MYSTERY

Cliffhanger: The Shadow goes to the rescue of Prescott and the others and becomes involved in a fight in the warehouse. Acid is leaking from some large drums, an oil lamp spills over, and there is a terrific explosion!

Chapter Eight: "The Shadow Rides the Rails."

Resolution: Once again falling beams brace against each other above The Shadow's head and give him protection from the collapsing roof.

Cliffhanger: While trying to prevent a train collision, The Shadow is overpowered and thrown across the track in the path of one of the speeding engines.

Chapter Nine: "The Devil in White."

Resolution: The Shadow recovers in time to roll free of the approaching train.

Cliffhanger: Margot Lane, disguised as Nurse Penfield, is caught along with Turner and Harry Vincent. All three are tied to the wall and the nullifying ray is turned on them. The Shadow overpowers the gang out in the hall and tries to break in to save them. Will he be in time?

Chapter Ten: "The Underground Trap."

Resolution: Yes! He shoots the lock of the door to the ray room and turns his gun on the ray machine itself. Margot, Turner, and Vincent leave by the window, followed soon after by The Shadow.

Cliffhanger: In search of the "One-Eyed Man of Anchor Street", The Shadow is drawn into an underground tunnel where an explosion is set off.

Chapter Eleven: "Chinatown Night."

Resolution: Once again, falling beams block the debris which should have killed The Shadow.

Cliffhanger: The Shadow sets a trap for The Black Tiger's men using Cranston's "Ray Nullifier" as bait. An electric explosive charge set by the gang is triggered by his entrance, there is an explosion, and a heavy safe falls on him. (This

"Ray Nullifier" will nullify the rays which nullify the airplane engines.)

Chapter Twelve: "Murder By Remote Control."

Resolution: The Shadow, only stunned, struggles to his feet and makes his escape before the police arrive.

Cliffhanger: The Cranston Ray is being demonstrated against The Black Tiger's ray. The Shadow bursts into the room at the airport to warn everyone of danger. The audience runs for it, but The Shadow is caught in the explosion.

Chapter Thirteen: "Wheels of Death."

Resolution: Once again, luck saves The Shadow. He reaches the edge of the explosion before the full force can harm him.

Cliffhanger: During a high speed chase, Cranston's car is struck and overturned by a truck driven by The Black Tiger's men.

Chapter Fourteen: "The Sealed Room."

Resolution: Cranston and Vincent climb out of their overturned car and Cranston sends word of The Black Tiger's plans via police radio.

Cliffhanger: The Black Tiger releases poison gas into the Cobalt Club where all are overcome. Even Cranston who has just trapped the Arch Lieutenant of The Black Tiger is trapped. Explosion!

Chapter Fifteen: "The Shadow's Net Closes."

Resolution: Cranston arises like the phoenix from the ashes of the explosion, a heavy table having shielded him and all of the others. The Black Tiger's mask is found by Cranston after the explosion, three distinct fingerprints on it proving conclusively that The Black Tiger is really one of the Corporation leaders who have been meeting at the Cobalt Club.

The Shadow Returns

(Monogram Pictures Corporation, 1946. 61 min., black and white) Kane Richmond (Lamont Cranston), Barbara Reed (Margo Lane), Tom Dugan (Shrevvie), Joseph Crehan (Inspector Cardona), Pierre Watkin (Commissioner Weston), Robert Emmett Keane (Charles Frobay), Frank Reicher (Michael Hasdon), Lester Dorr (William Monk), Rebel Randall (Lenore Jessup), Emmett Vogan (Brock Yomans), Sherry Hall (Robert Buell), Cyril Delevanti (John Adams).

Producer, Joe Kaufman. Director, Phil Rosen. Original Screenplay by George Callahan "based on the copyrighted stories published in the 'Shadow Magazine.'"   Assoc. Prod. George Callahan. Cinematographer, William Sickner. Film editor, Ace Herman. Music director, Edward Kay. Art director, Dave Milton.

This story of jewels, the key to a new plastics formula, smuggled into the country in a coffin was the first of three movies based partly on the pulp concept of The Shadow (as presented by Bruce Elliot at this time) and partly on the radio show. There is an effective scene behind the title credits on each film in which Lamont Cranston casts a shadow which is shown putting on the mask and cloak of The Shadow.

There is a brief scene involving the Burbank Detective Agency, one of whose agents is named Hawkeye, which should ring familiar bells with many Shadow fans. In the films, Lamont Cranston's presence is explained by making him the nephew of Commissioner Weston. The mask covers most of his face, leaving only the mouth free, the hat is a black fedora, and the cloak is a black overcoat. Everything is played in a light-hearted style (except for the graveyard scenes) and other themes are in keeping with what was currently in vogue in mystery films, including Margo Lane's pursuit of Lamont Cranston to marry him. Her character becomes the stereotypical scatter-brained girl Friday in the next films.

Behind the Mask

(Monogram Pictures, 1946. 67 min. black and white)
Kane Richmond (Lamont Cranston), Barbara Reed
(Margo Lane), George Chandler (Shrevie), Dorothea
Kent (Jennie), Joseph Crehan (Inspector Cardona),
Pierre Watkin (Commissioner Weston), Robert Shayne
(Brad Thomas), June Clyde (Edith Merrill), James
Cardwell (Jeff Mann), Marjorie Hoshelle (Mae
Bishop), Joyce Compton (Lulu), Ed Gargan (Dixon),
Lou Crosby (Marty Greane), Bill Christy (Copy Boy),
Nancy Brinkman (Susan), Dewey Robinson (Head
Waiter), Marie Harmon (Girl), Ruth Cherrington
(Dowager), James Nataro (Reporter), Jean Carlin and
Laura Stevens.

Producer, Joe Kaufman. Director, Phil Karlson.
Original screenplay by George Callahan (based on
"The Shadow" radio character). Cinematographer,
William A. Sickner. Film editor, Ace Herman.

This film also carries the title **The Shadow in
Behind the Mask**. When reporter-columnist Jeff Mann
is murdered, suspicion falls on The Shadow because
witnesses thought they saw him in Mann's office at
the time of the murder. Blackmail and a bookie
ring are part of the plot. Shrevie's girl friend,
Jennie Delaney is introduced in this film and the
attempts of Margo and Jennie to catch Cranston and
his assistant with other women make a strange
counterpoint to the otherwise good mystery mood.

The Missing Lady

(Monogram Pictures, 1946. 60 min. black and white)
Kane Richmond (Lamont Cranston), Barbara Reed
(Margo Lane), George Chandler (Shrevie), James
Flavin (Inspector Cardona), Pierre Watkin
(Commissioner Weston), Dorothea Kent (Jennie
Delaney), James Cardwell, Claire Carleton, Jack
Overman, Frances Robinson, Almira Sessions, Nora
Cecil, George Lewis, Dewey Robinson, Anthony Warde,
Bert Roach, also Gary Owen, Ray Teal, Jo-Carroll
Dennison, Ralph Dunn, and Douglas Wood.

Producer, Joe Kaufman. Director, Phil Karlson.
Original screenplay by George Callahan. Associate
Producer, George Callahan. Cinematographer, William

Sickner. Film editor, Ace Herman. Art director,
David Milton.

Also known as **The Shadow and the Missing Lady**,
this was the third and last film in the Kane
Richmond series. Much banter and confusion is made
of the identity of the "missing lady" of the title,
which turns out to be a jade statuette stolen when
an art dealer is murdered. Jennie and Margo are
still the jealous girl friends. Two interesting
characters are the old maid elevator operators,
Effie and Millie, who race their elevators (called
"Upsydaisy" and "Downsydaisy"). There is a good
crime story opening when a criminal named the Ox
finds a not very well disguised Lamont Cranston in
a flop house. Comparing Kane Richmond's profile
with the drawings of Lamont Cranston by Bob Powell
in **Shadow Comics** during this period suggests the
possibility that he used Richmond as a model.
(Powell did depict the features of radio actor Lon
Clark, who played Nick Carter on the air, in a try-
out for a newspaper comic strip about that Street &
Smith detective.)

The Invisible Avenger

(Republic, 1958. 60 min. black and white) Richard
Derr (Lamont Cranston), Mark Daniels (Jogendra),
Helen Westcott (Tara), Jeanne Neher (Felicia
Ramirez), Dan Mullin (Pablo Ramirez), Lee Edwards
(Colonel), Jack Doner (Billy), Steve Dano (Tony
Alcalde), Leo Bruno (Rocco), Sam Page (Charlie).

Producers, Eric Sayers, Emanuel Demby. Directors,
James Wong Howe, John Sledge, Ben Parker.
Screenplay by George Bellak and Betty Jeffries.
Cinematography, Willis Winford, Joseph Wheeler.
Film editor, John Hemel. Music director, Edward
Dutreil.

Re-released in 1962 as **Bourbon Street Shadows**
with additional footage added which was directed by
Parker. The murder of a New Orleans jazz player
leads The Shadow (who can become invisible like his
radio counterpart) to an exiled Latin American
dictator. (Not seen, comments and information
based on secondary sources, in particular, Jay
Robert Nash and Stanley Ralph Ross, **The Motion
Picture Guide**. Chicago: Cinebooks, Inc., 1985-

1987.)   There are two stills from the film in **The Shadow Scrapbook.**

Appendix E

Standing Ovation

Secondary Sources About Walter Gibson and His Works

Following is a selected list of the articles and books which include information about Gibson. Many of the standard reference works on the pulps devote space to The Shadow, but only a few discuss Gibson's career at any length. The only history of Street & Smith (Quentin Reynolds' **The Fiction Factory**) does not even mention his name, although by the time it was published (1955) it was no secret who the real person behind the name Maxwell Grant had been. Many of the interviews and newspaper articles repeat the same information since the interviewers tended to ask the same questions. The emphasis in most of these entries is nostalgia for the early days of The Shadow, but there is some material on the magic writing. Articles which are on The Shadow only and not on Gibson have not been listed. Entries have been selectively annotated.

Andrea Axelrod. "Superman Move Over Because Here Comes The Shadow," **Morning Call** (Allentown, Pa.), nd. (Probably between 1975 and 1980.)

"Behind the Curtain," **Street & Smith's Mystery Magazine**, 6 (June 1940): 5-6, 128-129. (Maxwell Grant receives a medal for the "best illusion of the year" published in **The Sphinx**.)

"Biography," **The Sphinx**, 19 (August 1920): 167. (Cover photo of Gibson.)

Harry Blackstone, Jr. **The Blackstone Book of Magic and Illusion**. New York: Newmarket Press, 1985. ("Blackstone in the Comics," pp. 84-85.)

Rob Borsellino. "The Shadow Returns," **Tempo** (Kingston, N. Y. **Sunday Freeman** magazine section), April 10, 1977, p. 4. (Gibson performs at the Murder Ink weekend at Mohunk Mountain House.)

Richard Buffum. "Help from The Shadow's Realm," **Los Angeles Times**, January 8, 1980, part 2, p. 8. (Among Gibson's contributions to magic were the invention of several of the coin tricks

manufactured by Carl Brema; Buffum is the author of
a monograph on Brema.)

Newgate Callendar [pseud.].   "Crime," **New York
Times Book Review**, February 5, 1978, n.p. (Review
of **Norgil the Magician.**)

Captain George's Penny Dreadful: A Weekly Review,
No. 425 (April 15, 1977).   (Cover by Frank
Hamilton, a double-profile of The Shadow and
Gibson.)

Nick Carr.   "A Man Named Gibson," **Echoes,** 5
(February 1986): 9.

Charles Chamberlain.   "A Conversation with 'The
Shadow,'"   **Nashua** (New Hampshire) **Telegraph,**
October 25, 1978, p. 26. (Gibson at the Bouchercon
in Chicago; AP wire service. See also "Shadow
Mania Brings Chuckle to Pulp Writer Who Likes
Magic," "Who is Walt Gibson?", and "Writer of 'The
Shadow' Still Active" in list below.)

Lewis Clifford.   "The Shadow: What Strange Spirit
Lurks in the Ancient Home at 12 Gay Street?"
Weekly World News, July 21, 1981, p. 17.   (The
former home of Walter Gibson is haunted by the
spirit of Lamont Cranston conjured up by Gibson's
creative energy.)

J. Randolph Cox. "Always Mysterious: Walter Gibson
in Memorium," **The Armchair Detective,** 19 (Summer
1986): 227-228.

_____.   "Memories in the Shadows," **The Pulp
Collector,** 1 (Spring 1986): 3-4.

_____. "That Mysterious Aide to the Forces of Law
and Order," **The Armchair Detective,** 4 (July 1971):
221-229. (An attempt to fit The Shadow into the
mainstream of mystery fiction; the first serious
study of the entire series though since superseded
by Sampson and Murray.)

Jim Detjen.   "Is He Gibson or Grant?...Only The
Shadow Knows," **Poughkeepsie** (NY) **Journal,** November
24, 1974, pp. 1-2.

Bernard A. Drew. "In the Days of The Shadow,"
Yesteryear, February 1980, pp. 6-7.

_____. "Philadelphia in the Pulps," **Discover** (**Philadelphia Sunday Bulletin** magazine section), August 6, 1978, p. 9. (Pulp stories with Philadelphia settings are discussed; 5 Shadow novels cited.)

_____. "The Turn-Ons of Yesteryear," **Gallery**, 7 (December 1979): 61-63. (Illustrated survey of the pulps with an emphasis on the "Spicies"; Gibson quoted.)

Ann Ehrenburg. "Who Knows What Magic Lurks in the Hearts of Men?" **Fort Worth Star-Telegram**, September 3, 1978, p. 24a. (Gibson interviewed while at a convention of Texas Association of Magicians.)

Frank Eisgruber. "Crime Undercover," **Pulp**, No. 4 (Spring 1972): 15-17. (The Shadow specialized in catching crooks known as "the hidden schemers.")
_____. **Gangland's Doom**: The Shadow of the Pulps. Chicago: Robert Weinberg, 1973. (Copyrighted 1974; the first book-length study of The Shadow series.)

_____. "Only The Shadow Knows," **Pulp**, No. 3 (Summer 1971): 28-37. (How The Shadow revealed his secret past yet kept it concealed.)

William Engle. "Letters Stump Author of 7,440,000 Words of Thrills," **New York World-Telegram**, May 15, 1937, n.p. (In his early days, Gibson could write for up to 10 hours a day, but had trouble answering letters. Photo of the author at his typewriter, behind him on the wall an original cover painting of the Shadow. This interview was delayed in publication by the story of the Hindenburg disaster.)

Chris Farlekas. "The Shadow Knows the Magic Tricks of Houdini, Duniger [sic]...and Tells All," **Sunday Record**, November 24, 1974, p. 12. (Gibson interviewed on the occasion of the publication of **Dunninger's Secrets**.)

[W. Robert Finegan]. "Walter B. Gibson '20: From Poker in the Dorm and Magic in the Classroom to The Shadow and Harry Houdini," **The Colgate Scene**, September 1975, pp. 1-3. (Gibson interviewed on the occasion of the 55th reunion of his college class.)

Tobie Geertsema.   "The   Shadow   Lives
Again...Eddyville's Gibson Crime-Fighter Returns,"
Tempo (Kingston, NY, **Sunday Freeman** magazine
section), June 22, 1975, p. 3.

Walter Gibson.   "A Million Words a Year for Ten
Straight Years," **Writer's Digest**, (March 1941):
23-27.   (A significant statement for writers by one
who considers one source of inspiration to be "a
good, swift, self-delivered kick in the pants.")

_____. "Paul & Co.," **The Magic World**, 4 (April
1920): 8-9. ("Anonymous" review of a performance
by Paul Kalbfleisch and Gibson who "executed some
unusual card work and finished with his
presentation of the Linking Rings.")

_____. "The Purple Girasol," in **The Duende History
of The Shadow Magazine**. Greenwood, Mass.: Odyssey
Publications, 1980. Pp. 100-101.   (Excerpt from
interview; remainder in **Duende**, No. 2. See "Out of
the Shadows--Walter Gibson" below.)

_____. **The Story of The Shadow**. A Sound Portrait
of the Greatest Crimefighter ever heard on radio as
told by Bret Morrison, Walter Gibson, Grace
Matthews, Gertrude Warner, Ken Roberts, Andre
Baruch and others!   Radiola, 4MR-3, 1985.
(Includes interviews with some of those involved
with The Shadow over the years and four radio
dramas: "The Vengeance of Angela Nolan" (June 27,
1954), "The White Legion" (March 20, 1938), "Friend
of Darkness" (February 19, 1939), and "They Kill
with a Silver Hatchet" (May 26, 1946).)

Wendel W. Gibson.   "On the Road with Blackstone,
Sr.," **The Magic Magazine**, 4 (March, April, August-
September 1977): Series in 3 parts.

William Gildea.   "Radio Author Remembers Shadow's
Heyday," **Los Angeles Times: Calendar** (July 16,
1978): 106.

_____. "The Shadow: The Crime Fighter Lives on in
Walter Gibson's 282 Novels," **Washington Post**, (May
13, 1978): C1, C3.

Ron Goulart. **Cheap Thrills**: An Informal History of
the Pulp Magazine.   New Rochelle, NY: Arlington
House, 1972) Pp. 43-54.

_____. "The Shadow Passes," **The Third** Degree
(Mystery Writers of America), April 1986, p. 4.
(See also Nancy Webb, below.)

Frank Gruber. **The Pulp Jungle.** Los Angeles:
Sherbourne Press, 1967. Pp. 105-106.

Jim Haviland. "The Man The Shadow Made Rich,"
Success Unlimited, 23 (April 1976): 56-63.

Marcia Hayes. "He Who Asked 'What Evil Lurks...'
Knew Beyond the Shadow of a Doubt," **Boston Globe,**
(October 10, 1971): n.p.

"Hocus Pocus Talks to Walter B. Gibson," **Hocus
Pocus,** 3 (January-March 1981): 16-23. (Continued
in issue following, second issue not seen.)

Edward T. Hollins. "W. B. Gibson and Assembly No.
4." Privately printed, n.d.; mimeographed; 2p.
(The founding of the Philadelphia Magicians' Club
and its affiliation with the Society of American
Magicians.)

"Howard Thurston and Walter B. Gibson." **The Sphinx,**
21 (September 15, 1922): 243. (Cover photo of
Thurston with Gibson.)

Claire Huff. "Time Stands Still for Author,"
Philadelphia Inquirer, (February 29, 1976): 2H.

Don Hutchison. "The Demented Shadow," **Echoes,** 5
(June 1986): 15-17. (A critique of Howard
Chaykin's comic book version of The Shadow.)

_____. "The Pulp File--Walter B. Gibson: The
Shadow's Shadow," **Wordsmith,** No. 4 (February 1986):
31-32.

_____. "The Shadow," **The New** Captain George's
Whizzbang, No. 8 (1970): 22-27.

Curtia James. "Magic," **Philadelphia Bulletin
(Books),** (June 20, 1981): n.p. (Review of **The Big
Book of Magic.)**

R. J. Kelly. "Friends Recall Walter Gibson,"
Sunday Freeman (Kingston, NY), January 12, 1986,
p. 5.

_____.   "Magician Gibson Dead, Created 'The Shadow,'"   Daily Freeman (Kingston, NY), December 6, 1985, pp. 1, 5.

_____.   "Shadow Still Lurking After 50,"   Sunday Freeman (Kingston, NY), July 5, 1981, pp. 1, 5. (The 50th anniversary of the creation of The Shadow is commemorated.)

Cliff Linedecker.   "Creator of 'Shadow' Gets Ideas from Twilight Zone,"   National Examiner, April 17, 1984, n.p.   (Comments based on a reissue of the Twilight Zone books in which Gibson claims telepathy as a source of stories. Cited from xerox copy.)

_____.   "The Day Houdini's Ghost Reached Out from the Grave,"   National Examiner, date and page not given.   (Gibson quoted in regard to a brush with death on the part of the Amazing Randi. Cited from xerox copy.)

_____.   "The Ghost of Gay Street,"   The National Tattler, date and page not given.   (Gibson's house, No. 12 Gay Street, Greenwich Village, was visited by the spirit of Lamont Cranston, a psychic image from the author's imagination.)

_____.   "Lady Magician Catches Bullet in Her Teeth,"   National Examiner, July 5, 1983, p. 2. (Gibson warned Dorothy Dietrich of the dangers in performing the famous bullet-catching trick.)

_____.   "'Shadow' Creator Credits Ideas to Psychic Vision,"   The National Tattler, July 21, 1974, p. 11.   (Original version of story from National Examiner of April 17, 1984 above. Longer text.)

Jay Maeder.   "The People Column," Miami Herald, July 15, 1981, p. 2A.   (The figure of Lamont Cranston appears in Greenwich Village as a psychic after-image.)

"Man Who Cast the Shadow," Newsweek, 69 (January 16, 1967): 10.

Walter E. Meyers.   Handbook of Contemporary English.   New York: Harcourt, Brace Jovanovich, 1974.   Pp. 438-439.   (Some statements about The Shadow demonstrate building a paragraph.)

Lon Murray. "The Shadow Treads on a Not-So-Innocent Creator," **Los Angeles Times:** Calendar, October 1, 1978, p. 6. (A former Street & Smith editor claims more credit than his due for shaping the character of The Shadow.)

Will Murray. "Batman vs. The Shadow," **The Comics Buyer's Guide,** January 4, 1985, p. 64.

_____. "The Five O'Clock Shadow," **The Comics Buyer's Guide,** March 21, 1986, pp. 26, 28, 30, 32, 34.

_____. "My Friend Walter Gibson," **The Comics Buyer's Guide,** January 3, 1986, p. 56.

_____. "Remembering Walter Gibson," **Echoes,** 5 (February 1986): 36-45.

_____. "The Top Twenty-Five Shadow Novels...and One Stinker," **The Age of The Unicorn,** No. 4 (October 1979): 3-17. (Inspired by lists of the top ten novels recommended by readers of **The Shadow** in the 1930s, five present day fans discuss their own favorites.)

_____. "Walter B. Gibson" in **Twentieth Century Crime and Mystery Writers** (2d ed.). New York: St. Martin's Press, 1985.

_____. "Walter B. Gibson: Casting a Giant Shadow," **Starlog,** 9.105 (April 1986): 59-62.

_____. "Walter B. Gibson Revisited" in **The Duende History of The Shadow Magazine.** Greenwood, Mass: Odyssey Publications, 1980. Pp. 114-122. (Interview.)

"Obituaries: Walter B. Gibson," **Variety,** December 18, 1985, p. 99.

"Obituary: Walter Gibson, 88, Creator of The Shadow," **The Comics Buyer's Guide,** January 3, 1986, p. 56.

Billy O'Brien. "Meyers and The Shadow Visit Today's Homecoming," **The Campus Lantern** (Colgate University), September 29, 1978, n.p. (News account: Gibson attends Homecoming activities at Colgate.)

"Old Time Radio to Be Recalled," **Northfield** (Minnesota) **News,** October 19, 1978, p. 18. (Local Arts Guild coffee house features a re-enactment of a Shadow radio play. This bibliographer portrayed The Shadow.)

Robert Ostermann. "Where Are the Pulp Fictioneers?" **National Observer,** May 17, 1965, p. 22. (Survey of the publications of Street & Smith and Gibson's work.)

"Out of the Shadows--Walter Gibson," **Duende,** No. 2 (Winter 1976-77): 33-46. (Interview taped at the Comic Art Convention, NYC, July 5, 1975.)

Judy Peet. "The Shadow: His Creator," **Sunday Call-Chronicle** (Allentown, Pa.), October 8, 1978, p. F8.

Bill Pronzini. "The Man Who Collected 'The Shadow'," **The Magazine of Fantasy and Science Fiction,** 40 (June 1971): 75-81. (A tale about a collector of nostalgia whose life is so centered in The Shadow that in the extraordinary fitness of things he becomes his hero in a moment of peril.)

The Pulp Collector, 1.3 (Winter 1986). **Walter Gibson Memorial Section,** 54p. (Contents: "Commentary" by John P. Gunnison; "Frank Hamilton's Walter Gibson Memorial Art Gallery;" "Walter B. Gibson, Friend," by John L. Nanovic; "Hooked," by Helen Deveny; "Rose-Colored Memories," by Frank Hamilton; "Walter Gibson on Walter Gibson: An Interview," by Will Murray; "Walter Gibson and Northeast High," by Albert Tonik; "His Master's Shadow," by Howard Hopkins; "Tribute to Walter Gibson," by Rick Lai; "Walter Gibson: A Man of Words Eulogized," by Will Murray.)

William V. Rauscher. **Walter B. Gibson, 1897-1985, Man of Letters and Literature.** Privately printed, 1986. 21p.

Wayne Robinson. "Who is Walter B. Gibson? The Shadow Knows," **Discover (Philadelphia Sunday Bulletin** magazine section), August 6, 1978, pp. 6-9, 18-19.

Franklin Rosemont. "From Indianapolis to Rangoon: Walter Gibson and the Biff Brewster Series," **The**

Mystery and Adventure Series Review, No. 18 (Spring 1987): 18-32.

_____. "A Last Talk with Walter Gibson," **The Mystery and Adventure Series Review**, No. 18 (Spring 1987): 26-27.

Robert Sampson. **The Night Master.** Chicago: Pulp Press, 1982. Illustrated. Not indexed. (The definitive study. Bibliography, pp. 182-187. Appendix B. (pp. 191-195) and Appendix C. (pp. 196-204) list reprints of Shadow novels and list the originals in the order in which they were written-- see also **The Duende History of The Shadow Magazine.**)

Wolfgang Saxon. "Walter B. Gibson, The Creator of 'The Shadow,' Dead at 88," **New York Times**, December 7, 1985. (This story appeared under varying titles in many newspapers that used **New York Times** wire services; "'Shadow' Creator Dies at 88," **St. Paul (Minnesota) Sunday Pioneer Press and Dispatch,** December 8, 1985, p. 9C.)

"Sequel: The Shadow Returns with Some Sweet Fruit for His Prolific Creator," **People Magazine**, November 29, 1975, p. 49.

Bill Severn. **Bill Severn's Guide to Magic as a Hobby.** New York: David McKay Co., Inc., 1979. Pp. 156-158.

"Shadow Mania Brings Chuckle to Pulp Writer Who Likes Magic," **Austin** (Texas) **American-Statesman,** October 29, 1978, p. H6. (Same article as Charles Chamberlain, "A Conversation with The Shadow." See above.)

"The Shadow Speaks, An Exchange Between Nick Carr and Walter Gibson," **Pulp**, No. 5 (Winter 1973). (Interview. Not seen.)

Allen Spraggett. "The Unexplained: The Shadow Returns," Syndicated column, copyright 1973, Toronto Sun Syndicate. (Walter Gibson and Litzka Gibson interviewed on personal examples of clairvoyant dreams and premonitions.)

[James Steranko]. **Shadow Secret Society Bulletin,** Nos. 1-2, Summer 1975-1976. (Included in membership kit in the Society--along with badge, membership card, official index of Shadow novels.)

_____. **Unseen Shadows.** Reading, Pa.: Supergraphics, 1978. (Artist's concepts for Shadow paperback covers; introduction by Steranko, Afterword by Gibson.)

Anthony Tollin. "The Man Who Created The Shadow," **The Shadow** (DC Mini-series), 1 (May 1986): 34. (See also issues of the comic book listed in Appendix D.)

Alice K. Turner. "Welcome, Ying Ko, to the World of Pulp Nostalgia," **Publishers Weekly,** 206 (October 7, 1974): 42-43.

"Walter B. Gibson." **Contemporary Authors.** Detroit: Gale Research Co., 1984. Vol. 110, pp. 204-209. (Interview with Gibson conducted by Jean W. Ross, May 5, 1982. Extensive checklist erroneously attributes an Australian romance novel, **Inherit the Sun** (1981), to Gibson because the writer was also named Maxwell Grant. Obituary notice in vol 118, 1986.)

"Walter B. Gibson," **The Magic World,** 4 (December 1920): 119.
"Walter B. Gibson: A Biography," **The Magic World,** 5 (December 1921): 115.

"Walter B. Gibson: Shadow's Creator Was 88," **The Globe and Mail** (Toronto), December 7, 1985, n.p.

"Walter Gibson, the Man Behind The Shadow," **The Magic Magazine,** 3 (November 1976): 20-21, 24-25.

Ray Walters. "Paperback Talk: Paperbacks--New and Noteworthy," **New York Times Book Review,** July 29, 1979, n.p. (Reviews **The Shadow Scrapbook** which contains bibliographies "whose thoroughness would do credit to a Shakespearean scholar.")

James Warren. "The Shadow Knows--and Tells His Secrets," **Chicago Sun-Times,** October 9, 1978, p. 9. (Gibson interviewed at time of the Bouchercon in Chicago, comments on his preferences in mystery writers...traditionalists.)

Nancy Webb. "The Shadow Passes," The Third Degree (Mystery Writers of America), April 1986, p. 4. (Memories of collaborating with Gibson on Blackstone, the Magic Detective.)

Robert Weinberg and Lohr McKinstry. The Hero Pulp Index. Evergreen, Colo.: Opar Press, 1971.

"Who is Walt Gibson? 'The Shadow' Knows," Boston Herald American, October 24, 1978, p. 36. (Same text as Charles Chamberlain article above.)

James J. J. Wilson. "Shades of the Shadow," The Comics Journal, No. 57 (Summer 1980): 49-50. (Review of The Duende History of The Shadow Magazine, The Shadow Scrapbook, and The Shadow Knows. This last is a collection of radio scripts.)

"Without a Shadow of a Doubt," Magick, No. 57 (September 8, 1972): 281-282, 284.

George Wolf. "The Shadow Speaks," Bronze Shadows, No. 14 (March 1968): 11-12. (Excerpts from Gibson's article from Writer's Digest, see above, this Appendix.)

"Writer of 'The Shadow' Still Active at Age 81," Hartford Courant, October 24, 1978, p. W31. (Same text as Chamberlain article, see above.)

John Zweers. "Walter B. Gibson: Magician of the Month," M-U-M, 66 (May 1977): 13-14.

A Walter Gibson
Checklist   ☞

A.1.   After Dinner Tricks
Columbus, Ohio: Magic Publishing Co., 1921.
30p. illus. paper covers.

A.2.   Practical Card Tricks
Hika, Wisconsin: E. R. Mill, 1921.
12p. paper covers.

A.3.   Money Magic
Philadelphia: Cooper Printing Co., 1926.
14p. illus. paper covers.

A.4.   Popular Card Tricks
New York: E. I. Company, nd [1926].
48p. illus. paper covers.

A.5.   Twenty New Practical Card Tricks
Hika, Wisconsin: E. R. Mill, 1926.
13-28p. paper covers.

A.6.   Howard Thurston's [Walter B. Gibson].
200 Tricks You Can Do
New York: George Sully and Co., 1926.
xiii, 126p. illus. cloth.

**A.7. The Book of Secrets, Miracles Ancient
and Modern With Added Chapters on Easy Magic
You Can Do**
Scranton, Pa.: Personal Arts Co., [1927].
159p. illus. cloth.

A.8.   The Bunco Book
Philadelphia: Walter B. Gibson, 1927.
96p. illus. paper covers.

A.9.   Wilber Gaston's [Walter B. Gibson]
First Principles of Astrology
New York: George Sully and Co., 1927.
186p cloth.

A.10.   Houdini's Book of Magic and Party Pastimes
New York: Stoll & Edwards Co., Inc., 1927.
32p. illus. paper covers.

**A.11.   The Magic Square: Tells Your
Past-Present-Future**
New York: George Sully and Co., 1927.
vi, 167p. cloth.

**A.12.   The Science of Numerology:
What Numbers Mean to You**
New York: George Sully and Co., 1927.
x, 186p. illus. cloth.

**A.13.   Howard Thurston's [Walter B. Gibson]
Book of Magic (New Edition-Number Nine)**
Philadelphia: Edward J. Murray, 1927.
16p. illus. paper covers.

A.14.   Two Dozen Effective Practical Card Tricks
Hika, Wisconsin: E. R. Mill, 1927.
29-44p. paper covers.

**A.15. Howard Thurston's [Walter B. Gibson]
200 More Tricks You Can Do**
New York: George Sully and Co., 1927.
187p. illus. cloth.

A.16.   The World's Best Book of Magic
Philadelphia: Penn Publishing Co., 1927.
319p. illus. cloth.

**A.17.   Howard Thurston's [Walter B. Gibson]
Fooling the World**
New York: Howard Thurston, 1928.
96p. illus. paper covers.

A.18.   Sixteen Master Card Mysteries
Hika, Wisconsin: Edward R. Mill, 1928.
16p. paper covers.

**A.19.   Howard Thurston's [Walter B. Gibson]
The Thurston Magic Lessons**
New York: Howard Thurston, 1928.
37p. illus. paper covers.

**A.20.   Harry Blackstone's [Walter B. Gibson]
Blackstone's Annual of Magic**
Philadelphia: Cooper Printing Co., 1929.
48p. illus. paper covers.

A.21. Harry Blackstone's [Walter B. Gibson]
Blackstone's Secrets of Magic
New York: George Sully and Co., 1929.
xv, 265p. illus. cloth.

A.22. Harry Blackstone's [Walter B. Gibson]
Blackstone's Tricks and Entertainments
New York: Jacobsen Publishing Co., 1929.
98p. illus. paper covers.

A.23. Howard Thurston's
My Life of Magic [as told to Walter B. Gibson]
Philadelphia: Dorrance and Co., 1929.
273p. illus. cloth.

A.24. Harry Blackstone's [Walter B. Gibson]
Blackstone's Magic: A Book of Mystery
Philadelphia: Shade Publishing Co., 1930.
64p. illus. paper covers.

A.25. Brain Tests; or, Your Brains, If Any
Boston: L. C. Page & Co., 1930.
xiii, 224p. illus. cloth.

A.26. Prof. A[lfred] F[rancis] Seward's
[Walter B. Gibson]
Facts about Brunettes and Blondes
Chicago: A. F. Seward & Co., 1930.
ii, 108p. illus. paper covers.

A.27. Houdini's Escapes
New York: Harcourt, Brace & Co., 1930.
xiv, 317p. illus. cloth.

A.28. Harry Blackstone's [Walter B. Gibson]
Blackstone's Modern Card Tricks
New York: George Sully and Co., 1932.
xiv, 204p. illus. cloth.

A.29. Houdini's Magic
New York: Harcourt, Brace & Co., 1932.
xi, 316p. illus. cloth.

A.30. Magic Made Easy
Springfield, Mass.: McLoughlin Bros., Inc., 1932.
121p. illus. paper covers.

A.31.   A[lfred] F[rancis] Seward's
[Walter B. Gibson]
Periodicity, the Absolute Law of the Universe
Atlantic City & Chicago: A. F. Seward & Co., 1932.
154p. paper covers.

A.32.   **Magician's Manual**
New York: The Magician's League of America, 1933.
140p. illus. cloth.

A.33.   Maxwell Grant's [Walter B. Gibson]
The Living Shadow: A Detective Novel
New York: Street & Smith, nd [1934].
245p. paper on boards.

A.34.   Maxwell Grant's [Walter B. Gibson]
The Eyes of The Shadow: A Detective Novel
New York: Street & Smith, nd [1935].
252p. paper on boards.

A.35.   Maxwell Grant's [Walter B. Gibson]
The Shadow Laughs: A Detective Novel
New York: Street & Smith, nd [1935].
252p. paper on boards.

A.36.   Joseph Dunninger's [Walter B. Gibson]
Inside the Medium's Cabinet
New York: David Kemp and Co., 1935.
vi, 228p. illus. cloth.

A.37.   Joseph Dunninger's [Walter B. Gibson]
How to Make a Ghost Walk
New York: David Kemp and Co., 1936.
viii, 82p. illus. cloth.

A.38.   **The New Magician's Manual**
New York: David Kemp and Co., 1936.
143p. illus. cloth.

A.39.   Maxwell Grant's [Walter B. Gibson]
The Shadow and the Voice of Murder
Los Angeles:Bantam Books, 1940.
100p. paper covers.

A.40.   The Great Blackstone's [Walter B. Gibson]
Complete Magic Show
[New York:] [Street & Smith,] 1941.
16p. illus. paper covers.

A.41. Maxwell Grant's [Walter Gibson]
The Shadow Annual [1942]
New York: Street & Smith, 1942.
160p. illus. paper covers.

A.42. Maxwell Grant's [Walter B. Gibson]
The Shadow Annual [1943]
New York: Street & Smith, 1943.
160p. illus. paper covers.

A.43. [Joseph] Dunninger's [Walter B. Gibson]
What's On Your Mind?
Cleveland and New York: World Publishing Co.,
1944. 192p. illus. cloth.

A.44. [Anonymous]
Blackstone, World's Super Magician:
Souvenir Program and Illustrated Trick Book
New York: Wm. C. Popper, nd [1945].
20p. illus. paper covers.

A.45. Secrets of Magic. A New Book of Tricks
You Can Do.
New York: Wm. C. Popper and Co., 1945.
50p. illus. paper covers.

A.46. [Anonymous]
Blackstone the Magic Detective Reveals Magic
Tricks Everyone Can Do
New York: Blackstone Magic Enterprises, Inc.1946
8p. illus. paper covers.

A.47. Julian J. Proskauer's [Walter B. Gibson]
The Dead Do Not Talk
New York: Harper and Brothers, 1946
xvii, 198p.cloth.

A.48. Professional Magic for Amateurs
New York: Prentice-Hall, 1947
xvi, 225p. illus. cloth.

A.49. Maxwell Grant's [Walter B. Gibson]
The Shadow Annual [1947]
New York: Street & Smith, 1947.
144p illus. paper covers.

A.50. Harry Hershfield's [Walter B. Gibson]
The Sin of Harold Diddlebock
New York: Bartholomew House, 1947.
155p. illus. endpapers. paper covers.

A.51. Harry Blackstone's [Walter B. Gibson]
Blackstone's Tricks Anyone Can Do
New York: Permabooks, 1948.
xvii, 232p. illus. pictorial board covers.

A.52. **A Blonde for Murder**
New York: Vital Publications, 1948.
128p. paper covers.

A.53. **Looks That Kill!**
New York: Current Detective Stories, Inc., 1948.
128p. paper covers.

A.54. **Magic Explained**
New York: Permabooks, 1949.
188p. illus. paper covers.

A.55. Walter B. Gibson's and Morris N. Young's
Houdini on Magic
New York: Dover Publications, 1953.
xv, 280p. illus. cloth and paper covered editions.

A.56. **The Book of the Presidents of the
United States**
New York: Vital Publications, 1956.
36p. (including cover) illus. paper covers.

A.57. Sy Seidman's [Walter B. Gibson]
Fun with Optical Illusions
New York: Padell Book Co., 1956.
32p. illus. paper covers.

A.58. Bill Barnum's [Walter B. Gibson]
Fun with Stunts, Tricks and Skits
New York: Padell Book Co., 1956.
32p. illus. paper covers.

A.59. **The Key to Hypnotism**
New York: Key Publishing Co., 1956.
96p. illus. paper covers.

A.60. Sidney H. Radner's [Walter B. Gibson]
Magic for Fun
New York: Padell Book Co., 1956.
93p. illus. paper covers.

A.61. **What's New in Magic**
Garden City, New York: Hanover House, 1956.
222p. illus. boards.

A.62.   Rufus Perry's [Walter B. Gibson]
How to Win with Racing Numerology
New York: Key Publishing Co., 1957.
92p. illus. paper covers.

A.63.   Sidney H. Radner's [Walter B. Gibson]
How to Play Poker and Win
New York: Key Publishing Co., 1957.
94p. illus. paper covers.

A.64.   Rufus Perry's [Walter B. Gibson]
How to Play the Horses and Win
New York: Key Publishing Co., 1957.
94p. illus. paper covers.

A.65.   Rufus Perry's [Walter B. Gibson]
How to Play the Trotters and Win
New York: Key Publishing Co., 1957.
91p. illus. paper covers.

A.66.   Sidney H. Radner's [Walter B. Gibson]
How to Spot Card Sharps and Their Methods
New York: Key Publishing Co., 1957.
95p. illus. paper covers.

A.67.   Rufus Perry's [Walter B. Gibson]
How to Win at Pinochle and Other Games
New York: Key Publishing Co., 1957.
92p. illus. paper covers.

A.68.   Teddy Nadler's [Walter B. Gibson]
Secrets of My Million Dollar Memory
New York: Jersam Publishing Corp., 1957.
64p. illus. paper covers.

A.69.   Sidney H. Radner's [Walter B. Gibson]
Sidney H. Radner on Dice
New York: Key Publishing Co., 1957.
96p. illus. paper covers.

A.70.   Sidney H. Radner's [Walter B. Gibson]
How to Win at Roulette and Other Casino Games
New York: Key Publishing Co., 1958.
96p. illus. paper covers.

A.71.   **The Key to Astronomy**
New York: Key Publishing Co., 1958.
96p. illus. paper covers.

A.72.   The Key to Camplife
New York: Key Publishing Co., 1958.
95p. illus.paper covers.

A.73.   Ishi Black's [Walter B. Gibson]
The Key to Judo and Jiujitsu [sic]
New York: Key Publishing Co., 1958.
95p. illus. paper covers.

A.74.   The Key to Space Travel
New York: Key Publishing Co., 1958.
96p. illus. paper covers.

A.75.   The Key to Yoga
New York: Key Publishing Co., 1958.
160p. illus. paper covers.

A.76.   Felix Fairfax's [Walter B. Gibson]
The Key to Astrology
New York: Key Publishing Co., 1959.
95p. illus. paper covers.

A.77.   Rufus Perry's [Walter B. Gibson]
The Key to Better Bowling
New York: Key Publishing Co., 1959.
95p. illus. paper covers.

A.78.   Andrew Abbott's [Walter B. Gibson]
The Key to Better Memory
New York: Key Publishing Co., 1959
95p. illus. paper covers.

A.79.   Andrew Abbott's [Walter B. Gibson]
The Key to Character Reading
New York: Key Publishing Co., 1959.
95p. illus. paper covers.

A.80.   Roy Masters' [Walter B. Gibson]
The Key to Chess Simplified
New York: Key Publishing Co., 1959.
96p. illus. paper covers.

A.81.   Walter Glass's [Walter B. Gibson]
The Key to Knots and Splices
New York: Key Publishing Co., 1959.
94p. illus. paper covers.

A.82. Andy Adams' [Walter B. Gibson]
Brazilian Gold Mine Mystery
New York: Grosset and Dunlap, 1960.
182p. illus. paper on boards.

A.83. Fell's Official Guide to Knots
and How to Tie Them
New York: Frederick Fell, 1961.
127p. illus. cloth.

A.84. Walter B. Gibson's and Morris N. Young's
Houdini's Fabulous Magic
Philadelphia & New York: Chilton Books, 1961.
viii, 214p. illus. cloth.

A.85. **Hypnotism Through the Ages**
New York: Vista House, 1961.
173p. illus. boards.

A.86. Maborushi Kineji's [Walter B. Gibson]
Judo: Attack and Defense
New York: Vista House, 1961.
136p. illus. boards.

A.87. Andy Adams' [Walter B. Gibson]
Mystery of the Mexican Treasure
New York: Grosset and Dunlap, 1961.
182p. illus. paper on boards.

A.88. Sidney H. Radner's [Walter B. Gibson]
Radner on Bridge
New York: Padell Book Co., 1961.
96p. paper covers.

A.89. Sidney H. Radner's [Walter B. Gibson]
Radner on Canasta, including Samba, Bolivia,
Calypso and Other Games
New York: Key Publishing Co., 1961.
95p. illus. paper covers.

A.90. Douglas Brown's [Walter B. Gibson]
Anne Bonny, Pirate Queen: The True Saga of
a Fabulous Female Buccaneer
Derby, Conn., Monarch Books, 1962.
138p. paper covers.

A.91. [Walter B. Gibson and Others]
Science and Mechanics Magic Handbook: 1962 Edition
Chicago: Science and Mechanics Publishing Co.,1961
160p. illus. paper covers.

A.92.   Walter B. Gibson's and Morris N. Young's
How to Develop an Exceptional Memory
New York: Chilton, 1962.
x, 266p. cloth.

A.93.   Andy Adams' [Walter B. Gibson]
Mystery of the Ambush in India
New York: Grosset and Dunlap, 1962.
170p. illus. paper on boards.

A.94.   Andy Adams' [Walter B. Gibson]
Egyptian Scarab Mystery
New York: Grosset and Dunlap, 1963.
170p. illus. paper on boards.

A.95.   Fell's Guide to Papercraft Tricks, Games
and Puzzles
New York: Frederick Fell, 1963.
125p. illus. paper on boards.

A.96.   Hoyle's Simplified Guide to the Popular
Card Games
Garden City, New York: Doubleday, 1963.
267p. illus. cloth.

A.97.   Magic Made Simple
Garden City, New York: Doubleday, 1963.
160p. illus. paper covers.

A.98.   Rod Serling's [Walter B. Gibson]
The Twilight Zone
New York: Grosset and Dunlap, 1963.
vi, 207p. illus. boards.

A.99.   Return of The Shadow
New York: Belmont Books, 1963.
140p. paper covers.

A.100.   Helen Wells' [Walter B. Gibson]
The Brass Idol Mystery
New York: Grosset and Dunlap, 1964.
173p. frontis. boards.

A.101.   Famous Lands and People Fun and
Activity Book
New York: Treasure Books, 1964.
80p. illus. paper covers/

A.102.   Fifty States Fun and Activity Book
New York: Treasure Books, 1964.
80p. illus. paper covers.

A.103.   How to Win at Solitaire
Garden City, New York: Doubleday, 1964.
vi, 152p. illus. cloth.

A.104.   Hoyle Card Games: Reference Crammer
New York: Ken Publishing Co., 1964.
160p. paper covers with spiral binding.

A.105.   Puzzles and Pastimes Fun and Activity Book
New York: Treasure Books, 1964.
80p. illus. paper covers.

A.106.   World Wide Fun and Activity Book
New York: Treasure Books, 1964.
80p. illus. paper covers.

A.107.   Year-Round Fun and Activity Book
New York: Treasure Books, 1964.
80p. illus. paper covers.

A.108.   Rod Serling's [Walter B. Gibson]
The Twilight Zone Revisited
New York: Grosset and Dunlap, 1964.
208p. illus. boards.

A.109.   Space and Science Fun and Activity Book
New York: Treasure Books, 1965.
80p. illus. paper covers.

A.110.   The Fine Art of Murder
New York: Grosset and Dunlap, 1965.
xi, 236p. illus. cloth.

A.111.   The Fine Art of Spying
New York: Grosset and Dunlap, 1965.
x, 243p. illus. cloth.

A.112.   Morris N. Young's and Chesley V. Young's
[Walter B. Gibson]
How to Read Faster and Remember More
West Nyack, N. Y.: Parker Publishing Co., 1965.
239p. cloth.

A.113.   The Man from U.N.C.L.E.: The Coin of El
Diablo Affair
New York: Wonder Books, 1965.
48p. illus. paper covers.

A.114.   Monsters: Three Famous Spine-Tingling Tales
New York: Wonder Books, 1965.
48p. illus. paper covers.

A.115.   Andy Adams' [Walter B. Gibson]
Mystery of the Alpine Pass
New York: Grosset and Dunlap, 1965.
170p. illus. pictorial boards.

A.116.   David Hoy's [Walter B. Gibson]
Psychic and Other ESP Party Games
Garden City, New York: Doubleday and Co., 1965.
141p. illus. cloth.

A.117.   Walter B. Gibson's and Litzka R. Gibson's
**The   Complete   Illustrated   Book   of   the   Psychic
Sciences**
Garden City, New York: Doubleday and Co., 1966.
xx, 403p. illus. cloth.

A.118.   The Fine Art of Robbery
New York: Grosset and Dunlap, 1966.
vi, 254p. illus. cloth.

A.119.   The Fine Art of Swindling
New York: Grosset and Dunlap, 1966.
255p. illus. cloth.

A.120.   How to Bet the Harness Races
Garden City, New York: Doubleday and Co., 1966.
148p. paper covers.

A.121.   Douglas Brown's [Walter B. Gibson]
The Key to Solitaire
New York: Crown, Ottenheimer, 1966.
142p. illus. paper covers.

**A.122.   The Master Magicians: Their Lives and Most
Famous Tricks**
Garden City, New York: Doubleday and Co., 1966.
xvii, 221p. illus. cloth.

A.123.   Walter Gibson's (alias Maxwell Grant)
The Weird Adventures of The Shadow
New York: Grosset and Dunlap, 1966.
216p. illus. pictorial boards.

A.124.   Secrets of Magic, Ancient and Modern
New York: Grosset and Dunlap, 1966.
147p. illus. pictorial boards.

A.125.   Winning the $2 Bet
Garden City, New York: Doubleday and Co., 1967.
146p. paper covers.

A.126.   [Anonymous]
The Key to Hoyle's Games
Owings Mills, Md.: Ottenheimer, 1968.
156p. boards.

A.127.   Magic With Science
New York: Grosset and Dunlap, 1968.
119p. illus. pictorial boards.

A.128.   The Complete Illustrated Book of Card Magic
Garden City, New York:Doubleday and Co., 1969.
xviii, 454p. illus. cloth.

A.129.   Maxwell Grant's [Walter B. Gibson]
The Death Tower
New York: Bantam Books, 1969.
138p. paper covers.

A.130.   Dreams
New York: Grosset and Dunlap, 1969.
127p. boards.

A.131.   Litzka R. Gibson's and Walter B. Gibson's
Mystic and Occult Arts: A Guide to Their Use in
Daily Living
New York: Parker Publishing Co., 1969.
224p. cloth.

A.132.   Rogues' Gallery: A Variety of Mystery
Stories
Garden City, New York: Doubleday and Co., 1969.
398p. illus. cloth.

A.133.   Family Games America Plays
Garden City, New York: Doubleday and Co., 1970.
vii, 275p. illus. cloth.

A.134.   Hypnotism
New York: Grosset and Dunlap, 1970.
124p. cloth and paper editions.

A.135.   Maxwell Grant's [Walter B. Gibson]
The Ghost Makers
New York: Bantam Books, 1970.
120p. paper covers.

A.136.   Maxwell Grant's [Walter B. Gibson]
Hidden Death
New York: Bantam Books, 1970.
138p. paper covers.

A.137.   Maxwell Grant's [Walter B. Gibson]
Gangdom's Doom
New York: Bantam Books, 1970.
166p. paper covers.

A.138.   Chesley V. Young's [Walter B. Gibson]
The Magic of a Mighty Memory
West Nyack, New York: Parker Publishing Co.,   1971.
249p. cloth.

A.139.   Mel Evans' and Walter Gibson's
What Are the Odds?
New York: Western Publishing Co., 1972.
128p. boards.

A.140.   Walter B. Gibson's and Litzka R. Gibson's
The Complete Illustrated Book of Divination
and Prophecy
Garden City, New York: Doubleday and Co., 1973.
336p. illus. cloth.

A.141.   Witchcraft
New York: Grosset and Dunlap, 1973.
149p. boards.

A.142.   Backgammon: The Way to Play and Win
New York: Harper & Row (Barnes & Noble), 1974.
144p. illus. paper covers.

A.143.   Maxwell Grant's [Walter B. Gibson]
The Black Master
New York: Pyramid Books, 1974.
174p. paper covers.

A.144. Joseph Dunninger's
Dunninger's Secrets (as told to Walter Gibson)
Secaucus, New Jersey: Lyle Stuart, 1974.
332p. cloth.

A.145. **Fell's Guide to Winning Backgammon**
New York: Frederick Fell, 1974.
166p. illus. boards and paper cover editions.

A.146. **Hoyle's Modern Encyclopedia of Card Games**
Garden City, New York: Doubleday and Co., 1974.
398p. illus. paper covers.

A.147. Maxwell Grant's [Walter B. Gibson]
The Mobsmen on the Spot
New York: Pyramid Books, 1974.
190p. paper covers.

A.148. **Pinochle is the Name of the Game**
New York: Harper & Row, 1974.
143p. paper covers.

A.149. **Poker is the Name of the Game**
New York: Harper & Row, 1974.
143p. paper covers.

A.150. Mark Wilson's
Mark Wilson Course in Magic (in collaboration with
Walter B. Gibson)
North Hollywood, Calif.: Mark Wilson, 1975.
472p. illus. boards.

A.151. Maxwell Grant's [Walter B. Gibson]
The Crime Oracle and The Teeth of the Dragon: Two
Adventures of The Shadow
New York: Dover Publications, 1975.
xxv, 163p. illus. paper covers.

A.152. **The Shadow: The Mask of Mephisto and**
Murder By Magic, as originally told by Walter
Gibson (Alias "Maxwell Grant")
Garden City, New York: Doubleday and Co., 1975.
xi, 179p. boards.

A.153. Maxwell Grant's [Walter B. Gibson]
Hands in the Dark
New York: Pyramid Books, 1975.
188p. paper covers.

A.154. Maxwell Grant's [Walter B. Gibson]
Double Z
New York: Pyramid Books, 1975.
189p. paper covers.

A.155. Maxwell Grant's [Walter B. Gibson]
The Crime Cult
New York: Pyramid Books, 1975.
157p. paper covers.

A.156. Maxwell Grant's [Walter B. Gibson]
The Red Menace
New York: Pyramid Books, 1975.
176p. paper covers.

A.157. Maxwell Grant's [Walter B. Gibson]
Mox
New York: Pyramid Books, 1975.
127p. paper covers.

A.158. Maxwell Grant's [Walter B. Gibson]
The Romanoff Jewels
New York: Pyramid Books, 1975.
143p. paper covers.

A.159. Maxwell Grant's [Walter B. Gibson]
The Silent Seven
New York: Pyramid Books, 1975.
143p. paper covers.

A.160. **Card Magic Made Easy**
New York: Harper & Row (Barnes & Noble), 1976.
iv, 91p. illus. paper covers.

A.161. **Fell's Beginner's Guide to Magic**
New York: Frederick Fell, 1976.
170p. illus. boards.

A.162. **The Original Houdini Scrapbook**
New York: Corwin, Sterling Publishing Co., 1976.
224p. illus. cloth and paper editions.

A.163. **Walter Gibson's Encyclopedia of**
Magic and Conjuring
New York: Drake Publishers, Inc., 1976.
x, 213p. illus. cloth and paper editions.

A.164. Maxwell Grant's [Walter B. Gibson]
Kings of Crime
New York: Pyramid Books, 1976.
160p. paper covers.

A.165. Maxwell Grant's [Walter B. Gibson]
Shadowed Millions
New York: Pyramid Books, 1976.
143p. paper covers.

A.166. **Kreskin's Mind Power Book**
New York: McGraw-Hill, 1977.
xi, 212p. cloth.

A.167. **Norgil the Magician**
New York: The Mysterious Press, 1977.
xv, 209p. frontis. cloth.

A.168. Maxwell Grant's [Walter B. Gibson]
Green Eyes
New York: Pyramid Books, 1977.
159p. paper covers.

A.169. Maxwell Grant's [Walter B. Gibson]
The Creeping Death
New York: Pyramid Books, 1977.
144p. paper covers.

A.170. Maxwell Grant's [Walter B. Gibson]
Gray Fist
New York: Pyramid Books, 1977.
174p. paper covers.

A.171. Maxwell Grant's [Walter B. Gibson]
The Shadow's Shadow
New York: Pyramid Books, 1977.
174p. paper covers.

A.172. Maxwell Grant's [Walter B. Gibson]
Fingers of Death
New York: Jove Books, 1977.
144p. paper covers.

A.173. Maxwell Grant's [Walter B. Gibson]
Murder Trail
New York: Jove Books, 1977.
159p. paper covers.

A.174.   Maxwell Grant's [Walter B. Gibson]
Zemba
New York: Jove Books, 1977.
160p. paper covers.

A.175.   Maxwell Grant's [Walter B. Gibson]
Charg, Monster
New York: Jove Books, 1977.
158p. paper covers.

A.176.   The Shadow: A Quarter of Eight & The Freak
Show Murders, as originally told by Walter Gibson
(Alias "Maxwell Grant")
Garden City, New York: Doubleday and Co., 1978.
xv, 248p. boards.

A.177.   Maxwell Grant's [Walter B. Gibson]
The Wealth Seeker
New York: Jove Books, 1978.
158p. paper covers.

A.178.   Maxwell Grant's [Walter B. Gibson]
The Silent Death
New York: Jove Books, 1978.
160p. paper covers.

A.179.   Maxwell Grant's [Walter B. Gibson]
The Death Giver
New York: Jove Books, 1978.
160p. paper covers.

A.180.   Norgil: More Tales of Prestidigitection
New York: The Mysterious Press, 1979.
xi, 208p. cloth.

A.181.   The Shadow: Crime Over Casco and The Mother
Goose Murders, as originally told by Walter Gibson
(Alias "Maxwell Grant")
Garden City, New York: Doubleday and Co., 1979.
xiii, 197p. boards.

A.182.   The Shadow Scrapbook
New York: Harcourt, Brace, Jovanovich, 1979.
v, 162p. illus. paper covers.

A.183.   The Complete Illustrated Book of Close-Up
Magic
Garden City, New York: Doubleday and Co., 1980.
xviii, 426p. illus. cloth.

A.184.   Walter Gibson's Big Book of Magic for All Ages
Garden City, New York: Doubleday and Co., 1980.
vii, 231p. illus. boards.

A.185.   The Shadow: Jade Dragon and House of Ghosts, as originally told by Walter Gibson (Alias "Maxwell Grant")
Garden City, New York: Doubleday and Co., 1981.
ix, 205p. boards.

A.186.   Attic Revivals Presents Walter Gibson's Magicians
Great Barrington, Mass., Attic Revivals Press, 1982.
8p. illus. paper covers.

A.187.   The Shadow and The Golden Master
New York: The Mysterious Press, 1984.
iv, 130, 114p. illus. cloth.

Index of Titles ☞

All titles of works by Walter Gibson are listed here alphabetically. Those titles which exist as independent units (books or pamphlets) are entered in bold face type; short stories, novels, or articles which are part of a larger unit (such as a magazine issue) are enclosed in quotation marks.

"The Accusing Corpse"   F.79.
"Adventures in Mind-Reading"   B.271.
"Adventures of an Escape Artist"   F.131.
"The Aerial Treasury"   B.83.
After Dinner Tricks   A.1, D.1.
"'Age of Torture' in Vogue Again"   D.26.
"Alias the Shadow"   B.804, B.893.
"Alibi Trail"   B.581, B.728.
"Along With Blackstone"   B.738.
"The Amazing Creations of Theodore DeLand"
      B.688, B.931.
"The Amazing Randi"   B.899.
"An Amazing Space Journey: A Tale of the Canadian
      West"   E.350.
"America Goes Endurance Crazy"   D.34.
"Among Only 5,000 Witnesses"   B.858.
"Among the Head-Hunters of Java"   B.277.
Anne Bonny, Pirate Queen   A.90.
"The Aquatic Thimbles"   B.32.
"Are You a Sucker for Marked Cards?"   B.851.
Arrow: The Family Comic Weekly   E.393.
["Arson"]   E.6.
"Arthur Lloyd, the Human Card Index"   B.122.
"Artistic Magic"   B.357.
"Ashes of the Phoenix"   B.914.
"Assignment Mousetrap"   B.785.
The Astrologer's Almanac and Occult Miscellany
      F.126.-F.130.
"At the Foot of the Gallows"   B.287.
"The Athenian,"   B.265.

341

Blackstone Haunts

"Blackstone Haunts Pirate's Cove"   E.178.
"Blackstone: [His Panama Adventures]"   E.159.
"Blackstone in the Adventure of 'the Jade Idol'"
      E.165.
"Blackstone in Voodoo Valley"   E.180.
"Blackstone Invades Cagliostro's Castle"   E.210.
"Blackstone Invades Crooks' Jungle"   E.230.
"Blackstone Invades the Castle of Doom!!!"   E.253.
"Blackstone Magic"   D.2.
"Blackstone Matches Magic with the Pirates of the
      Sargasso Sea"   E.160.
"Blackstone Meets Malbini, the Millionaire Mystic"
      E.207.
"Blackstone Meets Swami Simla, the Mystic Seer"
      E.194.
"Blackstone Meets the Algerian Assassins"   E.172.
"Blackstone Meets the Lady or the Tiger"   E.185.
"Blackstone Meets the Mad Magician"   E.191.
"Blackstone Meets the Pirates of Twin Island"
      E.197.
"Blackstone Meets the Shinto Wizards"   E.156.
"Blackstone Meets the Unlucky Seven"   E.223.
"Blackstone Meets the Water Wizards"   E.206.
"Blackstone Meets the Wizard of Wanga"   E.182.
"Blackstone Meets the Zombi Master"   E.209.
"Blackstone: Murder at Eight!"   E.263.
"Blackstone: Mystery of the Rajah's Ruby"   E.266.
"Blackstone on Incredible Island"   E.167.
"Blackstone on Skull Island"   E.166.
"Blackstone Outwits Dalban the Dervish"   E.221.
"Blackstone Outwits the Secret Six"   E.232.
"Blackstone Presents 'From Film to Life'"   E.249.
"Blackstone Presents Sawing a Woman in Half in the
      Haunted Theatre!"   E.224.
"Blackstone Reveals"   B.734.
"Blackstone: Riddle of the Third Face!"   E.264.
"Blackstone: 'Sahara Trail'"   E.173.
"Blackstone Shows You How to Do Magic"   E.255.
"Blackstone Solves the Riddle of the Rajpoot Ruby"
      E.219.
"Blackstone Solves the Riddle of the Vanishing
      Mummies"   E.258.
"Blackstone Solves the Sealed Vault Mystery"
      E.251.
"Blackstone Talks About Magic"   E.254.
"Blackstone: The Isle of Doom"   E.265.
Blackstone the Magic Detective   A.46.
"Blackstone the Magician and the Thugees of Kali"
      E.150.

Book Reviews

"The Case of the Vanished Bride"   B.835.
"Castle Doom"   B.424.
"Castle of Crime"   B.529.
"The Castle of Horrors"   B.833.
"Catherine Had a Date with Murder"   B.895.
"The Cellini Statuette"   F.63.
"Chain of Death"   B.388.
"A Changing Card"   B.68.
Charg, Monster   A.175, B.387.
"Charg, the Murder Monster"   E.9.
"The Chateau of Shadows: A Dr. Neff Mystery of the
        'Other' World"   E.279.
"The Chest of Ching Ling Foo"   B.526.
"The Chest of Chu-Chan"   B.671.
"Chicago Crime"   B.506.
"Chick Carter [and The Octopus]"   F.93.
"Chick Carter and the Shalimar Diamond"   F.92.
"CHick Carter [Meets The Bat]"   F.91.
"Chick Carter, Boy Detective, [Meets The Rattler]"
        F.89.
"Chick Carter: The Rattler and the Life-line of
        Oil"   F.90.
"Chinaman's Chance"   B.488.
"The Chinese Disks"   B.395.
"Chinese Magic"   B.292.
"The Chinese Primrose"   B.562.
"The Chinese Tapestry"   B.419.
"Chip Gardner, Private Eye: The Rock-a-Bye Baby
        Murder"   E.302.
"Chip Gardner: Death on the Run or The Case of the
        Darling Daughter"   E.312.
"Chip Gardner: The Case of the Buffalo Nickels"
        E.310.
"Chip Gardner: The Case of the Crooked
        Politician"   E.316.
"Chip Gardner: The Case of the Death's Head Ruby"
        E.314.
"Chip Gardner: The Case of the Jittery Patient"
        E.315.
"Chip Gardner: The Case of the King-Sized
        Miracle"   E.306.
"Chip Gardner: The Case of the Losing Winners"
        E.305.
"Chip Gardner: The Case of the Movie Star's
        Double"   E.311.
"Chip Gardner: The Case of the Ring That Cracked
        Itself"   E.313.
"Chip Gardner: The Case of the Substitute Nephew"
        E.303.

"Chip Gardner: The Case of the Vanishing Beauty
     Shops" E.309.
"Chip Gardner: The Escort Murder Case"   E.304.
"Chip Gardner: The Ostrich Murder Case"   E.308.
"Chip Gardner: The Payroll Bonus Murders & The
     Case of the Insistent Sister"   E.307.
"Chip Gardner: The Rabbit-Punch Murder Case"
     E.318.
"Chip Gardner: You'll Never Live to Tell"   E.317.
"A Cigarette Vanish"   B.101.
"The Circle of Death"   B.378.
"City of Crime"   B.441.
"The City of Doom"   B.432.
"City of Ghosts"   B.532.
"City of Shadows"   B.521.
"Clever Electric Swindle"   B.225.
"Clip Color"   B.585.
"Clue for Clue"   B.613.
"Clue Mysteries"   D.5.
"Clue of the Reptile Witness"   B.853.
"The Cobra"   B.380.
"The Coin of Cleopatra"   F.53.
"The Coin of Confucius"   F.45.
"Coin Sleights"   B.165.
"Coin Tricks Easily Learned"   B.237.
"The Coins of Death"   F.12.
[Commercial Comics], (First Series)   E.366.
[Commercial Comics], (Second Series)   E.367.
The Complete Illustrated Book of Card Magic
     A.128.
The Complete Illustrated Book of Close-Up Magic
     A.183.
The Complete Illustrated Book of Divination and
     Prophecy   A.140.
The Complete Illustrated Book of the Psychic
     Sciences   A.117.
Complete Magic Show   A.40.
"The Condor"   B.410.
"Confetti of Cathay"   B.601.
"Convention Magic"   B.746.
"The Coronation Murders"   B.848.
"Count Them Out"   B.624.
"Counterfeit Alibi"   B.799.
"The Cradle of Doom"   F.28.
"Crazy Quilt Guilt"   B.798.
"The Creeper"   B.414.
The Creeping Death   A.169, B.350, F.87.
"Crime at Seven Oaks"   B.552.
"Crime Caravan"   B.654.

The Dead Who

"The Dead Who Lived"   B.502.
"Deadman's Reef"   F.123.
"Death About Town"   B.606.
"Death Across the Tracks"   F.108.
"Death By Proxy"   B.442.
"Death Clew"   B.384.
"Death Counts Ten"   F.33.
"Death Dealt Double"   B.837.
"Death Defying Death"   F.80.
"Death Diamonds"   B.583.
"Death from Nowhere"   B.523.
The Death Giver   A.179, B.359.
Death Has Green Eyes   F.139.
"Death Has Grey Eyes"   B.690.
"Death in Mid-Air"   F.24.
"Death in the Crystal," B.669, F.69.
"Death in the Duffel-Bag"   B.836.
"Death in the Stars"   B.546.
"Death Jewels"   B.498.
"Death Meets the Boat"   F.29.
"Death Rides the Skyway"   B.425.
"Death Rings the Bell"   F.26.
"Death Ship"   B.516.
"The Death Sleep"   B.394.
"Death Token"   B.449.
The Death Tower   A.129, B.319.
"The Death Triangle"   B.369.
"Death Turrets"   B.471.
"Death Valley Scotty's Dash for Fame"   B.286.
"Death's Double Deal"   F.109.
"Death's Masquerade"   B.623.
"Death's Premium"   B.536.
"The Deathless Shots"   F.61.
"Debates on Magic: Should Magic Books Be Placed in
      Public Libraries?"   B.11.
"Deferred Coincidence"   B.643.
"DeLand Card Effects"   B.939.
"DeLand's Changing Cards"   B.714, B.938.
"DeLand's Ever-Ready Card Tricks"   B.709, B.933.
"DeLand's Floating Skeleton"   B.736.
"DeLand's Floating Smoke"   B.614.
"DeLand's Greatest Card Creation"   B.711.
"DeLand's Marked Card Creations"   B.696.
"DeLand's Mental Mysteries"   B.727.
"DeLand's Special Packs"   B.707, B.932.
"The Department of Death"   F.22.
"The Devil Master"   E.16.
"The Devil Monsters"   B.625.
"The Devil's Cauldron"   F.77.

"The Echo of Death"   F.107.
"Editorial"   B.116, B.155.
"The Educated Cards"   B.18.
"The Educated Dummy"   F.38.
"Effective Card Tricks"   B.304, B.306, B.310,
B.314, B.318, B.322, B.323.
Egyptian Scarab Mystery   A.94.
"80 Seconds to Solve It"   B.642, B.645, B.650,
    B.652, B.655, B.659, B.665, B.672, B.674,
    B.676, B.681, B.683.
"Elliman, Ace of Magic, and the Mysterious
    Sharpshooter"   E.239.
"Elliman, Ace of Magic, Battles 'Triple Crime'"
    E.240.
"Elliman, Ace of Magic, Exposes The Invisible
    Monster"   E.242.
"Elliman, Ace of Magic, Finds the Spanish
    Treasure"   E.238.
"Elliman, Ace of Magic, Meets the Wizard of the
    Everglades"   E.236.
"Elliman, Ace of Magic, Meets the Wizards of the
    North"   E.247.
"Elliman, Ace of Magic, Solves the Riddle of the
    Fifth Crook"   E.237.
"Elliman, Ace of Magic, Tricks the Crooks of
    Glenwood"   E.243.
"Elliman and the Baffled Burglars"   E.245.
"Elliman Does Magic in Miami"   E.283.
"Elliman Invades the House of Spooks"   E.235.
"Elliman Solves 'The Riddle of the Pyramid'"
    E.241.
"Elliman Solves the Riddle of the Rockies"   E.248.
"Elliman's Magic Baffles the Natives of The Twin
    Pools"   E.244.
"The Elusive Die: Another Improvement"   B.82.
"The Embassy Murders"   B.374.
"The Emerald in the Fish Bowl"   F.36.
Empire of Crime   F.137.
"Endowment for Murder"   F.106.
"Enigma"   B.1.
"Entre Nous: The Vest Pocket; Billiard Balls;
    Chosen Card   B.66.
"Escape from 'Living Burials'"   D.27.
"The Evil Eye Superstition"   B.275.
"The Expanding 'Three Card Trick'"   B.35.
"The Eyes of Shiva"   F.11.
The Eyes of The Shadow: A Detective Novel   A.34,
    B.309.

"Footsteps in the Night"   F.65.
"For Mr. Wise Guy"   B.160.
"For the First Time--The Shadow As He Appears on
    the Radio"   E.45.
"Foreword"   C.2, C.3.
"The Forgotten Alibi; or, Nick Carter Solves a
    Perfect Crime"   F.105.
"Forgotten Gold"   B.560.
"Formula for Crime"   B.587.
"Fountain of Death"   B.675.
"The Four Aces"   B.105, B.232, B.235.
"The Four Heaps"   B.57.
"The Four Keys to Crime"   F.67.
"The Four Porcelain Dragons"   E.84.
"The Four Signets"   B.399.
"Four-Forty in Holyoke's Holocaust"   B.859.
Frank Merriwell   F.94.
"The Freak Show Murders"   B.657.
"'Free' French Drop"   B.647.
Freedom's Trail Series   E.376.
"The Frozen Lady"   F.48.
Fun with Optical Illusions   A.57.
Fun with Stunts, Tricks and Skits   A.58.
The "Funline" Series   E.370.
"Further Adventures in India"   B.266.
"Further Famous Escapes of Harry Houdini"   B.270.

"Gabbatha"   B.772.
"Gabbatha and Jinxiana"   B.773.
"Gamblers Never Gamble, They Just Put the Game on
    Ice..."   E.325.
"Gamblers Won't Gamble"   E.321.
"Gamblers Won't Gamble, But Sometimes They Will
    Take a Chance"   E.322.
Gangdom's Doom   A.137, B.137.
"The Garaucan Swindle"   B.392.
"Garden of Death"   B.573.
"The Gay Divorcee and the Lover's Lane Slayer"
    B.824.
["Gem Robberies,"]   E.1.
"Gems of Doom"   B.551.
"The Getaway Ring"   B.539.
"Getting Away from Card Tricks"   B.621.
"Ghost Breakers (Letter Column)"   E.273.
"Ghost Breakers: One Hundred Years of Spooks and
    Spoof"   E.278.
"The Ghost from the Grave"   C.5.
"The Ghost in the Crypt"   F.78.
"The Ghost Maker"   B.253.

"How Good a Detective Are You? 'The Poison Dart
    Murder Case'"   E.291.
How to Bet the Harness Races   A.120.
How to Develop an Exceptional Memory   A.92.
How to Do Magic   F.134.
How to Make a Ghost Walk   A.37.
How to Play Better Basketball Series   E.373.
How to Play Poker and Win   A.63.
How to Play the Horses and Win   A.64.
How to Play the Trotters and Win   A.65.
How to Read Faster and Remember More   A.112.
How to Spot Card Sharps and Their Methods   A.66.
How to Win at Pinochle and Other Games   A.67.
How to Win at Roulette and Other Casino Games
    A.70.
How to Win at Solitaire   A.103.
How to Win with Racing Numerology   A.62.
"Howard Thurston's Magic Lessons"   B.685, B.689,
    B.693, B.697, B.700, B.936, B.940.
Hoyle Card Games: Reference Crammer   A.104.
Hoyle's Modern Encyclopedia of Card Games   A.146.
Hoyle's Simplified Guide to the Popular Card
    Games   A.96.
"Human Enigmas   D.8.
"The Hydra"   B.617.
Hypnotism   A.134.
"Hypnotism Can Cure"   B.907.
Hypnotism Through the Ages   A.85.

"I Am Shiwan Khan the Golden Master!...And I Am The
    Shadow"   E.20.
"The Icy Touch"   F.43.
"Ideas in Brief...Heard on the Road"   B.745.
"If This Social Set Hadn't Swapped Husbands"
    B.860.
"If You Can't Find Your Freak, Make It"   D.18.
"Impromptu Magic"   B.291.
"Improved Disc Mystery"   B.159.
"Improved 'Latest Rising Cards'"   B.54.
"Improved Nickels and Dimes"   B.764.
"In a Mask He Couldn't Take Off"   B.844.
"In Memory of My Friend 'The Great Raymond'"
    B.755.
"In the Pocket"   B.607.
"Incident at Powder River"   E.336.
Inside the Medium's Cabinet   A.36.
"Insured for Death; or, Nick Carter Takes a Premium
    on Life"   F.104.
"Intelligence Tests"   D.9.

The Magic of

"Murder Every Hour"   B.409.
"Murder for Sale"   B.495.
"Murder from Nowhere"   B.826.
"Murder Hits the Jackpot"   F.30.
"Murder House"   B.450.
"Murder in Bronze"   F.103.
"Murder in the crypt"   F.111.
"Murder in Wax"   B.515.
"Murder Lake"   B.634.
"Murder Mansion"   B.577.
"Murder Marsh"   B.393.
"The Murder Master"   B.481.
"Murder of the Carnival Buccaneer"   B.830.
"Murder on Skull Island"   F.112.
"Murder on Stage"   F.46.
"Murder Town"   B.434.
Murder Trail A.173, B.354.
Murder Unlimited   F.138.
"Murder Was the Keystone of His Career"   B.847.
"Murderer's Throne"   B.480.
"The Murdering Ghost"   B.616.
"The Museum Murders," B.622.
"My First Performance"   B.100.
My Life of Magic   A.23.
"Mysteries of Hindu 'Magic' Revealed"   D.23.
"The Mysterious Bowl"   B.12.
"The Mysterious Magazine"   B.65.
"The Mysterious Necktie"   B.20.
"Mystery Hangs Over Shop Where Dark Magic Rules,"
      B.207.
"The Mystery of Dead Man's Rock"   F.13.
"The Mystery of Moloch"   B.519.
"The Mystery of the 60-foot Phantom"   B.950.
Mystery of the Alpine Pass   A.115.
Mystery of the Ambush in India   A.93.
"The Mystery of the Giant Brain"   F.9.
"The Mystery of the Goona Goona Fan"   E.38.
"The Mystery of the Indian Hills"   E.339.
Mystery of the Mexican Treasure   A.87.
"The Mystery of the Old Red Mill"   F.98.
"The Mystery of the Sealed Box"   E.10, E.379.
"Mystery of the Secret Burials"   B.854.
**Mystic and Occult Arts: A Guide to Their Use in
      Daily Living**   A.131.
"Mystic Circle of Philadelphia (Reports)"   B.64.
"A Mystic Divination"   B.24.
"Mystic Ring"   B.171.
"The Mystic Skull"   B.79.
"Neff and His Great Show"   B.756.

On the Magic

"Practical Card Tricks [First Series]"   B.76,
    B.78, B.81, B.87, B.90, B.95, B.102, B.113,
    B.120, B.128, B.133, B.138, B.144, B.152.
"Practical Card Tricks, Second Series"   B.154,
    B.161, B.172, B.177, B.183, B.188.
"Practical Card Tricks, Third Series"   B.194,
    B.195, B.196, B.197, B.199, B.200, B.202,
    B.204, B.206, B.208, B.210, B.213, B.214.
"Practical Coin Tricks"   B.112, B.127, B.137,
    B.146.
"Prearrangement (Introduction)"   B.103.
"Presenting Harry Kellar"   B.943.
"Prizes for Puzzlers"   B.294, B.296, B.301, B.307,
    B.311.
"Prizes for Puzzlers-Answers"   B.295, B.300,
    B.302, B.308, B.312.
Professional Magic for Amateurs   A.48.
"Prohibition"   B.88.
Psychic and Other ESP Party Games   A.116.
"The Purloined Portraits"   F.102.
"Putting Your Lazy Hand to Work"   D.37.
"A Puzzle a Day"   D.40.
Puzzles and Pastimes Fun and Activity Book   A.105.
"The Python"   B.420.

"Q"   B.549.
"Quaint Chat from the Quaker City"   B.109.
"A Quarter of Eight"   B.708.
"A Question of Evidence"   B.838.
"Quetzal"   B.448.

"Racket Town"   B.475.
"The Rackets King"   B.493.
"The Radium Murders"   B.466.
Radner on Bridge   A.88.
Radner on Canasta   A.89.
"The Ragoff Brooch"   F.115.
"Rape Murder of the Co-Ed"   B.878.
"Rape Slaying of the Blonde Beauty"   B.871.
"Realm of Doom"   B.512.
"The Red Blot"   B.360.
"Red Light Vengeance"   B.898.
"The Red Men from Mars"   E.343.
The Red Menace   A.156, B.315.
"Red Trail of the Bludgeon Killer"   B.880.
"Regarding 'A Word with Mr. Howard Thurston'"
    B.114.
"Release from Reason"   B.670.
"The Reluctant Buzz Saw"   F.35.

The Shadow and the Adventure

"The Shadow and the Adventure of the Mayan Museum"
     E.21.
"The Shadow and the Bells of Doom"   E.112.
"The Shadow and The Black Ray"   E.51.
"The Shadow and the Chinese Torture Cage"   E.39.
"The Shadow and the Cliff Castle Mystery"   E.392.
"The Shadow and the Coils of The Python"   E.95.
"The Shadow and the Coins of Feng Huang"   E.110.
"The Shadow and The Creeping Death"   E.8.
"The Shadow and The Crime Wizard"   E.58.
"The Shadow and The Crystal Skull"   E.115.
["The Shadow and the Darvin Fortune"]   E.385.
"The Shadow and the Earthquake Machines"   E.390.
"The Shadow and the Ghosts of the Malden Manse"
     E.24.
The Shadow and The Golden Master   A.187.
"The Shadow and the Gray Ghost"   E.388.
"The Shadow and the Hand of Death"   E.37.
"The Shadow and the 'Hands of Doom'"   E.124.
"The Shadow and the Haunted Glen"   E.102.
"The Shadow and the Masked Headsman"   E.164.
"The Shadow and the Message of Death"   E.131.
"The Shadow and the Return of Althor"   E.391.
"The Shadow and the Riddle of the Astral Bells"
     E.85.
"The Shadow and The Riddle of the 'Hanging
     Skeleton'"   E.105.
"The Shadow and the 'Silver Skull'"   E.40.
"The Shadow and the Spotted Death"   E.41.
"The Shadow and the Star of Delhi"   E.389.
"The Shadow and the Two Gray Ghosts"   E.27.
"The Shadow and the Valley of Sleep"   E.80.
"The Shadow and the Vanishing Prisoners"   E.96.
The Shadow and the Voice of Murder   A.39.
The Shadow Annual   A.41, A.42, A.49.
"The Shadow at Ghost Manor"   E.60.
"The Shadow at Murder Circus"   E.72.
"The Shadow Baffles Berlin"   E.93.
"The Shadow Battles Crime Among the Aztecs"
     E.145.
"The Shadow Battles the Bund"   E.15.
"The Shadow Battles The Cloudmaster"   E.140.
"The Shadow Battles the Robot Master"   E.109.
"The Shadow Brings Terror to Tokio"   E.94.
"The Shadow: Calling Nick Carter"   E.82.
"The Shadow Conquers Crime in Centralba"   E.144.
"The Shadow Conquers The Hydra"   E.104.
"The Shadow--Convicts Judge Lawless"   E.134.

The Shadow Investigates

"The Shadow Investigates Midnight Murder"   E.141.
The Shadow: Jade Dragon and House of Ghosts
     A.185.
"The Shadow Jolts Landlubber's Haven, The Ship That
     Stays on Shore"   E.143.
The Shadow Laughs: A Detective Novel   A.35, B.313.
"The Shadow Matches Wits with Hoang Hu"   E.12.
"The Shadow Meets Damon the Nomad and His Unseen
     Horrors!!!"   E.117.
"The Shadow Meets Double Z"   E.130.
"The Shadow Meets Monstrodamus"   E.53.
"The Shadow Meets the Black Swami"   E.128.
"The Shadow Meets The Blur"   E.137.
"The Shadow Meets the 'Brain of Nippon'"   E.86.
"The Shadow Meets The Crime Master"   E.125.
"The Shadow Meets 'The Dagger'"   E.14.
"The Shadow Meets the Death Master"   E.77.
"The Shadow Meets the Green Ghoul and the Red
     Roamer"   E.91.
"The Shadow Meets the Mad Inventor"   E.103.
"The Shadow Meets the Mask"   B.571, B.673.
"The Shadow Meets The Seven Sinners"   E.106.
"The Shadow Meets the Spy Master"   E.61.
"The Shadow Meets The Tarantula"   E.97.
"The Shadow Meets The Wodahs"   E.122.
"The Shadow Nips the Nipponese"   E.25.
["The Shadow on Shark Island"]   E.382.
"Shadow Over Alcatraz"   B.508.
"The Shadow Protects His Country Against the Evil
     Plots of the Bund on the Ghost Fleet"   E.19.
"The Shadow Proves That Dead Men Live"   E.149.
"The Shadow: Red Mask"   E.75.
"The Shadow Saves the Game"   E.33.
The Shadow Scrapbook   A.182.
"The Shadow Seeks Solarus, the Space Master"
     E.89.
"The Shadow Sees...'Death in the Crystal'"   E.136.
"The Shadow Sets a Trap for Crime"   E.138.
"The Shadow: Seven Drops of Blood"   E.90.
"The Shadow Smashes Murderer's Row"   E.100.
"The Shadow Snares the White Dragon"   E.29.
"The Shadow: Solarus Returns"   E.99.
"The Shadow Solves The Hampshire Horror"   E.111.
"The Shadow Solves 'The Museum Murders'"   E.43.
"The Shadow Solves the Riddle of Professor
     Mentalo"   E.132.
"The Shadow Solves the Riddle of Seven Towers"
     E.78.

"The Silver Venus"   B.500.
Simplified Mind Reading   F.144.
The Sin of Harold Diddlebock   A.50.
"Sin Secret of the Murdering Mistress"   B.843.
"Siren Lure Traps Missing Killer"   B.795.
"The Sitter, the Baby and the Nice Boy Down the
     Street"   B.863.
"Six Men of Evil"   B.352.
Sixteen Master Card Mysteries   A.18.
"The Skeleton in the Closet; or, Nick Carter
     Settles an Old Score"   F.101.
"The Sledge-Hammer Crimes"   B.437.
"The Sleeve Swipe"   B.147.
"Sleight of Hand Tricks (Introduction)"   B.139.
"Smugglers of Death"   B.520.
"Some Good Card Tricks"   B.41.
"Some Thimble Sleights"   B.19.
"Something About Black Cats"   B.273.
"The Sometimes Deadly Spirits"   B.819.
"Soothsayer"   B.596.
Space and Science Fun and Activity Book   A.109.
"The Space Bronco"   E.348.
"Space Prospectors"   E.357.
"The Spaced-Out Card"   B.920.
"Special DeLand Effects"   B.729.
"Special Secrets, part 1: Paul's New Production
     Box"   B.118.
"Special Secrets, part 2: Astral Die"   B.140.
"Special Secrets, part 3: The Aerial Billiard
     Ball"   B.145.
"Special Secrets-Psycho Secrets, part 1: The Psycho
     Spirit Message"   B.163.
"Special Secrets-Psycho Secrets, part 2: The Psycho
     Sealed Answer"   B.164.
"Special Secrets-Psycho Secrets, part 3: The Psycho
     Spirit Slates"   B.168.
"Special Secrets-Psycho Secrets, part 4: The Psycho
     Spirit Smoke"   B.173.
"Special Secrets-Psycho Secrets, part 5: The Psycho
     Sealed Reading"   B.175.
"Special Secrets-Psycho Secrets, part 6: The Psycho
     Spirit Ball"   B.185.
"Spiderman and the Cakes"   B.810.
"Spirit Tricks"   B.247.
"The Spoils of The Shadow"   B.391.
"Spurs Jackson and his Space Vigilantes Battle the
     Red Menace beyond the Moon"   E.356.
"Spurs Jackson and his Space Vigilantes Face the
     Menace of the Meteor Men"   E.352.

The Vampire Murders

"The Vampire Murders"   B.610.
"Vanished Treasure"   B.503.
"The Vanished Victim"   B.850.
"The Vanishing Brooch"   F.82.
"The Vanishing Glass of Water"   B.84, B.143.
"The Vanishing Handkerchief"   B.132.
"The Vanishing Pearls"   F.51.
 "The Veiled Prophet"   B.543.
"Vengeance Bay"   B.586.
"Vengeance is Mine!"   B.446.
"The Vindicator"   B.514.
"Visit Spurs Jackson at His Spaceranch in
     Spaceman's Gulch"   E.354.
"Visit Spurs Jackson in Spaceman's Gulch"   E.361.
"The Voice"   B.505.
"The Voice from the Void"   F.72.
"The Voice of Crime"   F.96.
"Voice of Death"   B.540.
"Voodoo Death"   B.658.
"The Voodoo Master"   B.427.
"Voodoo Trail"   B.492.
"The Voodoo Treasure"   F.66.
"Voodoo," B.618.

"Walter B. Gibson Says: 'It Can't Be Wrong'"
     B.739.
Walter Gibson's Big Book of Magic for All
     Ages   A.184.
Walter Gibson's Encyclopedia of Magic and
     Conjuring   A.163.
"The War of the Moons"   B.809.
"Washington Crime"   B.451.
"Washington Irving Bishop"   F.121.
"The Wasp"   B.555.
"The Wasp Returns"   B.561.
"We Smashed the Philadelphia Dope Menace"   B.883.
The Wealth Seeker   A.177, B.375.
The Weird Adventures of The Shadow   A.123.
"Welcome from a Smothered Woman"   B.856.
"(Well I'll be--) Switched"   B.661.
What Are the Odds?   A.139.
"What's New in Books"   B.730.
What's New in Magic   A.61.
What's On Your Mind?   A.43.
"When the Hunter Becomes the Prey"   B.886.
"Where Is It?"   B.224.
"Which Murder Do You Want Me For?"   B.793.
"Which Rules the World--Blond or Brunette?"   D.30.
"The Whispering Buddha"   F.40.

"Yankee Vase"   B.646.
Year-Round Fun and Activity Book   A.107.
"The Yellow Band"   B.463.
The Yellow Disc Murder Case   F.141.
"The Yellow Door"   B.435.
"Yoga, to Keep Young and Healthy"   B.905.
"You Can't Fool the Monte Man"   D.21.
"You Won't Live to Tell It"   B.852.

Zemba   A.174, B.421.

Index of Names 👉

This is a selective index of some proper names, including pseudonyms, found in section A (books and pamphlets) as well as the Appendix, specifically Appendix C (The Other Maxwell Grants) and Appendix D (Casting Pale Shadows). Gibson pseudonyms are indicated by quotation marks. Characters are entered under their first names. Stage magicians are entered under their stage names with their birth names in parentheses. It is hoped that this will assist those who wish to check sources more quickly.